POP CULTURE WARS

Religion & *the Role of* Entertainment *in American Life*

WILLIAM D. ROMANOWSKI

InterVarsity Press
Downers Grove, Illinois

InterVarsity Press® is the book-publishing division of InterVarsity Christian Fellowship®, a student movement active on campus at hundreds of universities, colleges and schools of nursing in the United States of America, and a member movement of the International Fellowship of Evangelical Students. For information about local and regional activities, write Public Relations Dept., InterVarsity Christian Fellowship, 6400 Schroeder Rd., P.O. Box 7895, Madison, WI 53707-7895.

Cover photographs: Carlos Vergara and Johnson/Camerique
ISBN 0-8308-1988-6

Printed in the United States of America ∞

Library of Congress Cataloging-in-Publication Data

Romanowski, William D.
   Pop culture wars: religion and the role of entertainment in
American life/William D. Romanowski.
    p.   cm.
   Includes bibliographical references (p.   ).
   ISBN 0-8308-1988-6 (pbk.: alk. paper)
   1. Popular culture—Religious aspects—Christianity.   2. Popular
culture—United States—History—20th century.   3. Amusements—
Religious aspects—Christianity.   4. Amusements—United States—
History—20th century.   5. Christianity and culture—United States—
History—20th century.   6. United States—Religion—1960-
I. Title.
BR526.R65   1996
261.5'7—dc20
                                     96-16490
                                       CIP

18	17	16	15	14	13	12	11	10	9	8	7	6	5	4	3	2	1
11	10	09	08	07	06	05	04	03	02	01	00	99	98	97	96		

To
Michael and Tara
This be the land of adventure!

Acknowledgments

I would like to express my gratitude to a number of people without whose help and kindness it would have been much more difficult, if not altogether impossible, to complete this book. My colleagues in the Communication Arts and Sciences Department at Calvin College provided much support and encouragement, as did our support staff, Yvonne Posthuma and Jan Hennink, and our student assistant, Denise Avink. Many Calvin students contributed research on specific topics or helped with projects related to this book: Brad Bergman, Judy DeJager, Maria DeRose, Amy Faber, Emily Girard, Chris Smit, Brad Van Arragon and Char Weening. Special thanks to Jim Bratt and Carl Plantinga for their careful reading of the manuscript and helpful commentary. I received assistance from Laura Kasier at the UCLA Film and Television Archive, Scott Curtis at the Margaret Herrick Library of the Academy of Motion Picture Arts and Sciences, the Motion Picture Association of America's Worldwide Market Research Department, the Classification and Rating Administration, the Calvin College Library (especially Conrad Bult, Glenn Remelts and Kathleen Struck) and the Free Library of Philadelphia.

My editor Rodney Clapp, an accomplished author himself, demonstrated great patience during the writing process and skill, camaraderie, good sense and humor during the editorial phase. I also want to mention Del Willink and Keith Hammersma (the master builders), Jahan Parirokh at Video Master and John and Mary Loeks at Jack Loeks Theatres; and I offer a note of thanks to friends and neighbors whose daily acts of kindness toward my family kept this project in motion and continue to enrich our lives. I especially want to express my appreciation to my good friend Terry Thomas, a heavenly fool who taught me a long time ago to live by grace and with gratitude, and after more than twenty years still keeps me self-aware and amused.

My mother has never stopped encouraging me and has helped so much by taking care of her grandchildren. My wife, Donna, labored right along with me during this project, helping with the research, staying up late at night viewing films, reading the manuscript and picking up the extra slack around the house at times. Through it all, morning by morning new mercies we continue to see. My children, Michael and Tara, made plenty of sacrifices too, while also helping me to see the popular arts from a kid's perspective. It is to them that I dedicate this book.

1
. . . . .

Total
Recall

During the Christmas season of the Bicentennial year, American moviegoers crowded theaters to see a film about a down-and-out fighter from Philadelphia named Rocky Balboa, the "Italian Stallion." Audiences acted as if they were sitting ringside, jumping out of their seats at a knockdown, cheering for Rocky, and booing his opponent, Apollo Creed. Rocky's triumphant individualism and poignant rags-to-riches story captured the American imagination. By the end of April 1977, the film had grossed over $50 million in the United States and Canada, and it topped the $100-million mark by the end of the summer.

I was doing ministry that summer with a youth group on a work project at an urban church in Philadelphia. During our stay we took in the sights, making the regular tourist stops at the Liberty Bell, Constitution Hall and Betsy Ross's house. But the students were eager to drive around the working-class neighborhoods on the south side of Philadelphia and see the Italian market. Most of all, they wanted to visit the Philadelphia Museum of Art. They were not, however, the least bit interested in the museum's striking Greek Revival architecture or the priceless collection of art housed inside. What they wanted to see was the museum's steps—all seventy-two of them.

When we arrived at this major artistic institution, these young people jumped out of the vans and raced up the huge stone steps, their own personal recreation of Rocky's energizing run as he prepared to fight for the heavyweight championship of the world. To my surprise, we were not the only ones reenacting Balboa's workout ritual, as young and old alike documented their visit with photographs of themselves, arms raised above their heads and the breathtaking panoramic view of the City of Brotherly Love in the background. The *Rocky* films turned the museum's doorstep into an internationally famous attraction that is today included among the city's historic sights. According to the director of Philadelphia's Visitors Bureau, the inquiry "Where's Rocky?" is second only to "Which way to the Liberty Bell?"[1]

Sylvester Stallone, who wrote the original screenplay and starred in the role of Rocky, commissioned a bronze statue of the now famed fighter to be used in a 1982 sequel *(Rocky III)* and remain afterwards as a gift to the city. The film's producers, Chartoff-Winkler Productions, commissioned Thomas Schomberg to create the sculpture. Schomberg's work had been exhibited at Super Bowls and World Series and in galleries around the world. He modeled the statue after classical tributes to ancient Roman gladiators, and was confident that his sculpted boxer held "as much power aesthetically as any piece in that (museum) courtyard."[2] Members of the Philadelphia Art Commission, the Fairmount Park Commission and the museum board approved the placement of the statue atop the steps, under the condition that it be relocated "to a more suitable location" (the Spectrum sports arena in South Philadelphia was suggested) immediately after filming was completed. "Rocky belonged anywhere else," a Philadelphia writer later explained. "He was a boxer, after all, a hero of the masses; hardly one of the cultured elite. Put him in front of a stadium, a gym, a sporting-goods shop—certainly not at the entrance of a major artistic institution."[3]

A citywide controversy erupted over the statue's value to the city and its location; local newspapers carried the debate in editorial and opinion columns. One side argued that the statue was not "great art" and "nothing short of outstanding deserves a pedestal like the museum's doorstep." Besides, the statue has "commercial hype written all over it." The leader of a group that successfully petitioned to keep the statue in the city by placing it at the Spectrum unpretentiously said, "It ain't a bad piece of art." Stallone, who thought the whole statue controversy was "blown out of proportion," said, "I didn't mean to force the sculpture on anyone," and arranged to have it taken back to California.[4]

City officials and community leaders implored Stallone to leave the eight-and-a-half foot, 1,800-pound monument in Rocky's hometown, but with no location approved by the end of filming, the statue was shipped back to Los Angeles. A petition drive ensued, and in December 1981, the city council announced an ordinance to accept Stallone's gift to the city. The statue was transported back to Philadelphia. A compromise was worked out with the art commission to exhibit the statue at the museum from the May 24 premiere of *Rocky III* until July 11, when it was to be moved to its permanent place at the Spectrum. Apparently, with the publicity behind them, the film company abandoned the statue and the museum got stuck with the moving bill. According to a spokesperson, the museum had to pay "$12,000 out of pocket that we were not reimbursed for" to haul it off to the Spectrum.[5]

At the beginning of 1990, Stallone returned to Philadelphia to shoot the final sequel in the Rocky saga *(Rocky V)*. The statue and art museum steps, the symbolic scene of Rocky's triumph, were critical to the story line of the fighter's return to his roots. Despite protests from the museum administration and supporters, the Rocky monument was returned to the museum's grand entrance, and the controversy renewed.

The local press and many Philadelphians may have been bothered by Stallone's hubris in 1982, suggesting that a bronze effigy of himself be immortalized in a prominent public place in the city. By 1990, however, the *Rocky* films had done wonders for Philadelphia's image, brought additional revenues and demonstrated the city's potential for filmmakers. (The award-winning *Philadelphia,* starring Tom Hanks and Denzel Washington, was shot there.) Rocky had become an international symbol of the spirit of Philadelphia along with the Liberty Bell, and secured a place in the history of the American cinema. The statue had become a popular icon, "a tribute to the indomitable spirit of man," as one writer described it.[6]

Public sentiment intensified and shifted in favor of the statue residing permanently at the art museum. "Why not highlight a statue that uplifts and inspires so many, not only in Philadelphia, but around the world?" a writer in the *Philadelphia Inquirer* asked. "Philadelphia's reputation in the art world is secure. We don't have to worry about snobs sniffing their noses at such vulgar common art so prominently displayed. They want fine art, let them walk around to the other side of the Art Museum and gawk at Jacques Lip-

chitz's statue of Prometheus strangling a chicken. Or a vulture. Whatever."
Another writer pointed out that wealthy patrons originally objected to the
Statue of Liberty "on aesthetic grounds," and that as a statue "exemplifying
the triumph of an individual against great odds," the Rocky sculpture "must
fit within one of the many definitions of art." A state senator, who introduced
a resolution suggesting the museum keep the statue atop the East Terrace
steps, called it "a symbol of the spirit of Philadelphia and it captures and
represents the hopes and aspirations of the common person in true art form."[7]
Museum officials and benefactors, however, refused to accept defeat. With
strong financial backing and political connections they forced the removal of
the statue of Rocky to the Spectrum sports arena where it stands today.

At issue in the debate about the Rocky statue and its appropriate location
was the artistic value and cultural significance of both the statue and the art
museum. The event itself can be viewed as a contemporary symbol of long-
standing cultural divisions in America.

Founded in 1682, Philadelphia had become one of the most prominent
cities on the east coast by the mid-1750s, a center for education, art, trade,
industry, architecture, and politics. The city was far less cosmopolitan and its
population more homogeneous than New York, but it had its Revolutionary
past, a collection of historic shrines, libraries and museums, the American
Philosophical Society and later the Pennsylvania Academy of Fine Arts. Beginning in the late eighteenth century, Philadelphia also became one of the
major theatrical centers along the Atlantic seaboard. By 1828 there were three
theaters in operation in Philadelphia, presenting Shakespeare, opera, ballet,
and European and American plays.

For two centuries William Penn's Anglo-Saxon descendants, who occupied
the exclusive Main Line and expensive suburbs, dominated the city's cultural
life. The Main Line families of Philadelphia, like their counterparts in other
eastern cities, represented the upper-class "Old American" families and
guarded their social status and genteel cultural tradition. Philadelphia was
rocked by cultural conflicts during the Revolutionary period and again in the
1840s, when violent religious and ethnic riots erupted between Catholics and
native-born Protestants over politics, economics and Catholics' use of their
own version of the Bible in schools. At the turn of the twentieth century,
cultural distinctions were heightened again as waves of impoverished Italians
settled in row houses lining hundreds of streets in the working-class neighborhoods in the city's south side. The two groups staked out their territories,

cultivating different lifestyles and values that reflected the city's cultural divisions. "The art museum, concert halls, and theaters belonged to the Main Liners," one writer said. "The sports stadiums, pizza joints, and street corners belonged to South Philadelphia."[8]

The Rocky statue was a symbolic invasion of the physical space of the city's "high" or elite cultural tradition by "low" or commercial popular culture. One writer, for example, explained the debate over the statue as "fundamentally a battle for territory," a cultural conflict that manifested itself in the significance of physical space. "The control of land has historically been associated with power, and the creation of buildings, spaces and the streets that link them have been expressions of authority, whose purpose is to tell the populace who is in charge," he wrote. The city's layout and architecture signified a social hierarchy. The Benjamin Franklin Parkway, a boulevard stretching about a mile from City Hall to the museum, "links the heart of the city to a romantic natural landscape. The buildings that terminate it represent two aspects of human life: the worldly issues of politics and justice and the eternal values of art," he explained. "The Rocky statue raises what at first seems to be a trivial set of issues, but ultimately, it comes down to what values we choose to celebrate."[9]

This event represents long-standing tensions between high and low cultures in America. These cultural categories form one aspect of the controversies over entertainment that are taking place in today's "culture wars." Their entrenchment in American life coincided with the emergence of the entertainment industry in the early decades of this century, another period of cultural and religious conflict of no less magnitude than that of today, but then between native Protestants and the arriving immigrant groups. Public discourse about the role and influence of entertainment has been a consistent feature of twentieth-century American life. After a century of growth, the entertainment industry is a pervasive, multibillion-dollar global business. And yet, despite its ubiquitous presence, we remain unsure about its role in society, perplexed by its awesome appeal, and uneasy about its potential influence.

Terminate Hollywood: The Sequel

Entertainment has long been a source of controversy in American life. It may be, as *Time* noted of popular culture in general, "the ultimate instance of American mixed feelings."[10] On the one hand, entertainment has been criticized as trivial, mindless, and escapist amusement. At other times (and we are in the midst of one now), attacks on entertainment range from charges of debasement of taste to the destruction of values, with critics charging that the popular culture industries represent a dangerous threat to the maintenance of the social order, wielding an influence that could potentially overwhelm the combined efforts of family, school and faith communities. But entertainment cannot be trivial and dangerous at the same time; it is either one or the other.

American entertainment is enormously popular, capable of amusing and thrilling (as well as alarming and appalling) audiences around the world. Almost half of the movies shown in theaters in Japan are produced in the United States; two-thirds of movie admissions in France, Germany and Italy are for Hollywood productions. There are over one billion television sets in use around the globe, and American programs are consistently among the top-rated shows. Sales of prerecorded music and music videos in the United States leaped a record 20 percent in 1994, reaching $12 billion. Worldwide sales totaled $35.5 billion that year, a 16.5 percent increase over the previous one, and grew to $41 billion in 1995. MTV—music television—reaches over 257 million homes in sixty-eight territories on five continents. A recent satellite venture, STAR TV (Satellite Television Asia Region) has the potential to reach three billion people from Israel to India, representing two-thirds of the world's population. A 1990 cover story in *Fortune* celebrated "America's Hottest Export: Pop Culture," reporting that together, American movies, music, television programming and home video generated an annual trade surplus of some $8 billion.[11]

But while the financial world lauded the commercial success of the American entertainment industry, other sectors of society intensified their criticism of its content. A spate of films aimed at young viewers in the early 1980s— *Gremlins, The Karate Kid, Indiana Jones and the Temple of Doom*—drew criticism for scenes containing violence. Consumer and religious groups demanded a revamping of Hollywood's rating system and the PG-13 rating was created to differentiate movies not suitable for children under 13. In 1985 a group of parents formed an organization called Parents Music Resource Center (PMRC) and lobbied Congress for a record-rating system to warn parents about the sexual and violent imagery in the lyrics of many rock albums. The following year the Recording Industry Association of America (RIAA) agreed to place a warning label ("Explicit Lyrics—Parental Advisory") on records containing lyrics parents might find objectionable.

Public discourse about entertainment exploded into controversy in the 1990s, as institutions of cultural transmission and communication became critical in the cultural conflict that has marked this final decade of the twentieth century. In his now famous "Murphy Brown" speech, former vice president Dan Quayle denounced Candice Bergen's television character for bearing a child out of wedlock. Quayle politicized the discourse about entertainment by proposing that a nebulous "cultural elite," found in "newsrooms, sitcom studios, and faculty lounges across America," was behind a liberal attack on the moral values of average Americans. Quayle created a mythical "Us versus Them," the "Us" being the silent majority of middle Americans pitted against film and television producers, artists, journalists and academics, those "left-wing, out-of-step, valueless Democrats."[12]

Even though most people thought the whole affair was a distraction from the real issues of the campaign, Quayle's speech did much to align the entertainment industry with other institutions of cultural transmission on one side of the much publicized culture wars. This became a common theme among conservative critics of the media. James C. Dobson, president of Focus on the Family, wrote in his monthly newsletter that following Quayle's remarks "the forces of hell were unleashed against intact families and the principles on which they are based." Republican presidential candidate Pat Buchanan said "the adversary culture, with its implacable hostility to Judeo-Christian teaching" had subverted values "from the public classroom to the TV screen, from the movie theater to the museum." This was also the thesis of a controversial book, *Hollywood vs. America: Popular Culture and the War on Traditional Values*. "Tens of millions of Americans now see the entertainment industry as an all-powerful enemy, an alien force that assaults our most cherished values and corrupts our children," conservative film critic Michael Medved wrote. "The dream factory has become the poison factory."[13]

Quayle's speech grabbed instant headlines and one-liners on late-night television, and while his comments were meant to amass support for the Bush campaign, they sounded a chord that awakened a debate that has been on and off over the course of this century. A cover story in the *Los Angeles Times* "Calendar" asked, "Is Hollywood Ruining America?" Surveys in the 1990s showed that the majority of Americans thought there was too much sex and violence in movies and that television was more influential than parents. News magazines ran cover stories like "Killer Movies: *Basic Instinct* Pushes the Boundaries of the Hollywood Mainstream," "The Selling of Sex" and "X Rated."[14]

The religious community entered the discussion. In 1992 the National Council of Churches declared: "We deplore the increasing glorification of violence and sexual violence in the visual media," adding that these "violent portrayals damage the common good and threaten media freedom." Empirical studies were used to argue that the media "are powerful teachers and conditioners of individual attitudes and behavior," and that some action short of censorship, was needed to "hold broadcasters and film makers to higher levels of responsibility."[15] The following year, Southern Baptists accused the television networks of contributing to "the moral breakdown in our society." The content of television programs was exerting a corruptive influence, the denomination declared at its annual convention, encouraging immoral sexual behavior and violence: "The viewing public is bombarded with themes, plots, images and advertisements which promote and glorify sexual promiscuity, violence and other forms of immorality."[16]

Ted Baehr of the Christian Film and Television Commission composed a revised version of the Motion Picture Production Code of 1930 that he wanted the film industry to adopt. The Roman Catholic archbishop of Los Angeles, Cardinal Roger M. Mahoney, refrained from endorsing Baehr's updated code. Instead, he issued a pastoral letter to the entertainment industry. Mahoney offered general criteria from a "human values perspective" for producers to follow in carrying out their social responsibility to the common good and the well-being of the population.[17]

In the meantime, Time-Warner, the world's largest communication company, released several projects that generated enormous controversy: Oliver Stone's movie *JFK*, Ice-T's recording *Body Count*, Madonna's *Sex* book and Spike Lee's film *Malcolm X*.[18] Facing increasing competition from the cable networks and the deregulation of the television industry during the 1980s, the major networks introduced more violence and sexuality in programming. *NYPD Blue* debuted in the fall of 1993 amidst a storm of controversy and campaigns against the show. Stations covering 20 percent of the country refused to carry it, and advertisers fearing consumer boycotts stayed away. Under pressure from the American Family Association, one of my local ABC affiliates did not carry the cop show, but oddly received no complaints about its *Baywatch* replacement, a "T&A" program facetiously known as "Babewatch."[19]

Even though overall crime rates remained steady through the 1980s, statistical reports on escalating violent crime coincided with monitoring groups reported increased levels of violence in TV programming. The National Council for Families and Television sponsored an industrywide conference on television violence in August 1993. The following year, St. John's University sponsored the International Conference on Violence in the Media. Public opinion polls documented America's growing concern about violent crime, bringing governmental officials into the fray over the role and effects of entertainment. Attorney General Janet Reno threatened government intervention if the industry did not voluntarily reduce levels of violence in programming. Senator Paul Simon (D-Ill.) led a crusade of legislators who introduced bills calling for a ban on TV violence during children's viewing hours, the establishment of monitoring and enforcement agencies, an MPAA-like rating system for TV shows, and mandatory "V-chip" technology to allow parents to block out shows containing violence. President Bill Clinton implored entertainment industry leaders for self-restraint, and in his 1995 State of the Union address chastised the industry for its proliferation of "incessant, repetitive, mindless violence and irresponsible conduct that permeates our media all the time."

Entertainment executives complained that the industry was being scapegoated for larger problems in society: poverty, drugs, lack of education and opportunity, domestic abuse, easy access to guns. And there were many journalists who thought the campaign against the entertainment industry was so much political posturing, and largely a smoke screen to avoid grappling with the more significant issues. Even so, cable programmers and the major television networks agreed to include parental advisory warnings and to establish an independent monitoring organization to dodge TV violence legislation. FCC Chairman Reed Hundt said, "The time has come to reexamine, redefine, restate and renew the social compact between the public and the broadcasting industry."[20]

In the spring of 1995, *U.S. News & World Report* noted an increase in "family friendly" movies in the previous year and recorded the pleasure of conservative media critics Michael Medved and Ted Baehr.[21] Still, according to a survey conducted by the Gallup Organization for the Catholic Communication Campaign in April, 60 percent of Americans said that under half of the movies they saw in the past year portrayed their values. Respondents said they wanted to see less crime and violence, sex and profanity, and more "positive" values including honesty, integrity, family life and family values, moral and Christian values, respect for self and others, fidelity, kindness, tolerance for others, decency and trust.[22]

Just when reports indicated that the entertainment industry was making some efforts to accommodate its critics, Republican presidential hopeful Bob Dole reignited the controversy. Dole lashed out at the entertainment industry for producing "nightmares of depravity" with portrayals of "casual violence and even more casual sex" that threatened to undermine the character and social values of the nation. Mimicking Medved's thesis, Dole charged that "a line has been crossed—not just of taste, but of human dignity and decency. It's crossed every time . . . Hollywood's dream factories turn out nightmares of depravity." Like Quayle's earlier remonstration, Dole's attack on Hollywood smacked of political expediency as he tried to gather support for his candidacy by addressing the moral agenda of the culturally conservative wing of the Republican Party.[23]

Columnist Ellen Goodman wrote that the succession of strikes on the entertainment industry began to look like a series of Hollywood sequels: "Terminate Hollywood IV. Die Hollywood with a Vengeance." But as reporters observed, criticism of the entertainment industry was an issue that transcended party politics and resonated with the American public. Surveys showed that the majority of Americans were concerned about the amount of violence and sex depicted in the entertainment media and the effect it might be having, especially on children. At the same time, after the Oklahoma City bombing, comparisons were made between cop-killer rap lyrics and radio talk-show host G. Gordon Liddy's suggestion to "aim for the head" when greeting federal law-enforcement agents at your door. Goodman wrote, "Whether we are talking about hate radio or gangsta rap, about Oklahoma City or Hollywood, there is a growing understanding that ideas, words, and images matter, especially in raising children."[24]

In December 1995 former secretary of education William Bennett and Senator Joe Lieberman (D-Conn.) launched a campaign to clean up daytime talk shows, soap operas and prime-time television shows. In his 1996 State of the Union address, Clinton called for a White House summit with television programmers to improve children's television and urged legislators to pass a telecommunications bill that included a V-chip requirement. FCC chair Reed Hundt pressed for a children's educational programming quota for all commercial broadcasters. Predictably, there were quarrels over what constituted "educational" programming, and the National Association of Broadcasters (NAB) and many industry executives had difficulty with government imposition on programming and were concerned about First Amendment issues.

The running debate today has revived issues about American entertainment that have spanned the twentieth century: free speech and censorship, the roles and purposes of contemporary entertainment, and its relation to other social institutions. We have reached a pivotal moment in the public discourse, a time of transition not unlike others in the past when various social, cultural, political, and religious groups are working to redefine the role of entertainment with the intent of influencing its future direction.

Art and Entertainment

The main inquiry of this book is the confluence of religion and culture and its relation to the nature and role of entertainment in American life. Specifically, I am concerned with the identification of a cosmic spiritual battle between good and evil with historically conceived cultural categories; this has been a consistent feature of the discussion about entertainment and popular culture throughout the twentieth century. For that reason I concentrate on two forces in American life that largely defined the discussion about entertainment—the one intellectual and the other religious—as they serve to highlight the cultural and moral aspects of the debate.

The former is represented today by the flood of research from scholars and government committees published in books, academic journals and bureaucratic reports. The latter is represented not only by church denominations but also by organizations like the American Family Association, the Christian Film and Television Commission and the Dove Association. Working at a grassroots level are various advocacy organizations like the Parent's Music Resource Center and Children Now, for example, which continue the efforts of earlier reform groups that tried to influence movies, radio and comic books. The efforts of these at times overlapping groups can be traced back to struggles going on in the evolution of the American theater in the nineteenth century involving the religious community and the educated and wealthy elite.

At that time the Victorian social system held the two together to some degree, but already in the late nineteenth century they were separating, with marked suspicion emerging between them. Cultural elitists derided popular culture on grounds of aesthetic taste; religious moralists feared its influence and yearned for disciplinary control. By the 1920s, with the full emergence of modernism, the conflict between these groups was as sharp as their quarrel with the popular arts. That aspect of this subject receives only parenthetical treatment in the effort here to give a context for today's reform movement. The concerns of earlier reformers and those of today lead them into a myopic perspective that in our contemporary cultural conflict results in curious distinctions between high and popular, contemporary and traditional culture. Today's reformers have no particular love for high art (but do promote the classics) and little use for aesthetic theory and purposes. They are invariably middle-brow, preferring the simple and Pollyannaish, and campaigning on moral rather than aesthetic grounds.

American popular culture is as old as the colonies, but the appearance of high and popular culture as distinctive categories in American life occurred around the turn of this century. As Lawrence Levine showed in his book *Highbrow/Lowbrow,* a "cultural hierarchy" emerged that divided American life into "high" and "low" culture as a primary means of social, intellectual and aesthetic separation.[25] "Cultural hierarchy" refers to the establishment of certain cultural forms and practices of one group as superior in value and contribution in life to those of other groups. This suggests a hegemonic system with the dominant culture exerting at least symbolic, if not social, control over subordinate groups. A shared culture binds members of a group together while also marking outsiders. As cultural analyst Paul DiMaggio observed, "Particularly in the case of a dominant status group, it is important that their culture be recognized as legitimate by, yet be only partially available to, groups that are subordinate to them."[26]

The high and low divide created boundaries between cultural forms and social groups. We customarily think of the traditional arts (the visual arts, music, poetry, drama and literature) as high culture and contemporary entertainment (movies, popular music, pulp fiction and television) as low culture. As crude as these distinctions might be, they are often related to class, wealth, and education; the upper classes associated with appreciation of high culture, and the lower classes with low culture.

High and *low* are not merely categories that describe created products. They are ways of thinking and acting that affect the polices and practices of institutions, like schools and museums, for example. These categories were historically conceived and socially constructed, based on a set of underlying assumptions necessary for their continued maintenance. In that sense they are fluid and arbitrary, shifting in time and according to prevailing ideas and tastes. Though commonly used, they are not necessarily accurate descriptions of the way things are, nor are they a necessary model for the way things ought to be. Regardless, the establishment of this cultural hierarchy, with different institutions and standards, greatly affected the ways twentieth-century entertainment forms developed and the roles they served.

There is nothing intrinsic to the traditional arts that qualifies them as art. It is not the particular technology or forms that distinguish art from "craft" or "entertainment." As they are used to distinguish particular art forms, the terms *art* and *entertainment* are really superficial and problematic for study of contemporary culture. In everyday conversation *art* refers to the symphony, painting, sculpture, theater and literature; *entertainment* implies movies, television and popular music. But film, for example, is both art and entertainment, and so for that matter is the theater or symphony. And so throughout this narrative I use terms like "entertainment industry," "entertainment forms," "popular arts," "traditional arts" or "high arts" rather loosely to acknowledge commonly accepted notions while also trying to diminish these distinctions.

Art can be discussed in terms of formal properties like symbolic suggestiveness, quality and complexity, but the arts acquire their status by the way they function and are used, and the social institutions within which works are produced, distributed and consumed. The value of the earliest works of art was related to the functions they served in both religious and secular rituals and was not limited to aesthetic contemplation as it usually is today.[27] Art serves no one particular purpose, but fulfills a diversity of roles in human life. One way of understanding the arts is by analyzing these roles.

The arts have been recognized as giving form and meaning to life, offering a deeper understanding of our own lives and the lives of others. They have been studied as expressions of the "spirit" of an age or people. They also provide diversion from the cares and concerns of life, and can satisfy desires unfulfilled in our everyday lives. For our purposes here, I will focus on four important roles or functions that have historically been associated with art in society: transmitting culture, doing social criticism, providing social cohesion, and contributing to the collective memory.[28]

These roles are not exclusive of particular art forms, although each form has its own unique and specific properties used in fulfilling them. For example, literature does not have a monopoly on historical explanation or contemporary social criticism; films like *JFK* or *Boyz N the Hood* demonstrate the potential of this medium to communicate interpretations of the past and the present. Artists and audiences are not always intentional about these functions as they create and experience art, nor are they blatantly obvious in particular works of art. Nevertheless, art carries out these roles in many ways, and whether consciously or not, most people understand this and employ them in these ways. It is in the capacity of serving these roles that art, by which I mean both high and popular art forms or "entertainment," contribute to the improvement of our quality of life.

An effect of the American cultural hierarchy was to delineate the traditional arts from contemporary entertainment forms. On the one hand, the high arts were largely divorced from any meaningful purpose in the everyday lives of most people, existing now only for disinterested aesthetic contemplation. On the other hand, popular art forms labeled *entertainment* increasingly served roles and functions historically associated with art. Even so, *entertainment* still lacks a clear definition, and is often defined as that which is not art, usually by virtue of its being a commercial product designed for mass consumption. But this understanding is based on assumptions about art that today seem outmoded as we have come to recognize how much high and popular culture have in common as social practices.

Art has always had a commercial and industrial base, whether supported by royalty, merchants and aristocrats, the church and national governments, or the marketplace. Prior to the Renaissance, what we think of as the "high" or traditional arts existed alongside the crafts. The work of poets, painters, sculptors and architects was not distinguished from that of silversmiths, carpenters, stone cutters and armorers. As the idea evolved that the purpose of the "fine" arts was something different than the crafts, the two were differentiated beginning with the separation of artists from trade guilds in the sixteenth century under the influence of Vasari, a writer, architect and painter. Even so, while painting, sculpture, architecture, music and poetry had won a level of distinction from the crafts, artists had to acquiesce to the dictates of king, pope or wealthy businessman under the patronage system. And like today's commercial artists, few criticized their means of production.[29]

Our modern system of the "fine arts" emerged in the late eighteenth century; the visual arts, poetry and music were grouped together having pleasure as their end and distinguished from the usefulness of the crafts or mechanical arts. The idea that art had a unique and single purpose, existing only for aesthetic contemplation, followed. Nineteenth century "aesthetes," as they were called, argued that "art was to be in bond to no man: art is not for the infallible pope and his red hat church, it is not for the kings—may they be decapitated—and keep your money! art is for nobody! art is good for nothing! art is for art's sake!" as aesthetician Calvin Seerveld so colorfully put it.[30] As all this reveals, the various arts change not only in terms of their content and style but also in their relation to one another and their social and cultural status. In certain periods, the novel, instrumental music and canvas painting did not have much importance; at other times the sonnet, the epic poem, stained glass, mosaic, fresco painting, tapestry and pottery were all major arts. On the other hand, there was no place for the motion picture as a means of artistic expression in the established system of the fine arts around the turn of the twentieth century.

The idea of a pure art that grew out of the Renaissance cult of beauty stripped high art and music of social functions, leaving disinterested delight as the sole or highest purpose of art. One museum curator around the turn of the twentieth century, for example, wrote that "joy, not knowledge, is the aim of contemplating a painting by Turner or Dupre's 'On the Cliff,' nor need we look at a statue or a coin for aught else than inspiration and the pleasure of exercising our faculties of perception. . . . The direct aim of art is the pleasure derived from a contemplation of the perfect."[31] Philosopher Nicholas Wolterstorff, however, observed that this "is characteristic neither of institutions of art in other societies nor of our own society's total institution of art."[32] But the cultural elite became "bewitched" by this assumption that authentic art was art for contemplative delight; other purposes somehow denigrated art, and works intended to serve other roles were deemed inferior cultural products.

Contemporary entertainment cannot be understood apart from its economic base, in this case, the mass production and consumption of culture that characterizes twentieth-century society. But neither can it be limited by this aspect, for entertainment forms are more than a commercial product, and in that sense, cannot be understood apart from the artistic purposes they serve. This entanglement, as it affects the nature of entertainment, is a constant theme and source of tension in debates about the entertainment media throughout this century.

Under the conditions of the cultural hierarchy, the traditional high arts were detached from the marketplace, as though profit and financial success degraded the quality of art. The "legitimate" theater, opera, symphony, museums and galleries were funded by wealthy patrons in order to present and preserve the best of the Anglo-European tradition. Those who did not belong to the American cultural elite, however, still desired art that entertained as well as expressed their ideals and problems, tastes and values. "Popular" theater, especially vaudeville, indigenous African-American music, Tin Pan Alley and the new silent motion pictures competed in the commercial marketplace by expressing the dreams and realities of the working and middle classes.

The bifurcation of high and low culture took place during the profound transformation in American life brought about by the forces of modernism—rapid industrialism and urbanization, the rise of individualism, and the advent of a mass society. These were accompanied by huge population growth fueled by immigrants from Europe and Asia, and African-Americans migrating to the North. Modernism created a crisis for the American cultural elite made up of prosperous native Protestant groups, especially from the new urban middle class. They practiced and espoused the ideals and values of Victorianism, which defined the culture of the middle and upper classes in the late nineteenth and early twentieth centuries. The Victorian elite became the self-appointed guardians of the Anglo-European tradition which they claimed was the pinnacle of human development, and the standard by which other cultures were to be judged.

A different culture, however, was forged in the cities reflecting the beliefs and values of the new industrial democracy. Cultural historian Warren Susman described it as a fundamental conflict between an older "producer-capitalist culture, and a newly emerging culture of abundance" that belonged to the new white-collar middle class. Like our cultural conflict today, the "battle" at the beginning of the century, Susman wrote, "was between rival perceptions of the world, different visions of life. It was cultural and social, never merely or even centrally political."[33] It was in this traumatic setting that movies, the phonograph and radio were born. The role of entertainment was determined as the separation between high and low cultures became entrenched in American life.

The technology-based art forms we call "entertainment" were immediately perceived as different than the traditional arts in their form, function, status and relation to their audience. With the emergence of twentieth-century mass culture, the advent of the cinema, for example, took storytelling to an unprecedented scale as American films were shown to general audiences, not only in the United States but around the world. The virtue of this new "democratic" art is also the reason it continues to draw such hostile criticism. While popular art forms have demonstrated a keen ability to carry out the functions of art, they are not limited to a sophisticated and mature few, but reach a wide and undifferentiated audience. Modern entertainment, then, was a unique phenomenon that required new definitions of art, amusement and leisure.

For working-class immigrants, participating in the urban amusements—dance halls, amusement parks, vaudeville and movie theaters—was not like attending the symphony or opera, nor for that matter was it like attending the church revival meeting, which was not high art but heavily instructional. High art was for aesthetic contemplation, moral or spiritual elevation, intellectual refinement. But there were other functions for art that the entertainment of the day was fulfilling. The "amusements," activities that filled their recently acquired leisure hours, were something new in the industrial and urban environment. City dwellers needed a justification for fun, a way to understand the pleasure and importance they derived from and attributed to entertainment. In other words, they needed to understand the role and purpose of their own art and culture. The popular arts are a significant part of the artistic fabric of our society today, but our judgment of their role and significance continues to be hampered by the lingering assumptions of the high and low divide.

The Cheap Amusements

The entertainment industry is in the midst of a seismic shift today, and it is worthwhile to examine previous transitional periods and the issues that preoccupied industry leaders and reformers to both inform and give context to current struggles. The historical survey presented in this book is divided into four periods, each marked by changes within the entertainment industry, the introduction of new technologies, shifting markets, and renewed discussions about the roles of art and entertainment that matched changing social and cultural realities. Contemporary entertainment was an important aspect of the changing urban landscape in the opening decades of this century. Transformations in work, leisure and courtship began trends that continued and in some ways expanded throughout the century.

In this changing world, the youth culture and entertainment became significant influences on the behavior of the young. Parents concerned about the amount of time their children spend watching TV and movies or listening to music today may be surprised to find that their counterparts at the beginning of the twentieth century also worried about the effects of vaudeville theaters, the new dance halls and nickelodeons, and later radio and comic books. Parents were reluctant to grant young people the freedom they demanded to use leisure hours as they pleased, and young people's participation in entertainment was a major source of family clashes even then.

The city's amusements became places where young men and women could meet, flirt, court and enjoy an evening of inexpensive entertainment. As historian Kathy Peiss wrote, the "cheap amusements" were viewed as "the embodiment of American urban culture, particularly its individualism, ideology of consumption, and affirmation of dating and courtship outside parental control."[34] Participation in the world of urban entertainment was a visible display of integration into modern American life, not only for the young but also for newly arrived immigrants.

The silent cinema especially became an important means of communication for foreign immigrants unfamiliar with the English language; silent movies served as an introduction to American culture and values. "More vividly than any other single agency," film historian Lewis Jacobs wrote, the cinema "revealed the social topography of America to the immigrant, to the poor, and to the country folk. Thus from the outset the movies were, besides a commodity and developing craft, a social agency."[35] Perhaps more than the other urban amusements, the movies symbolized the cultural conflict that accompanied the social transformation of the time. As such it became a contestable arena as the cinema evolved apart from other established institutions and beyond the control of the middle class. There were repeated efforts at censorship of movies, and in the aftermath of a controversy over *The Birth of a Nation* in 1915, the U.S. Supreme Court declared the cinema a "business pure and simple" and not an art form to be protected by the First Amendment. The movies, then, could be regulated as a consumer product.

By the mid-1910s, film entrepreneurs wanted to distance their entertainment programs and establishments from their origins in the music and burlesque halls and arcades in order to make them more attractive to the respectable middle class. Eventually the appeal of this captivating medium brought middle-class patrons into movie theaters, and as the composition of its audience changed, so did the role of the cinema in conjunction with other factors. The "progressive" films of the 1920s aimed at the urban working class diminished as the film industry followed the course of vaudeville and began pursuing a middle-class patronage.

Extensive research conducted after the advent of sound in motion pictures made it clear that movies played a significant role in American life. Unlike the high arts, however, which were limited to the wealthy and educated classes, twentieth-century films reached an undifferentiated audience composed of men, women and children of various classes and educational backgrounds. How would American society deal with this influential and pervasive art? Religious groups wanted movies to reflect high moral standards. Educators wanted movies to teach lessons to young people. Civic leaders wanted films to affirm the authority of the state. These groups coalesced around the belief that the cinema was a powerful means of communication. As such, it was perceived as a potential threat to the maintenance of middle-class culture and institutions. That the industry was controlled by "foreigners"—that is, first- and second-generation Jewish immigrants—was not lost on movie reformers; religious antagonisms were clearly behind the crusade against the "menace of the movies."

Without constitutional protection, the film industry was vulnerable to censorship. Economic misfortunes during the early years of the Depression, fears of government regulation and tremendous pressure from the newly formed Catholic Legion of Decency forced the Hollywood studios to agree to self-regulation. This led to the institution of the Production Code of 1930, which wed box office lure with religious morality: filmmakers could deal with sex and crime as long as their treatments were sanitized and the guilty perpetrators were punished in the end. The code worked to control film as a means of cultural transmission and criticism.

Industry self-regulation relegated movies (and the other popular art industries) to a specific role as a provider of harmless or innocent amusement for the entire family. Every movie made had to be suitable for viewing by a twelve-year-old. Prior censorship freed the film industry from outside interference, and while it morally sanitized their pictures, it allowed the studios to keep control of their product. But it also prohibited film from maturing and serving the roles for art. "Admitting that the movies were entertainment—not primarily a medium for culture, or education, or propaganda—it was clear that the level of such entertainment could not rise very high if left wholly dependent upon the desires (as interpreted by Hollywood) of a movie-going public which included all elements among the American people," Foster Rhea Dulles later observed. "A natural consequence of the democracy of this nationwide audience was a lag between possible artistic and cultural standards and those which the public would support."[36]

Prior censorship and standardized production ran counter to the prevailing assumptions about what constituted genuine art and made films appear more like an assembly-line production than imaginative artistry. Furthermore, as film historian Robert Sklar observed, the code "cut the movies off from many of the most important moral and social themes of the contemporary world."[37] In this respect at least, it is understandable that critics and educators did little critical analysis of the cinema and perceived no need to incorporate the popular arts into the school curriculum.

By this time the division between high and low culture was reified in American life. The cultural elite now included not only Protestants but also Catholics and Jews, as well as progressive modernists who had no devotion to the preservation of Victorian values and had a marked suspicion of moralist reformers. A full treatment of this development is beyond the scope of this study, but as immigrant groups were transmuted in the American assimilation process, members moved into the middle and upper classes. As sociologist Will Herberg has shown, religious and cultural differences were allayed as the three religious communities—Protestant, Catholic, Jew—became branches of a larger common civic faith which provided an overarching sense of unity despite differences of religious belief, class, region and culture. Belief in technological and economic progress, nationalism, a Judeo-Christian morality and the supposedly self-evident superiority of Western civilization became the foundation for a common American faith and means of national consensus. It was during the 1930s that the phrase "American dream" came into common usage, and as Susman has observed, "Americans then began thinking in terms of patterns of behavior and belief, values and life-styles, symbols and meanings" in reference to an "American way of life."[38]

Movie moguls recognized the potential profits from films that appealed to people's ideals and dreams during the renewed nationalism of the New Deal era. Jewish immigrants who saw themselves as having a marginal status in society seized the moment to legitimize the film industry and redirected the energies of Hollywood. Instead of challenging the Victorian ethos, the film industry now joined the guardians of American culture, employing the powers of the cinema in the service of building a national cultural consensus during the malaise of the Depression. The payback was a large national audience, high profits and no federal censorship.

This period extended into the years after World War II when a combination of factors created a crisis for American entertainment that resulted in dramatic changes in the industry structure and its artistic role. This period was also marked by a significant shift in audience, from the general family market to a specific segment, the under-thirty group. Radio, record and film industries all faced falling revenues and audience shares, the result of many changes in American life after the war and competition from television, the new "family" medium. Radio and the recording business capitalized on the advent of rock'n'roll music beginning in the mid-1950s and its popularity among a new social group in America called "teenagers."

The film industry, plagued by a host of internal and external problems, was slower to respond to the demographic changes taking place in its audience. Despite a devastating box office decline, Hollywood continued to make movies for a general audience until the late 1960s, when film studios reoriented their production and marketing strategies around the youth audience. Competition from television and the collapse of the studio system not only created economic stress for the industry, but also made self-regulation difficult to enforce. In a series of decisions, the Supreme Court reversed its earlier position, extending the free speech protection of the First Amendment to film and later differentiating obscenity standards for adults and minors. These events diminished the influence the church had on the movie industry. Shifting social attitudes made the Production Code seem antiquated, and when the economic and national crises were over, the Legion's boycotts were less effective.

In the 1950s, Hollywood, record companies, comic book publishers and the television networks all heeded various production codes plainly designed to eliminate those elements (overt sexuality and profanity) and themes (drug addiction, homosexuality) that might offend members of the middle-class family audience. Eventually the events mentioned above led to the dissolution of the Production Code and the establishment of the MPAA rating system. The rating system was intended to give filmmakers freedom of expression while also acting as a consumer guide to help parents decide which pictures to allow their children to see. Films were now classified based on (im)morality and suitability for different age groups.

The Supreme Court created a new role for the cinema as a legitimate and uncensored art in society, and there were good indications that audiences wanted more mature and sophisticated movies, as the interest in international art cinema suggested. Film producers now had constitutional freedom, but still pursued the largest possible audience in order to maximize profits. Increasingly throughout the 1950s and 1960s, however, the largest proportion of the moviegoing audience became the under-thirty age group, and especially sixteen- to twenty-four-year-olds. In the interest of expanding profits, the entertainment industry homed in on the youth market beginning in the late 1960s, but with the judicial freedom to explore controversial topics and in an explicit manner better suited for more mature adult audiences than pubescent teens.

This period lasted until the late 1980s, when the entertainment industry entered another transitional period that continues today. Now in the 1990s, aging baby boomers are returning to the theaters, and along with their children and other groups are altering the movie marketplace. The advent of satellite, cable and video technology and the growth of the international market are powerful forces shaping an industry that is increasingly consolidated under the umbrella of a few huge multinational corporations that exercise synergy as an industry byword and practice.[39] At the same time, as an important means of communication, new definitions and roles for entertainment are being negotiated amidst our contemporary culture wars.

Today's changing social landscape and cultural conflict, anxieties about the current generation of youth, and advancing technologies create some interesting parallels with the period at the beginning of the century. As social, political and religious leaders search for solutions to the strain and confusion of our time, like their counterparts in the past, they recognize that the entertainment media and popular culture industries are among our most active and vital processes, capable of enthralling audiences around the world, setting fashions, selling products and communicating ideas. Over the course of this century, entertainment has become a significant social institution centering on human needs for leisure and artistic interpretations of our lives and times. It involves many rituals and practices that are commonplace in American life: a couple going out to the movies on a date, a group of friends renting a video for viewing at home, or journalists discussing a national trend brought into the limelight by a movie release. These activities are as familiar as going to work, school or church.

But as a commercial enterprise, the entertainment industry exists quite independent of other social institutions. Consequently, these institutions often adopt an adversarial position, treating entertainment as a threat to cultural excellence, institutional life and ultimately a democratic society. In part a result of the segregation of high and low culture, entertainment has been peripheral to the "curriculum" of these institutions. Consequently, they have been hindered in their role to help define and give direction to the popular arts. Instead of critically engaging entertainment as it performs the functions of art, the most vocal response has been limited to consumer tactics, quelling the real force these institutions wield in American life. Even as we lack agreement on definition, roles, and the significance of popular art forms, the ubiquitous presence of the entertainment media in our society, and especially the youth culture, has instead redefined the roles of other social institutions, suggesting the need for reform in our social arrangement.

*   *   *

The purpose of this book is to examine the world of entertainment and the forces that affect its role in our lives and society. This study is an interdisciplinary work examining the interaction of cultural and intellectual trends, social and religious institutions, technology, art, economics and forces of production. Beyond the development of my own thesis about the confluence of religious and cultural forces in American life, I have synthesized original source material and the work of many film and media scholars, historians and cultural analysts. This historical approach leads to the consideration of perspectives generally overlooked in today's discourse about entertainment that nonetheless could be fruitful for our understanding of the issues and efforts to transform our situation. The analysis here is guided by the principle that people as well as institutions evaluate their present condition in the context of the past, and in light of the possibilities for the future.

This is not meant to be a comprehensive history. Instead I have focused on certain pivotal moments in the history of American entertainment as they relate to the overall thesis of the book. By "pivotal moments" I mean periods of confusion and adjustment that arise when, because of conflicting pressures and demands, a social institution has difficulty either establishing or maintaining its distinct identity. That identity, in my judgment, is based on its service to people, the roles and functions it carries out in the formation, maintenance and growth of a culture and a community.

The popular arts are both art and popular, cultural artifacts and commercial products—an observation that immediately introduces a level of ambivalence in this study. Our society has not entirely come to terms with the role of the popular arts as such, though these conflictions are the source of much of the controversy over entertainment today. Reformers cannot escape the ambiguity in their desire for moral and disciplinary purpose in entertainment that is produced and consumed in a free commercial market. As I will show in the historical narrative that follows, if they recognize the artistic role of the entertainment media they do not regard them as art, preferring instead to use consumer tactics to assert a reduced role for the media based on moralistic concerns. This is a serious oversimplification that evades pertinent industrial, artistic, social and cultural considerations.

My own ambivalence is rooted in the commercialization that makes possible the democratization of the arts but also restricts a deeper and more pluralistic development of the arts. In the narrative that follows, I show how the popular arts serve the roles of art in society, and I draw attention to entertainment that does so by developing artistic functions and qualities. This is part of an effort to establish the artistic roles and capabilities of the popular arts and show that reformers have disregarded these potentials in order to establish social control over the popular media. At the same time I examine the commercial process of cultural production that can be prohibitive of artistic development yet is critical to the popularizing or "democratizing" of entertainment forms and prevents them from becoming an entirely elitist affair. The massification of society and culture in the twentieth century occurred, however, at the expense of distinct folk and traditional subcultures, a paradoxical development that fueled the rise of democractic culture while also diminishing personal, ethnic and religious identities.

Thus it is that throughout the twentieth century, queries about artistic quality and moral concerns, free expression and free market—the basic terms of the discussion about entertainment—have of necessity taken a paradoxical stance. Entertainment defies expectations and limitations associated with high and low culture, freely mixing artistic functions with a crass commercializing that can be morally and aesthetically disturbing or delightful. The result is products that can be profound and intriguing, captivating and exciting, dull and mediocre, shoddy and exploitative, or even a curious combination of these. Nevertheless, in this treatment of entertainment I have tried to approach the subject from several different angles in an effort to map out an understanding of the popular arts that explains these tensions at the nexus of art, commerce and morality, while also suggesting a way forward.

My intent is not to exonerate the entertainment industry from any abuse of its artistic freedom, its exploitation of markets and its often blatant disregard for roles it serves other than appeasing corporate investors—all of which rightly deserve criticism. Nor am I trying to dismiss the efforts of reformers and critics. Rather, my aim is to explain why the industry and its many critics acted as they did, while revealing their strengths and weaknesses, in order to develop a healthy and responsible approach today.

For a number of reasons I have focused my discussion on the cinema (and mostly the mainstream Hollywood cinema), which was at the vanguard of the technology-based art forms that came to dominate entertainment and leisure in twentieth-century America. Because this book has a general historical arrangement, focusing on one aspect of the entertainment industry gives greater coherence to the overall design, making it easier to trace and develop themes. Much of what I have written about film can be applied to radio, the recording industry and television.

Finally, I do not intend to answer all questions about whether teens should listen to heavy metal music or whether Beavis and Butthead inhibit the development of analytical thinking among the young. These kinds of questions are certainly not unimportant, but in my judgment we lack a right context for asking and responding to them today. In the course of this research I have discovered, somewhat to my surprise, that beyond titles and stars, most people actually know very little about entertainment. They are largely unaware of the most significant events in the development of the entertainment media, solutions applied to problems in the past, how the industry operates, the composition of its audience and especially how entertainment established the role and force it has in our society today. It is hoped that this study will provide such a context for understanding and dealing with contemporary issues related to American culture, the organized religious community and entertainment.

2

• • • • •

Religion &
"Worldly"
Amusements

In 1993 the Roman Catholic Diocese of Scranton, Pennsylvania, bought fifty commercial spots on MTV and VH-1 in the hope of interesting young men in the priesthood. The thirty-second recruitment ads showed young priests explaining what the ministry meant to them. *Tonight Show* host Jay Leno quipped, "Just think, a future Pope could be watching *Beavis and Butthead* right now!"

The idea of using MTV to recruit for the priesthood is both amusing and revealing. The humor is based on a widely shared assumption about a basic incongruity between organized religion and entertainment. Historically the relation of religion and entertainment, in the United States at least, has been something like a pendulum swinging back and forth between vicious attack and uneasy cooperation. What has remained constant, however, is a level of antagonism between the two.

Long before the high and low disjunction in American life, the church condemned spectacle entertainment as such. The more conservative religious groups have always been leery of the influence of media on family and religious life and have a long history of protesting new forms of communication. Today religious conservatives have made the entire entertainment industry an arena for battle in the wider culture wars. Though not alone in their criticism, they have been the most outspoken on their side in the cultural conflict that sociologist James Davison Hunter described as "ultimately a struggle over national identity—*over the meaning of America*, who we are now, and perhaps most important, who we, as a nation, will aspire to become in the new millennium."[1]

While the term "culture wars" is derived from the German *Kulturkampf*, its popular usage today suggests an allusion to George Lucas's Star Wars films, which pitted a cosmic "Force" of good against evil in a struggle for ultimate control of the universe. Though science-fiction fantasy, it is a fitting metaphor for our contemporary struggle, because many religious groups have interpreted today's cultural conflict as a real manifestation of the spiritual battle between God and the demonic world. This was also true of the social and cultural turmoil at the start of the twentieth century.

Today's cultural conflict, which is perceived as a full-fledged assault on Christian civilization, includes both high and low cultures; the same arguments were used in the hot debates over Robert Mapplethorpe's photographic exhibit and 2 Live Crew's rap record, the one being high culture and the other popular. Today's defenders of the faith have employed (with some variation) the same apocalyptic scheme as earlier reformers in their attack on entertainment.

It is worthwhile to examine the confluence of religious and cultural forces in American life around the beginning of the twentieth century and their effects on the burgeoning entertainment industry, especially the cinema. That is the case because the relationship between entertainment and the American religious community reveals a historic passion in the church that dates back to its beginnings. The current controversy over entertainment it not something new, but has precedents, and historical analysis reveals reform efforts to be not just a simple matter of morality but an entanglement of religious, cultural and social forces.

Most of what today's reformers have to say about entertainment harks back to speeches and sermons from earlier battles throughout the twentieth century. "There can be no doubt that the movies with their sensationalism, their false standards, their pornography, and their open exhibition of moral laxity and lawlessness are influencing our young people today far more than the church, and seriously counteracting the combined stabilizing influence of the school and the home."[2] This statement appeared in an article in *The Christian Century* in 1930. Near the end of World War II, during which Hollywood produced a profusion of extremely patriotic films, a U.S. congressman launched an investigation of the film community "to expose those elements that are insidiously trying to spread subversive propaganda, poison the minds of your children, distort the history of our country, and discredit Christianity."[3] Even in 1948, celebrated as a peak year in movie attendance, legislators were not satisfied with Hollywood productions. "The American people like pictures which are clean and wholesome," Congressman Clare E. Hoffman said, distressed by recent movies. "They do not care for barroom scenes. They do not care for any of those things which a dissolute, decaying nation sometimes sanctions." The congressman based his appeal to Hollywood on the profit motive, arguing that if "clean pictures" were shown in movie houses, adult housewives and businessmen who "would like just a little clean fun on the screen" would flock to the theaters and "educate the producers as to what the American picture audience really wanted."[4]

Comparable arguments are used by media critics, clergy and politicians today. The survey in chapter one shows that their rhetoric is laced with the same inflammatory and apocalyptic imagery as that of earlier reformers and clergy: the entertainment industry produces "nightmares of depravity" and is "an all-powerful enemy, an alien force." Images of war and crisis ("the forces of hell were unleashed") are used to heighten and dramatize the problems they see with entertainment and to mobilize their constituencies. As was the case with reformers in the past, while the rhetoric of the debate emphasizes family, children and "traditional" values, these are only one aspect of a larger social and political agenda. Nevertheless, they have set the tone and, in many respects, the terms of the current discussion about entertainment, at least in the popular press. As we shall see, the controversies and notions of the early twentieth century have been long-lasting and continue to adversely affect the church's analysis and subsequent strategies for transforming the role of entertainment in American life.

Since the Days of Rome

The Preamble to the Motion Picture Production Code of 1930 referred as far back in history as the "gladiatorial combats" and "obscene plays of Roman times" to argue that different forms of entertainment have been either "HELPFUL or HARMFUL to the human race." As this suggests, the animosity between the church and entertainment can be traced back to the days of the Roman Empire, when Christians in the early church distinguished themselves from the pagans by refusing to attend the Roman games. "The frightful debaucheries and cruelties which constituted the sports of the Romans merited the holy indignation with which the disciples of the early days denounced them," Washington Gladden, a leading figure in the social gospel movement, wrote in an essay on "Christianity and Popular Amusements" in 1885. His description is worth quoting at length.

When we know that the best actor was the one who could behave the most obscenely; that the chariot races at the circus, where there were seats for three hundred and eighty-five thousand spectators, were deemed most successful when horses and men were killed in the contest; that the spectacles at the amphitheater derived all their relish from the butchery of gladiators by scores and hundreds in their battles with wild beasts and with one another; that the public executions also offered a delectable entertainment for the populace, the condemned sometimes appearing "in garments interwoven with threads of gold, and with crowns on their heads, when suddenly flames burst from their clothing and consumed them," all for the amusement of the people,—we are not disposed to find fault with the protest of the early Christians against the popular diversions. "Bread and games!" was the cry of the Roman populace. "Work and prayer!" was the watch-word of the Christians. Against the indolence and savage frivolity of the people about them, they lifted up their standard of industry and soberness.[5]

First-century Christians must have perceived the Roman amusements as a real live manifestation of the spiritual struggle between God and Satan, and the amphitheater itself as an all-too-real symbol representing the arena in which the cosmic battle between good and evil was waged.

The church's crusade against the amusements of the day continued for centuries after the Roman spectacles had ceased. But the association between amusements and the campaign of the devil was somehow woven into the cultural fabric of the religious life. One way of looking at this is to examine the church's association of entertainment with basic principles in Christian theology. Evangelical Protestants believe that God's general or "common grace" is an ever-present reality that restrains the power of sin; believers and unbelievers alike are given good gifts to use in service of the "cultural mandate," God's command to human beings to explore and cultivate the possibilities of the creation (Gen 1:28; 2:15). And yet there exists a fundamental and universal spiritual opposition or "antithesis" between the dominion of God and that of Satan, the ruler of "this world."

The doctrine of common grace and the cosmic struggle between good and evil, light and darkness, can be found in some form or other, with greater or lesser emphasis, in all Christian denominations. The earth is the arena where this spiritual warfare takes place, a struggle between cultural activity in faith and that in unbelief, waged in human affairs, that leaves no aspect of life untouched.[6] Righteousness characterizes faithful Christian living, "worldliness" the compromise with sin. Against this theological background, in the past as well as today, devout Christians have sometimes interpreted times of social upheaval and cultural stress as moments when human affairs approach the edge of the apocalypse.

This is especially true of those Christian fundamentalists and evangelicals who retreat from culture rather than trying to influence it. Instead of understanding sin as having a corrupting influence on all of life, these groups tend to identify evil with certain aspects of life. At different times alcohol, sex, modernism, communism, liberalism and—of special interest here—popular culture have all been branded by conservative evangelicals as demonic.

Of course some evangelical pietists have completely rejected all culture, regardless of high and low categories, as unspiritual. Nineteenth-century revivalist Charles Grandison Finney, for example, declared, "I cannot believe that a person who has ever known the love of God can relish a secular novel. . . . Let me visit your chamber, your parlor, or wherever you keep your books. What is here? Byron, Scott, Shakespeare and a host of triflers and blasphemers of God."[7]

Finney complained about the great popular-culture issue of his time—novel reading—with all the vigor today's champions of literature employ in disdaining the visual media. But while he denounced the content of popular art, he embraced its format as a vehicle for revivalist theology, drawing criticism from the cultural elite. Finney preached producer values, religious purity and moral discipline, but his methods and oratory style drew from the spectacle format.

This approach has been used by many evangelicals who condemn the content of the popular arts but justify their employment of entertainment media and formats by an appeal to a higher "sacred" purpose, such as evangelization or worship. Billy Sunday's sensational style of preaching and revivals was very much a product of mass entertainment, even though he was critical of it. Evangelist Charles D. Fuller used national radio broadcasts in the 1940s to spread the gospel. In the 1950s and 1960s Billy Graham employed television and movies for the same purpose.

Graham and earlier revivalists used popular music in their crusades, and young evangelicals christianized secular rock music with religious lyrics in order to save lost youth in the late 1960s and early 1970s. By the 1980s the contemporary Christian music (CCM) industry was a multimillion-dollar business combining religious worship and evangelism with entertainment. At the same time, televangelist Pat Robertson established the Christian Broadcasting Network (CBN), a satellite network designed to beam the Christian gospel around the world.

Ironically, while conservative evangelicals today rail against contemporary popular culture and the media as part of an assault on "traditional values," they are rejecting some aspects of church tradition in their "praise and worship" services, turning to contemporary music and television programming as modes of expression. Some evangelicals who condemn popular culture may think high culture is superior. Most, however, recognize the importance of the popular media, evidenced by their employment of it, and want it scrubbed morally and spiritually clean by their standards. Still, their critique and strategies for reform are rooted in assumptions about art and entertainment embodied in the bifurcation of high and low culture.

Evangelicals and Cultural Reform

Most American Christians in the late nineteenth century were in a general sense what we call evangelicals today. Evangelicalism is the branch of Protestantism most characterized by fervor to spread the gospel of salvation from sin through personal faith in the atoning work of Jesus Christ. During the nineteenth century, evangelical Protestantism was the dominant religious force in America. In a short time, however, between the 1890s and the 1930s, evangelicalism lost its tremendous cultural influence to the challenge of modernism.

The collapse of evangelical influence also coincided with the rise of the social gospel movement. Responding to the strain created by rapid industrialization and urbanization, mainline churches worked for social and legal reform in child labor, factory working conditions and the duration of the work week. The social gospel movement was different from evangelical reform movements, in that the former was rooted in Protestant liberal theology and emphasized concern for human welfare and social conditions over personal evangelism and piety. Church historians explain,

> While not necessarily denying the value of the traditional evangelical approach of starting with evangelism, social gospel spokesmen subordinated such themes, often suggesting that stress on evangelism had made American evangelicalism too otherworldly (concerned about getting people to heaven) and individualistic (concerned with personal purity more than with the welfare of one's neighbor). Such themes fit well with the emerging liberal theology of the day, which was optimistic about human nature, ethical in emphasis, and hopeful about establishing the principles of the kingdom in the twentieth century.[8]

In reaction to these trends in the church, some evangelicals became fundamentalists, militantly upholding the evangelical faith against the encroachment of modernism and Protestant liberal theology. Fundamentalists professed the inerrancy of Scripture in matters of faith, history and science; modernists emphasized its human origins. The debate over creation versus Darwinian evolution in the Scopes trial in 1925 typified the intellectual and cultural tension between fundamentalism and modernism. Fundamentalists defended the "fundamental" doctrines of the evangelical Christian faith, which modernists commonly denied.[9]

By the 1930s it was clear that reform from within church denominations was not effective in turning the tide of modernism. Many fundamentalists began separating themselves from the mainline denominations, establishing their own denominations or, more often, independent churches and parachurch organizations. Instead of trying to influence American culture, fundamentalists retreated from it. This represented their approach to the "worldly amusements."

The prominent role of the Catholic Church in reforming the film industry during the 1930s illustrates the shift in power in the religious community. Even so, Catholic reformers also saw themselves in a cosmic struggle between good and evil and along with evangelicals assumed that Christianity was the only basis for a virtuous people and a healthy civilization. "Religion was the basis for true virtue; the purer the religion, the higher the morality. Christianity was the purest religion," religious historian George Marsden writes, adding, "The supposedly self-evident superiority of Western civilization and especially northern Europe was clearly due to the influence of Christianity and

Protestantism in particular."[10]

Religious leaders were committed to maintaining a cultural system consistent with Christian beliefs and supported by other social institutions like the family, church, school and government. The preservation of these values and institutions was considered crucial to ensure both faithful Christian living and the moral, social and political welfare of the nation. Any threat to the welfare of the country, then, was perceived as an attack on the kingdom of God and righteousness.

An understanding of this apocalyptic setting is critical to any explanation of the church's response to entertainment, for the meaning of social and cultural affairs was amplified because these events were treated as manifestations of the cosmic cataclysm between the spiritual powers of good and evil. The more powerful entertainment became as a force in American life, the greater the fear in the religious community, and especially among more conservative groups, of its potential as an instrument of evil. This explains in large part the emotional furor, inflammatory prose and rhetoric, and depth of conviction that religious leaders brought to their attacks on the entertainment industry.

This reaction was not unprecedented, however, and as we shall see, it continues today. Second-century church father Tertullian condemned the theater on the grounds that it reflected the pagan spirit of Rome. John Calvin banned it in Geneva in the sixteenth century. In Elizabethan England, Puritans wrote books condemning the theater in the harshest terms as an instrument of the devil. In the American colonies, the House of Representatives of New Hampshire banned an acting company in 1762 on the grounds that the theater has a "peculiar influence on the minds of young people, and greatly endanger[s] their morals by giving them a taste for intriguing, amusement and pleasure."[11]

There are some common themes in the church's disdain for the theater. For centuries actors were characterized as immoral (especially in their sexual behavior), lazy and slothful; in contrast to the virtue of hard work, the acting profession was criticized as "play." Even attending the theater was considered a waste of time and money, better spent on the poor or in prayer. Mendel Kohansky, a theater historian, has suggested an even more compelling reason for such opposition:

The church sees in the theatre a competitor, because the theatre opens vistas to the audience that religion considers its exclusive domain. The power of the actor to lead the audience beyond the limits of everyday experience, to experiences of much greater intensity and purity, is a direct threat to organized religion. The church claims to be the sole possessor of this power.[12]

Competition between institutions that communicate religious and cultural traditions and offer social criticism has remained a central issue in conflicts throughout the twentieth century.

The Devil's Workshop?

For centuries American Protestant groups criticized the theater as inimical to religiously defined values, especially hard work and the restraint of passion. Throughout the colonies there were strict regulations enforcing work and prohibiting all amusements; the stern rule of Puritanism demanded a consecrated observance of the "sabbath" (Sunday), including mandatory church attendance. There was nothing inherent in Calvinistic theology to justify such disapproval of pleasure. But in their condemnation of the worldliness of the church, Puritan reformers associated the moral laxity of their opponents (who generally belonged to the more privileged classes) with their amusements. The amusements symbolized a lack of spirituality in Puritan thought, but this association was also rooted in a social bias.

As long as the survival of early pioneer society depended on a tradition of hard work and the cooperation of the entire community, the Puritan work ethic and denunciation of leisure served the colonists well. But as the economic justification for these ideals diminished, it threatened their way of life, and many Puritan leaders responded by intensifying their enforcement of this rigid code of conduct. "Having convinced themselves that all idle pursuits were a Satanic trap to lure the godly from the path of duty, strict followers of the New England way could no more tolerate frivolity than heresy," according to one writer. "Their conscience would not let them enjoy worldly pleasures themselves; it would not let them permit others such enjoyment."[13]

As the population of non-Puritans increased, however, the exaltation of endless work and rigid self-restraint and the equation of pleasure with sin became intolerable: people needed normal recreational outlets for their fears and frustrations, tiredness and discontent. In the absence of other entertainment, many people took to heavy drinking, and taverns sprang up as friendly places offering a selection of drinks to satisfy people's tastes and need for sociable activity. Drunkenness, in turn, fostered other social problems and led to further prohibitive measures. Eventually state and church suspicion gave way to encouragement of healthy recreation and amusement, but the Puritan spirit exerted a strong and long-lasting influence on American attitudes about work and leisure.

The belief that amusement of any sort is sinful had a powerful hold on evangelical Protestant groups and—since evangelicalism was the dominant religious force in America during the nineteenth century—on the society at large. "The only enjoyment deemed strictly legitimate for the eminent saint was religious rapture," Washington Gladden wrote in criticism of the evangelical church. "It was the implicit, if not the avowed, doctrine of the Church, that all kinds of diversions were substitutes for this holy ecstasy, and as such sinful."[14] The most conservative Christian groups absolutely separated a life of godliness and virtue from leisure and pleasure. And so it was difficult for "the average Protestant church-member" to associate "a genuine piety . . . with cheery manners and a hearty joy in the good things of this life," or to take a "diversion without some compunctions or questionings of conscience," according to Gladden.[15]

Throughout the nineteenth century, evangelicals almost universally condemned the theater on moral and theological grounds. It was estimated that 70 percent of the American population in the middle of the nineteenth century thought theater attendance was sinful.[16] Religious leaders considered the theater a "worldly amusement," along with card playing, dancing, horse racing and sometimes novel reading. Such amusements, it was believed, distracted people from their vocation and worship of God; the theater, or "devil's workshop," was charged with appealing to the sinful nature, fostering laziness, impiety and immorality. The clergy recognized that the theater was competing with the church for the time, the money and even the souls of its congregants. For these reasons they forbade attendance and condemned the stage as "the synagogue of Satan."

Entertainment clearly represented values and practices that nineteenth-century Protestant leaders considered a threat to their notion of an ideal society based on the Bible. Relaxation, play, amusement and idle time were called "diversions," reflecting the belief that they "divert" people from the higher tasks of life associated with work and piety. The religious community feared entertainment as a social institution that often conflicted with the values fostered at home and in church. As the moral and spiritual center of the Victorian world, the home was considered essential to the well-being of the church and the moral health of the nation. Entertainment represented a threat to this social order, a threat that could eventually undermine the values of hard work and restraint that came to characterize Victorian culture, as they had characterized Puritanism.

Instead of encouraging believers to work in the industry to provide attractive and wholesome entertainment, and instead of providing general principles Christians could use to evaluate the amusements, the church adopted the strategy of arbitrary regulation of amusements, allowing some diversions and not others. But as Gladden observed, religious groups soon became bogged down in a host of ridiculous questions about "whether dancing was sinful, and whether billiards are worse than croquet, and whether cards are always an abomination, and whether church-members ought to be disciplined for attending the theater or the opera."

By the turn of the century, the church's admonitions against entertainment seemed largely futile and conspicuously out of touch with modern life. According to Gladden, even as early as 1885 people were most willing to spend "three times as much as a seat in a church would cost on the theatre and variety show" (here he refers to the practice of renting a family pew).[17] Albert F. McLean Jr. indicates that vaudeville patrons thought prohibitions against the amusements and "the appeal to purity and uplift [were] more a snobbish identification with upper-middle class taste than . . . a matter of religious conviction."[18]

Despite religious condemnation, the lower classes discovered that the amusements helped them navigate through the complexity of the modern world, not only through what they communicated but also by providing a stimulating escape from the drudgery of urban life and work. Prohibitions were constantly violated, and the church could do little to discipline offenders.

A Softening Attitude

The clergy recognized that they were waging a losing battle in their denunciation of the amusements. In 1904 a general consensus emerged among mainline Protestant and Catholic leaders that the church should take a more moderate position. A restrictive, legalistic attitude was replaced by an emphasis on the individual conscience and personal discernment of the believer. To be sure, clergymen still thought the amusements were not necessarily spiritually uplifting and did not always meet the moral standards the church preached. That did not mean, however, that participation would destroy a person's moral character or threaten his or her spiritual well-being. "When the Christ-life is enthroned," a United Brethren minister said, "the Kingdom of God has nothing to fear from innocent amusements, and ecclesiastical legislation is not necessary to keep out those which are sinful."[19]

There were two reasons for this change. First, denominational leaders acknowledged the need for leisure as a humanizing element to compensate for the boredom, monotony and routinization of work and life in the industrial city. "Play lubricates the stiff, grating machinery of workday life," a leading Presbyterian minister wrote. Second, banning the amusements, they realized, was inconsistent with biblical principles. "Many churchmen have erred greatly by their indiscriminate denunciation of all amusements" and their adoption of "positions which neither common sense nor holy Scripture can enable them to maintain," one Baptist minister said. An Episcopal bishop summarized the new position:

> Religion should be the guiding principle in every department of life, of which amusement is but one. The Christian man is not under bondage, but under the law of liberty, and his conduct is to be determined not by a series of superficial and martinet directions, but by his own instinctive sense of what is fit and proper. It is not therefore in my judgment within the office of the Church to regulate his amusements for him.[20]

Instead, various clergy proposed, Christians should be given the prerogative to decide for themselves in the matter of amusements, using biblical principles as their guide.

The subsequent participation of middle-class churchgoers contributed to the general boom in entertainment over the next decade and dramatically increased the size of the potential audience for motion pictures just prior to the advent of the nickelodeon. Ministers at that time still believed the church's teaching was sufficient to counter what negative effects there might be in entertainment. By the late 1920s, however, clergy would not be so confident. As the entertainment industry grew enormously and greatly expanded its audience, religious leaders began to look at the movie industry in particular as a social institution with influence in American life that could overwhelm the combined impact of family, church and school.

Victorianism on the Wane

Americans were aware that they were living in a new age that demanded the development of new values. As scarcity gave way to abundance, belief in self-denial and the Protestant work ethic had to be reconciled with immediate gratification and the new consumer status. As people paid more attention to satisfying their personal needs, a new morality replaced the strict Victorian code, and new ideas about work, leisure, courtship, companionship as a basis for marriage, birth control and childrearing became possible. The rapid pace of change during this social transformation created a conflict for many who saw the new values as fundamentally and socially destructive. From a wide range of perspectives there was a shared sense that American civilization was in crisis.

As chapter three will show, the forces of modernism combined with the social upheaval caused by rapid industrialization, urbanization and population explosion put enormous strain on traditional Victorian culture. Protestant and Catholic leaders interpreted this transformation as an attack on the Christian faith. Modernism, they feared, would ultimately tear apart the fabric of civilization by undermining the Victorian values they considered essential to the maintenance of Christian society. Darwin's theory of evolution negated even the possibility of morality by presupposing that "men and women were merely animals from whom only animal morals could be expected," Father Daniel A. Lord, a coauthor of the Motion Picture Production Code of 1930, argued.[21] Church leaders believed that Freud's theory of the unconscious could only unleash passions, undermining the value of restraint and leading to moral ruin. Likewise, industrial patterns of work and leisure, the increase in women working for wages outside the home and the growing use of radio, automobile and movies were all cited as contributing to a breakdown in the family—and, it followed, the spiritual and moral welfare of the nation.

Noting the changes brought about by modernism and World War I, Will H. Hays, president of the Motion Picture Producers and Distributors Association of America (MPPDA), wrote that the battle over the movies "was often a case of inherited American standards—products of a Christian civilization—against alien customs variously considered 'modern,' 'liberal,' or 'pagan.' Hosts of Americans clung firmly to their own ideals and strongly resisted the alien invasion."[22] In defense of Christian theology, morality and society, members of the middle class proclaimed themselves leaders in the advance of civilization and staked a claim for the righteousness of their way of life. The ascendancy of other cultures, they believed, would lead to debauchery and barbarism.

Protestant and Catholic leaders infused the social and cultural turmoil around the turn of the century with a spiritual dimension, mingling religious beliefs with culturally conceived ideals, values, assumptions and even practices. To say that church leaders simply identified high and low culture with righteousness and sin, respectively, would be an oversimplification, for as we shall see, the situation reveals a greater complexity. Evangelicals may have lauded high culture, but they loved pious hymns and stories that were anything but high art and detested modernist painting, music and pieces of literature that were exclusively high art. Their critique and tastes were founded on moral, not cultural or aesthetic, concerns as a defense against perceived threats to their religious and folk tradition. But they also wanted the social respectability and acceptance in American life that was associated both symbolically and socially with the traditional high arts.

Already in the first quarter of the twentieth century, distinctions between high and low, traditional and contemporary appeared in the cultural discourse. Such cultural categories and sociological assumptions did inform evangelicals' thinking, discussions and tactics on the matter of entertainment, indicated by the designation *worldly* that was used by some. For that reason the distinction between high and popular culture as it relates to the spiritual antithesis is a good entry into the American discourse about entertainment.

Consider this critique of the movies by a conservative Protestant minister. The motion picture apparatus may have been a "wonderful invention" and movies "a valuable production of art, especially for educational purposes," he wrote in 1909. But the film industry catered to public desires for the "spectacular and exciting," producing films designed to "appeal the most to the corrupt taste of the largest portion of the masses." Rather than urge Christians to transform the burgeoning film industry, this minister concluded that "God's name can never be glorified, and His kingdom will never be furthered by cooperating with such institutions of the world."[23] The line of the antithesis was drawn, sequestering church members from the movies and other amusements and consequently prohibiting them from distinguishing redemptive aspects and establishing appropriate Christian participation.

As zealous as religious reformers were, however, they did not take entertainment seriously enough: their rhetoric overstated the problem on the one hand, while their response underplayed it on the other. This remains true of today's critics as well. Entertainment has become a significant institution in American life. Already in the first quarter of the twentieth century, the theater,

47

movies and new styles of music were having an effect on the family and did represent a challenge to the authority of established religious and social institutions. These observations could have developed into important insights and strategies for affecting the emerging structure of modern society, but instead Christian leaders were overwhelmed by a pietistic concern with the (im)morality of entertainment. Instead of responding to the entertainment industry as to any other aspect of life that is corrupted by sin and in need of transformation, church leaders perceived it as part of a spiritual attack on Christian values and social institutions that imperiled not only the nation but also the kingdom of God and righteous living.

Influenced by assumptions of the disjunction between high and low culture, the church subjugated the artistic possibilities of the cinema to its perceived potential for evil. Roman Catholic and Protestant leaders worked to render entertainment harmless by regulating it with industry production codes that removed elements considered offensive to middle-class religious and cultural values. The more conservative denominations regarded movies and other entertainment as apostate cultural forms beyond redemption. While different religious groups were more or less restrictive, the list of activities prohibited by the most conservative ones included card playing, dancing, listening to popular recordings and the radio, novel reading, and vaudeville or movie attendance; some even banned the legitimate theater. One denomination forbade members to attend movies or the theater on the grounds that their general influence put them "on the side of Satan against the Kingdom of Christ."[24]

But this scheme represents a denial of the universality of the spiritual antithesis, insofar as the divide between high and low culture carved the creation up into aspects worthy of Christian participation and others to be abandoned to the forces of secularism. A genuinely biblical perspective affirms the opposite: no individual, group of people, human endeavor or aspect of life is immune to the corrosive effects of sin, and it follows that none of these should be excluded from redemptive activity. If the earth and everything in it belongs to God, as the psalmist wrote (Psalm 24), then popular art forms deserve to be critiqued and cultivated just as much as the traditional arts or other aspects of reality.

In effect, both abstinence and regulation restricted the transformative role of the church in culture. The church (and other institutions as well) did not engage contemporary entertainment forms as art, trying to discover fitting roles for these new and pervasive media in our modern democratic society, but instead either eschewed them or worked to mitigate their impact by ensuring control over their ideological and moral content.

As spiritual lines were drawn across the affairs of life, however, they became cultural and sociological categories that were distinctly unchristian in their assumptions. The tastes of unbelievers and those of the masses were too easily equated in this theological view of culture, resulting in the denigration of groups of people and their cultural products, but not simply on the basis of religious belief or disbelief. Spiritual distinctions that were drawn were often based on class, cultural or ideological differences, or race and ethnicity—a practice rejuvenated by some at the end of the twentieth century.

Spiritual distinctions were also identified with certain human activities. Obviously prayer and church attendance were assumed to contribute to a godly life. But as I will show in following chapters, the high arts were also invested with a level of divinity. In contrast, immigrant amusements and African-American musical styles, it was believed, fostered the influence of the devil. The urban amusements, and movies in particular, became a major arena in the cultural conflict at the beginning of the twentieth century—a conflict that was portrayed as an apocalyptic contest between good and evil, civilization and barbarism. The same rhetoric and debate about entertainment have been rejuvenated in our contemporary culture wars.

The Menace of the Movies

Although most denominations removed official prohibitions after the turn of the century, religious leaders continued to view the encroachment of entertainment on the family and religious circle with great skepticism. Many Christian groups reduced the spiritual battle against "worldliness" to immorality, and particularly sexual impurity. Sensual "animal" dances (like the grizzly bear and foxtrot), double-entendre humor on vaudeville, and risqué movies lacked the moral and spiritual quality that clergy desired. One religious conservative wrote, for example, that because human nature is sinful, "movie patrons demand the salacious, the suggestive, the naughty, to make really good movies profitable."[25]

Lurid advertising provided ample evidence of moral corruption and was a constant source of contention. Exhibitors regularly tried to lure moviegoers with ads like these:

Social secretary tells all. The bold facts, shocking but true. Reveals the private affairs of New York's fastest-stepping crowd of millionaires, from boudoirs to speakeasies.

She lured men. Her red lips and warm eyes enslaved a man of the world . . . and taught life to an innocent boy! Hot tropic nights fanning the flames of desire. She lived for love alone.

The scarlet truth about a reign of terror broken by a night of love! The smart set sought her secretly and compromised her privately.

A blonde intruder made scandal of her marriage. So she thumbed her nose at convention and gave them something worth talking about.

She stopped at nothing. She wanted happiness, fun, romance, but the things she sought were denied, so she stopped at nothing to get what was forbidden. The shockingly real drama of a modern girl.[26]

These advertising blurbs can hardly be distinguished from those on the covers of today's romance novels, tabloid magazines or the *Night Eyes* video series. Regardless, they can be construed as offensive, and the fact that the strategy is almost a century old does little to mitigate fears about their corruptive influence today.

Movies, even more than the other amusements, came to represent the cultural transformation that seemed seriously threatening to a Christian-based society. Perhaps this was because motion pictures were an industrial art form, a technology-based medium that was an enormously popular form of entertainment. As modern ideas and values were incorporated into movies, they became an even greater threat, because motion pictures were accessible to an unsophisticated mass audience that was worldwide in scope. By the late 1920s, concerned religious leaders and social reformers saw the movie industry as a loose cultural cannon.

The tremendous popularity of the movies made them a competitor not only of the church but also of other entertainment operations, including saloons, vaudeville and the legitimate theater. Reformers at first actually praised the nickelodeons because they put a good number of saloons out of business. A Chicago police inspector observed in 1909, for example, that "nickel theaters have done more to injure the saloon business in Chicago than any other factor."[27]

But it was much more than that the "church collection plate had lost much of its jingle," as film historian Lewis Jacobs quipped, that irked religious leaders.[28] Conservative religious groups wanted to establish themselves in America without imitating its secular practices; they remained devoted to their religious tradition and producer-oriented values while also hungering for social respectability in their new country. The movie industry, with its godlike stars and opulent exhibition palaces—resembling cathedrals right down to the massive organ—symbolized both the culture of consumption and a competing religious order. It was no wonder, as Warren I. Susman has observed, that "some more fundamentalist Protestant religionists forbid movie-going to their congregants. They know a surrogate or competing religious order when they see one."[29]

In addition, as a fundamental agent of communication and socialization, the entertainment media challenged the authority and communal control that family and church had over the nurture and enculturation of their members. Add to that the risqué content of many motion pictures, and it is easy to see why church leaders viewed the movies as a threat to religious and moral purity, as well as a force that could completely homogenize and nationalize any ethnoreligious community.

Religious conservatives relentlessly condemned the movies as "degrading, polluting, ruining souls and bodies and poisoning the minds of men, especially the young and inexperienced." The cinema was repeatedly referred to as "godless," a "moral bubonic plague," a "maelstrom of iniquity," and even the place "where Satan has his throne." As late as 1947, one writer described the cinema as "one of the most effective inventions of the devil to seduce our covenant-children and drag them into the streets of this modern Sodom and Gomorrah."[30]

Remarkably, the film industry was sometimes vested with supernatural power—such a great evil, one religious conservative said, "that even the combined efforts of the home, the school, and the church to overcome that influence, where it can be prevented, is bound to fail in most cases."[31]

This anxiety was shared by the mainline denominations and the Roman Catholic Church as well. Martin Quigley, a Catholic who participated in crafting the Motion Picture Production Code of 1930, wrote that film "exerts a power and influence capable of either advancing or retarding the mightiest efforts of the church, the school, and even the home."[32] Even more striking was Fred Eastman's conclusion to a series of articles in *The Christian Century,* a mainline Protestant publication. The cinema's "portrayal of life . . . has lost all sense of spiritual values," he wrote. "The conflict between the standards portrayed in the movies and those upheld by the home, the school, and the church has created confusion, not only in the minds of growing children, but also in the minds of our foreign neighbors who see our movies but do not see our homes and schools and churches."[33]

Eastman left no doubt that he viewed the cinema as a diabolic force assaulting the institutions of righteousness. Likening the campaign to censor films to the American Revolution, the abolition of slavery and the Civil War, he called on churches, schools, parent-teacher associations, women's clubs, Rotary, Kiwanis and Lions clubs, the American Legion, and "all the rest" to "stand up and be counted" in the crusade "to convert this industry from public enemy to public friend."[34] Eastman urged support for prior federal censorship ("We cannot cut the devil out of a picture with a pair of scissors"), legislation to outlaw the industry's monopolistic practices, and the establishment of a state commission to monitor and restrict films in their foreign distribution.

Mainline and conservative church leaders alike were also upset that exhibitors violated the sabbath by opening on Sunday (which was prime leisure time for working men and women). This line of criticism gives us another insight into the "spiritual" battle over the movies. Protestant evangelist Billy Sunday preached in 1921 that "no foreign bunch can come over here and tell us how we ought to observe the Lord's Day. The United States is a God-fearing and a God-loving nation."[35] This reference to the immorality of immigrants alludes to the fact that by that time first- and second-generation Jewish immigrants had acquired complete control of the American film industry.

The controversy over the "menace of the movies" occurred during a time when African-Americans, immigrants and Jews were openly persecuted for not being "100 percent American." This was not a prominent element in the public discourse about movies, but religious antagonisms were clearly behind the crusade for Christian civilization. One religious lobbying group in 1920 voted "to rescue the motion pictures from the hands of the Devil and 500 unChristian Jews."[36] The following year an article appeared in the anti-Semitic *Dearborn Independent* maligning Jews in the film industry: "As soon as the Jews gained control of the 'movies,' we had a movie problem, the consequences of which are not yet visible. It is the genius of that race to create problems of a moral character in whatever business they achieve a majority."[37] The Methodist publication *Churchman* accused the Hays Office of being a "smoke screen to mask" the "meretricious methods" of "shrewd Hebrews who make the big money by selling crime and shame."[38]

The comments of Joseph Breen are even more revealing. Just prior to becoming head of the Production Code Administration (PCA), the office that approved films for distribution, Breen expressed his dissatisfaction with his boss, MPPDA president Will Hays, and the lack of enforcement of the Motion Picture Production Code. He wrote from Hollywood in 1932 that Hays "sold us a first-class bill of goods when he put over the Code on us. . . . It may be that Hays thought these lousy Jews out here would abide by the Code's provisions but if he did then he should be censured for his lack of proper knowledge of the breed." He went on to denigrate the Jews in the film industry: "They are simply a rotten bunch of vile people with no respect for anything beyond the making of money. . . . Here we have Paganism rampant and in its most virulent form. . . . These Jews seem to think of nothing but money making and sexual indulgence. . . . They are, probably, the scum of the scum of the earth."[39] Such anti-Semitic propaganda, articulated both in public and in private, understandably produced a climate of fear for Hollywood Jews.

Clearly, then, in some cases religious prejudice was intermingled with a Christian conviction that the cinema had to be turned into an instrument for the advance of civilization and the moral and spiritual improvement of the human race.

Hollywood Versus America in the 1990s

As the cultural conflict escalated in the 1990s, opinion polls indicated that a majority of Americans thought there was an excessive amount of profanity, sex and violence in the media. Sensing a mood of discontent, a number of individuals and organizations proclaimed themselves representatives of a silent majority of Americans who were "fed up" with the immoral character of entertainment. Among the religious-oriented ones are the Reverend Donald Wildmon's American Family Association, Ted Baehr's Christian Film and Television Commissions, and the Michigan-based Dove Foundation. While their immediate goals and strategies vary, today's reformers have much in common with each other, and with their counterparts in the first half of the twentieth century as well. They argue that as guardians of public morality, they have to protect the family from corruption by the outside world. They too fuse spirituality and culture and invest their campaign with the authority of God.

Today's skirmish over entertainment does not have specific church denominational support. It is centered in parachurch and other organizations located in the conservative end of what George Marsden has called "neo-evangelicalism," although it also includes social conservatives who would also affirm

Judeo-Christian morality. The neo-evangelical movement began to take shape after World War II, as a combination of the biblical orthodoxy of fundamentalism and the cultural calling of evangelicalism to evangelize and serve as moral guardians of American culture.[40] During the tumult of the Vietnam era it remained largely buried. Near the end of the 1960s, however, neo-evangelicalism emerged as a distinct movement, and it became the mainline religion of the 1970s, embodying an array of denominational churches and parachurch organizations, including black evangelical churches and nondenominational campus and youth ministries.

What is unique about today's reform movement in the church is its confluence of religious convictions and conservative political ideology. Social and religious conservatives have redrawn the spiritual and cultural battle lines; the entertainment industry has become one of the battlefronts in what James Dobson of Focus on the Family has called a "Civil War of Values."[41] "It's a spiritual war for the souls of those who constitute our civilization," Ted Baehr wrote. "The warfare of ideas and thoughts has exploded through the use of movies and television, revolutionizing our way of thinking. We are fighting against an enemy that is using every possible tactic to control our minds: materialism, secularism, humanism, Marxism—all the isms that conflict with Christianity."[42]

These critics tend to identify faithfulness to God with the defense of conservative values, summed up by Michael Medved as "hard work, traditional family, a strong national defense, and material acquisition."[43] In effect, they have taken values that were historically conceived and culturally defined, and have turned them into absolutes. It followed that American institutions embodying these values are sacred in their minds, and any attack on them they consider an attack on the kingdom of God.

After the fall of Soviet communism and the 1992 election of a Democratic president in the United States, the liberal tradition in American politics became the new demonic threat to Christian civilization. President Ronald Reagan himself had made the word *liberal* something profane by referring to it as the "L-word." Congress, the White House, the news media, academia, the arts and entertainment were all blasted as taking part in a liberal attack on "traditional" America, as institutions of communication and cultural transmission were increasingly drawn into the fire.

The line of the cultural hierarchy and the religious antithesis as it is drawn today pits contemporary culture, both high and low, against historic elite culture. Conservatives have campaigned to eliminate funding for the National Endowment for the Arts (NEA) and the National Endowment for the Humanities (NEH); on another front, evangelicals battling television and pornography have escalated their campaign for decency into a full-fledged indictment of the entire entertainment industry.

In brief, their charge is that the entertainment industry is a liberal-minded community resolved to subvert American culture. The Hollywood elite, they argue, are even willing to forsake profits in a determined effort to undermine "traditional" American values. "There is simply no way that the single-minded pursuit of profit can account for Hollywood's ongoing war on traditional values," Medved wrote.[44]

This is a curious charge. Surveys do indicate that people in the media industries are more progressive than most Americans. But it takes a major leap in logic and argumentation to claim that ideology, and not financial profit, drives the entertainment business, which is a supreme example of unbridled free-market economics. Regardless, conservative critics maintain that the entertainment industry is not driven by profit but by ideological warfare. The effect, once again, is to equate the spiritual battle line between good and evil with social, political and cultural groups and categories.

In Medved's 1992 book *Hollywood vs. America* (a foreboding-sounding title, suggesting an end-times ideology), he traced the source of Hollywood's assault on "traditional" values to the "counterculture's comprehensive conquest of Hollywood" in the late 1960s.[45] According to the former scriptwriter, the golden age of Hollywood ended when liberals took over and corrupted the entertainment industry by promoting their leftist agenda and (im)morality throughout the world. Since then, Medved and others submit, entertainment has been out of touch with the values of the majority of Americans.

Medved did much to bring public debate about entertainment into the limelight by tapping into widespread fears about the current generation of youth and concerns about the impact of entertainment amid the declining influence of family, school and faith community. By drawing the entertainment industry into the culture wars, he asserted the place of moral and ideological criticism.

Beyond that, however, he has been soundly criticized for his superficial and faulty scholarship.[46] As will become apparent throughout this study, his historical analysis is largely uninformed and at critical points is based on misinformation. He never considers, for example, that changes in motion pictures after World War II might have resulted from a Supreme Court decision that extended First Amendment protection to film. His examination of weekly box-office trends in the late 1960s is based on an erroneous source; the actual figures undermine his hypothesis. Even fundamental contradictions in Medved's work have not gone unnoticed by some. His basic contention is that the entertainment media are destroying American values and institutions, but his appeal to Hollywood producers for more wholesome family entertainment is based on the idea that the majority of the population live a "conservative lifestyle." Either movies are not having such a negative effect, or they are not nearly as out of touch with the tastes or values of American moviegoers as Medved claims.

At a later point I will return to Medved's analysis to examine in more detail certain fundamental and related issues in the effort to reform entertainment today. That these same issues, which have been constant in the debate throughout the twentieth century, continue to dominate public discourse and frustrate proposals for change demonstrates the inadequacy of the assumptions on which our conceptions about art and entertainment are based.

Conclusion

Medved is probably the most visible conservative media critic. His ideas, which have been parroted by politicians and other media critics, have also had an impact on the evangelical church's attitude and response. The wide and uncritical acceptance of the conservative critique among evangelical Protestants (and some Catholics) is of particular interest for this study of the nexus of religion, culture and entertainment. *Hollywood vs. America* told its audience, in this case evangelical Christians, in simple terms what they wanted to hear—Hollywood is an "all-powerful enemy, an alien force that assaults our most cherished values and corrupts our children."[47] Medved cast a cultural and ideological struggle in a moral and spiritual framework that evangelicals could understand.

What is most alarming, however, is that serious flaws in Medved's analysis and the weakness of his proposals went completely unquestioned by evangelicals. Instead, Medved received hearty endorsements from evangelical leaders. He was featured in evangelical publications and radio and television programs, and was invited to speak to the National Religious Broadcasters, the Gospel Music Association, and Regent University and other Christian liberal arts colleges. Such uncritical acceptance lends credence to the contention of

Os Guinness, himself an evangelical Christian. "Failing to think Christianly, evangelicals have been forced into the role of cultural imitators and adapters rather than originators," he wrote. "In biblical terms, it is to be worldly and conformist, not decisively Christian."[48]

As I have already suggested, there are some striking parallels between today's culture wars and the conflict and social upheaval at the beginning of the twentieth century. Entertainment was a critical arena then, as it is in our cultural struggle today. During the striking transformation in American society around the turn of the century, the contemporary entertainment industry was born. The phonograph, motion pictures and radio were among the scores of technological developments that occurred around that time. These media dramatically changed the means of communication in American life, creating a mass society. Entrepreneurs exploited the "amusement" potential of the media, and huge, competitive companies evolved into the entertainment industry as we know it today. The entertainment industry, then, did not emerge in a vacuum, and understanding the context in which the entertainment industry evolved will shed much light on our current concerns and discussion.

3

· · · · ·

High & Low
Culture
Wars

As the twentieth century progressed, groups in the American cultural order were increasingly identified by the categories highbrow, middlebrow and lowbrow. As these cultural distinctions became reified in American life, the connotations of *highbrow* extended beyond wealth and family, finding a locus among intellectuals, especially those with esoteric interests. Noting that the old American industrialists like the Carnegies or Morgans were being replaced by a new intellectual elite composed of scientists, artists, writers and commentators, *Harper's Magazine* examined the three categories at midcentury. "What is a highbrow?" the writer asked, followed by three replies. "A highbrow is a man who has found something more interesting than women," Edgar Wallace, a writer of crime novels and thrillers once said. *Harper's* writer thought that too vague, but that Columbia professor and author Brander Matthews came closer with "a highbrow is a person educated beyond his intelligence," and that perhaps humorist and playwright A. P. Herbert came closest with "a highbrow is the kind of person who looks at a sausage and thinks of Picasso." "It is this association of culture with every aspect of daily life," the writer asserted, "that distinguishes the highbrow from the middlebrow or the lowbrow."[1]

Before midcentury, the separation of high and popular culture was firmly established in American life, but although the original class distinctions they represented had faded, these categories continued to have an impact on ideas and discourse about the nature of art and entertainment in mass society.

America was transformed by the modern industrial world that emerged around the turn of the twentieth century. Between 1860 and 1900, American capital invested in industry leaped from one to ten billion dollars; the value of goods manufactured in the United States soared from two to thirteen billion dollars. The wealth of natural resources in America fueled the oil, steel, agricultural and textile industries, making the United States one of the world's leading industrial powers by the turn of the century. Railroads, telegraph and telephone lines crisscrossed the country fostering transportation and advancing the means of communication.

The cities, which were the centers for manufacturing and distribution, were most affected by this tremendous industrial and population growth. The U.S. population increased from sixty-three million in 1890 to seventy-six million in 1900 to nearly ninety-two million by 1910. In that same span of time, some twenty-eight million immigrants from Canada, Latin America, Asia and Europe reached the shores of America. Others left family-owned farms or small towns from all across the country and poured into the nation's cities, hoping to procure a better life for themselves and their children. To meet the employment demands of this rapid industrialization, they became laborers in the mines and mills, factory workers, or bookkeepers and clerks.

In the period between the Civil War and 1920, the urban population grew from 28 to 52 percent; almost fifty million Americans inhabited the nation's cities.[2] Cities became kaleidoscopes of neighborhoods established on ethnicity, social and economic groups, tapestries of customs, habits and practices and a confusion of languages. By the early 1900s there were some thirteen hundred foreign-language newspapers and magazines published in the United States.

As American cities became places of both work and entertainment, the changes brought about by industrialization and urbanization also affected patterns of courtship. Dating and leisure in general centered around the commercial amusements, a dynamic that helped amplify the presence and role of entertainment in American life. Dance halls, amusement parks, restaurants, movies and vaudeville theaters became public places where young people could mingle with members of the opposite sex. Especially for women, going out into the world of amusements—alone, with friends or on a date—was actually a new practice in the early twentieth century, something that had previously been expressly forbidden. This contributed greatly to the popularity of the city's amusements and the subsequent growth of the entertainment industry. At the same time, it fueled the controversy about entertainment as it related to the family, and especially the young.

The country at that time was not a fully unified society. There were continued hostilities between North and South and suspicions between East and West. Emancipated blacks struggled to find a place in American society. There were conflicts with Native Americans. Established Americans were threatened by, and even feared, the immigrant groups. The newer immigrants were discriminated against by ethnic groups that arrived earlier. Asians were openly persecuted, and tensions persisted between Protestants, Catholics and Jews.

The tumultuous social change and cultural conflict in America around the turn of the century created a search for a unifying principle, a common faith or set of convictions, that would hold the people and the nation together. Ideas from several fields were fused into a kind of creed. The belief in technological and economic progress gave a sense of purpose and direction for the country. Nationalism provided a collective identity for immigrants who were expected to leave the "old world" behind and adopt the practices of their new country. The Judeo-Christian tradition offered a transcendent morality. Most important for this study, Matthew Arnold's concept of culture as "the best that has been thought and said in the world" gave the Protestant cultural elite the intellectual justification they needed to assume social and cultural power and authority. They proclaimed Victorian culture as the pinnacle of human development and expected foreign immigrants and other racial groups to embrace its ideals and standards in order to solidify American life. Instead, a different culture was forged in the cities reflecting the beliefs and values of the new industrial democracy. This urban-industrial culture of the immigrants and African-Americans often conflicted with the WASP culture—a term not meant to be derogatory but referring to Anglo-American Protestant culture.

American life was profoundly affected by the "culture wars" around the turn of the century, and my treatment of the development of the cultural elite begins here. One effect of this conflict was the fragmentation into "highbrow" and "lowbrow" cultures. These categories emerged from the cultural strife of the time and became reified as general descriptors of American culture and life, to be accepted not only by Anglo-American Protestants but also by other religious groups and modernists in the twentieth century. It is important to understand, however, that this model was historically conceived; the emergence of a cultural hierarchy in America was rooted in a social experience that was characterized by cultural elitism, racial and ethnocentric anxieties, and religious discord. It was based on certain assumptions about what constitutes art and the role of entertainment in society. The emerging world of public entertainment or "amusements" became a critical arena in these cultural battles. These categories and accompanying myths, fears and attitudes continue to shape the discussion about entertainment.

Victorian Secrets

The cultural elite in America during the nineteenth and early twentieth centuries were the prosperous native Protestants, the "Victorians." They came from the oldest and wealthiest American families whose ancestors were among the first to settle in the colonies. Graduates of colleges or universities, or at least public or private secondary schools, they championed Victorian ideals, values and practices and set the tone for the middle class. There were, of course, other groups existing in the United States at this time, including Native Americans, African-Americans and the Spanish-speaking people living in the lands taken from Mexico. There were also some intellectuals—Walt Whitman, Herman Melville and Edgar Allan Poe among the most famous— who rejected the norms of the Victorian middle class. Most notably, the huge influx of ethnic immigrants brought a tremendous level of cultural diversity and conflict to the United States. But there is little question that Victorianism was the dominant cultural force during the crucial transformation to modernization.

Victorian culture can be characterized as Anglo-Saxon and Protestant. That it was named for Queen Victoria, who ruled in Britain from 1837 to 1901, shows the connection between Britain and the United States. In contrast to Britain, however, where Victorianism was identified with the nobility, aristocratic patterns in the United States were weak. American Victorianism was the culture of the urban middle class which controlled the social, economic, political and communication institutions. The Victorian era was shaped by the great evangelical Protestant revivals that swept the country during the Second Great Awakening between 1800 and the Civil War. Victorian and Protestant values were fused together into a set of principles that held the social order together providing a basis for public morality and behavior.

Victorianism, then, does not simply describe a group of people. The popular stereotype of wealthy, genteel men and women who were very formal and smug, emotionally restrained and sexually repressive only touches the surface of the nineteenth-century Victorian middle class. Instead, Victorianism is best understood as a culture, the particular way of life of a group of people. While diversity and contradiction existed in American Victorianism, the Victorians shared a common set of ideals, values and assumptions about life. These cultural motifs shaped what became known as the Protestant work ethic, and represent much of what social and religious conservatives today call "traditional family values."[3]

In brief, the Victorian way of life was based on individual self-reliance, democratic opportunity and social mobility. Self-sufficiency was the ultimate goal for individuals and the basis of their social model. They envisioned America as a vast land of opportunity for all, both on the western frontier and in the eastern cities. Those who worked hard—even to the point of compulsion—and lived an upright moral life, according to Puritan standards, could achieve economic independence. People dedicated to improving their lives through ceaseless labor, the Victorians thought, would develop a sense of duty, virtue, moral obligation and social responsibility. They would learn to value punctuality, hard work, order, self-control and delayed gratification—values necessary for an efficient industrial work force. The goal was to develop within individuals an internal character, based on these values, that would serve as a guiding force for the individual in a changing world. Further, the Victorians assumed that such devotion to continuous work would result in personal betterment and ultimately perfection, both for the individual and society.

The core of this confining life perspective was a "humanistic self-cultivation, Protestant self-denial" in the name of the pursuit of individual perfection, historian Daniel Walker Howe wrote.[4] Every activity in life was meaningful insofar as it furthered the goal of self-sufficiency. Entertainment, or amusement, then, was perceived as contradictory to the Protestant work ethic.

Obsessed with work and self-improvement, the Victorians elevated the spirit above the body—reason above passion. Sensual emotions were considered vulgar and commonplace, and were disassociated from the ideal of romance. Not surprisingly, they discouraged behavior and participation in activities they thought might lead to sexual temptation, deter one from work or hinder the process of self-improvement. The Victorians placed restrictions on sensuality, drinking and amusements, all of which seemed to them antithetical to a society devoted to work and progress. That there were human needs associated with these was undeniable, but the Victorians sought only to repress or control them, even if it meant hypocrisy. For example, they discretely sanctioned the brothels and saloons in the vice districts in the major cities—Chicago's South Side, New York's Bowery and the French Quarter in New Orleans. There young men could find release for their sexual passions apart from family and work. The Victorian middle class "rarely distinguished between these vices and the festivals and dances of the immigrants where men and women often mingled freely," film historian Lary May noted. "Both symbolized social and sexual anarchy."[5] It was against this background that they judged the new forms of entertainment that originated in the cities.

There was an air of cultural superiority among the Victorians that was manifested in their aggressive efforts to convert others to their way of life. They were also extremely didactic in their approach; the primary, if not sole purpose of literature and the other arts was to instruct and elevate the tastes of the audience. The transmission of their cultural tradition, they thought, was assured by the control they exerted over schools and the dominant means of communication—the print media, and later telegraph and telephone. The Victorian communication system, however, was based on the English language, unlike the new silent movies which had great appeal to non-English-speaking immigrants. The new visual form of communication was quickly taken over by "aliens." These were Jewish immigrants who perceived it not as a didactic art form, but as a business.

The Crisis with Modernism
Victorian culture was thrown into a crisis in the 1890s. The 1890 census marked the closing of the frontier of free land in the West. Frederick Jackson Turner argued in his famous "frontier thesis" that the continuous westward expansion of civilization into the wilderness was perhaps the most significant factor in the development of the American character and democratic institutions. It was widely believed that the western frontier was the real Darwinian-like setting for the cultivation of Victorian values. Pioneers had to become economically independent and self-sufficient in order to survive in the wilderness. The frontier setting, "the meeting point between savagery and civ-

ilization" as Turner called it, has been used by filmmakers in countless classic Westerns to explore American mythology and values.[6]

The boom in urbanization and industrialization created an even greater threat to the preservation of Victorian ideals and values than the passing of the frontier. The frontiersman had a mythic counterpart in the city in the figure of Horatio Alger, but the possibility of economic independence was largely lost to social mobility within existing corporations. Greater security and affluence compensated for the implausibility of reaching the exclusive ranks at the top of the corporate world. There was little correlation between the Victorian sense of "character" and corporate life. The need for consistent product quality or service and people who could work smoothly with others, the nature of work on the interchangeable assembly line, and new occupations in administration, sales and engineering did not require someone with frontier values the likes of Daniel Boone. The damage the corporate world caused to Victorianism, one writer said, "was subtle, but lethal."[7]

Diminishing the goal of self-sufficiency undermined the significance and value of ceaseless labor. Consequently, ideas about success changed, and Victorian values became less meaningful and more difficult to enforce. Industrialization increased the general standard of living and reduced the work week. The emphasis on hard work and productivity, self-denial and postponed gratification conflicted with the realities of the new consumer society. With the increase in the production of manufactured goods, a larger consumer market was needed in order to keep the economy expanding. The goal of economic independence was largely replaced by the consumption of goods and the enjoyment of newly acquired leisure time. Workers pressed for higher wages and shorter work hours to get some relief from their continuous and boring labor. A study conducted in New York City in 1908 showed that workers spent much of the money they earned above the subsistence level on entertainment.[8]

A host of problems accompanied the rapid urbanization and industrialization in the United States. The gulf between rich and poor widened. While the national wealth quadrupled in the last half of the nineteenth century, it was estimated that 1 percent of the population possessed about 50 percent of that wealth and 12 percent owned over 90 percent of it.[9] Unfortunately, the leading industrialists felt little obligation for social welfare, and American institutions did not offer enough protection from exploitation. Workers were paid and fed poorly, crowded into wretched housing in appalling ghettos. Work was boring, mundane and depersonalized. There were constant worries about employment. Crime and poverty rates increased, as did political corruption. One immigration official writing in 1913 described the cities as "a horrible modern Frankenstein."[10]

Fearing that these social ills would lead to the collapse of the social order, the "progressives" spearheaded reform movements in the first quarter of this century. Made up of well-educated businessmen and professionals, Progressive leaders came from the established native Protestant families. Although they harbored their own prejudices against the new immigrants—Catholics and Jews among them—they believed in the democratic tradition, the Victorian code of self-reliance and Puritan morality. In essence, they tried to impose the Victorian social model on the new urban-industrial world, and their culture and values on the foreign immigrants.

The focus of the reform movements was on the perceived decline of the family in urban life. While such fears can be traced back at least as far as the 1830s and 1840s, they became prominent among reformers in the first quarter of the twentieth century. The perceived deterioration of the family was seen against the backdrop of a supposed golden age in the nineteenth century. In brief, Victorian social life was organized by gender; there were clear and distinct "spheres" for men and women. The public sphere belonged to men as economic providers; women inhabited the domestic sphere as homemakers and mothers. The urban work and leisure environment brought about dramatic changes in the family, including the breakdown of the rigid distinctions in life based on gender. Released from productive chores, the emphasis of the middle-class Victorian home was now on the education and socialization of children. The home, and in particular the woman, became the most important means for the transmission of Victorian principles.

Social trends in urban America, however, seemed to be tearing the family apart. In the emerging "culture of abundance," as cultural historian Warren Susman called it, personal fulfillment now competed with values associated with marriage and family. The proportion of both single and married women earning wages outside the home (if only for the financial survival of their families) increased dramatically in the first quarter of the century. As children adopted the ways of the urban world they related more closely with their peers than their parents; generational tensions developed. In addition, increasing divorce rates, declining fertility rates, and a rise in the marriageable age marked trends that have continued to the present.

It is easy to see, then, why the Victorians idealized women and the family. They considered the Victorian home the moral and spiritual center of the commercial world; the extension of these values into the broader society was needed to curb the greed and ambitions of competitive industrialists. The reformers tried to protect the Victorian model of the family, based on the assumption that it would serve as a humanizing force against the fierce competition and exploitation unleashed by industrial capitalism. Social welfare legislation and child labor laws, the regulation of business practices, minimum wages, reduced working time and improved working conditions were all designed to diminish the harmful effects of industrial life on the family. In effect, these magnified expectations for the family. The home was supposed to make up for social deficiencies; the fate of the nation rested upon it. The family, then, was seen as a haven against the sweeping changes occurring in American life. Consequently, there was an increased privatization or isolation of the family from the larger community in an attempt to block out the corruption of the outside world. As much as any other aspect of modern life, the new patterns of courtship in the early twentieth century, and their affinity with the city's amusements, broke down barriers between the home and the public world.

Going Out on a Date

In the early years of the twentieth century, dating, or going out into the public world for male and female companionship, became an important part of urban life, and a great concern of the middle class. The practices and conventions of dating represented profound changes in the nature of courtship and intensified the cultural conflict. In the nineteenth century Victorian world, courtship and marriage were kept within the experience of home and family, considered the woman's realm. Prospective suitors secured an invitation in order to "call" on a young woman at her home. In the calling system, courtship took place in the domestic sphere; the primary means of entertainment were the parlor piano, conversations on the front porch swing, or community social events. The woman's parents, and especially her mother, did everything from screening suitors to deciding proper topics of conversation and the amount of chaperonage.

All that changed in the urban centers after the turn of the century. Four to six people crowded in two-bedroom apartments in tenement houses was not a pleasant arrangement for entertaining guests. Between 1890 and 1920, the practice of dating replaced the chaperoned visit in urban life. Young people were increasingly leaving the cramped quarters of their small apartments to find entertainment and intimacy in the world of the city's amusements. The practice of dating turned the Victorian social world upside down. It completely transformed generational and gender roles in courtship, first among the working and then the middle class. The parents' role in selecting potential marriage partners was all but eliminated. Young women and men could meet at work or at places of public entertainment, making dating more a matter of choice between individuals and not primarily a family affair based on class and ethnicity as in the calling system.

Dating in the world of commercial amusements created what historian Kathy Peiss has called a "heterosocial culture" by breaking down distinctions between Victorian and immigrant cultures, the classes and the sexes. Both at work and at play, women were venturing outside the domestic sphere to participate in the public "male" domain, an arena considered dangerous for respectable women, who were thought to be more delicate in mind and body than men.

Studies conducted in New York showed that between 1903 and 1909 the average working-class family, typically four to six members, received average annual earnings of about eight hundred dollars, or fifteen dollars a week. More important, the father was the sole means of support in under 50 percent of households. According to the Victorian ideal, a woman's primary social obligation was in the home; she was to inspire her husband on to success in the business world and nurture their children in Victorian values and principles. But if only for the financial survival of their families, women began entering the labor force in unprecedented numbers in the first decade of this century. While women worked for wages during the nineteenth century, the context and relationship between work and leisure changed with the industrial revolution. Instead of doing domestic service, household production or sweatshop labor, women now worked in department stores, as clerks in factories or offices, and as secretaries and sales personnel. Young, single working-class women dominated the female labor force from 1880 to 1920. In 1900, four-fifths of the women working for wages in New York were single, and almost 60 percent of all women sixteen to twenty years old worked outside the home in the early 1900s.[11]

Instead of instilling Victorian values, "good business habits, discipline, and a desire for quiet evenings at home," Kathy Peiss, author of *Cheap Amuse-*

ments: Working Women and Leisure in Turn-of-the-Century New York explains, the work environment actually fostered the desire to get out and have a good time. Leisure became "a separate sphere of independence, youthful pleasure, and mixed-sex fun," that stood in opposition to, and was "a reaction against the discipline, drudgery, and exploitative conditions of labor," she explained. "A woman could forget rattling machinery or irritating customers in the nervous energy and freedom of the grizzly bear and turkey trot, or escape the rigors of the workplace altogether by finding a husband in the city's night spots."[12] The necessity of earning a living became an experience that defined and organized leisure activities.

Wage-earning women now had at least some money and greater social freedom. They could go to restaurants, amusement parks, dance halls, vaudeville theaters and nickelodeons. But although women had access to these places, most could not, however, afford to go to them on their own. Working women's earnings were below the "living wage"; what they did make was quickly consumed by room, board and clothing. With little discretionary income to spend on recreation, women had to depend on men to "treat" them. Dating was understood as a kind of exchange relationship; women reciprocated by offering sexual "treats." Peiss wrote, for example, that young women offered "sexual favors of varying degrees" in return for the drinks men would buy them at the saloons and dance halls. Even though this most often amounted to "only flirtatious companionship," women were still "capitalizing on their attractiveness and personality," behaving according to the cultural rules of dating. Likewise, at the amusement parks, as David Nasaw has written, "single working women, unable to afford a day's vacation on their meager wages, looked for men who could treat them—and not ask too much in return."[13]

The middle class feared (and with good reason) that the breakdown of social barriers and the mixed-sex amusements were undermining the Victorian ethos. Sex was considered dangerous to both personal life and their work-oriented social order (as were drinking and amusements). Any respectable woman who ventured into the public world, especially without a male escort, risked losing her virtue, or at least tarnishing her reputation. A woman's moral chastity and sexual purity were vital to the preservation of the Anglo-Saxon race. And now working women from all classes were patronizing urban entertainment establishments that had previously been the province of men and prostitutes.

In their campaign to prevent the degeneration of women's morals, middle-class reformers connected the new freedom in women's fashion, the use of cosmetics (also associated with prostitutes) and more liberal sexual mores with the popularity of the city's amusements. The mixed-sex amusements were equated with promiscuous sexual behavior. In contrast to the reserved and high-cultured Victorian lifestyle, reformers saw the dance halls, amusement parks and nickelodeons as "appealing to the 'low' instincts of the masses, debasing womanly virtues, segregating youth from the family, and fostering a dangerously expressive culture," Peiss wrote.[14] The new dances, which were based on African-American musical styles, emphasized sensuality, and were especially linked with women's morality as a symbol of the heterosocial culture. So much so that many people, and especially religious groups, simply barred any form of dancing.

All things considered, it is not surprising that the presence of women among the audience for commercial amusements steadily increased throughout the first quarter of the twentieth century. Young women across a wide social spectrum fueled the new dance crazes just after the turn of the century. They accounted for one-third of the vaudeville audience in New York in 1910; according to recreation surveys, women and children together made up almost 50 percent of the vaudeville audience in the major cities. Working-class women fueled the nickelodeon boom that began in 1905; they constituted 40 percent of the working-class audience in New York in 1910. One survey estimated that forty thousand children in greater New York went to the movies daily without a parent or guardian. The cheap price of a ticket and safe environment of the neighborhood nickelodeon made the movies affordable and available to unescorted women, and especially those who did not want to engage in the negotiations of treating. The flirtatious mingling and sexual risks at the dance halls and amusement parks were not eliminated but were largely reduced at the nickel theaters. It was estimated that the percentage of women among the general moviegoing audience increased from 40 percent in 1910 to 60 percent in 1920; *Moving Picture World* put the figure at 83 percent in 1927, a number that increasingly included the middle class.[15] These figures, in turn, heightened middle-class anxieties about the potentially corrupting influence of entertainment and the urban environment.

Obviously, middle-class reformers viewed this fascination with entertainment as yet another threat to their ideal of the family. Industrialized work took family members away from the home. Now it seemed the commercialized amusements did the same, dividing family members in their leisure time. Vaudeville and the movies could provide outings for the whole family, but there seems little doubt that age groups coalesced around different kinds of amusements. Fathers continued going to saloons, mothers went to vaudeville or the movies, adolescents converged on the dance halls, young children played in the streets. Even the movies, according to historian Elizabeth Ewen, "became less identified with family entertainment and were utilized increasingly by the young as a space away from family life, a place to escape, to use a hard-won allowance, to sneak a date."[16]

Under these circumstances, it seemed impossible to realize the Victorian ideal for family in working-class homes that had become "nothing but eating and sleeping places," as one report put it.[17] Consequently, reformers set out to counteract the amusements. Social and educational clubs substituted for the absence of family control. As an alternative to saloons and dance halls, neighborhood centers provided dancing, sports and entertainment designed for the entire family. These efforts, Peiss said of New York reformers, "were designed to provide working-class youth with family-oriented, wholesome recreation, an alternative to the age-segregated, promiscuous amusements provided commercially."[18] A number of institutions were created to protect and help working women. The Young Women's Christian Association (YWCA) provided meals and lodging along with educational classes, a library, concerts and entertainment. Other clubs, including the church-based group The Girls' Friendly Society, offered instruction, entertainment, lodging, sex education and even insurance coverage and employment referrals. Reformers lobbied for legislation to regulate the commercial amusements. Chicago's noted social worker Jane Addams even started an experimental theater that showed travelogues and literary adaptations at her settlement-house project, Hull House. The cinematic venture was short-lived, however, as it could not compete with neighboring theaters that featured films like *The Pirates, The Defrauding Banker, Adventures of an American Cowboy* and *Car Man's Danger.* A neighborhood resident explained, "Oh, it's a good show, all right, but it ain't lively enough. . . . People like to see fights and fellows getting hurt, and robbers and all that stuff. . . . This show ain't even funny, unless those big lizards from Java was funny."[19]

There are some interesting similarities between our own day and this period at the beginning of the century. New delivery systems have increasingly lessened parental control over their children's entertainment choices, and increased fears and anxieties about the influence of entertainment media. The amusements in the first quarter of the century represented a challenge to the authority of the home (and church), and therefore, a threat to Victorianism. Entertainment was thought to be a moral and spiritual peril not only for individuals but for the whole social order. But at that time young people still went out of the home to dance halls, vaudeville performances and nickelodeons. Over the course of the century, radio, the phonograph, and later broadcast and cable television and VCRs eventually brought the world of entertainment, as well as news and information, directly and more immediately into the home than previous forms. The same concerns and charges have been rejuvenated today by middle-class families who find they are unable to barricade themselves from the outside world because of advancing technologies. A significant basis for much of the contemporary debate about entertainment, as well as the proposed solutions, is the same Victorian assumption that the family, and especially children, must be protected from the outside world, even in the form of dramatic portrayals of that world. These are especially dangerous, it seems, because the cultural commentary in entertainment was, and still remains, powerful, in part because of its accessibility to a large population. Consequently, the continual struggle to control these images has taken on various forms, including production codes and ratings systems, monitoring organizations, economic boycotts or funding restrictions, and new technologies like the "V-chip," which lets households block out violent programming.

Attack of the Goths and Huns

For a time, the immigrant groups that arrived in America around the turn of the century retained their own cuisine, eating and drinking habits, language, literature, churches, social organizations and amusements. The native Protestants, however, saw these as interfering with the assimilation process. It was not that the immigrants simply rejected Victorian culture in its entirety. Hard work did bring the benefits of tangible rewards and social mobility. But the promotion of Victorian norms often meant the rejection of the culture of recent immigrants and fueled conflicts between them and the native Victorians. The ethnic immigrants "scorned temperance in favor of their traditions of public festivals celebrated with dancing and drinking, and camaraderie at the corner saloon," May explains. "They came from traditions where work went according to the task or season—not the regulation of the assembly line or the clock. When these groups retreated from public education to establish their own parochial schools, or used politics to protect their festivals and ethnic neighborhoods, it sparked an even more militant desire among the natives to outlaw the sports, games, and entertainments of the recently arrived immigrants."[20] Leisure and entertainment were critical arenas in the cultural conflict between the Victorians and immigrants arriving around the turn of the century. That this was so demonstrates that entertainment forms were perceived as more than mere diversion and amusement. They were recognized, and consequently feared by the cultural elite, because of their potential power as a means of cultural transmission and social criticism.

American leaders were confronted with a crisis that was most dramatic. The growth of cities and suburbs was rapidly transforming America, presenting a host of moral, social, political and ethical problems that strained their paradigm. How would the Victorian culture of middle-class Protestants survive the onslaught of these foreign cultures? What would distinguish the Anglo-Saxon character from the immigrant groups? Could American cultural unity be preserved now that American society was characterized by such a wide variety of cultural traditions, languages, religious differences, customs and practices? Believing in democracy, the Victorian elite had no choice but to learn to live with religious and cultural pluralism. But industry, social and religious leaders worked to preserve the essence of the Victorian social model while adapting it to the modern industrial society.

During the nineteenth century, Americans had an "open arms" attitude toward immigration, based on two traditional ideals: America was an asylum for the oppressed of Europe, and a "melting pot" that mystically transformed foreigners into Americans. But "the majority of Americans did not view this melting pot as a process of cultural fusion by which each immigrant group contributed its share to a national mosaic," one immigration official explained. "Rather, it was generally believed to be a smelting process in which the immigrant was stripped of his old-world characteristics and recast in a standard American mold."[21] The idea, then, was not to create a multicultural society—one composed of a diverse population of racial and ethnic groups from different religious and cultural traditions. Rather, it was thought that foreigners would shed their past and embrace the culture of their adoptive country. In other words, immigrants were supposed to leave their cultural baggage—religious practices, language, customs, habits and personal behavior—on Ellis Island. Life, liberty and happiness were to be pursued according to Victorian ideals and practices.

The native Protestants assumed that those who sought economic independence and self-sufficiency would learn to value self-reliance, moral virtue and social obligation. But as early as 1849, a college president wondered if the melting pot was having the opposite effect on the nation's population. "The multitude of emigrants from the old world, interfused among our population, is rapidly changing the identity of American character," he said in a public lecture. "These strangers come among us, ignorant of our institutions, and unacquainted with the modes of thought and the habits of life peculiar to a free people." The American character and the survival of American institutions were at stake. "Shall these adopted citizens become a part of the body politic, and firm supporters of liberal institutions, or will they prove to our republic what the Goths and Huns were to the Roman Empire?" he asked.[22]

Shifts in the makeup of immigration intensified fears about the threat of foreigners to Protestant American culture. The pre-Civil War immigration of Irish Catholics challenged the hegemony of Anglo-American Protestants, but during the wave of immigration after the war most immigrants to the United States came from northwestern European countries, Great Britain, Germany, the Netherlands and Scandinavia, until the 1880s. They came from the same stock as the country's founders and adhered to most of the same social, political and religious values. Over four million immigrants arrived in the two decades before the Civil War, a number surpassing the total population in 1790, when 85 percent of white Americans were Protestant. Among this "tyrannical mob," as native Protestants referred to them, were Roman Catholics from Ireland, Scotland and Germany.[23]

The population of Roman Catholics, though itself fragmented by ethnic diversity, grew from thirty thousand in 1790 to over three million in 1860, making it the nation's largest denomination. Between 1860 and 1900, the membership in the major Protestant denominations tripled from five to sixteen million, but the number of Catholics quadrupled from three million to twelve million. Their culture and customs were decidedly foreign to Protestant Americans. They built "beer gardens" in the face of Protestant campaigns for abstinence and violated the sabbath by participating in amusements. They ignored American institutions, establishing their own newspapers, schools, political and social organizations. Among many Protestants the rise of Catholicism was perceived as a significant threat to the social and moral welfare of the nation. The native Protestants never questioned the superiority of their cultural and moral values, but by the turn of the century they became increasingly concerned about their survival.

As the rate of immigration continued to increase, the fears and anxieties of native Protestants were heightened. By 1890, immigrants from northwestern European countries were outnumbered by those from southeastern Europe—Italy, Poland, Austria and Hungary. They were mainly Catholics and Jews, fleeing political or religious persecution and unacquainted with democratic institutions. These "new" immigrants came from countries ruled by kings, emperors, czars, sultans, shahs and presidents, every political form from absolute monarchy to socialism. They represented a diversity of religions, including Protestantism, Roman and Greek Catholicism, Buddhism, Confucianism, Judaism and Islam. And they spoke a host of languages and unfamiliar dialects. By 1910, the foreign born represented more than twice the total population and almost three times the number of native Anglo-Saxons in the six New England states.[24]

Distinctions between the older and newer immigrant groups became value judgments. A "hierarchy of races existed in the United States," one writer explained, "with 'Nordics' [the Germanic peoples of northern Europe and Scandinavia] on top, recent immigrants from Southern and Eastern Europe far down but above migrants from Mexico and Orientals, and, at the very bottom, Negroes."[25] Southeastern Europeans were constantly referred to as an "alien flood" and a "barbarian horde." Members of Congress argued that these newcomers had failed to "melt" and that the country was suffering from "alien indigestion." There was much speculation about what effect this "volume of ignorance" might have on American culture and society.[26]

The country's unrestricted immigration policy came under serious attack. On the one hand, immigration satisfied the enormous labor demands of rapid industrialization. Industrial leaders wanted a steady stream of foreign immigrants because their cheap labor kept wages down. But immigrants also brought potentially dangerous ideas about socialism, communism and anarchism that could threaten democracy and capitalism. Labor strikes in the coal, steel and textile industries in the early years of the twentieth century increased fears about the revolutionary potential of foreign ideologies, especially after the Bolshevik Revolution in 1917.

Protecting democracy and capitalism from foreign ideologies and "keeping pure the blood of America," as one House representative put it, became the rationales for restricting the immigration of southern Europeans in the

1920s.[27] Immigration laws were passed limiting a country's annual quota to a percentage of nationals already living in the United States. They were clearly based on racist distinctions between "superior" and "inferior" national and racial affiliations, and demonstrated an explicit bias against people from southeastern European and Asian countries. The congressional debate over the establishment of a quota system centered on racial and cultural homogeneity as a basis for the preservation of American democracy and culture. But as one writer observed, the Immigration Act of 1924 actually "reflected a denial of faith in the American tradition" and "the principle of individualism." Potential citizens were judged by their racial and national affiliations, rather than by their individual character and ability. "This application of group criteria to individualism," he said, "ignored the wide range of individual difference in a nation's population and reduced all the people of a country to a generalized stereotype."[28]

Immigration restrictions along hereditary lines were strongly supported by the eugenics movement in the United States. The theory behind eugenics is that heredity determines the character and intelligence of individuals, not environmental factors. It was widely believed that the native Anglo-Saxons were a superior stock to the new immigrants from southeastern Europe. That democracy and Victorian culture came from this racially and culturally homogeneous group of Anglo-Saxons was proof enough. The flood of alien races and cultures was perceived as a threat to the foundations of American culture and society. A prominent eugeneticist wrote in 1911, for example, that "the hordes of Jews that are now coming to us from Russia and the extreme southeast of Europe, with their intense individualism and ideals of gain at the cost of any interest, represent the opposite extreme from the early English and the more recent Scandinavian immigration with their ideals of community life in the open country, advancement by the sweat of the brow, and the uprearing of families in the fear of God and the love of country." He feared that the "influx of blood" from southeastern Europeans would destroy the American character, resulting in an increase in crime, sexual immorality and insanity.[29] Eugenicists supported immigration restriction and also prescribed sterilization and laws prohibiting interracial marriages. By 1931, sterilization laws were passed in thirty states and thousands of Americans, those considered mentally unfit (including epileptics) or criminally insane were involuntarily sterilized.[30]

The association of eugenics with race, social class and the emerging ideas about "highbrow" and "lowbrow" cultures was unmistakable. The terms themselves were first used around the turn of the century to describe people of intellectual or aesthetic superiority (highbrow) or inferiority (lowbrow). They were derived from phrenology, a nineteenth-century practice widely used in determining racial types and intelligence by studying the size and shape of the skull with the presumption that the cranial shape indicated a person's mental faculties and character.[31] Louis Reeves Harrison, one of the early film critics, employed this terminology to distinguish audiences and taste. He suggested that movies featuring gratuitous violence were "not only inartistic, but are ineffective save with the few low-brows who like them. . . . They are repellent to the cultivated, and even cease in the course of time to stimulate the jaded appetites of the unwashed."[32]

The appropriation of high art and culture by the wealthy and educated elite was a means to distinguish themselves from others they considered socially and culturally inferior, both in America and in other parts of the world. In the progressive scheme, the government acted as a "benevolent guardian," and they believed that only an "educated elite" could govern effectively. The WASP elite became the self-proclaimed guardians of American culture and society, and as Henry Seidel Canby wrote in *The Age of Confidence*, the immigrant "needed only be Americanized to make no trouble for the right-minded."[33] Elitist notions about culture that originated in the late nineteenth century provided an intellectual context, and even justification, for the subordination of other people. As DiMaggio has observed, the American elite identified cultural taste with morality, and that with social class. "In high culture, the upper classes of late nineteenth century America found both a common currency and a refuge from the slings and arrows of the troubled world around them," he wrote.[34]

The Pursuit of Culture

After the Civil War, the American elite were increasingly influenced by European trends, including Darwin's theory of evolution and Matthew Arnold's concept of Culture. The Anglo-Saxons who settled in New England in the seventeenth and eighteenth centuries believed they were replacing the Jews as God's chosen people, establishing a holy "city on a hill" in the New World. This conviction about their manifest destiny was combined with ideas about progress and evolution in the nineteenth century. Anglo-Saxon Protestants considered themselves leaders in the progress of civilization and ahead of other racial groups in the evolutionary process. Even Darwin suggested that the American character and progress were the favorable result of the process of natural selection.[35]

The Victorians were also fascinated by Matthew Arnold's idea of Culture. Arnold was a British Victorian poet and social and literary critic. In his judgment, the middle-class Victorians valued industriousness, religion and moral virtue, but America was not yet that "type of civilization combining all those powers which go to the building up of a truly human life—the power of intellect and knowledge, the power of beauty, the power of social life and manners, as well as the great power of conduct and religion."[36] In other words, American culture, dominated as it was by the large middle class, was distinctly lacking in the cultural refinement of the British aristocracy. Arnold acknowledged the benefits, even necessity of the social world of industrial capitalism, its religious organizations, political dogma, wealth, recreation and material products. But in Arnold's scheme, those who pursued these as ends in themselves relinquished their lives to a lesser course. The value of a human being was not based on wealth or achievements, like building railroads or church buildings, but on his or her progress toward culture.

By culture, Arnold meant the "pursuit of our total perfection by means of getting to know, on all the matters which most concern us, the best which has been thought and said in the world." His usage denied the more general understanding of a people's way of life, or system of meaning, by appropriating the term to describe a particular value system and lifestyle that had to be acquired by individuals primarily through education. Affirming the Victorian ideal of the perfected individual, he described culture as an "internal condition," an individual process of intellectual, aesthetic and spiritual refinement by which humans distinguished themselves from their "animality." The connection with the evolutionary process was unmistakable; those who sought after culture reached a higher level of humanity than the "raw and uncultivated" masses. Arnold proposed that a "best self" would emerge from this pursuit of perfection, serving as the supreme authority in art, literature, religion and politics. While in principle this "best self" transcended class distinctions, it was clear that culture, as he defined it, was the limited domain of the wealthy and educated descendants of the Western tradition.[37]

Arnold argued that the guidance and governing of a remnant of cultured elite was essential for the survival of democracy. He suggested that "the refinement of an aristocracy may be precious and educative to a raw nation as a kind of shadow of true refinement; how its serenity and dignified freedom from petty cares may serve as a useful foil to set off the vulgarity and hideousness of that type of life which a hard middle class tends to establish, and to help people to see this vulgarity and hideousness in their true colours."[38] There is no question that Arnold's saving remnant was composed of the wealthy, educated and most prominent Anglo-Saxon Protestants who eagerly, and uncritically, accepted his ideas. Those of Anglo-Saxon descent, Arnold said, were "of the most moral races of men that the world has yet seen, with the soundest laws, the least violent passions, the fairest domestic and civil virtues."[39] They were the exclusive possessors of the tradition that embodied the best that had been thought and said in the world, which for Arnold and his followers was a synthesis of the Greek and Hebrew traditions, the two major forces in Anglo-Saxon culture, or what is generally meant today by Western civilization.

When Arnold arrived in the United States in 1883, he was greeted by Andrew Carnegie, one of the nation's leading industrialists. During his lecture tour, he visited the exclusive men's clubs and was hosted by the most prominent and wealthy citizens of the cities on the eastern seaboard. The Victorian elite found Arnold most appealing during the transformation to modernism. His idea about culture vindicated the separation of the educated minority from the industrial masses on the grounds that this was necessary for the survival of a democracy. At the same time, it affirmed the superiority of Anglo-Saxon culture and gave the Victorian middle class a paternalistic responsibility to convert others to their way of life, which to the Victorians meant to raise the standards of other groups in society, especially the ethnic immigrants. Arnold's ideas, of course, were greeted with much acclaim by the educated elite in the United States.[40]

Arnold's idea of culture was thoroughly humanistic. He deified the human capacity for rational thinking, as though reason was not corrupted by sin. A careful look at Arnold's idea of culture reveals an absolute faith in reason as the supreme authority. He said, "Only in right reason can we get a source of sure authority; and culture brings us towards right reason." The effect of culture, then, was "that we might be partakers of the divine nature." From a Christian perspective, Arnold attributed to the intellect and reason that which belongs to the more fundamental religious impulse of humans.[41]

Arnold's concept of culture amounted to a religion of culture, a "faith in the progress of humanity towards perfection," which for Arnold and his followers was a unilinear process that culminated in the refinement of nine-teenth-century British and European high culture. Arnold expressed the epit-ome of cultural chauvinism, as though nineteenth-century European culture was the pinnacle of humanity, and the people of Asia and Africa had no culture, or at best a horribly inferior one not far from their "animality." Culture replaced religion as the means of perfection or salvation both for the person and society. To ensure this course for American life, the educated elite had a social responsibility to preserve "the best which has been thought and said in the world," and simultaneously to raise the cultural and intellectual stan-dards of the mass of society. This privileged minority became the "sovereign educators," Arnold said, "the true apostles of equality," making "the best knowledge, the best ideas of their time" prevail among "the raw and un-kindled masses of humanity."[42]

Cultural hegemony was Arnold's social ideal. In other words, he envisioned one group in society, those of Anglo-European descent, subordinating all others to its social, moral and cultural values. That the "culture" of the elite prevail as the moral, social, aesthetic and intellectual standard was imperative to secure the political order. It was necessary, then, that the masses "get" the culture of the Victorian elite.

Other obvious problems followed the creation of a cultural hierarchy in America. As Levine points out, it "led the arbiters of culture on the one hand to insulate themselves from the masses in order to promote and preserve pure culture, and on the other to reach out to the masses and sow the seeds of culture among them in order to ensure civilized order"[43] Howe thinks the reification of "high" and "low" culture was "a symptom of the disintegration of Victorian culture."[44] The cultural elite were no longer in a position of influence regarding the public opinion of the masses. To the contrary, there was now a degree of animosity between the classes, and the amusements symbolized this tension.

So while the intent of the elite was to "sow the seeds" of Victorian culture among the masses, pretty much the opposite occurred. As following chapters will show, in the first quarter of the century it was the immigrant amuse-ments—vaudeville, nickelodeons, dance halls and amusement parks—that became enormously popular among the middle and working classes. In con-trast, traditional high art was increasingly removed from the fabric of daily existence for the vast majority of people. The "best" of Western civilization became the exclusive property of the cultural elite, who thought it too complicated for the average person and believed that the educated alone could understand and appreciate it.

An Arnoldian Legacy

Arnold's ideas and the establishment of a cultural hierarchy in America at the beginning of the twentieth century had a formative and lasting impact that continues to inform discussions about contemporary culture and entertainment. As a result of the civil rights and feminist movements of the 1960s, rigid elite and popular cultural distinctions based on race, class and gender have dissolved today without entirely disappearing. Courses at the university level now reflect the diversity of American society, including groups and activities formerly considered the province of low culture: workers, immigrants, women, Native Americans, African-Americans, Asian-Americans and Latinos, as well as the study of entertainment and popular and folk cultures. Scholars now examine radio, movies, romance novels, popular music styles and television programs in their study of American life and culture. In fact, a condition of postmodernism is the blurring of traditional categories and distinctions like high and low culture.

But the erosion of the barriers between high and low culture challenged the hegemony of the Anglo-American Western tradition, and educational institutions became battlefields in the contemporary culture wars. In reaction, cultural conservatives rejuvenated Arnold's ideas about culture and education.

The book that best captured this phenomenon was Allan Bloom's *The Closing of the American Mind.* Bloom spoke of culture in Arnoldian terms as "something high, profound, respectable—a thing before which we bow"— and something that must be acquired through a liberal arts education. As Levine has observed, Bloom's diatribe strongly resembled the reproofs and proposals during the cultural conflict at the beginning of the twentieth century. Like the Victorians, Bloom contended that American culture was deteriorating, and in no small measure he blamed the proliferation of popular culture. He made absolute qualitative distinctions between high and low culture, seeing "no relation between popular culture and high culture" and lamenting that "the former is all that is now influential on our scene." He thought classical music, for example, was "probably the only regularly recognizable class distinction between educated and uneducated in America . . . a class distinction between high and low." But classical music was "dead among the young" today, he asserted, supplanted by young people's addiction to rock music, which along with the newest technology has made life "into a nonstop, commercially prepackaged masturbational fantasy."

Bloom portrayed young people as "uncivilized" and quite uneducable, and proposed that the solution rested in an educational curriculum based on the great books of Western civilization.[45] Actually, such courses were first instituted during the 1920s to resolve the cultural struggles at that time. The idea was to establish a common knowledge of general human history based on Western civilization as a unified and continuous progress toward a more perfect future. The educational curriculum, then, became a means of cultural transmission to be used to advance the process of civilization itself.[46]

I will return to this topic in a later chapter, but suffice it to say at this point that the paradigm of Bloom and his followers is problematic insofar as it identifies one cultural tradition as embodying the Truth (with a capital *T*) over against others that are perceived as having a corrupting effect on civilization. This approach assumes that true knowledge is the exclusive province of one group of people, based on race and nationality, and leads to the denigration of other cultures—even those that share a Christian tradition. And it has become all too easy for evangelicals to equate the culture and values of the Anglo-American tradition with spiritual transcendence and moral righteousness, which explains in part why they have aligned themselves with the cultural conservative movement today.

Based on the standards and institutional structure of Anglo-American high culture, for example, African-American culture has been considered primitive, vulgar and even sinful by many. But the black church is one of the most dynamic illustrations of the integration of faith and culture in the twentieth century. Bonded together not only by a history of oppression but also by their racial and religious identity, African-Americans fashioned a distinct cultural tradition rooted in the Christian faith, not only in sermons and worship but also in social life, politics and the arts. The black church was the central institution in the modern civil rights movement.

Black musicians and musical styles were the impetus for every vital new movement in American popular music, representing America's greatest contributions to the world of music. African-American music "brings together the background of African music, the reforming power of Christian faith, Puritan psalm-singing, the hymns of Isaac Watts and Charles Wesley, European ballad singing and mountain fiddling, as well as the realities of cultural, social and spiritual alienation," a music analyst noted. "These all produced a music that faces life in a brutally honest fashion, with the honesty including the grace of God and the hope of renewal and redemption that it provides."[47]

Though African-Americans represent only 13 percent of the population, "they dominate the nation's popular culture: its music, its dance, its talk, its sports, its youths' fashion; and they are a powerful force in its popular and elite literature," one scholar has observed. "A black music, jazz, is the nation's classical voice, defining, audibly, its entire civilizational style."[48] Certainly there is something of the "best that has been thought and said" in African-American life for Christians to learn about cultural transformation and the struggle with secularization.

The Bible offers a very different understanding of culture, however, from the Arnoldian notion of human improvement and perfection. To be human is to be created in God's image as an inherently cultural being. As caretakers or stewards over God's creation, Christians are commanded to "do" culture, or in other words to cultivate the creation, by exploring and opening up the possibilities inherent in "things" God created so that they serve their intended purposes. Through the Bible, empirical study and historical experience, humans are to discern God's laws or norms and apply them to specific situations. But norms are complex, and love, justice, faithfulness and stewardship can be both violated and applied in myriad ways to a host of complicated human situations: interpersonal relationships, family, church, art, schooling, journalism, advertising, international relations, politics, computer technology, business, communication and the mass media. A biblical idea of culture as the mandate to explore and cultivate the possibilities woven into God's creation allows for cultural pluralism, while affirming the existence of a world ordered by God.

4

•••••

To Be or Not to Be: The Theater in American Culture

The religious community and the educated and wealthy elite were both powerful forces shaping the nature and role of entertainment in American life. The efforts of these at times overlapping groups can be traced back to struggles going on in the evolution of the theater in the nineteenth century. While these two groups serve to highlight the moral and cultural aspects of the continual debate about entertainment, at least in the nineteenth century they still had much in common. The American cultural elite was made up of prosperous native Protestant groups, especially from the urban middle class. While they became an increasingly smaller percentage of the population as the rate of immigration increased, their Victorian ideals, values and assumptions remained a powerful cultural force until the 1920s.

This chapter focuses on the impact religious and cultural leaders had on the development of the theater, which was the hub for entertainment in American life throughout the nineteenth century. Specifically, the shattering of the theater as a place of social unity and the emergence of an elite and popular theater will be examined. While the theater once served as a symbol of social unity and affirmation of the dominant belief system, the fragmentation of theatrical entertainment in America along class and cultural lines had direct implications for audience attendance and the financial survival and power of the theater as a cultural institution. The cultural fragmentation into elite and popular worlds was a primary means of social, intellectual and aesthetic separation in American society, and these cultural distinctions, which were put into practice at the beginning of this century, continue to inform the way we think about life and art, its roles and functions in our lives and society.

A Worldly Amusement

The church's prohibition of amusement could not suppress people's desire for it. In the late nineteenth century, all forms of entertainment from opera houses and concert halls to beer gardens and "less reputable places of diversion" were well patronized. It was reported that two opera houses in an inland city of sixty thousand people collected one hundred thousand dollars in box-office receipts for the year, much more than the support received by all the Protestant churches. Considering all the money spent at other halls and rinks, pubs, circuses and other outdoor shows, and for billiards, dances, baseball, horse races, alcohol and prostitution, Washington Gladden concluded that "it is safe to say that the people of this country spend every year for amusements more than they pay for their schools, and three times as much as they pay for their churches."[1] As I noted earlier, the church's effort to regulate participation, allowing some amusements and not others, floundered over questions about the degree of sinfulness of one activity over another and discipline for offenders.

Despite inconsistent and even irrational thinking about the amusements, the religious community's concerns were not without merit. If Gladden's observations are to be trusted, the entertainment of the late nineteenth century "tends to the degradation rather than the elevation of the people," and "the business of diverting the people is largely in the hands of men and women whose moral standards are low, whose habits are vicious, and whose influence upon those with whom they come in contact must be evil."[2] Clergy loudly protested the immorality of the theater. Theater personnel acquired a reputation for drunkenness, divorce and an inability to repay debts (probably due to the poor financial state of most theaters). However true or exaggerated, these transgressions were as likely to be found among patrons (and critics) as the performers. But it was perhaps the nature of the theater experience itself that created the most controversy.

The theater reflected the sense of classlessness that pervaded the social mind in the nineteenth century—a manifestation of the idea that all Americans could improve their status in life by living according to Victorian norms. It was a meeting place for all classes of society. Larger buildings were constructed and ticket prices reduced in order to attract both the social elite and the middle and lower classes. Theaters in the major cities could hold between twenty-five hundred and four thousand people, and their size forced them to keep admission prices low and cater to the general public. One observer in 1838 noted that American theaters were "not much frequented by the more opulent and intelligent classes, but sustained by the middle and humbler ranks." By drawing "all ranks of the people together" for a common activity, the theater was a microcosm, or miniature version of American society in the first half of the nineteenth century.[3]

People from different classes saw the same plays in the same theaters, though from different locations. Most theaters were divided into three sections and price ranges, which in effect corresponded to and affirmed the social divisions in the world outside the theater. The middle classes filled the pit or main floor, the wealthy sat in the boxes (symbolically) looking down on the crowd below, and the lower class, blacks and prostitutes were restricted to the gallery or balcony in the back. The heterogeneity and behavior of the nineteenth-century audience resembled the audience at the Globe Theatre for a Shakespearean play in Elizabethan England. (In some respects it can be compared to a crowd today at a World Wrestling Federation Main Event.) The audience participated collectively in the action on stage. Applause, whistling, foot stomping, and shouting demonstrated their appreciation; boos and hisses signaled their disdain for a performance, and it was not uncommon for patrons in the gallery to bombard the actors, musicians in the orchestra, or even other patrons, with rotten vegetables. One writer described the gallery noise in an American theater as "somewhat similar to that which prevailed in Noah's Ark; for we have an imitation of the whistles and yells of every kind of animal . . . and they commenced a discharge of apples, nuts and gingerbread on the heads of the honest folks in the pit."[4]

The contrast with attending the theater or symphony today points to a serious change in cultural understanding regarding the theater experience. Today, food and drink are restricted to the lobbies. Inside the theater, talking, or even whispering, is not allowed. Laughter and applause should be mild and polite, and not loud and raucous; shouting and foot stomping are forbidden. Huge bins of cough drops in the lobby are often made available to symphony patrons to prevent a tickle in the throat from interrupting the performance. These differences in audience behavior represent the change from thinking of the theater as a popular activity to seeing it as a refined and respectable event.

It was the gallery, or "third tier," that was the source of much of the theater's immoral reputation. At some theaters a bar serviced the balcony, contributing to the unruly behavior the rest of the patrons complained about regularly. Prostitutes made initial contacts with customers there and set up arrangements for the rest of the evening. Apparently some even consummated their business in the balcony. Perhaps this explains why there were so few religious dramas produced in the nineteenth century. When the manager of the Park Theatre in New York tried to appease critics by staging a religious play, "The Israelites in Egypt, or the Passage of the Red Sea," a letter to the *New York Herald* noted the contradiction: "Look at the inconsistency of the production of sacred drama in a temple devoted to the harlot."[5] Primarily for financial reasons, managers resisted pressure from the religious community and the press to close the galleries, even though it meant alienating "respectable" patrons.

A Polite and Elegant Theater

The theater was also attacked by the nineteenth-century cultural elite, those "persons better educated and of a more refined taste," as theater historian David Grimsted puts it.[6] They did not condemn the theater outright, because they recognized its potential for social and moral instruction. Always anxious to convert others to Victorian principles, they reasoned that as much could be learned from a good drama as from a sermon; an educated person should be as fluent in Shakespeare as in the Bible. Even so, the wealthy and leisured class deplored the American theater, considering it a "total debasement of a polite and elegant source of rational amusement." A more refined theater was what they desired, one that appealed to the intellectual life and elevated the aesthetic tastes of the general audience. In particular, they wanted the American theater to emulate the vogue of the British aristocracy, even though the rise of a large, affluent middle class in America diminished the strong social distinctions that characterized British and European society. Instead, as the theater began to thrive in America, it developed a level of independence from the British stage. The cultural elite disdained American productions for indulging "the depraved taste of a corrupt multitude." Even so staunch an advocate of democracy as Walt Whitman reprimanded theater managers for catering to "the million" when they should be trying "to please the select few who guide, (and ought to guide,) public taste."[7]

The American theatrical entertainment that emerged from these struggles was condemned from the pulpit on moral grounds and criticized by the social elite in magazines and the press for catering to the tastes of the lower classes. The upper class preferred to have its own theater, but as one woman explained in 1848, "unfortunately we of ourselves are not sufficiently numerous to support an Opera, so we have been forced to admit the People."[8] Theater managers, if only for financial survival, were responsive to the desires of the paying public. Increasingly, American theatergoers wanted to be entertained by plays that embodied and reflected their own beliefs and values, explored their ideals and problems using distinctly American motifs, characters and settings.

This is an important element of American entertainment, and the beginning of a specific trend that lasted through the mid-twentieth century. In order to survive financially, the entertainment industry tailored its product to appeal to the large middle-class audience. Entrepreneurs sought to provide affordable entertainment for the widest—and therefore largest—possible audience, meaning from children to their great-grandparents and everyone in between. This was both a marketing and a profit-making strategy that had immediate implications for the content of entertainment. In order to be "popular," entertainment had to appeal to a lowest common denominator in society by reflecting the dominant value system, and be able to communicate with a wide range of people from different educational, social, economic and religious backgrounds. During periods of cultural conflict this becomes more difficult because of the loss of wide cultural consensus. It is important to see that this is a commercial-based aesthetic. In contrast to the traditional high arts, the features and functions of the popular arts are made subservient to moneymaking. The demands of the marketplace, as industry executives perceive them, largely govern the production of entertainment. This in turn greatly affects the roles and functions of entertainment in society.

The criticism from the educated class was directed at the very elements that made the American theater so popular and appealing to a wide range of people across social lines. The "depraved taste" of American audiences referred to their love for the melodrama, a dramatic form in which simple but powerful stories were acted out by characters based on prototypes. Some idealized state is disrupted by an outside force or diabolical act. A villainous landlord shatters a happy home by demanding unpaid rent or the hand of the tenant's beautiful daughter as a substitute. Enraptured young lovers are separated or forced apart by those opposed to their marriage. The standard plot, as theater historian Oscar G. Brockett explains, is familiar to most: "a virtuous hero (or heroine) is relentlessly hounded by a villain and is rescued from seemingly insurmountable difficulties only after he has undergone a series of threats to his life, reputation, or happiness."[9] The hero or heroine overcomes these obstacles and restores the idyllic state by the end of the story.

Melodrama was not a distinctly American form. Most of its elements were common in drama since the sixteenth century, and it was a powerful force in the theater both in Europe and the United States during the nineteenth century. But critics treated the melodrama as an inferior form to tragedy. While "classical tragedy from Aeschylus to Shakespeare dealt with kings, queens, princes, and other figures of social importance whose actions determined the fate of cities, principalities, kingdoms, and nations," melodrama portrayed the fate and fortunes of ordinary people, couples and families, those Grimsted has called the "historically voiceless."[10] Although tragedy appealed to all classes, it emphasized the aristocratic social order and values. In melodrama, the values that distinguished characters were those of the middle class.

Melodramas portrayed the conflict between good and evil in contemporary social settings and encouraged the audience to support the underdog. Characters were not judged by their social status but by their moral integrity, natural talent and ability for genuine love. The strength of heroes and heroines came from their virtuousness, a quality available to all regardless of class. In contrast, villains were driven by evil.

The American melodrama featured sentimental tear-jerking scenes, suspenseful plots, high action, comedy, music and dance. Some productions included lavish spectacle and elaborate theatrical effects, including volcanoes, waterfalls, floods and battles. It was a dramatic form conducive to the portrayal of life in the budding democracy and easily understood by the diversity of theatergoers in the nineteenth century. The Victorian idealization of women was affirmed in plays exhorting female chastity. The moral preaching of the melodrama, despite its oversimplification, allowed for social commentary; happy endings reaffirmed the ultimate triumph of justice and democratic values.

As a theatrical form, however, the melodrama was terribly flawed. The realities of life were subjugated to the ideal of the Victorian moral vision. There was no room for moral ambiguity or complex characterization. With few exceptions, virtue was a matter of individual character, and not the result of circumstances or a corrupt society. And yet it had tremendous appeal in the young democracy. "It took the lives of common people seriously and paid much respect to their superior purity and wisdom," Grimsted explains. "And its moral parable struggled to reconcile social fears and life's awesomeness with the period's confidence in absolute moral standards, man's upward progress, and a benevolent providence that insured the triumph of the pure."[11] The impression we get is that the American theater through the mid-nineteenth century was both highly instructive and wildly entertaining. The tremendous popularity of melodrama among middle-class theatergoers in the nineteenth century was not lost upon early silent filmmakers. The melodramatic style, with its emphasis on mood and emotional appeal, proved an effective way to communicate ideas and feelings without dialogue.

Enter Stage Right: William Shakespeare

The American theater survived in a precarious environment, a situation that continued to define the entertainment industry throughout this century. Its financial survival depended on its ability to meet the tastes and demands of a widely diverse audience in terms of education and social class. Under these circumstances it is not surprising that Shakespeare, whose reputation towered above all other dramatists, was the most popular playwright in America. Shakespeare served to legitimize the theater, thereby expanding its audience in the face of attacks from religious moralists and the cultural elite. Both groups were appeased by productions of Shakespeare that also attracted large audiences, much to the delight of theater managers. Shakespearean drama, then, played a key role in establishing and expanding the American theater amid the elitist and moral/religious criticism of the time.

This is ironic, for while Shakespeare has become an icon of highbrow culture, in his own day he was considered not a literary genius but a public dramatist, with a reputation lower than that of some of his peers (such as Robert Greene, Ben Jonson or John Webster). It is worth examining the theater in Shakespeare's time, for like the entertainment industry in the twentieth century, the Elizabethan theater was shaped by religious, political, legal and commercial pressures. A "flashback" to sixteenth-century Elizabethan

England will dispel some of the notions people use to distinguish art and entertainment today. Far from being an autonomous artist, Shakespeare was wed to and shaped by social and cultural forces of his time, and especially the marketplace.

When Queen Elizabeth took the throne in 1558, she sought to gain control over the various forces that fueled the religious and political discord raging in England. During previous reigns, drama had been used as a weapon in these controversies. At the time there was little organization and supervision of actors; any nobleman could serve as a patron, and theatrical troupes could do as they pleased while out on tour. Many illegal companies working under the false pretense of noble patronage performed plays that aroused religious and political contention.

To establish order, the queen immediately banned unlicensed performances and forbade playwrights from treating religious or political subjects altogether. The absence of partisanship and particular religious perspective led to a secularization of the theater, with plays simply portraying a universal moral force at work in human affairs (the fate of the classic Hollywood cinema). Eventually the crown restricted troupe patronage to those noblemen above the rank of baron and required other companies to obtain a license. These laws reduced the number of drama troupes but also legitimized and protected licensed companies.

The crown's patronage, then, was not primarily economic in the sense of commissioning works but in the form of government regulation, social recognition and legal sanction. The Elizabethan public theaters became commercial institutions, their existence ensured—and also supervised—by the government, which collected fees and issued licenses for plays and theaters. Theater companies had to be cautious in their presentation of topical material for fear of upsetting the political authorities who could close down theaters, putting companies out of work, and even jail individuals.

The success of the Elizabethan theater was as much a result of commercial interests as of artistic creativity. Shakespeare was not only an actor and playwright but also an investor in the Globe Theatre. He and the other leading figures in the Elizabethan stage did not come from the professional classes but from the yeoman class, the ranks of artisans and tradesmen. They aspired to the status of upper-class merchants and the gentry and entered the theater for financial reasons, not artistic ones. The theater provided them with enormous financial opportunities unavailable to artisans and tradesmen. From the

Globe Theatre alone Shakespeare earned more in a single day than an artisan or tradesman earned in a month. His total annual income was equal to that of the middle ranks of the lower gentry and more than the average artisan could hope to earn in a lifetime.

Historian James H. Forse has shown that nearly every aspect of the Elizabethan theater, including playwriting, was "shaped by the demands of profit and business management."[12] There was an intense rivalry between theaters. They capitalized on the large and concentrated London population with low admission prices; buildings were constructed to accommodate audiences of two to three thousand people across many classes and social backgrounds. As Robert Weiman has suggested, "It was precisely because the London theater was *not* exclusively a courtly, academic, or guild theater that there developed a stage and a mode of production the theatrical possibilities of which were as diverse as the models and sources from which it drew."[13]

Box-office receipts and not artistic merit determined the stage life of a play. Not unlike the contemporary entertainment industry, commercially successful productions spawned imitations. The blood and gore and "feigned" madness scenes in the enormously popular *Spanish Tragedy* (c. 1587), for example, were used repeatedly by Shakespeare (in *Titus Andronicus, Hamlet, King Lear* and *The Taming of the Shrew*) and other dramatists. Apparently the popularity of the character Falstaff in both Henry IV plays prompted Shakespeare to bring him back in the comedy *The Merry Wives of Windsor*. The same can be said of the repeated use of sensational devices (like ghosts), murder and revenge stories, pastoral and romantic comedies, and the inclusion of historical events and classical mythology.

Not unlike commercial artists today, Shakespeare produced works that exploited the popular mood and preoccupations. For example, during the heightened English nationalism in the second half of the sixteenth century, travel and history books were tremendously popular. Shakespeare averaged one history play a year from 1590 to 1599. Then suddenly he turned his attention to Greco-Roman stories. There had been no decline in nationalistic spirit, but the publication of history books had fallen off somewhat. Tapping into the new popularity of Greco-Roman sources, between 1599 and 1607 Shakespeare produced a new Greco-Roman play on the average of every eighteen months. Often within a year or two after the publication of a best-selling book, Shakespeare would create the play version, relying on the simplified translations that reached the working classes as his inspiration.

Market research and profit-making played powerful roles in shaping Shakespeare's art. Brockett writes, "Shakespeare gave little thought to preserving his plays, which in his time were looked upon as momentary diversions (much as television dramas are today)."[14] It is easy to see why managers edited Shakespeare for the Victorian audience in America. Shakespeare's plays were filled with bawdy humor, including flatulence jokes, sexual puns and innuendos. They contained risqué encounters and references to illicit sex and masturbation. Racial and ethnic tensions of the time were apparent in the treatment of characters (Othello was black, Shylock Jewish). Plays depicted child abuse, gender relations, homoeroticism and violence. Julius Caesar is butchered onstage by his conspirators. *Hamlet* begins with a murder, followed by a suicide, a poisoning and a suggestion of incest, and it ends with the stage filled with corpses. *Macbeth* is a virtual bloodfest, with bodies falling act by act.

Not unlike today's commercial artists, Shakespeare made use of conventional forms and characters in his approach to playwriting. Typically the main characters and situations are clearly established in the opening scenes. The action develops out of this initial exposition, with several independent plot lines interwoven until all serve to resolve each other in the end. Beyond the structure of his plays, the economy of cast and scripting of roles for specific actors reveals a business orientation. That he limited his productive output to avoid flooding the market and did not seek the publication of his plays is further evidence that he considered them "company assets, meant to generate profits for the acting company; they were not meant to be vehicles designed to propel their author into respectability within the literary circle," according to Forse.[15]

By today's measure, Shakespeare was not an autonomous artist with a vision for society that could be understood only by the educated and wealthy. Instead he was a popular artist, comparable to today's filmmakers, recording artists and television producers, communicating the issues of the day in a popular medium and in the contemporary vernacular. His productions were designed to attract a wide audience from all social and economic classes in order to be financially profitable.

Until 1870, Shakespeare made up a large portion of the theatrical repertory in America. It was estimated that almost one-quarter of the theatrical season in eastern cities was given to Shakespearean plays, and touring companies staged performances in small towns across the country. *Romeo and Juliet,*

Richard III, Hamlet, Macbeth, Othello and *King Lear* were among the most popular and most frequently performed. The usual theatrical evening featured a full-length play followed by a parody or farce. Interspersed between acts and productions, the orchestra played popular songs of the day, or a wide range of contemporary entertainment was presented. Audiences were treated to animal acts, magicians, dancers, singers, jugglers, acrobats, minstrels and comics—the slate of variety acts we now associate with vaudeville. Shakespeare, then, was integrated into nineteenth-century American culture.

Shakespearean plays were loved for their treatment of moral issues: the importance of fidelity and the bonds of family, the "problem" of tyranny and murder, jealousy and ambition. The plays focused on individuals who bore the responsibility for and consequences of their actions. But as you can imagine, some religious writers were critical of Shakespeare's sense of morality, and Elizabethan humor was not always appropriate in Victorian America. Theater managers did not hesitate, some in fact felt a moral obligation, to adapt Shakespeare in order to better accommodate the melodramatic tastes of the nineteenth-century American audience. Sometimes changes were made to shorten the play or to improve it for stage production; minor characters were consolidated and speeches shortened or even deleted. More importantly, Shakespeare's plays were adapted in order to heighten those qualities that most appealed to the moral tastes of Victorian America. Sexual allusions were omitted or changed, ambiguity in good and bad characters was eliminated to emphasize clear distinctions between good and evil and a sense of ultimate justice. Unlike Shakespearean productions today, these modified versions appealed to the moral and aesthetic tastes of both the educated elite and the general populace. In other words, until the mid-nineteenth century, Shakespearean drama was both popular and elite. People from all social and economic groups found pleasure and enjoyment in it, while it also affirmed their basic values and beliefs about life.[16]

While Shakespearean and other standard plays comprised a good part of the theatrical repertory, many of the long-running productions were new plays. A popular theater emerged that met the needs and desires of the majority of the people, increasingly adding the Protestant middle class to its audience. As the theater developed in the nineteenth century, a number of native dramatists acquired a level of fame, as did actors like Edwin Forrest and Charlotte Cushman. American plays employed American themes, characters and situations; they explored the ideals and anxieties of the time while providing vicarious romance and adventure. There were Indian plays like John Augustus Stone's *Metamora* (1829) and George William Custis's *Pocahontas* (1930), "Yankee" plays like Charles Matthew's *A Trip to America* (1824), and Benjamin Baker's *A Glance at New York* (1848), which featured the "city boy." Anna Ogden Mowatt's comic satire on New York social life, *Fashion* (1845), and William Henry Smith's morality play *The Drunkard* (1844) both enjoyed extensive theatrical runs. Charles Hoyt's satirical musical comedy *A Trip to Chinatown* broke performance records in New York in 1891, and sheet music sales for "After the Ball," a song from the musical, reportedly sold over five million copies. Edward Harrigan wrote a series of hilarious comedies about urban immigrant life that were extremely popular. John Brougham's spoof of the "noble savage" play called *Po-ca-hon-tas, or The Gentle Savage* (1855) and George L. Fox's parodies of *Macbeth, Hamlet* and *Richard III* demonstrated the continued popularity of burlesque. Ironically, the minstrel shows, which featured black caricatures, reached their peak of popularity between 1850 and 1870, just as the first stage versions of Harriet Beecher Stowe's novel *Uncle Tom's Cabin* (1852) appeared.

Producers described *Uncle Tom's Cabin* as "a moral, religious, and instructive play," and more than any other single production, it brought the respectable Protestant middle class into the "immoral" theater.[17] *Uncle Tom's Cabin* ran for a staggering 325 performances in New York in 1852-1853 and was possibly the most popular production of the period. Productions played in every major city and hundreds of touring companies logged thousands of performances that lasted until the 1930s. In New York at one time, *Uncle Tom's Cabin* was playing eighteen times a week to sold-out houses. It was estimated that the play was performed over a quarter of a million times to audiences totaling more than the population of the United States.[18]

As the hub for all kinds of entertainment, the American theater flourished throughout the nineteenth century. Philadelphia, New York, Boston and Charleston became major theatrical centers, and other cities established permanent theaters as well. Touring companies followed the westward expansion, and riverboats brought the New York stage to the shores of the Ohio and Mississippi rivers. In many respects, the theater compared with the church in cultural importance. The theater as an institution symbolized American life. It was a projection of nineteenth-century democratic ideals and values.

Social Unity to Discord

Just as the theater began making inroads with the large Protestant middle class with plays like *Uncle Tom's Cabin,* a dramatic change began to take place in the makeup of the theater. Increasingly, after the mid-nineteenth century, class lines drawn by box, pit and gallery were replaced by separate theaters for the upper and lower classes. The term "legitimate theater" came into use to describe "serious" or classical drama, and to distinguish it from the contemporary or "popular" theater of the day.

One event, though bloody and tragic, illustrated the momentous changes occurring in American culture and the theater. A long-standing rivalry existed between a very popular British actor, William Charles MacCready, and his American counterpart, Edwin Forrest. Forrest's exuberant acting style and outspoken patriotism made him an American favorite, while MacCready's cerebral style and aristocratic manner identified him with the wealthy elite. On May 7, 1849, the two played opposite each other in productions of *Macbeth* in New York. Forrest's performance at the Broadway Theatre was greeted with thunderous applause, but Forrest's admirers packed the gallery at the new and exclusive Astor Place Opera House and created such a disturbance that the British actor MacCready was unable to complete his performance. Amid the booing and hissing were cries of "Three groans for the English bulldog!" and "Down with the codfish aristocracy!"[19] MacCready's repeat performance three nights later was protested by a mob of some ten thousand outside the Astor Place Opera House who threw stones at the theater and shouted, "Burn the damned den of the aristocracy!" When the crowd tried to storm the entrance, policemen and a militia squadron opened fire, killing at least twenty-two and wounding over 150 others.

The Astor Place Riot demonstrated how important the role of the theater was as a social institution. There was always a certain uneasiness about the format of the early nineteenth-century theater with its combination of Shakespearean drama, opera, farce, acrobats and equestrian acts. But the social experience itself was part of the attraction; people from all social and economic groups came together for a common event. They found pleasure and enjoyment and had their basic values and beliefs affirmed in an evening of theatrical entertainment. The Astor Place Riot marked the end of both this prominent role of the theater in society and the social mixture of the audience. The theater had become a cultural arena for expression of both intense nationalism and class antagonism.

Trying to interpret the Astor Place Riot, a Philadelphia newspaper observed that "there is now in our country, in New York City, what every good patriot has hitherto considered it his duty to deny—a *high* class and a *low* class."[20] The separation of entertainments mirrored an increase in the population and class differentiation. As Grimsted notes, "One roof, housing a vast miscellany of entertainment each evening, could no longer cover a people growing intellectually and financially more disparate."[21] Where formerly the theater was something like the town square, a center for entertainment and a symbol of social unity, now it represented harsh divisions in American life: high art and culture for the wealthy and educated class, lowbrow entertainment and popular culture for the industrial masses.

The role of theater as a microcosm of American society ended with the segregation of audiences, actors and acting styles. Social and cultural lines were drawn (however inadequately) between the legitimate theater and vaudeville, the "popular" theater that flourished from the 1890s to the early 1930s. As following chapters will show, the advent of motion pictures around the turn of the century accentuated these divisions even more, although eventually movies would provide the social cohesion in the first half of the twentieth century that the theater did in the previous one.

Lawrence Levine has fittingly called this transformation in America a "sacralization" of culture.[22] The effect was to delineate certain aspects of culture as "sacred," something to be set apart from ordinary life, protected against abuse and made immune from criticism. Shakespeare, for example, was in effect transformed in American life from popular to elite culture, from a public playwright into a literary classic belonging to a more educated and elite circle. Instead of belonging to a public culture as in the nineteenth century, his plays were turned into sacred texts that had to be protected by the cultural elite from abuse by editing producers, melodramatic actors and the unlearned public. By direct implication other aspects of culture, specifically those regarded as popular or lowbrow, were depreciated even to the point of condemnation.

Two aspects of the sacralization of culture should be emphasized here. First, the term *sacralization* suggests a collusion of religion and culture. In the late nineteenth century, the cultural elite often associated the high arts with spirituality. Writing in 1892, concert pianist Edward Baxter Perry likened the symphonic musician to a "high priest in the temple of the beautiful." Onstage, a musician should lift his audience above the "trivial, petty phases of mere sensuous pleasure or superficial enjoyment, to a higher . . . plane of spiritual aesthetic gratification."[23] Renowned orchestra conductor Theodore Thomas wrote in his autobiography that "the master works of great composers contain more good brain and soul than the prettiest waltzes" and that "there is a deeper joy and a nobler spirituality to be gained from familiarity with the higher art forms than . . . the lower."[24] If classical music was sacred, it followed that other kinds of music belonged in a lower secular realm. Thomas wrote that "popular music" represented "nothing more than sweet sentimentalism and rhythm, on the level of the dime novel," and referred to it as "the sensual side of art [that] has more or less the devil in it."[25]

Second, as aesthetician Susan Sontag has noted, the distinction between high and low cultures was based in part on an evaluation of the difference between unique and mass-produced objects.[26] This argument was first presented in 1936 by the German critic Walter Benjamin. He maintained that the "age of mechanical reproduction" shattered traditional values associated with the unique existence of a work of art. In traditional elite culture it was the individual painting, sculpture, manuscript or live performance that was highly valued or held "sacred." But the technique of mass reproduction "substitutes a plurality of copies for a unique existence," Benjamin wrote. It was inconceivable, then, that technology-based cultural forms, like film and recorded music, could become socially significant apart from the "liquidation of the traditional value of the cultural heritage."[27] In other words, these new cultural forms demanded a change in values. As long as the tradition of esteem for a unique object continued to be dominant, contemporary art forms would remain inferior regardless of quality and service in society.

Based on this value system, however, high and low categories were institutionalized and reified in American life, distinguishing Art (with a capital *A*) from popular or "mass" culture. High art represented the "best" forms of culture, while popular art was seen not only as mediocre but as debasing of high culture. Contrasts between individuality and the mass audience, and between means of production—the individual creation of a unique work against commercially produced ones for mass consumption—became the basis for theories of mass culture beginning around midcentury.

The mass culture theorists claimed that popular art exerts a harmful effect on the moral and intellectual fabric of society. Dwight Macdonald, for example, argued that mass culture corrupted the aesthetic purity of high culture, that the "bad stuff drives out the good by mimicking and debasing the forms of High Art."[28] Based on the assumptions of the cultural hierarchy, critics like Macdonald argue that popularization inevitably debases the quality of art by corrupting the aesthetic standards of high art, and that the pursuit of high culture uplifts people while popular culture leads to personal corruption. It all sounds very Arnoldian. Macdonald initially thought it was possible for the masses to be integrated into high culture, or in Arnoldian terms that by aspiring to high culture the lower classes would raise their standards. Later, however, he resigned himself to the separation of high and popular art, seeing these cultural lines as "dikes against corruption." Macdonald created three categories—high culture, "midcult" and "masscult"—and saw midcult as the most dangerous to high culture because it "pretends to respect the standards of High Culture while in fact it waters them down and vulgarizes them." He wrote: "So let the masses have their Masscult, let the few who care about good writing, painting, music, architecture, philosophy etc., have their High Culture, and don't fuzz up the distinction with Midcult."[29]

Macdonald can be understood as advocating a kind of distinction in the arts that resembles proposals for greater differentiation in the production of movies, for example—an approach that will be explored later. But for now it is important to note that his theory reveals basic tensions in the elitist critique of American popular culture. As communications scholar Joli Jensen has observed, "Macdonald's two-culture 'compromise' is an uneven, but characteristically American, attempt to support the possibility of participatory, pluralistic American culture, while arguing for the existence of elite sensibilities that require protection from the taint of popular cultural forms."[30] The underlying premise that seems unavoidable in mass culture theories is that the general populace has an instinctual desire for the "bad stuff." Democratic values, however, deny the inherent superiority of some citizens over others, making it difficult to defend evaluative standards based on cultural and social distinctions in the name of democratic culture, especially when the cultural forms disparaged by critics are the most popular among the general population. These theorists, however, mitigate what is a harsh view of people by endowing the media with extraordinary powers of seduction as a way to explain why people choose to participate in what these critics believe are worthless and even dangerous activities.

The condemnation of popular culture as tasteless, vulgar and largely homogeneous is based on historically conceived cultural values and aesthetic standards applied in evaluation of high art forms that also affirm the virtue of the culture of the privileged. In part the debate about popular culture revealed anxieties about the popular arts as they fulfilled the roles of art for the masses, and with the expansion of the media industries as important sources of news and information. As Maltby explains, it became a "question of where cultural power was situated in Western democracies. The 'democracy of images' protected the political and economic elite from social criticism, but it equally endangered their role as protectors of 'culture.' "[31] These remain important issues in the current debate about art and culture and the university curriculum.

Patterns of cultural consumption and the diversity of the popular arts did not match the predictions of mass culture theorists, however. Other avenues of research emerged with scholars arguing that high culture was not intrinsically superior to popular culture, and that the lines between them were blurred for a number of reasons. The traditional and popular arts borrow from one another, and because their respective audiences overlap they do not have distinctive followings. Also, the popular arts are often more dynamic than the traditional ones.[32]

Scholars began examining the arts as they reflected social conditions and changes or public tastes. First published in 1957, Reuel Denney's *The Astonished Muse* inaugurated study of the relationship between media, artistic forms and sociological factors, and pioneered journalistic analysis of the popular arts and the academic field of popular culture studies. Other sociologists like Herbert Gans examined the audiences for the arts (both high and popular) as taste groups based on demographic characteristics.[33] Sociologist Howard Becker considered the production of artworks as part of a cooperative social network or "art world." Becker demonstrated that artists, audiences, critics and numerous laborers (editors, actors, recording engineers, distributors, marketers, manufacturers and so forth) form institutionalized art worlds with established conventions, each producing its own artworks of varying quality for groups of people. Within an art world, rationales and philosophical justifications take shape identifying the roles of art and standards of aesthetic evaluation.[34]

The Advent of a "Legitimate" Theater

There was little effort to distinguish between art and entertainment or between culture and commerce before 1850, but in the process of reification, high and low categories were given an institutional structure that created social distinctions and gave these cultural constructs the appearance of being "natural." The classification of high and popular culture worked to insulate high culture and institutions not only from popular art and commercial interests but also from the masses themselves. The traditional high arts were secluded in museums and symphonic concert halls, divorced from the dynamics of everyday life, and especially the forces of commercialism. Eventually they were almost exclusively funded by a patronage system that included wealthy individuals, corporations, foundation grants and government support. Conversely, the new entertainment forms became available to an audience of unprecedented size that included both the more educated and the masses. But because they were in large part defined by commercialism, the urban popular arts were not afforded the status and legitimate roles of high art. Entertainment forms were wed almost exclusively to the marketplace, their value or popularity determined by box-office receipts or the number of units sold.

It is important to emphasize again that artists have always had some kind of economic base in society and a specific audience that they served.[35] For centuries artists were organized by different forms of patronage. Sculptors, painters and poets were retained and commissioned at various times by the nobility or ruling class, the church, wealthy businessmen or politicians. Historically there is a long overlap of the patronage system and the production of art as a commodity to be sold directly in the market. With the later arose the salaried professional and the need for distributors, copyright laws and the royalty payment. The advent of the new media in the early twentieth century—cinema, radio, recording and later television—was accompanied by the creation of a whole complex industry with salaried specialists employed to produce, market and distribute art on a huge mass scale. The patronage system declined after the Industrial Revolution, but patron relations continue in the traditional arts, painting, sculpture, theater and symphonic music; in the case of funding raised by taxation, a government agency acts on behalf of the general public as patron. But the contemporary patronage system is minor in comparison with the cultural importance and presence of entertainment forms based on the technology of satellites, CDs, videocassettes and laser discs. Far from having a marginal status in today's society, the cultural institutions of publishing, radio, the recording industry, television and the cinema are integral to our economy and social life.

With the emergence of high and low cultural categories around the turn

of the century, distinctions were created between "commercial" art, or entertainment, and nineteenth-century "high" art, that which was considered creative and authentic. This occurred even though these are really the same
cultural practices carried out in different social institutions for different audiences and according to different standards of success and value. The creation of a "legitimate" theater was intended to give the culture of the elite a
superior status and to prevent it from being corrupted by the pressures of the
marketplace. In reality, the legitimate theater was by no means immune to
business and economic trends or unaffected by them. Divorcing it from the
general public actually worked against the endeavor to preserve and promote
the high culture tradition.

After 1870, the legitimate theater followed the course of many other industries. Local community theaters were replaced by a centralized production
system and standardization of product. Combination companies were formed,
mounting entire productions with cast and scenery for tour at theaters in cities
across the country. These forced local stock companies out of business and
led to the centralization of the legitimate theater in New York; by 1880 the
majority of productions were organized there. Local independent theater
managers, who once selected plays, cast and often directed them, now only
booked productions which originated in New York. They established circuits
to acquire more bargaining power; eventually these came under control of
powerful individuals.

In 1896, Marc Klaw and A. L. Erlanger merged with several other theater
owners to form the Theatrical Syndicate, which virtually monopolized the
booking and theater business. The number of theaters controlled by the
Syndicate rose from thirty-three in 1896 to seventy in 1903; the number of
one-night-stand theaters for traveling shows brought the number to five
hundred.[36] The Shubert brothers (Sam, Lee and Jacob) were the only competition for the Syndicate. Together they controlled virtually all of the legitimate theater activity in the United States. By the beginning of the nickelodeon era, they owned or leased over fifty theaters, including six in New York
City.[37] These men, and their counterparts in vaudeville, were ruthless businessmen engaged in an intense competition. This will be pursued in a later
chapter, but for the time being I want to show the effects of the cultural divide
on theater and movie attendance.

A survey of theaters in Boston showed that by 1909 vaudeville and movie
theaters could accommodate over 85 percent of the potential weekly au-

dience, the legitimate theater only 13.5 percent, and opera a mere 1.1 percent.[38] People in the theatrical business worked under what had become a commonly held assumption that in distinction from the nineteenth-century audience there was a wide gap between the tastes, attitudes and outlooks of the different socioeconomic groups. Theater entrepreneurs considered the fare of the legitimate theater—Shakespeare and other highbrow theatrical productions—to be "of little interest to the masses and therefore of slight potential profit to producers," according to Levine.[39] As a result, legitimate productions were staged almost exclusively for the upper class and formally educated. Shakespearean productions, for example, were deemed too complicated for the average person and therefore unsuitable for a mass audience. The Boston survey revealed that theaters running Shakespeare could accommodate less than 1 percent of the potential weekly audience, a dramatic contrast with the previous century.

The legitimate theaters constructed around the turn of century were built to accommodate a smaller audience. Some argued that this was because the production of the new modern realism in drama demanded a smaller, more intimate theater that allowed for the new natural acting style, which was inaudible in the balcony. This more subtle acting was obviously quite different from the energetic and flamboyant technique of melodrama which was necessary to engage a crowd in a larger hall. It may seem that managers were no longer interested in appealing to the gallery crowd, but as theater critic Walter Prichard Eaton pointed out, theater managers, who he said "would not care a snap about the proper presentation of intimate drama if they could fill the Metropolitan Opera House with it improperly presented, or with something else," discovered they simply could not fill the larger houses for legitimate productions.[40] Consequently, most of the new theaters were built without galleries as legitimate theater managers increasingly catered solely to the upper classes.

Actually, the loss of the gallery audience was cited by critics at the time as a major contribution to the decline of the legitimate theater throughout the first quarter of the century. First vaudeville, and then the movies drained away the theater's audience among the lower income groups and some of the working class. Admission costs were certainly a factor. In 1915, a man could take his wife and three children to the movies for the same cost as one gallery seat at the legitimate theater. Also, the movie theater was closer to home and there was no separation of the classes in the movie theater. Eaton said, "It will require a tremendous deal of 'educating' before you can persuade such a man to invest a dollar and a quarter instead of twenty-five cents, out of a yearly wage of five hundred dollars, on a single evening's entertainment, and to invest it in a theater where he enters by the back stairs." As Eaton suggested, the change in the theatrical audience was more than a simple matter of economics. The theater critic noted that in the past when Shakespeare played at the Manhattan Opera House in New York, "the galleries were always packed with a proletarian audience." And the "automobiles parked two deep along the curb in front of a motion-picture theatre" suggested that the wealthy patronized the movies. Nevertheless, he concluded that "in the larger towns, where the higher-priced drama coexists with the motion-picture plays, the line of cleavage is sharply drawn in the character of the audience, and this line is the same line which marks the proletariat from the *bourgeoisie* and capitalist class."[41] Attending the theater itself was an activity loaded with meaning regarding class and culture. As I have shown, until around the mid-nineteenth century the theater symbolized democratic ideals; afterward the legitimate theater, vaudeville and the movies increasingly symbolized class distinctions.

Conclusion

The theater, which was the center for entertainment around the turn of the century, was fragmented into high or "legitimate" art for the wealthy and educated class and popular "amusement" for the industrial masses. As chapter nine will show, a parallel development occurred with opera and the symphony. Near the end of the nineteenth century, orchestra leaders complained about "the indifference of the mass of the people to the higher forms of music" and resisted the general desire for "music of a lighter character."[42] They wanted to establish a permanent orchestra in order to maintain the highest standards of performance of the great works of the great composers to the exclusion of more popular pieces. Such an orchestra, however, could not survive on box-office receipts alone. To cover increasing deficits, a patron system was established putting control of the symphonies in the hands of a board of wealthy sponsors.

The cultural clash between high culture and low made it virtually impossible for the former to be assimilated with the consumer economy that emerged in the twentieth century. Instead different social institutions, audiences and artistic standards were eventually established for the traditional high arts and popular arts. Increasingly after the mid-nineteenth century, the wealthy and educated elite financially sponsored and attended the legitimate theater—Shakespearean drama, opera, ballet and symphony. The middle- and working-class immigrants became the audience for the circus, burlesque, minstrelsy, baseball, boxing, and especially vaudeville and the new silent movies.

Popular cultural forms remained the primary means of artistic expression and communication for immigrant groups, women and minorities. After World War II popular culture was increasingly associated with youth culture, not only in the United States but around the world. As the significance of issues surrounding race, gender and multiculturalism mounted in the second half of the century, challenging the existing dichotomy between high and low culture, popular culture began to be taken seriously. The entertainment industry came under attack from a wide range of social and religious groups, conservative and liberal, although for assorted reasons. Despite conflicts and differences in critique and conclusions, entertainment was recognized by most as an influential and pervasive social institution that plays an important role in shaping individual life perspectives and society at large.

5

. . . . .

Highbrow
Stuff
Never Pays

The entertainment industry as we know it today developed during the dramatic cultural struggle between Victorian and modern industrial life in the first quarter of the century. As I showed in chapter three, the Victorians controlled the dominant means of communication, and therefore cultural transmission, during the nineteenth century. Traditionally the task of cultural transmission belonged to the family, clergy, educators, artists, political and business leaders and other organizations. Members of the "Old American" elite served on the boards of private schools, colleges and state universities, as well as museums and art galleries. They were also the leading industrial and political figures of the day. These institutions, then, embodied and supported their culture and values.

The influx of ethnic minority cultures and the rise of a mass society, however, dramatically changed the means of communication. While Victorian culture was still transmitted through elite art forms, educational and other social institutions, the culture and urban experience of immigrants and minorities was conveyed through the popular media—movies, radio, recordings. These new media served as means of both entertainment and communication. The movies especially presented a serious challenge to established American social institutions responsible for communicating cultural values among people and between generations. Although the movie talent (stars and directors) was still very powerful and largely Anglo-Saxon, Jewish immigrants owned much of the industry by the midteens. Thus for the first time in American history a powerfully persuasive means of communication and cultural transmission was controlled by a group considered "foreigners" or "aliens." Despite their status as lowbrow amusements, however, these media did more than transmit the culture of the urban masses. They were also effective means for social criticism, pointing out class, economic and social injustices.

The effect of immigration was the creation of an incredibly heterogenous population representing widely disparate cultural backgrounds with an array of traditions, customs, habits and practices. American popular culture became "the means through which the enormously varied cultural traditions that immigrants brought with them were assimilated into American life," Richard Maltby writes. "It worked to level differences between ethnic groups and social classes."[1] Adjusting to urban industrial life was a traumatic experience for newly arrived immigrants and those who left rural life behind in their move to the cities. Crowded together in urban centers, they shared common fears and anxieties, social and economic pressures, dreams and desires. Unable to rely on the ways of the old country or the social institutions in urban America, these people "sought out the vaudeville theater and listened to what it had to say about the bustling, energizing, affluent life of the cities," according to Albert F. McLean.[2]

Vaudeville became the most popular form of entertainment in the United States around the beginning of the twentieth century. At one-fourth the cost of the legitimate theater, vaudeville theaters attracted the family fare from the middle and lower classes. Vaudeville entrepreneurs were shrewd, ruthless and intensely competitive businessmen. By 1900, vaudeville theaters were consolidated into chains controlled by a single booking company. The nation's largest was built by B. F. Keith and Edward F. Albee. Their United Booking Office controlled the theaters east of Chicago; Martin Beck's Orpheum Circuit, which operated theaters west and south of the Windy City, was their only real competition. The two merged in 1927, and according to one source the Radio-Keith-Orpheum Circuit had an average weekly attendance of some twelve million people at its seven hundred theaters, although by then the vast majority of them were programming vaudeville and movies.[3]

Vaudeville became the model for mass entertainment by instituting mass-marketing and standardization practices that popularized entertainment on a national scale but also worked to diminish differences between ethnic and religious subcultures. The vaudeville circuit furnished the initial exhibition network for films. As you can imagine, the tremendous popularity of first vaudeville and then the movies had a significant impact on the legitimate theater. An analysis of the interaction between these competing enterprises gives us some insight into the nature of contemporary entertainment and the industry that provides it.

Entertainment for the Whole Family

There was a wide range of entertainment in the cities in the late nineteenth century, including pool halls and roller-skating rinks, dime novels and illustrated papers, circuses, amusement parks and professional sports. Theatrical entertainment splintered into a number of types that reflected the growing class, social and cultural differences. By 1880 the northern cities had a large number of theaters offering different kinds of entertainment to a wide audience. Located in the affluent areas, the legitimate theaters catered to the upper classes. The smaller seating capacity and higher admission costs effectively kept out the masses. The cheap theaters or foreign-language theaters that catered to working-class immigrants continued to play melodrama until shortly after 1900, when it lost its audience to vaudeville. Audiences at the melodrama hissed at dastardly villains, shouted warnings to damsels in distress and sang along on the chorus as the orchestra played "Harrigan" during intermission.

In the vice districts (where no respectable woman of the Victorian middle class would be caught dead) were the "music halls." The music halls served particular ethnic groups, sometimes an audience of mixed sexes, but primarily an exclusively male clientele. They were basically saloons or honky-tonks with a back room or cellar converted into a concert hall. Using a variety show format that included circus and minstrel acts, the music halls mostly provided risqué entertainment—crude jokes, bawdy comedy sketches and female bodies put on display for drinkers. They became the source of an array of entertainment that developed and thrived between the mid-nineteenth century and the 1920s. The burlesque theater, for example, continued the erotic elements of the music hall in song and dance, slapstick and double-entendre comedy.

Beginning auspiciously with *The Black Crook* (1866), the musical comedies combined musical and dramatic elements. Florenz Ziegfeld's *Follies* was perhaps the best-known of the "revues," which were musical extravaganzas that relied on song, dance and plenty of scantily clad women.

It was vaudeville, however, that took the variety format to new heights and reigned as the most popular form of entertainment in America from the 1880s until the late 1920s. Vaudeville attracted larger audiences than all the other forms of entertainment at the time combined, including the legitimate theater. Its weekly audience in 1896 was estimated at one million.[4] Vaudeville entrepreneurs Tony Pastor and Benjamin Franklin Keith and partner Edward F. Albee recognized the profitability of providing theatrical entertainment that would appeal to people of all classes, and especially the respectable middle class who were led into the theaters by the morality plays. These businessmen tailored the variety show to the tastes and practices of the urban and suburban family audience.

The first move they made was to "clean it up" and disassociate it from the unsavory reputation of the saloons and burlesque. Chase Theatres in Washington, D.C., advertised that "it is the constant aim of the management to prevent the use of a single word, expression, or situation that will offend the intelligent, refined and cultured classes."[5] The use of profanity, off-color jokes or sexual innuendo in songs or stories was expressly forbidden; performers who persisted in the use of these were blacklisted. Some acts undoubtedly tested the limits of censorship, as the habitual warnings from theater managers (including notices posted backstage) would seem to indicate. One patron in 1910 complained, for example, that "if your wife or your daughter goes to a vaudeville theater at the present time the chances are at least seventy-five in a hundred that she will hear some jest or some song that reeks of the barroom or worse."[6]

But descriptions of vaudeville as "clean, wholesome, respectable entertainment, suitable for the entire family,"[7] though probably exaggerated to one degree or another, were still not far from the truth. Vaudeville was "clean," but not too clean. It still reflected its origins in the male subculture of the saloons; the entertainment was subdued, but yet suggestive, testing conventions of respectability. Still, in one of the earliest works on vaudeville, Caroline Caffin said that vaudeville managers tried to make their theaters "places of harmless amusement and recreation for all classes of society, to which women and children might go unescorted without fear."[8]

That vaudeville had acquired a reputation for family entertainment is clear from a story in the *American Mercury* in 1924. A reporter said (not without some exaggeration and sarcasm) that the moral authorities of the time thought vaudeville "to be so pure that it needs no Christian supervision. . . . Eminent moralists of all wings and from all over the country, both clerical and lay, have endorsed the vaudeville theater as an almost ideal scene of amusement for the whole family, from grandma to the baby." He told of a woman who sent a letter to Albee saying that his New York vaudeville house "was the one place of entertainment she could attend on the Sabbath and still feel that she was in direct communion with God."[9] Of course this was meant to be humorous, but it became increasingly difficult for the social elite and clergy to condemn the "family entertainment" the vaudeville program offered. After the turn of the century more and more people began to see the beneficial role of entertainment as a relief from the monotony and routine of urban industrial life.

In a sense vaudeville was, as Russel Nye has called it, "the ultimate democratic theater."[10] This requires some qualification, however, for there is nothing *inherently* democratic about popular art forms that would distinguish them from the high arts. Inferences about their democratic nature are usually derived from their general accessibility made possible by low cost and medium, whether a large vaudeville theater, movie prints or broadcast radio and television. The mass-market revolution coincided with American democratization in the early twentieth century; both put tremendous pressures on the survival of individual groups, whether ethnic or religious, and particular perspectives. This created a paradox, because the standardization and lowest-common-denominator model employed for mass entertainment worked to abate the kind of pluralism that should characterize genuine democracy. Beginning with vaudeville and then the movies, the entertainment media have demonstrated a tendency to level social and cultural differences by propagating a national mythology in order to appeal to large-scale audiences. In addition, this approach hindered the artistic development of the popular arts, which in turn contributed to their exclusion from serious evaluation by other social institutions.

Vaudeville admission prices were kept low, ranging anywhere from a dime to a dollar (depending on the seat and attractions), but still making entrance to a vaudeville theater one-half or even one-quarter the cost of the legitimate theaters. Vaudeville theaters were usually located in the business or shopping districts and attracted both city inhabitants and suburban shoppers. Each act on the bill was intended to appeal to a specific audience segment: animal acts thrilled younger children, slapstick comedians made adolescent boys laugh, and female singers attracted women shoppers. For the male saloon crowd, vaudeville managers announced the scores of hometown games and booked boxers, baseball players and other athletes to perform or celebrate their victories on the vaudeville stage.

In 1894 the continuous-performance format was instituted; the classic nine-act program was repeated continuously from late morning until midnight. Those who worked during the day could catch evening performances, but this new format also made vaudeville available to those who had leisure time during the day, mostly women and children. It was estimated that by 1900 children made up as much as one-half of afternoon audiences and one-quarter of the evening audiences at vaudeville theaters.[11] One survey showed that about 16 percent of the metropolitan population in New York went to a vaudeville show at least once a week.[12]

The creation of "refined" or "high class" vaudeville in the 1890s further attracted the upper classes, in turn, influencing vaudeville. Drinking and smoking were not permitted in "high class" vaudeville theaters. Vaudeville managers even began to expect audiences to behave more like those in the legitimate theater. Men were asked by the management not to smoke in the theaters and to "kindly avoid the stamping of feet and pounding of canes on the floor." Theater employees handed out printed notices to patrons requesting that they "don't talk during acts, as it annoys those about you, and prevents a perfect hearing of the entertainment."[13] It was reported that members of the social elite of Boston and New York attended the opening of B. F. Keith's first vaudeville palace theater in 1894, demonstrating that "high class" vaudeville was "the cup of tea for the swanks as well as the dish for the masses."[14]

Vaudeville did appeal to a wide social and economic range of people, from the urban working class to the social and economic elite. "Watch the audience trooping into a New York vaudeville house," Caffin said. "There is no more democratic crowd to be seen anywhere."[15] According to Albert F. McLean, however, the expanding class of white-collar workers (managers, professionals, technicians, salespeople, clerks, engineers) accounted for the largest portion of vaudeville's regular audience.[16] Their experience was urban and not rural. They were success-minded and aspired to the middle class. They believed in material success and social progress, valued immediate satisfaction and happiness in the present. These people desired and enjoyed their increased leisure time, and found pleasure and affirmation in the amusements available in the city. This group was perhaps best represented by what McLean has identified as the new folk culture that emerged out of the urban and industrial environment. As the above description of vaudeville suggests, the new middle-class indulgences aspired to those of the upper classes, whose wealth had enabled them to elevate "culture" to a height of luxury and enjoyment. For the upper classes "culture" was a product of abundance and a matter of leisure-time consumption, an attitude that set the tone for the expanding white-collar class.

With the emergence of a consumer economy, the masses were not seen as simply workers or producers, but as, importantly, consumers. The Victorian ethos with its demand for compulsive work, productivity, order and self-control was replaced by a new mass democratic culture of novelty that encouraged leisure, pleasure and consumption. The white-collar class was no longer willing to look beyond this life to a heavenly reward; urban life emphasized immediate satisfaction and happiness in the present, not only for the economically privileged but for people of all classes. The belief in material success triumphed over a "pie-in-the-sky" deliverance from earthly toil. The demands of industrial life intensified people's need for recreation while also limiting the possibilities for diversion, since people were crowded in urban centers. The Protestant work ethic was reshaped by this desire for leisure and amusement in urban industrial life. These changes coincided with a new attitude toward amusement, which was now accepted as a legitimate part of life, not only for the leisured classes but across the social spectrum. The decrease in working hours and increase in wages corresponded with an explosion of low-priced mass entertainment around the turn of the century. Symbolizing the modern era, machines created new vistas for amusement as movies replaced the theater, radio brought entertainment directly into the home, and automobiles expanded the range of recreational possibilities.

Vaudeville was a ritual celebration of the new urban folk culture. It both reflected and influenced social and cultural patterns in the cities, entertaining people with the materials of their own environment. At its center was the "Myth of Success" that lured most people to the cities in the first place. Even though it may not have reflected the realities and experience of urban life, this myth still maintained a strong hold on the popular imagination. Vaudeville was, as McLean describes it, "both an escape from the moment and a

tangible promise for the future. Its glittering promises of pleasure and fulfillment, its easy answers for immediate problems, its roots in middle-class
values, and its cheerful materialism."[17]

Vaudeville thrived on the novelty and variety that audiences demanded and,
as a result, mirrored the complexity and perpetual motion of the city itself.
Vaudeville treated changes in American humor, ethnic stereotypes, urban
affairs and modifications in family life. The humor, drama and cast of characters were drawn from the city: the glamorous and the mundane, the successful and the downtrodden, the industrious and the lazy, authority figures,
the naive and the innocent. The vaudeville program, then, reflected urban
culture and values. "Not the happy ending but the happy moment, not fulfillment at the end of some career rainbow but a sensory, psychically satisfying
here-and-now were the results of a vaudeville show," McLean writes. "Its
concern was not the making of money but the enjoyment of it. It offered, in
symbolic terms, the sweet fruits of success neither as a reward nor as a
promise, but as an accessible right for all those participating in the new life
of the cities."[18] Vaudeville's modular format, which evolved during the 1880s
and 1890s, gave managers great flexibility in programming. They could easily
incorporate new types of entertainment and respond quickly to public taste
and sentiment and reflect it on the stage. Vaudeville drew from every source
of entertainment available at the time: the music halls, minstrel shows, circuses, dime museums, opera, symphony, pantomime, choreography, farce
and the legitimate stage.

Despite its dazzling array of talent from around the world, vaudeville was
by intent "mass-produced entertainment geared to the broadest denominator
of middle-class taste," Nye writes. "It had no pretensions to art, nor did it
make any consistent appeal to a serious audience."[19] Regardless of the social
range of their patronage, vaudeville managers thought of themselves as primarily in the business of providing "popular" entertainment for a "lowbrow"
audience. Caffin wrote that in vaudeville the designation *highbrow* was considered a "taboo epithet," a "hideous demon" that vaudeville managers vig-
ilantly exorcised from their programs. The established rule for commercial
success was that "highbrow stuff never pays."[20]

As I explained earlier, the programming decisions of both vaudeville and
legitimate theater managers were based on assumptions about their respective audiences and the cultural distinctions resulting from the bifurcation of
American culture. The notable exceptions and critical commentary of the time

expose their arbitrariness. In practice, the lines that existed between these were often blurred. Caffin insisted, for example, that there was no act that was "too good" for vaudeville. The dancing of Ruth St. Denis she called "the wonder and delight of all lovers of the beautiful." Caffin said: "For so entirely was her conception that of an artist . . . so impersonal and abstract was her performance that it became something more than mere amusement and claimed a place in the category of art."[21] Likewise, she was enamored by the vaudeville performance of Sarah Bernhardt, the world-famous star of the legitimate stage. Caffin noted that many people came to see the French actress, not because she was an "artist" but because she was a "celebrity." Even so, she said, if audiences supported vaudeville's inclusion of such talent, "we know that there is ambition enough among the managers to supply whatever demand is made."[22]

These illustrations suggest that the cultural assumptions and expectations by which theater managers operated were not necessarily in sync with the American audience. The crossover between legitimate and vaudeville stages of both acts and audience suggests that the cultural hierarchy did not necessarily describe real distinctions in American life as much as it fostered taste and attitudinal differences, and especially class antagonism. Regardless of whether people from different social backgrounds enjoyed and appreciated the entertainment provided by the theater or the movies, actual attendance at the theater or cinema represented class and cultural distinctions and animosities.

In his observations about the effect of the movies on the theater in 1915, Eaton offered a poignant illustration. In a New England industrial city with a population of thirty-five thousand, fully twenty thousand did not, and would not, attend a play at a legitimate theater. Several wealthy men in that city purchased a theater, installed an excellent stock company, and reduced gallery seats to ten cents to compete with the movies. "But the theatre was on the 'fashionable' side of town," Eaton explained. "It was looked upon by the six thousand mill operatives and their families . . . as something that belonged to the other class—and they would not go near it." The well-intended venture was a failure, he said, "while the movies continued to flourish as the green bay tree."[23]

During the golden years of vaudeville, between the 1890s and 1920s, there were thirty-seven vaudeville theaters in New York, thirty in Philadelphia, twenty-two in Chicago, and outside the cities some two thousand smaller theaters that also booked vaudeville.[24] The competition between them was extremely intense; the battle for the biggest stars and the search for the newest novelty was unceasing. Vaudeville entrepreneurs tried to gain the competitive edge by using huge salaries to lure stars of the legitimate theater to the vaudeville stage. It comes as no surprise, then, that a New York vaudeville theater gave top billing to "Edison's latest marvel," the vitascope. The moving images projected on a screen were greeted with "vociferous cheering" by the crowd at Koster and Bial's Music Hall on April 23, 1896.[25] Immediately after their debut in the spring of 1896, projected films were quickly incorporated into the versatile vaudeville program.

Nickelodeon Madness

Initially movies were not projected on screens but shown in kinetoscopes, which were moving-picture peep shows. Kinetoscopes, slot machines, phonographs and other novelties filled the penny arcades. The arcades were male hangouts with seamy reputations that kept families away and made them a dangerous environment for women. As one would expect, many of the kinetoscope peep shows featured women in underclothes or getting undressed, glimpses of ankles and limbs, long embraces and kissing. These very brief movies shown in kinetoscopes were regarded as curiosities for the urban working class. Thus the movies gained an early association with lowbrow amusements that alienated members of the respectable middle class.

The vaudeville theatrical circuit, however, provided an instant exhibition network for projected movies. It supplied a large national audience of largely middle-class people who were used to seeing various types of novelties in an evening's entertainment. Within three months of the Koster and Bial exhibition, film shorts were being shown in vaudeville houses throughout the East and Midwest. The vitascope was called "the best drawing card ever presented" at the Bijou in Philadelphia and was credited with attracting "hundreds of people who have never attended a vaudeville house before" to the Hopkins Theatre in Chicago.[26] Comic and trick films, like George Melies's *Trip to the Moon* (1902), which was particularly appealing to children, as well as early narrative films like Edwin S. Porter's *Life of an American Farmer* and *The Great Train Robbery* (both 1903), were first seen in vaudeville theaters.

The popularity of these early one-reel films, lasting no longer than about fifteen minutes, fueled the competition in the entertainment world. Two vaudeville businessmen, Harry Davis and John P. Harris, opened the first of the nickelodeons in a defunct opera house in Pittsburgh on June 19, 1905. For a five-cent admission, the audience watched *The Great Train Robbery* to piano accompaniment. The nickelodeon boom began the following year, and by 1907, there were some twenty-five hundred nickelodeons in the United States.[27] Two years later they numbered about eight thousand. At the peak of the nickelodeon craze in 1910, there were over ten thousand theaters across the country, creating a demand for between one and two hundred reels of film each week.[28] Nickelodeons were small, makeshift movie theaters, often converted storefronts that seated about one hundred people. The standard nickelodeon program consisted of about six short films, usually including an adventure, a comedy, an informational film and a melodrama.

Downtown workers used the noonday lunch to visit the nickelodeon, an experience that "must have been an exhilarating—and slightly scandalous—break from routine," David Nasaw comments. "The trip to the nickel theater was an act of almost pure hedonism—in the middle of the workday, where it most certainly did not belong."[29] And their behavior resembled that of the gallery crowd at the melodrama. As Kathy Peiss writes, "The working-class crowd audibly interacted with the screen and each other, commenting on the action, explaining the plot, and vocally accompanying the piano player."[30]

Going to the movies became a weekly outing for many families. By the most conservative estimates, some twenty-six million Americans, slightly less than 20 percent of the national population, attended the nickelodeon weekly. More than 25 percent of the New York City population went to the movies every week, as did an incredible 43 percent of Chicago residents. National gross receipts in 1910 totalled ninety-one million dollars.[31] The most prominent vaudeville businessmen had no choice but to begin converting their palaces into movie theaters (the fate of the Astor Place Opera House in 1914).

As the competition intensified, a hybrid form called "small-time vaudeville" was created by combining the low admission cost and film program of the nickelodeon with the vaudeville acts and comfortable surroundings of the "high class" vaudeville theater. Small-time vaudeville had great appeal to the middle class and demonstrated the potential for film exhibition in large theaters. By capitalizing on the immediate popularity of the feature film around 1912, movie theater managers could offer an alternative to both the nickelodeon and high-class vaudeville; employing fewer vaudeville acts reduced costs, which meant lower admission prices. Small-time vaudeville paved the way for the full-length feature film and the spectacular motion-picture palaces, the first being the luxuriant Strand Theatre, built in New York in 1914 with thirty-three hundred seats, marble interior, plush carpeting and crystal chandeliers. These two developments marked the end of the nickelodeon era and increased the appeal of the movies for the American middle class.

The motion picture industry completely revolutionized the entertainment world by the 1920s, ultimately spelling disaster for both vaudeville and the legitimate theater. Between 1895 and 1906 the number of vaudeville theaters increased to over four hundred, a figure roughly equal to the legitimate theaters at that time. Both the number of legitimate theaters and vaudeville houses topped one thousand between the 1890s and 1920s, the period considered vaudeville's golden age. By 1926, however, only twelve "big-time" vaudeville houses remained; the Keith-Orpheum Circuit was purchased by the Radio Corporation of America in 1928 to be used as a film exhibition network named Radio-Keith-Orpheum (RKO).[32]

The last traces of vaudeville coincided with the introduction of sound in motion pictures in 1927. Vaudeville went out of existence as a form of theatrical entertainment, but its basic approach to entertainment and audience continued as the foundation for twentieth-century entertainment. In a sense, vaudeville was simply transferred to the new media—radio, movies and later television—which absorbed both vaudeville's talent and audience. Many former vaudevillians made the transition to radio or film; the variety format survived in Milton Berle's *Texas Star Theatre* and *The Ed Sullivan Show*. The vaudeville playlets, brief dramas with recognizable characters and formulas, contributed to television sitcoms and dramas.

At first motion pictures had no effect on the legitimate theater. Prior to 1910, movies were controlled by respectable Anglo-Saxon Protestants, who created a virtual monopoly in the film industry between 1908 and 1912 with the formation of the Motion Picture Patents Company (MPPC), known as "The Trust." Thomas Edison and the other members of the Trust thought that improving the quality of films would increase production costs, resulting in higher rental fees and admission prices. They argued that this would be unacceptable to patrons and only hurt business. Initially the novelty of moving pictures attracted the urban audience and especially the working class that "had been effectively disenfranchised from the older arts," as Russell Merritt observes.[33] The prevailing assumption among members of the Trust was that this audience "did not have the mental capacity to understand, let alone appreciate, longer films," according to film analyst Tino Balio. Consequently, the Trust restricted film production to the standardized one-reelers (ten- to fifteen-minute films). In doing so, however, they ignored the pleas of exhibitors for "better and longer films, ones that told well-developed and sophisticated stories that could attract a more intelligent clientele," Balio notes.[34] In effect, this policy limited the market for movies "to a segment of society which rarely frequented legitimate theaters and were unaccustomed to anything beyond triteness, low humor, pie-throwing, and train chases," according to theater historian Robert McLaughlin.[35]

Independent producers and distributors, however, thought otherwise. In 1912 Adolph Zukor purchased the rights to a three-and-a-half-reel French film, *Queen Elizabeth,* which starred renowned stage actress Sarah Bernhardt. Prohibited by the Trust from using the normal distribution channels, Zukor booked the film in a first-class legitimate theater, the Lyceum on Broadway; admission was an unprecedented one dollar. The full-length feature film was an enormous hit, despite the high price of a ticket (compared to the nickel and dime charged at nickelodeons), and demonstrated that there was a market for longer narrative films featuring a star. *Queen Elizabeth* and other feature films that followed attracted the more prosperous and sophisticated audience among the middle and upper classes.

Movies initially attracted a new audience among immigrant city dwellers, many of whom had never been to the legitimate theater. In the course of resisting the Trust, independent producers and exhibitors made legitimate and vaudeville theatergoers into moviegoers. The independents launched the full-length feature film and, in contrast to the Trust's policy of keeping actors appearing in films anonymous, developed a star system modeled on vaudeville. Each movie was now advertised as a unique product in its own right. These new players in the high-stakes game of entertainment came from the immigrant ethnic groups who had been effectively disenfranchised from traditional high culture. In contrast to prevailing ideas about the traditional arts, they saw entertainment as a competitive business, and not a didactic art form as the Victorians hoped it might become.

By the advent of sound in motion pictures in 1927-1928, Adolph Zukor, Carl Laemmle, Samuel Goldwyn, Louis B. Mayer, William Fox, Marcus Loew, Harry and Jack Cohn, and the Warner brothers (Harry, Albert, Sam and Jack) had built movie empires, increasing their control over every aspect of the business—production, distribution and exhibition—through the vertical integration of the major film studios. The extraordinary overnight success of the "talkies" gave Hollywood studio heads enormous power in the entertainment business. "Being unable to eliminate each other," drama critic Arthur Mann observed, "they settled down to the task of killing off the remainder of the opposition, which consisted chiefly of legitimate [theater] productions."[36]

Decline of the Legitimate Theater

As mentioned earlier, the first sign that the movies were having an impact on the legitimate theater was the loss in the gallery audience. "Even the most successful plays on Broadway, plays which are 'selling out' down-stairs, often show tiers of empty benches under the roof," Eaton wrote. "This is usually attributed to the movies."[37] But the movies attracted patrons from the down-stairs as well. Writing in the thirties, just after the introduction of sound in the movies, theater critic Arthur Mann observed that younger patrons, who were "spurned" by the legitimate theater, now gave "their money to the girl in the gilded cage outside the picture palace." He said they were lured away from the theater by the "awesome, cathedral-like structures" and glamorous "motion-picture beauties." Glamorous movie stars were apparently too much competition for legitimate actresses, who the critic described as "a regiment of husky-voiced, flat-chested heroines who couldn't bestir the imagination of a half-wit."[38]

More important, the legitimate theater was now the exclusive property of the social and wealthy elite; others were simply not welcome. Mann pointed out that "the entire structure of the drama, from reviewer and wise-cracking columnist up and down, has been framed during the past decade for the top-hatted patron of the orchestra." Legitimate performers played to the audience in the front rows, critics, business executives and others who could afford the $4.40 tickets "quite beyond the reach of a normal income."[39] It was commonly understood by producers, critics and audience alike that the legitimate theater was a "sacred precinct" for the cultural elite, who it was assumed, were the only ones who could understand and appreciate "so-called first-class drama" and the naturalistic acting style.[40] The fact that gallery seats were no longer available eliminated the lower classes from the legitimate theater audience.

Not surprisingly, as the cinema replaced the theater in cultural significance for most people, it moved to the center of American life in the early twentieth century. One observer in 1913 noted that the theater had "hardly impressed itself upon the popular mind in this country," being "a subject for profession-als and 'highbrows.' " In contrast, the movies were more than popular spectacle in that they had "enter[ed] into the daily thought of the masses." According to this writer, "The crowds not only throng to the shows; they talk about them, on street corners, in the cars, and over the hoods of baby carriages, . . . [discussing] the technique of the moving-picture theatre with as much interest as literary salons in Paris or London discuss the minutiae of the higher drama." Filmmakers, he wrote, "have achieved an extraordinary triumph. They have converted their entire audience into first-nighters."[41]

Movies not only drew away the audience for stage plays but also brought about a dramatic change in the economic structure of the theater. As movies increasingly appealed to the American middle class, they lured away the audience for the legitimate theater with admission prices one-fifth those of a stage play. Touring companies quickly became unprofitable. Prior to 1910, the financial success of a play was largely determined by the 250 to 350 road companies that toured plays which were originally produced in New York. Between 1910 and 1920, however, the number of companies on tour during an average week dropped from 236 to 34.[42] During that decade, production costs increased two to three times, forcing companies to either lower production standards or increase admission prices. The cheap price for a movie ticket made the latter impossible. Instead, touring companies lowered the quality of productions to cut costs and even resorted to dishonest advertising. Audiences felt exploited by legitimate productions and were eager for a substitute for the poor plays and high prices of the legitimate stage.

Further, as production companies increased their share of the box-office take, local theaters began closing their doors or featuring vaudeville and motion pictures. As a result, the number of theaters available for legitimate productions outside the major cities dropped significantly. According to a *Billboard* survey, the number fell from 1,549 to 674 between 1910 and 1925; by 1930 there only 500 theaters available for legitimate plays outside of New York, and the number continued to decline.[43]

The combined effect of talking pictures and the economic plight of the Depression proved to be devastating for the legitimate theater. In 1915 there were still about fifteen hundred legitimate theaters outside New York and the number of productions on Broadway continued to increase until the season of 1927-1928, when about three hundred plays were mounted. The sound era of motion pictures began that season with *The Jazz Singer,* starring renowned vaudeville star Al Jolson, marking the beginning of a dramatic decline in live theater. By the mid-thirties, legitimate road activity had dwindled to an average weekly total of only about twenty productions; only twelve cities besides New York were capable of supporting legitimate theater. A mere eighty new productions were launched during the 1939-1940 season.[44]

Theater managers began throwing together shows in order to keep their theaters open, but the talkies continued to drain away the audience. Only 35 out of a total of 225 new productions during the 1928-1929 season were financially successful, or just over 15 percent, as compared with 31 percent that had showed a profit the previous season. By the 1931-1932 season a pattern was established whereby 80-85 percent of all productions failed to secure a profit during their Broadway runs. If shows did not prove to be big hits with long runs, they were closed immediately. In order to survive, legitimate theater managers began showing films and by the fall of 1931, almost 20 percent of all New York legitimate stages were involved in alternate bookings of live drama and movies.[45]

Between 1928 and 1933 the number of stock companies in the United States dropped from 165 to 35. The 410 cities in North America that hosted Broadway plays "on the road" were reduced to a mere 12 outside of greater New York. Only 15 of 152 tent shows were still in existence. The Shubert Theatre Corporation folded. The loss of revenues from the road put enormous pressure on productions to have a substantial run on Broadway. Rising costs and risks resulted in the "hit-flop syndrome"; plays that showed little potential for long, lucrative runs were closed immediately. A production had to play to a near capacity crowd for ten weeks for the producer to recoup the investment.

"It is Broadway or bust," Mann wrote, "and, of late, it is usually bust."[46] Some eighty-five hundred actors and actresses and over four hundred union stagehands, carpenters and electricians were out of work. Most of the managers either left the business or went bankrupt, and the majority of New York theaters were taken over by mortgage-holding banks. Even a slash in ticket prices in January 1933 did not curtail the loss of gross receipts.[47]

As the need for cinematic material increased with the demand for talking pictures, film executives mined the legitimate theater for talent. Legitimate performers replaced those silent stars who could not make the transition to sound or worked in radio. Actors, directors, producers and playwrights received higher wages and more job security in the film industry. Broadway producers discovered they could realize production expenses from the sale of motion picture rights alone, and they began selling Broadway productions to film studios even before rehearsals began.[48]

The legitimate theater took a serious blow in the competition with the cinema. Producers of serious drama had to focus on the most popular plays in order to secure profits. But critics eventually recognized and rightly lamented the loss of the theater's institutional role in society. "Needless to say, our concern is not with the displacement of sophisticated comedy by musicals but with the decline of serious drama," two writers in *The Yale Review* said in 1959. "After all, the theatre has for a long time been an important forum in which to present serious social, psychological, and political problems; and the narrowing of this forum is a loss to society."[49] Economic circumstances made the theater less willing to perform traditional functions of art, especially social criticism.

According to one source, between the 1927-1928 and 1952-1953 seasons there was a decline of 69 percent in the number of New York theaters, 55 percent in the number of road companies, 46 percent in the number of stock companies and 81 percent in the number of New York first nights.[50] Increased costs and risks and falling demand continued to plague producers, forcing them to rely on hit shows with longer runs and quickly close those that flopped. From the advent of sound until World War II, the film industry prospered financially while the theater dwindled to the point where it was no longer an economic threat to Hollywood.

Conclusion

Entrepreneurs in the legitimate field tried to counter the threat from vaudeville and the movies. According to Oscar Brockett, after 1900 the Syndicate "refused to accept works not likely to appeal to a mass audience and favored productions that featured stars with large personal followings."[51] The Shubert brothers and Klaw and Erlanger even tried to arrange a deal to put vaudeville acts into their theaters.[52] In what was an unprecedented move at the time, the Shuberts began showing ten-cent movies at one of their Boston theaters, igniting a fierce nickelodeon price war during the slow summer months in 1909.

Such attempts to popularize the legitimate theater, however, did not make it commercially viable enough to withstand the threat that motion pictures asserted in the late 1920s. As a result, the theater moved in a more esoteric direction. This in turn, however, made for an even more distressing financial situation. "From an artistic standpoint, the talkies may have been a godsend to the theatre, but from an economic standpoint, even this prospect added to an already serious dilemma," Robert McLaughlin notes. "It was becoming more and more costly to produce the kind of productions that people would pay to see."[53]

The legitimate theater had in effect, if only partly by intent, cut itself off from a more general audience and subsequent success in the commercial marketplace. This was an accidental byproduct of the strategy to preserve traditional high culture while also employing it to raise the standards of the "raw and unkindled masses of humanity." Legitimate theater became an esoteric art form associated with the tastes of the upper classes. There were some critics who argued that as the quality of motion pictures improved they would breed new audiences for the legitimate theater. But such optimism overlooked the social barriers represented by these different activities. "Each is an amusement, the pastime, of a separate and antagonistic class," Walter Prichard Eaton observed in 1915.[54]

But while the legitimate theater became an activity exclusive of the upper classes, the cinema appealed to all classes, providing an integrating social experience rather than a fragmenting one. "Movies breathe the spirit in which the country was founded, freedom and equality," film magnate William Fox declared. "In the motion picture theaters there are no separations of classes. . . . The rich rub elbows with the poor and that's the way it should be. The motion picture is a distinctly American institution."[55] A twentieth-century art born in the turbulence of the emerging modern industrial society, the cinema was a genuine art of the populace. As film entrepreneurs saw it, movies operated as a kind of participatory democracy, with tickets acting as ballots. In contrast to the theater in the first quarter of the century, the cinema developed the reputation of being a "democratic" art form, replacing the theater as a social microcosm of American society.

6
· · · · ·
The Not-So-Silent
Moving Picture
World

The movies originated among the city's amusements and symbolized the conflict between Victorian and modern culture. The depreciation of the popular arts, despite their amazing popularity, had a negative effect on the way people thought about the movies and the course of their development. Initially the possibilities of the cinema went largely unrecognized. Filmmakers approached their work along the lines of manufacturers of a consumer product and not as part of an artistic community. Critics paid scant attention to movies; when they did it was usually to demean them as a second-rate entertainment that carried on the popular tradition of nineteenth-century melodrama.

Regardless, moving pictures became an important aspect of the new urban culture by finding a niche serving the needs and desires of the working-class immigrants who struggled through the often traumatic transformations of urban and industrial life. In contrast to the traditional arts, the origin of film was among the lower classes and not the wealthy and educated elite. The movies emerged as an urban folk art. The earliest film shorts simply recorded movements like railroad trains, fire engines and workers leaving a factory. The source of many early movies were nineteenth-century paintings and post-cards, comic strips, popular songs, newspaper headlines, vaudeville and bur-lesque routines, magazines and dime novels.

In an important essay on the origin and nature of the cinema, Erwin Pa-nofsky shows that these early films gratified a basic sense of justice by reward-ing virtue and industry and punishing vice and laziness. They exhibited a plain sentimentality, sensation in the form of blood and violence, a taste for mild pornography and a crude humor called slapstick. These primal elements of movies as a folk art, Panofsky writes, "could blossom forth into genuine history, tragedy and romance, crime and adventure, and comedy, as soon as it was realized that they could be transfigured—not by an artificial injection of literary values but by the exploitation of the unique and specific possibil-ities of the new medium."[1]

The motion picture industry evolved foremost as a profitable business and not an artistic enterprise. By the second decade of the century, film produc-tion was industrialized; the primary purpose of manufacturing and distribut-ing movies was to make a profit. Foster Rhea Dulles suggests that the com-mercial mass marketing of the early film producers "represented an approach to the development of this new amusement which would not have been possible in any other country. It reflected a democratic concept of the general availability of popular entertainment which was thoroughly American."[2] The cinema in European countries, meanwhile, followed a different course. "There filmmaking was not as much a business as an extension of the intel-lectual and cultural world of the fine arts," film historian Douglas Gomery writes.[3] Government subsidies lessened commercial pressures and fostered the development of national cinemas and styles—French Impressionism, Ger-man Expressionism and Soviet montage are the most prominent examples—which, although they did not have the worldwide appeal of American pictures, eventually had an impact on Hollywood filmmakers.

At first going to the movies was a kind of "slumming" for the middle and upper classes—participating in a cultural activity associated with working-class immigrants. Nickelodeons were on a par with saloons, dime museums, dance halls, roller rinks, amusement parks and vaudeville. Movie entrepre-neurs, however, wanted to expand their audience into the middle class. At the same time, middle-class crusaders feared the influence of the movies. Instead of giving the cinema a place in American life to evolve as a legitimate art form, they tried to establish authority over the industry. This proved significant in determining the role movies would serve in American society, at least until the end of World War II. Like the theater before it, the movies (and the other urban amusements) became contested ground in the cultural struggle in the first quarter of the twentieth century.

A Shabby Occupation

After the turn of the century, the high art tradition became disaffected with the general population. This left the false impression that artistic activity (actually the aesthetic dimension of human life) was a specialized and esoteric affair to be equated with the high art tradition. Entertainment forms were relegated to an inferior status as cheap amusement for the masses. This in turn affected their development as art forms. It was within this framework of the cultural hierarchy that entrepreneurs developed the new technology-based art forms of the twentieth century. In the face of condescension from the religious community and the cultural elite (and tremendous profit potential from the working and middle classes), enterprising businessmen and artists developed entertainment forms primarily along the lines of a commercial product and only secondarily as art. The entertainment industry was perceived as a business that profited by providing amusement for a large and diverse population.

In this context, film companies instituted a production system designed to manufacture movies quickly and efficiently. Early film studios were called "factories," and filmmakers considered themselves along the lines of factory workers; theirs was a lowbrow occupation, simply grinding out cheap films for entertainment purposes. In the early years, no one received screen credit; film executives knew from vaudeville that a popular "star" with a public reputation could demand higher wages. Early film historian Lewis Jacobs wrote that "most of the directors, actors, and cameramen who had come to the movies were more or less ashamed of their connection with them; they stayed in their jobs because they needed work, and they gave little thought to the medium's possibilities or opportunities. Nearly everyone still regarded moviemaking as a shabby occupation."[4]

This attitude retarded serious development of film as an art form; filmmakers were slow to explore the medium's unique properties. "There was none of the intellectual excitement and creative ferment which we might expect to find at the birth of an art form," film historian David A. Cook writes, "because no one was yet equipped to acknowledge that birth, and so between

1903 and 1912 the industry's level of artistic and technical competence scarcely ever rose above the marginally adequate."⁵ Even D. W. Griffith, considered the cinema's first great *auteur,* was embarrassed by his occupation and worked in anonymity for years. Griffith wanted to be a writer of novels in the tradition of Victorian high literature and thought the movies were a vulgar medium. It is somewhat ironic, then, that Griffith pioneered the narrative language of film and is credited with elevating the medium to an art form. It was not until *The Birth of a Nation* in 1915, however, that he actually took credit for his over 150 films, proclaiming himself "Producer of all great Biograph successes, revolutionizing Motion Picture drama and founding the modern technique of the art."⁶

To create a "popular" cinema, American filmmakers relied on the popular theater tradition from the nineteenth century. They consciously developed a cinematic style with standardized formulas to facilitate communication with the working- and middle-class audience. The evolution of the "classical Hollywood style" of filmmaking was shaped as much, if not more, by economic considerations and the need for efficiency in production, than the inspiration to develop the creative potentials of a new art form. In brief, the classical Hollywood film is character-centered. The story moves along a tight linear narrative structure, the consequence of one action or event leading to the next. All of the problems are resolved in the end. This narrative pattern and attending cinematic style of filmmaking allowed for rapid and efficient production of new works and became the basis for Hollywood genres. Genres are based on standard formulas (like boy-meets-girl, boy-loses-girl, boy-gets-girl-back) that are generally repeatable and therefore familiar to both the scriptwriter and the audience. Genres also make it easier to advertise movies; audiences know what to expect from a western, romantic comedy or action-adventure film.

By the dawn of the cinema, the American intellectual community had demarcated high and low culture. Taking their cue from Matthew Arnold, most educators believed that they should impart the best and most distinguished achievements of Western civilization. Unfortunately, movies did not fit the bill. Consequently, the kind of criticism that might have contributed to the development of the early cinema as an art form did not take place.

Critics knew the film industry was controlled for the most part by people who sought financial profits. Film production seemed more like an assembly line than a process for creative expression; this violated the Romantic ideal of the individual artist, or *auteur,* offering a personal vision through a creative work. The filmmaking process is a communal one that depends on the combined efforts of writers, directors, producers, cameramen, editors, actors and cinematographers. Also, by the standards of the high culture tradition, art had to be free from the negative influences of commercialism to be authentic.

These elitist attitudes about art and the cinema were expressed in an interview with British dramatist George Bernard Shaw, published approvingly in an American magazine. American author and literary critic Archibald Henderson began the discussion by suggesting that "the film industry is, for the most part, directed and controlled by people with imperfectly developed artistic instincts and ideals who have their eyes fixed primarily on financial rewards." Shaw concurred, using commercialism to distinguish high and popular art: "If the capitalists let themselves be seduced from their pursuit of profits to the enchantments of art, they would be bankrupt before they knew where they were. You cannot combine the pursuit of money with the pursuit of art." Shaw recognized the movies as a "new art" and suggested that "movie plays should be invented expressly for the screen by original imaginative visualizers." Still, he regarded film, like the melodrama, as "a second-class entertainment not to be confused with comedy and tragedy." The movies made "mediocrity compulsory" in his estimation, because they had to appeal to a large and diverse international audience for commercial viability, "the average of an American millionaire and a Chinese coolie, a cathedral-town governess and a mining-village barmaid." For that reason he thought films could not "afford to meddle with the upper-ten-per-cent theater of the highbrows," asserting further that "democracy always prefers second bests."[7] Here again we see the ambivalence about the confluence of art and commerce in entertainment forms.

The division between high and popular culture gave the cinema a secondary status as art, but the establishment of a market-oriented production system did not prevent filmmakers like Griffith and others from developing the artistic potentials of the medium. And by the mid-teens, serious books had been written about film. In *The Art of the Moving Picture* (1915), Vachel Lindsay tried to distinguish the properties that made film unique from other arts. Hugo Munsterberg's *The Photoplay: A Psychological Study* (1916) examined the psychology of film viewing. In contrast to Europe, where intellectuals and artists immediately embraced the cinema as an art, the educated class in America continued to regard movies as mere amusement. Writing in 1913,

Walter Prichard Eaton bemoaned the growing popularity of what he called the "canned drama" of the movies and concurrent decline in the "so-called first-class drama" of the serious theater. But despite the obvious change in cultural priorities, Eaton said, "we have still our ancient faith in the abiding worth of true dramatic art and the abiding imagination of humanity."[8] Consequently, the magazine for which he wrote was not about to begin a regular column on movie criticism. In contrast, the *London Evening News* began a column in 1912 called "Round the Picture Palace" to give serious coverage to the movies as part of the artistic world.

Even though the cinema was thought of as a commercial amusement and not a legitimate art form, in reality it still performed the functions of art, but outside the control of the cultural elite. As such, the cinema initially found a niche serving the needs and desires of the urban working class. Movies, Lewis Jacobs writes, became the "first art child of democracy."[9]

The Silent World of Urban Movies

Early silent films transcended language barriers and appealed to the urban working and middle classes; they could identify with characters and situations that reflected the realities, hopes and disappointments of their lives. In many early films, the central hero was the common man or woman navigating through the urban world of tenement housing, industrial work and amusements. Films like *The Eviction, The Need for Gold, She Won't Pay Her Rent, Neighbors Who Borrow, The Miser's Hoard, Bertha, The Sewing Machine Girl* and Edwin S. Porter's *The Kleptomaniac* and *Eleventh Hour* treated issues of poverty, economic injustice and the struggle for survival in the urban centers. Newspaper stories inspired many silent films that treated the exploitation of immigrants, the corruption of city politics or the scandal of the white slave trafficking. *Hop, the Devil's Brew* (1916) was about opium smuggling, and *Where Are My Children?* (1916) attacked abortion while also defending birth control. Especially for illiterate and foreign-born immigrants, nickelodeons were centers not just of entertainment but of information. They became "the academy of the working man, his pulpit, his newspaper, his club."[10]

Since the initial audience for the movies was the working class, many of the early movies resembled the popular melodramas of the cheap theater with stock characters and plots and painted backdrop scenery. Also, silent shorts employed the salacious sexual imagery and risqué humor of the saloons and the kinetoscope peep shows. But production of these kinds of risqué films

declined as the movies moved out of the penny arcades and into the nickelodeons that attracted a female audience. Voyeurism, titillation and suggestiveness continued, however, in comedies that reflected urban culture. Films
like *My Best Girl* (1927), starring Mary Pickford, depicted romance and sexual
encounters between men and women in the social context of the city, using
places of work and entertainment as locations. The values they celebrated—
youthfulness, sexuality, personal freedom, romantic companionship—reflected the social world and upwardly mobile consumer society.

Early filmmakers were aware that movies and the other amusements represented class and cultural distinctions, and many early silents challenged proper middle-class sensibilities. Some films made fun of the sincere efforts of
moral reformers, temperance advocates and feminists who argued for political
equality and new roles for women. With the notable exception of D. W.
Griffith, movies reflected the new mood in America, characterized by a repu-
diation of "the 'old morality' of Victorian idealism for a fashionable materialism which emphasized wealth, sensation, and sexual freedom," Cook wrote.[11]
Early silents existed outside the moral world of respectable middle-class society. They not only explored the ambiguities of everyday life in the city but
also poked fun at Victorian values and social conventions, mocked authority
and satirized the respectable ruling class. Silent filmmaker Mack Sennett
thought his characters had an approach to life that was "earthy and understandable." He said, "I especially enjoyed the reduction of Authority to ab-
surdity, the notion that Sex could be funny, and the bold insults that were
hurled at Pretension."[12] Sennett's Keystone Kops mocked traditional authoriy;
his bathing beauties defied social propriety. Likewise, Charlie Chaplin satirized Victorian values and industrialized work and bureaucracy, while Douglas Fairbanks exalted the joy of play and sports over the tediousness of
routinized work. In the comedy *Safety Last,* Harold Lloyd's scaling of a modern skyscraper is a powerful metaphor for both the high ambitions of the
urban white-collar class and the personal ordeal and risk necessary for survival
in this social and economic world.

Images of women and men in early silent films expressed what Kathy Peiss
calls the "heterosocial culture" of urban work and amusement. The preoccupation with romance was reflected on the screen; one-third of the comedies
produced between 1898 and 1910 treated heterosexual relationships.[13] Wom-
en were featured prominently in the early silents. The silent "serial queens"
also brought wage-earning women to the screen in weekly features. Titles like

The Perils of Pauline (1912-1914) and *The Hazards of Helen* (1912-1915) reveal the influence of melodrama. While still resembling their Victorian predecessor, however, these self-reliant, adventurous and modern heroines represented new possibilities for love and marriage. "America's sweetheart," Mary Pickford, portrayed working women who were liberated from Victorian moral standards. Trapped by the corporate system and repressive middle-class home, Pickford's characters escaped into the immigrant culture and amusements. There "she became more sexually attractive to males, and also mingled more widely, bringing her into contact with a wider choice of potential spouses," film historian Lary May explains. "In this way, her personality promised to chip away at class, ethnic, and sexual divisions of the past."[14]

The cinema developed as a place for romance and sexual expression not only in the social space of the theater, but also in the thematic content and imagery of the movies projected on the screen. Hollywood filmmakers were aware that they were entertaining couples out on dates. Romance became a prominent feature of Hollywood films, as suggested by many titillating titles such as *A Shocking Night, Luring Lips, Rouged Lips, Red Hot Romance, Virgin Paradise, Scrambled Wives, The Truant Husband, The Fourteenth Lover, Her Purchase Price, Plaything of Broadway, The Daring Years, Sinner in Silk, Women Who Give* and *The Queen of Sins.* The film *Alimony* was advertised as "brilliant men, beautiful jazz babies, champagne baths, midnight revels, petting parties in the purple dawn, all ending in one terrific, smashing climax that makes you gasp." Another, *Flaming Youth,* was promoted with the promise of "neckers, petters, white kisses, red kisses, pleasure-mad daughters, sensation-craving mothers, by an author who didn't dare sign his name; the truth, bold, naked, sensational."[15] More than simply a pleasurable experience while on a date, movies introduced young people to lovemaking techniques (at that time kissing and hugging) and promoted the new morality of urban culture. This became a major issue for middle-class reformers, who were concerned about the effects of this shifting moral climate and feared the loss of their cultural authority and control over the behavior of the immigrant working class.

An Affair to Remember

Initially, members of the middle class may have thought that urban amusements were trivial and hardly worth serious attention, but places that provided entertainment quickly became important centers of communication and cultural transmission. As the popularity of the nickelodeons increased among the working class, movies became of greater concern for public officials, clergy and reformers. Reacting to the effects of modernization on the children, family and society, urban reformers treated the movies as a new urban vice, associating them with the saloon and with alcohol. They attacked the safety and sanitary conditions of the cheap theaters, as well as the content of movies. Questions about the effects of sexual and violent images on the impressionable young were already a matter of public discourse. The Protestant clergy especially wanted movie and vaudeville theaters closed on the sabbath. "There are far too many of them, and children on their way to Sunday school are lured and dragged into them," one Protestant minister said.[16]

While similar events occurred in other cities, the battle over the movies reached a pivotal point in 1907-1908 in New York, which was the center for film production and had the largest number of movie theaters—about eight hundred—with a daily attendance of over 400,000 people.[17] During 1907 several nickelodeon managers were arrested for violating Sunday observance laws and showing indecent pictures. Mayor George B. McClellan heard arguments from both clergy and exhibitors at what was described as "one of the biggest public hearings ever held in City Hall." One prominent minister, Canon William Sheafe Chase, said, "These men who run these shows have no moral scruples whatever. They are simply in the business for the money there is in it."[18] Charles Sprague Smith of the People's Institute of New York, a social research bureau, defended the movies saying, "There are more things rotten in New York than motion pictures."[19] The working-class people in the gallery burst into applause, and apparently women cheered as loudly as men. Many observed that the working class was actually the target of the attacks on the nickelodeons and entertainment on Sunday. According to a newspaper account, among those who protested the closing of the theaters were "chubby Irishmen as well as Hungarians, Italians, Greeks and just a handful of Germans, but the greater portion of the assembly were Jewish Americans."[20] Very quickly the movies, like the theater before them, had become a new arena in the cultural conflict.

Under pressure from clergy and reformist groups, McClellan closed all the movie houses on Christmas Day 1908 on the grounds that they were safety hazards. The procedures for license renewals, however, showed that the agenda of clergy and reformers had prevailed with the mayor. New licenses were to be issued after theaters passed inspections. In addition, however, exhibitors had to agree to remain closed on Sunday. Further, the license of any exhibitor would be revoked if thereafter films were shown "which tend to degrade or injure the morals of the community," the mayor said.[21] Predictably, McCellan's action threw the amusement business into chaos; however, the day after Christmas, film producers and exhibitors obtained an injunction preventing the mayor from carrying out this and any future actions of the kind.

It is important to point out that McCellan's edict was intended to affect only the nickel theaters that paid a $25 licensing fee and not the ten-cent houses that paid $150 a year. Later, the Motion Picture Ordinance of 1912 raised the theatrical licensing fee from $25 to $500. The clear intent was to bring "better" businessmen into the exhibition business, or in other words, to give the middle class greater control of the industry. Similar episodes occurred in other cities. In Chicago, the second largest movie market in the country, an ordinance was passed in 1907 requiring a police permit for every film shown in the city; two years later a censorship commission was established.

If only to avoid being arrested, movie producers and exhibitors began to cooperate with reformers. But there was another more important reason for their interest in establishing what had the potential to become a mutually beneficial relationship. Despite the regular support of the blue-collar worker and his family, exhibitors dreamed of getting out of the urban ghettos and constantly complained that the nickelodeon audience lacked "class."[22] In their efforts to include the respectable middle class in the moviegoing audience, however, film producers and exhibitors had run up against seemingly insurmountable obstacles. The upper classes attended public amusements in the exclusive neighborhoods or high-priced theaters. The cheap movie theaters, like other urban amusements, posed a threat to the class and sexual divisions of Victorian life, especially regarding the protection of women. As Russell Merritt has shown, the most ambitious exhibitors followed the path of vaudeville and sought to attract the larger, middle-class audience that patronized vaudeville and legitimate theaters. One theater inspector observed in 1910 that exhibitors not only improved the health and safety conditions at their theaters, but "there is an evident desire to secure the patronage of the better people of the neighborhood," indicating they were also seizing the moment to establish a middle-class patronage.[23]

As cities and states across the country passed licensing laws and formed review boards, fear of censorship and the desire for respectability made filmmakers willing to acquiesce to reformers' demands for movies that taught moral lessons as a means of social control and reform. Temperance dramas and morality plays preached traditional middle-class values of hard work, home and family, while showing drinking and sin as leading to suffering, shame, poverty and death. These films also benefited from free publicity. A trade journal reported that

the uplift picture receives the enthusiastic support of all those influences which are ordinarily opposed to the motion pictures. The cooperation of . . . municipal boards of health, of anti-tuberculosis leagues, and social bodies in general, inevitably leads to the cooperation of big newspapers. The secret of the commercial success of the uplift film lies after all in the vast amount of free publicity it secures.[24]

In addition, film adaptations of works by literary greats like Shakespeare, Poe, Dickens, Thackeray and Browning were made, as well as movies with biblical and historical themes.

These efforts to promote the educational value of movies paid off. By 1912 schools were using travelogues in the classroom, and films were shown in school auditoriums in the evening as part of the effort to create alternatives to the nickelodeons. Biblical films were shown at evening church services and in Sunday schools, and even the fundamentalist Moody Bible Institute used movies to lure people into its revival meetings, a use of motion pictures justified by evangelism. According to one historian, the arrival of these new types of movies between 1908 and 1915 "gradually won the reformers' approval, and the appearance of films in churches, schools and social centers paved the way for the entrance of the middle classes."[25]

Nickelodeons were built in the shopping centers on the edge of the cities, making them more accessible to both urban and suburban people. Managers especially wanted to appeal to the middle-class woman and her children. Women were central in the modern economy, accounting for as much as 85 percent of consumer spending. According to Maltby, "Middle-class women constituted a new leisure class, spending their time at shops, theater matinees and hairdressers."[26] But there were reasons other than simply boosting box office receipts. The very presence of middle-class women symbolized respectability, and exhibitors wanted them frequenting their movie houses. Some theaters gave women free admission to pre-noon shows, while most charged women and children half fare at all screenings.

In the years before World War I, the most powerful nickelodeon owners began purchasing legitimate theaters and converting them into movie palaces.

When legitimate theaters were used for film exhibition they were seen as places the respectable middle and upper classes could pay full fare to see movies on a regular basis without embarrassment. As Merritt observed, a hierarchy of movie theaters developed between 1910 and World War I.[27] Movie patrons and exhibitors began to classify theaters by size and quality, comparing the first-class movie houses to the legitimate theaters and distinguishing them from the cheap nickelodeons. In order to be more acceptable to middle-class patrons, theater owners were anxious to disassociate the movies from their disreputable origins in the arcades and storefront theaters that still catered to the working class. The construction of the lavish picture palaces reveals the depth of their aspirations.

Beginning around 1910, the urban working class was joined in the movie houses by vaudeville and legitimate theater patrons and middle-class individuals who, despite religious sanctions against such activities, were beginning to explore the city's entertainments. The addition of the large middle-class family to the moviegoing audience swelled box-office figures. In actual numbers, movie attendance almost doubled, increasing from twenty-six million persons per week in 1908 to about forty-nine million in 1914.[28]

At the same time, film producers, who were as eager as exhibitors to expand into the middle class, began improving the "quality" of movies. Fearing renewed threats of government intervention and the continued pressure from social and religious groups, film companies agreed to work in cooperation with a review board. The Board of Censorship of Motion Pictures (renamed the National Board of Review in 1915) was established in 1909 in cooperation with the newly formed Motion Pictures Patents Company (MPPC).[29] Although the initial idea was for the board to "censor" all films shown in New York City, within months its mandate was expanded to include the entire country. Even though the Board consisted mostly of wealthy and respectable Protestant leaders, moviemakers now had a group of prestigious citizens to help them draw up criteria for acceptable films. Based on the composition of the Board, however, such standards would obviously represent Anglo-Saxon Protestant values, even though the movie audience was still largely composed of ethnic immigrants. Even so, from its inception the Board was hounded by outspoken critics whose individual tastes varied enormously. The National Board operated on the principle that movies had the freedom guaranteed by the First Amendment. Ultimately, however, the board was unable to establish standards for the moral and social improvement of movies that were universally accepted, even among the middle class. This became the goal of writers of the Motion Picture Production Code of 1930.

Paralleling the distinction between theaters was a double standard regarding the kinds of films that could be shown in the different theaters. The purview of the National Board of Review was over the cheap theaters. That the Board did not allow the white slavery pictures (about urban prostitution rings) and sex education shorts to be shown in nickelodeons did not prevent the dollar theaters from exhibiting them.[30] As this suggests, middle-class reformers did not consider these pictures harmful for everyone but wanted to regulate the content of motion pictures exhibited for the lower classes.

This feature of the reform movement is also true of today's efforts to change the entertainment industry. The moral charges of today's reformers are also lined with racial, class and cultural connotations. For example, when members of advocacy groups argue that children should not be exposed to the imagery on *N.Y.P.D. Blue*, which airs at 10:00 p.m. EST, whose children do they have in mind? Theirs are probably in bed at that hour, or perhaps watching it with critical commentary from parents or prohibited from seeing it altogether. Moreover, are these critics all that fearful that their children will become more promiscuous or turn to criminal behavior simply because of seeing sexual and violent imagery on television? It is not difficult to conclude that in their protest these critics are referring to the children of the lower classes (especially minorities) or those in single-parent homes—two groups that have been the primary targets in the political debate about welfare reform and have been stereotyped as irresponsibly using the television as a baby-sitter (although most parents, I would guess, have felt guilty about that at one time or another). The real fear is that people raised or living in an environment in which mediating factors like family, church or school are weak will be vulnerable to any effect the media might have. Studies indeed confirm that the media are more effective in such a situation. Rather than deal with other, perhaps more important social factors like poverty, unemployment, poor education or dysfunctional families, however, these critics isolate the media as a negative influence and source of society's ills. The effect of this myopic attack on the media is the same today as it was at the beginning of the twentieth century—to prevent the lower classes from seeing programming that does not promote the values and lifestyle of moral guardians. Conversely, there was no criticism of rap music from the white middle class until the urban sound became popular in the suburbs.

As a scene of cultural conflict, the uproar over the cheap theaters resembled the Astor Place Riot. The battle over the movies happened during the nickelodeon boom, when movies were recognized by the middle class as a potent means of cultural communication and social criticism for working-class immigrants. The conflict that erupted in New York was one of many like it that affected the course of the movies and shaped their role in American life, at least until the end of World War II. Ironically, the result was the opposite of the Astor Place incident, which represented the fragmentation of theatrical entertainment along class and cultural lines. The New York incident marked the beginning of an effort to make motion pictures an instrument of consensus in American life based on American middle-class values.

Guess Who's Going to the Movies

At first, middle-class influence over the film industry seemed secure. The most prominent filmmaker, D. W. Griffith, affirmed Victorian values and urged social reform in his movies. When Griffith's masterpiece, *The Birth of a Nation,* opened at a New York legitimate theater on February 8, 1915, it was heralded as an unprecedented cinematic achievement—"like writing history with lightning," President Wilson reportedly said after seeing the Civil War saga.[31] But the film's idealization of the Victorian woman and affirmation of Anglo-Saxon superiority generated a fierce controversy because of its racist attitudes. Even middle-class reformers who shared Griffith's Victorian vision joined the NAACP in petitioning the National Board of Review to cut certain racist sections.[32]

During the same period, as movies were becoming popular among the middle class, power shifted from the industry's Anglo-Saxon pioneers to the immigrants who headed the independent companies. Edison's Trust was inoperative by 1914 and was officially dissolved in 1918 as the result of an antitrust suit. Control of the film industry now resided with the immigrant groups the middle class hoped to influence. It was not lost upon the religious and cultural elite that the independent companies were run by Eastern European Jewish immigrants with little formal education. The Jewish moguls, as they were called, all began as independent exhibitors who outmaneuvered the Trust. In a sharply competitive struggle, they rose from nickelodeon managers to producers, then distributors, and now reigned over an entertainment empire with a potential audience that was 90 percent Protestant and Catholic.

The independent producers and exhibitors pioneered the film industry's efforts to include middle-class patrons among their audience. This was a crucial factor in the demise of the MPPC. In their resistance to the Trust, the independents established the full-length feature film, paving the way for the extraordinary success of *The Birth of a Nation.* They relocated the industry in Hollywood and instituted the star system. The Hollywood studio system emerged as an efficient and standardized way to produce movies on a year-round basis. Executives began the vertical integration of their studios by adding international distribution arms and chains of theaters. Profits soared during the economic boom before World War I, but so did costs. Just as the movies were moving to the center of American cultural life, the guardians of middle-class culture realized they had little control or even authority over this burgeoning entertainment industry. In other words, instead of the middle class controlling the motion pictures and spreading high culture among the lower classes, the opposite occurred. To the chagrin of the cultural elite, the immigrant entertainments seemed to be moving out of the urban ghettos and were attracting middle-class patrons.

Amidst America's cultural diversity, the movies, more than other social institutions, demonstrated the capacity to transmit a common public culture. "Not since the Elizabethan Age in England had the high culture of the middle and upper classes been a truly popular culture, accessible to all social groups," film historian Robert Sklar writes. "But the nickelodeons could restore the past: movies would bring high culture back to the people."[33] As reformers saw it, what potential the movies had as an instrument for evil could be converted into a means for good. Unlike other urban amusements, movies could be centrally regulated at the point of production, before being widely distributed to thousands of theaters across the country. Middle-class reformers hoped to use the new communication medium to propagate WASP culture.

Middle-class custodians began a concerted effort to control the course of movies, which had demonstrated their enormous potential as a popular mass medium during the nickelodeon boom. Instead of exploring the new values emerging in the modern world, "movies would serve to counter the forces that were undercutting the Victorian world," May explains. "Urban Progressives hoped that modern amusements would no longer solely tap the desire for a release from work or sexual experimentation."[34] Instead, they hoped the movies would become a tool for spreading WASP norms throughout the population. Consequently, they worked to control entertainment as a means of cultural transmission and a form of social criticism by turning it into an instrument by which to forge a cultural consensus in American life according to the design of middle-class reformers.

At the same time, and to the delight of film moguls, this in effect sanctioned movies and the other commercial amusements for the middle classes. By 1910 critics like Louis Reeves Harrison were imploring film producers to make movies that would "interest the intelligent class throughout the country as to bring in the desirable patronage of those who have the means and leisure to go every day to the picture exhibition." In his appeal, Harrison made the industry's case for middle-class patronage. Increasing the quality of films, he said, would allow the exhibitor "to charge more for desirable seats, would fill his house at better rates, and would tend to elevate the quality of the average audience without decreasing its numbers."[35] From a business perspective, that was exactly what film producers and exhibitors hoped would happen.

By the mid-1910s the role of the cinema began to shift as a result of events that took place both within and outside the industry. Instead of focusing on the working-class world, filmmakers began to turn their attention to interpreting the new morality and urban culture for the more educated middle-class audience.

More than any other American filmmaker, Cecil B. DeMille made the new morality fashionable in his domestic dramas. DeMille redefined the subject matter of movies in such a way that made them alluring to both the working and middle classes by tapping the pulse of cultural life after World War I. Film historian Arthur Knight observes that DeMille exploited a "basic duality in his audiences—on the one hand their tremendous eagerness to see what they considered sinful and taboo, and on the other, the fact that they could enjoy sin only if they were able to preserve their own sense of righteous respectability in the process."[36] Apparently as a result, DeMille was one of the most successful filmmakers during this period.

DeMille's films continued to explore the sexual dynamics of the new morality, but instead of using urban settings, he took audiences into the luxuriant and intimate lives of the rich—not only their mansions but indeed their bedrooms and baths. *Old Wives for New* (1918), *Don't Change Your Husband, Male and Female* (both 1919), *Why Change Your Wife?* (1920), *Forbidden Fruit* (1920) and *The Affairs of Anatol* (1921) fused sex and romance, marriage and money into a fantasy world that articulated what Elizabeth Ewen considered "a crucial myth of modern culture: metamorphosis through consumption."[37] (This was a theme, I might add, of the 1990 hit *Pretty Woman*, starring Julia Roberts and Richard Gere.) In contrast to the restrictiveness of Victorianism, DeMille portrayed sex and eroticism as exciting and necessary elements for a strong marriage. However voyeuristic, these were still caution-ary tales showing promiscuity as destructive to both personal life and society.

DeMille's films were both scandalous and enormously profitable, grossing between five and ten times their production costs. As a cultural representa-tion, they entwined and legitimized, and even made fashionable, the consum-er lifestyle and the new morality of urban culture. "For second-generation immigrant women, one step away from arranged marriage and family obliga-tion, these new movies were manuals of desire, wishes, and dreams," Ewen explains. "Out of DeMille's movies came a visual textbook to American cul-ture. . . . Here was guidance their mothers could not offer. By presenting an illusory world where 'a shop girl can marry a millionaire,' these movies evoked a vision of the American dream for women and the means to its feminine realization."[38]

Ewen's description of the fascination with DeMille's films reveals their value and the important place the movies now occupied in people's lives. Movies both reflected and promoted the "new ways" of urban democracy and the choices and possibilities it gave to young people concerning friends, spouse, occupation and leisure pursuits. This same situation would recur beginning in the post-World War II period, a time once again of profound change in American life. Entertainment continues to serve this function today. It is not difficult to see why religious and educational groups over the course of the twentieth century have at different times regarded movies, radio, comic books, rock music and television as competing institutions and even hostile to their goals.

A Business Pure and Simple

The banning of *The Birth of a Nation* in Ohio because of its racist portrayal of southern blacks led to a Supreme Court decision in 1915 that resolved, at least for the time being, questions and fears about the social and psycholog-ical impact of the movies. This ruling also had a long-lasting effect on the role of the cinema in American society. In the momentous case *Mutual Film Corporation* v. *Ohio,* the Supreme Court refused to grant movies the free-speech protection of the First Amendment. In this far-reaching decision that stood for nearly forty years, the Court created a legal definition of movies that made clear that entertainment was an important arena in the cultural conflict of the time. Motion pictures were not "speech" or art, the Court declared, but entertainment along the lines of a circus. The "exhibition of moving pictures," the decision read,

> is a business pure and simple, originated and conducted for profit, like other spectacles, not to be regarded, nor intended to be regarded . . . as part of the press of the country, or as organs of public opinion. They are mere representations of events, of ideas and sentiments published and known; vivid, useful, and entertaining, no doubt, but . . . capable of evil, having power for it, the greater because of their attractiveness and manner of exhibition.

The effects of the cultural hierarchy can be seen in the dubious assumptions upon which this decision rested. That the movies were a commercial enterprise—"a business pure and simple"—contributed to the conclusion that they were not a means for artistic expression or the communication of ideas. This criterion had not been used before to determine whether some form of speech should be censored. Newspapers, for example, are private enterprises that depend on profit-making for their survival. Furthermore, the fact that the movies were run by profit-minded businessmen somehow put the industry in an adversarial position with the general community. Movies were "capable of evil," and the community had to defend itself against the potential misuse of the medium by unethical entrepreneurs, who all happened to be Jewish and from the immigrant class. Reflecting contemporary fears, the Court dramatized this by noting that in their power for both amusement and education, the movies attracted a mixed-sex audience that included children. This made movies "more insidious in corruption . . . if they should degenerate from worthy purpose," since "a prurient interest may be excited and appealed to" in this general audience.[39]

Second, the court delineated between the transmission of culture and the provision of entertainment, and relegated movies to the fulfillment of the latter. This is most ironic, because the film that led to this case, Griffith's *The Birth of a Nation,* had demonstrated the power and potential of film as an intellectual and artistic medium. Now, however, movies were lowbrow entertainment not just by cultural category but by legal definition as well.

Film was defined as a consumer commodity; its potential for evil could be rendered harmless by regulation. As a result of the Court's decision, not only was the film industry vulnerable to state or federal censorship, but movies were by law restricted in their performance of the functions of art. The effect was to cut this most influential and culturally significant art form off from the major social, intellectual, political and moral issues in American society. In this way the cultural elite did not need to have ownership in the industry in order to control its output and decide what would be permitted to the lower classes.

Film producers yielded the artistic freedom the First Amendment guaranteed to other creative arts like theater, literature, painting and even still photography. Unlike these other art forms, movies would be evaluated along the lines of consumer goods. The major film companies accepted this role as providers of commercial amusement and not creators of artistic works. The industry could fend off state or federal regulation by presenting its product as harmless entertainment that did not affect people's behavior in any important ways. Moreover, this line of defense was assured if movies appeared to be superficial and escapist, lacking substantial commentary on the real world. These same debates about the role and influence of entertainment continue even today as politicians, critics, religious leaders and producers of entertainment spar in the media.

7

· · · · ·

The Yellow
Brick Road
to Respectability

As we have seen, the movies played a central role in the social and cultural conflicts in the first quarter of the twentieth century. According to Robert Sklar, "No cultural force as strong as movies had ever established itself so independently of the proprietors of American culture."[1] The entertainment industry had become a powerful social institution communicating ideas and values, but with few ties or commitments to other institutions traditionally responsible for that task, like family, school and religious community.

The controversy over the movies continued to mount throughout the 1920s, as the American elite had come to realize the great potential of film as a medium of communication. As the "democratic art," movies could make accessible to virtually the entire population ideas that previously were exclusive to small elite groups of readers and theatergoers.[2] This was perceived as both a blessing and a curse. A powerful instrument of progress and communication, the cinema was controlled by first- and second-generation Jews and not members of the Anglo-American middle class.

Although not an organized mass movement, a number of religious groups and social organizations coalesced around the "menace of the movies." Educators, clergy, academics and reformers all attacked the movies as harmful to moral, social, political and religious life. Extensive research conducted around 1930 confirmed their worst suspicions. It was shown that young people learned about dating and sexual behavior from movies, were persuaded by various racial and ethnic stereotypes and were dissatisfied with many aspects of their own lives when compared with screen portrayals they saw. The effects of the movies on children became a major concern of religious and civic leaders, who were also dismayed by the lack of influence educational and religious institutions had in the development of movies.

Attempts to supervise or censor movies were frustrated. Local censorship, either by police or censorship boards, proved futile; there were far too many theaters to make oversight possible at this level. Beginning in 1907, several states established censorship boards which were more effective. But varying standards between state boards meant that film companies had to release different versions of movies, a costly effect that producers resisted in court. Reform groups began lobbying Congress for federal censorship.

As a consensus began to emerge from the cultural struggles at the beginning of the century, religious and cultural leaders recognized the cinema could play a significant role in the development of a national culture. Advocates of reform changed their tactics. The question became how to turn this powerful entertainment medium into an instrument of progress and human betterment. Instead of condemning and trying to destroy the motion pictures, they now hoped to use the movies as an instrument to spread moral and civic values.

The combined force of religious, educational and social groups reshaped the role of the cinema. During the 1930s and 1940s, designated the "studio era" or "golden era," Hollywood films affirmed American mythology and middle-class culture. This role was assured by the industry's agreement to self-censorship by adhering to the provisions of the Motion Picture Production Code of 1930. Studio executives agreed to self-regulation for a number of reasons, all related to staying in business; there was much money to be made as one of the nation's most powerful transmitters of American culture during the malaise of the Depression.

The "progressive" films of the teens and twenties, exploring urban culture, dissipated during 1930s. The film industry's role was redirected as a provider of innocent and culturally homogenized amusement meant to appeal to the entire middle-class American "family," an amorphous entity that in theory transcended age, sex, racial, ethnic or class distinctions. How and why this dramatic shift in the role of the cinema occurred is the substance of this chapter.

Hollywood's Compensating Values

After years of continual growth, there was a decline in movie patronage in the early 1920s. Movies were faced with new competition for leisure time and money, especially from commercial radio, which brought live entertainment directly into the home. Also, installment plans made the automobile more available to working people and opened up yet new possibilities for leisure time. Moral crusaders, however, claimed that disappointing box-office figures were the direct result of public displeasure with salacious and violent movies and the decadent lifestyles of some movie stars. Hollywood, they declared, was out of touch with the realities of American life, a charge some critics would make again in the 1990s.

A content analysis at the time revealed that three categories—love, sex and crime—constituted over three-quarters of the films produced during the 1920s.[3] Seventy-five percent of the characters shown were between the ages of nineteen and forty; only 15 percent of the adult characters were married as against 60 percent in the general population. Of a group of 115 movies, 66 percent showed alcohol consumption, 43 percent intoxication and 78 percent contained "liquor situations." In 45 films there were 71 deaths, 59 cases of assault and battery, 17 robberies and 21 kidnappings. Of the 449 crimes attempted, 406 were successful (meaning that the robbery or murder was accomplished). The hero's goals in order of frequency were winning another's love, marriage for love, professional success, revenge, crime for gain, illicit love, thrills or excitement, conquering a rival, financial success, enjoyment, concealment of guilt and marriage for money—only 9 percent of which were deemed "socially desirable in nature."

The objectionable content of movies was linked with a series of scandals in the early 1920s. Mary Pickford secretly divorced her husband to marry co-star Douglas Fairbanks. When a young actress died at a party with bootleg liquor in the hotel room of Roscoe "Fatty" Arbuckle, the comedian was charged with rape and murder (he was, however, acquitted). William Desmond Taylor, director and president of the Screen Directors Guild, was found murdered in his apartment. Handsome, all-American actor Wallace Reid died of a drug overdose. These stories became tabloid headlines that fueled a public fascination with Hollywood as a Babylonian empire of stars and starlets with extravagant salaries, lavish surroundings and promiscuous lifestyles. In the era of Prohibition, this led to a mounting protest against the film industry from Protestant reformers, educational groups and women's organizations, including the General Federation of Women's Clubs, the Lord's Day Alliance, the Central Conference of American Rabbis and the National Congress of Parents and Teachers.

In response, the film industry formed the Motion Picture Producers and Distributors Association (MPPDA) in 1922 with Will H. Hays as president. Hays had both the moral credentials and administrative abilities for the position. He was Protestant, an elder in the Presbyterian Church; as former postmaster general of the United States and national chairman of the Republican Party, he had strong political connections. The job of the "Hays Office" was to improve the public image of the film industry and to fend off threats of government censorship while establishing a policy for industry self-regulation. But according to historian Joel Spring, a more basic design of the organization was to help film entrepreneurs "function in an environment that was hostile to both immigrants and Jews," since as has already been noted, most attacks on the film industry came from Protestant evangelicals and were laced with anti-Semitism and class antagonism.[4]

To accomplish this, Hays developed a level of cooperation between the film industry and the leaders of various social organizations and other groups with religious, cultural, educational or economic purposes. In part the purpose of the MPPDA was to work through differences to reach a general agreement about the role of the cinema, a public dialogue that has not abated. From the perspective of film producers and their financial investors, movies were first and foremost a profit-making business. They wanted movies judged by their audience, which cast its votes at the box office. Producers argued that the social influence of film had been exaggerated. Movies were primarily entertainment, with no more educational value than a newspaper story, and certainly not the enemy of morality.

Religious and civic-minded reformers, however, recognized film's potential for informal instruction. Based on the Victorian ideal, they sought to protect the family from the intrusion and corruption of the outside world. Movies, they argued, existed to teach moral and social lessons, especially to children. The larger cultural conflict in which movies played an important part was veiled in the campaign to protect children from the supposedly harmful influence of the cinema. This tactic, still employed today, masked religious, class and cultural antagonisms that were also at the crux of the conflict. These crusaders did not want film production governed by public preference, and insisted that movies abide by the moral standards and cultural values of established institutions. That a comparable debate continues in the 1990s is revealing, for it shows not only that these issues remain unresolved and contentious but also that attacks on the entertainment industry serve symbolic purposes as they are inextricably connected with other cultural concerns and agendas.

The MPPDA's statement of purpose tried to combine these mixed purposes. Producers pledged to maintain "the highest possible moral and artistic standards in motion picture production, by developing the educational as well as the entertainment value and the general usefulness of the motion picture."[5]

The formation of the MPPDA by no means resolved the inherent tension between the business of Hollywood and the desires of its critics. As expected, the same ingredients film studio heads deemed important for box-office success were the ones that received the most frequent complaints from censorship groups. Universal president Carl Laemmle, for example, polled theater owners in 1916 and claimed that "instead of finding that 95 per cent favored clean pictures, I discovered that at least half, and maybe 60 per cent, want the pictures to be 'risqué.' . . . They found their patrons were more willing to pay money to see an off-color than a decent one."[6]

To increase the moral quality of movies without dulling box-office attractiveness, Hays first established the overarching principle of "compensating values" as the standard for motion picture production: virtue had to be rewarded, sin punished, and good always had to triumph over evil. The way Hollywood studios interpreted this, Arthur Knight explained, was that "they could present six reels of ticket-selling sinfulness if, in the seventh reel, all the sinners came to a bad end, and that they could go through all the motions of vice if, at the last moment, virtue triumphed."[7] And so DeMille could show a drunken, orgiastic feast around the golden calf while Moses was receiving the Ten Commandments on Mt. Sinai above.

But this theory forced the movies into a formula that echoed the nineteenth-century melodrama in predictability, stock characters and contrived happy endings. On the one hand, the standardization of Hollywood films appeased censors while also facilitating rapid production and easier marketing of movies. But this approach was not conducive to artistic experimentation and hampered the development of the cinema as an art form and its recognition as such. European films appeared much more honest and real than these formulaic Hollywood productions.

Finally, the introduction of sound in motion pictures in 1927 revolutionized the entertainment industry, while also intensifying the argument over the movies. People flocked to the theaters to see the new "talking" pictures. Paid admissions in 1927, the last year of the silent era, totaled sixty million dollars; by 1930 they reached ninety million, a 50 percent increase. Among those ninety million in attendance were an estimated forty million minors, including seventeen million children under the age of fourteen.[8] This means that on an average basis, by the end of the 1920s, every man, woman and child in the United States between the ages of six and sixty went to the movies about once a week.[9]

The amazing popularity of talking pictures dramatically increased movie attendance, giving the industry the appearance of an even more ominous presence in American life. Moral crusaders had yet another worry about the danger of offensive language now that movies "talked." Sound also added an element of screen realism that enhanced the artistic power of film and expanded the possibilities for subject matter. The illusory dream world of the cinema was now much more lifelike and dynamic, making movies a more potent force for communication and cultural transmission in American life. The middle class became even more anxious about the magnitude of impact the talking pictures might have.

The Payne Studies

There was much speculation about the impact of the movies on young people but very little valid research was done on the subject prior to the late 1920s and early 1930s. The efforts of reformers lacked the support of empirical evidence that would confirm their suspicions about the harmful effects of the cinema and support their argument for outside control of the industry. As the controversy over the movies mounted, the Payne Fund, a private philanthropic foundation, awarded a significant grant to the Motion Picture Research Council to study the effects of movies on young people. Among the elite members of the Research Council were Dr. A. Lawrence Lowell, president emeritus of Harvard University, Mrs. August Belmont (formerly Elanor Robson, a renowned American actress) and former First Lady Mrs. Calvin Coolidge.

The Council was unquestionably procensorship; it was clear from its inception that movies were prejudged as evil and harmful to children and to the social welfare of the nation. The overall design of the project was to provide the empirical research necessary to argue for movie censorship on the grounds of protecting the young. A group of scholars was commissioned to conduct a series of studies from 1929 to 1932, which were subsequently published in twelve volumes between 1933 and 1937.

The Payne Fund Studies proved that film served most effectively as art. It was difficult to deny now that in combination with other cultural and environmental factors, the cinema had become a powerful force in American life. The researchers found that movies were an effectual learning format, especially for young people. Films affected attitudes toward different national and racial groups and influenced views on social issues like war, crime, capital punishment, Prohibition and the treatment of criminals. But while movies offered models of behavior and shaped interpretations of life, they also tended to reaffirm already existing values and attitudes in moviegoers.

The most striking and consistent feature of these studies was their disclosure that whatever effect the movies had was specific to individuals and particular films and tempered by a host of factors including age, sex, personal experience, family and home conditions, neighborhood, education, community standards, and social and economic status. Hard conclusions were difficult to reach. Regarding the study of attitudes, for example, it was found that "the influence of the community far overshadows in importance the influence of the movie."[10] Concerning the ability of movies to incite criminal behavior, the authors wrote, "The movies may help to dispose or lead persons to delinquency and crime or they may fortify conventional behavior."[11] On the one hand, movie portrayals of women as aggressive in lovemaking ran counter to accepted social mores, but in the treatment of children by their parents, democratic action and racial tolerance, movie depictions exceeded social standards.

It followed that the impact of the cinema was mitigated by the strength or weakness of other social institutions responsible for the well-being of children. "The influence of motion pictures seems to be proportionate to the weakness of the family, school, church, and neighborhood," the authors of one study wrote, echoing the conclusions of others. "Where the institutions which traditionally have transmitted social attitudes and forms of conduct have broken down, as is usually the case in high-rate delinquency areas, motion pictures assume a greater importance as a source of ideas and schemes of life."[12] Movies could fill gaps left by family, church and school, even if what they presented conflicted with the standards and values these other institutions sought to impart. Such conclusions weakened arguments about the force of movies by showing that the cinema was only one of many influences on young people that could have either a positive or a negative effect. Cautious interpretations of specific authors suggested that movies were not entirely good or evil, but their impact was only one among many factors that hinged upon each other.

These ideas were elaborated in a report by Paul G. Cressey. For some unknown reason, this study was never published in book form, possibly because it conflicted with the censorial designs of the overall project. Its conclusions did, however, appear in an essay in *The Journal of Educational Sociology*. Cressey concurred with other Payne researchers that the cinema was a "quasi-educational enterprise" with unparalleled potential among social institutions for influence in American life.[13] He too found children to be especially vulnerable to the cinema's influence because they tended to be more receptive to and less discerning about screen images.

Cressey was quick to point out, however, that this influence, though dynamic, was "by no means uniform as to extent and content," but was instead a very individualized process that could only be understood in the context of each individual's social background. He highlighted two specific situations in which the cinema had greater influence than usual. The first was during the uncertainty and self-consciousness of adolescence. "For such young people," he wrote, "the motion picture's portrayal of attractive adults of both sexes provides a ready basis for the acquisition of personality patterns, standards of dress and conduct, and even philosophies and schemes of life." The second was during the conflict between immigrant parents and their American-born children as they both adapted to American culture. Cressey explained, "Especially where the other agencies and institutions in a young person's life do not adapt themselves adequately to his psychological and cultural situation, the cinema may very well be, and, in fact, often is, the refuge to which the individual goes to discover that which he considers is really 'American.' "[14]

This proved to be an important insight about the role of entertainment. Circumstances after World War II combined the two situations Cressey described for postwar adolescents. Traditional institutions had a difficult time keeping pace with the rapid changes taking place in America. Consequently, the role of the new rock'n'roll music, television and movies was enhanced among youth, who needed help understanding the emerging age-segregated youth culture they now inhabited, along with postwar American ideals.

Cressey also observed that films could be categorized by levels of maturity and the corresponding interests of certain age groups. And Hollywood had something for everyone. There were animated cartoons, slapstick comedy and animal pictures for small children. For those a little older there were westerns and melodramas, then mystery thrillers and war films, followed by sports pictures, murder films and gangster films. During adolescence, movies depicting love and romance were especially appealing, and these were followed by an interest in travelogues, historical dramas and films treating psychological or philosophical problems. These findings about audience segmentation and tastes could have provided reformers with a basis to argue for the production of different kinds of movies based on age and maturity. Instead, reformers established guidelines to ensure that all films were made acceptable for viewing by twelve-year-olds. Again, movies were regulated as a consumer product and restricted in their service of various artistic and social functions for different audiences.

As a result of this research, Cressey concluded that the cinema should be engaged at the institutional level. As a storytelling medium, he argued, movies possessed "unique pedagogical advantages" over schools, but he also noted that "the cinema is here to stay and it is well that the school adopt a more enlightened attitude towards it." He suggested that schools introduce film appreciation courses "to exert a positive influence in the child's selection and response to photoplays."[15] In chapter thirteen we will return to the issue of media literacy and school curriculum in our own day.

Unfortunately, the discourse that followed the release of the Payne Studies took place on two different levels. The serious scholarly inquiry, with statistical findings and carefully qualified conclusions, was lost in academic journals and books. Instead, the first published volume in the series, Henry James Forman's *Our Movie Made Children* (1933), set the tone for the public debate. Unlike the other publications that followed, Forman's book was intended for a popular audience. The caution of the other researchers was completely absent in his summary of their work. Forman used selective material and employed inflammatory rhetoric to sensationalize the investigation. His reinterpretation was misleading, taking evidence out of context and generalizing about research without mentioning specific qualifications. He reported, for example, that the aggressiveness of women in lovemaking as depicted in movies was out of line with accepted social standards, but he failed to mention that portrayals of racial tolerance, democratic practices and parenting were better than social mores. Despite evidence to the contrary, Forman allowed readers to conclude that movies had a uniform and harmful effect on young people, as suggested in his sweeping conclusion that the cinema was "a gigantic educational system with an instruction possibly more successful than the present text-book variety."[16]

Reviewing the Payne Studies in the *American Journal of Sociology* in 1935, Kimball Young called Forman's book a "genuine disservice" to the academic community, "a form of propaganda evidently stimulated by those supporters of the original research project who felt that the motion pictures constitute a serious menace to public and private morals."[17] Such criticism went unheard. Forman's synopsis, however unethical, was what reformers wanted to hear. The book was widely read and was summarized in religious and popular magazines like *The Christian Century, Parent's Magazine* and *Survey Graphic*. The "wave of sentiment against the movies" inspired by *Our Movie Made Children* put the industry on the defensive. MPPDA members reaffirmed their dedication to "the highest possible artistic and moral standards" in the movies they produced. But this was perceived by crusading reformers as a redundant and empty promise; they wanted established guidelines for the regulation of movies.

Increased fears of federal or state regulation coincided with economic misfortunes that beset the industry during the early years of the Depression. Weekly box-office receipts plummeted from ninety million in 1930 to sixty million by 1932.[18] Financial survival made the studios extremely vulnerable to attack and more agreeable to change. If ever there was a time to force a change in the course of the cinema, this was it.

The 1930 Production Code

Catholic and Protestant reformers shared a belief that movies should be morality plays, illustrating proper social behavior and supporting established moral and political values associated with family, church and government. The first production code, known as "The Don'ts and Be Carefuls," was instituted in 1927, but without any enforcement procedures. It had little effect on Hollywood productions. Within three years the Hays Office adopted a more formal code, the Motion Picture Production Code of 1930, but adherence remained voluntary.

The Code was written by Martin I. Quigley, a Catholic layperson, and Father Daniel A. Lord, a Jesuit priest, to establish a standard for movies that would be acceptable to both Catholics and Protestants. Father Lord envisioned the Code as an opportunity "to tie the Ten Commandments in with the newest and most widespread form of entertainment."[19] The Code's basic tenets represented a synthesis of the general principles of Judeo-Christian morality and the ideals of American middle-class culture. Like its 1927 predecessor, the Code imposed limitations on the portrayal of human behavior on the screen based on a general religious morality that set earthly events in the context of judgment from heaven. Evil or sinful acts, like adultery and murder, could be shown, but they had to be put in the context of ultimate judgment. Such acts could not be glorified and transgressors had to be punished. The General Principles of the Code prohibited the production of films "which will lower the moral standards of those who see it" or ridiculed natural or human law, allowing only those films that portrayed "correct standards of life." What this amounted to, however, was a self-imposed set of taboos, or a list of offenses that violated middle-class culture, implying that it was sacred, its values and standards immune from criticism.

In the aftermath of the Payne Studies, producers now acknowledged in the Code's Preamble that while they "regarded motion pictures primarily as entertainment without any explicit purpose of teaching or propaganda, they know that the motion picture within its own field of entertainment may be directly responsible for spiritual or moral progress, for higher types of social life, and for much correct thinking." In other words, as "primarily" entertainment, motion pictures had special moral obligations to contribute to the improvement of the human race and the elevation of the "whole standard of the nation."

On the other hand, movies had "the same object as the other arts, the presentation of human thought, emotion, and experience, in terms of an appeal to the soul through the senses." And in this regard also, film had a moral responsibility to be uplifting in its presentation of ideas and ideals. The writers of the Code recognized film's place alongside the traditional arts and even considered movies to be a more powerful means of communication. This situation was complicated, however, in that in contrast to the high arts, movies reached a broad, undifferentiated audience, "appealing at once to every class, mature, immature, developed, undeveloped, law abiding, criminal," reaching "places unpenetrated by other forms of art." The mass audience composed of men, women, children and the "morons of the world," as one writer of the Production Code of 1930 put it, were thought to be more susceptible to ideas introduced in motion pictures than the more sophisticated box-seat theater crowd. By virtue of its artistic power and the breadth of its audience, it was decided that film, the "art of the multitudes," simply could not be given the "latitude" of the other arts.[20]

Since no individual or group was given authority to enforce the Code, filmmakers continued to follow their own instincts regarding box-office acceptability, despite growing public controversy. Social and religious reformers were especially disturbed by the sensational sex films and the increasing number of gangster pictures, which they thought eroded the moral and social fabric of society. Illicit love affairs, risqué situations and sympathetic portrayals of prostitutes or kept women were featured in a number of films in the early thirties, including *Confessions of a Co-ed* (1931), *Bachelor Apartment* (1931), *Beauty for Sale* (1932), *Red Dust* (1932) and *Back Street* (1932). Marlene Dietrich seduced an aging professor in *The Blue Angel* (1930) and became the mistress of a wealthy gangster in *Blonde Venus* (1932). Greta Garbo turned to prostitution in *Susan Lenox, Her Fall and Rise* (1931). Maureen O'Sullivan skinny-dipped with the ape-man in *Tarzan and His Mate* (1934).

Gritty and realistic gangster films like *Little Caesar* (1930), *The Public Enemy* (1931) and *Scarface* (1932) were interpreted by church leaders as mocking hard work, sacrifice and respect for institutional authority. These films were so popular that Hollywood released some fifty gangster films in the years following. But reformers thought these portrayals of underworld criminals flaunting money, flashy clothes and beautiful women created sympathy for criminals and had a negative influence on impressionable youth (even though mob leaders were all punished with death). Though enormously popular with audiences and critics alike, the pictures of Mae West irked reformers the most. "In word and gesture Mae West was the living mockery of all the Code's pieties," film analyst Alexander Walker writes. "But Hollywood made her welcome for one excellent reason: her films were enormous moneymakers."[21]

An Uneasy Alliance
The very nature of Protestantism made the mainline denominations uncomfortable with, and at times even resistant to, censorship. The Protestant Ref-

ormation doctrine of the final authority of Scripture over tradition, ecclesiastical power or any other cultural manifestation of the eternal truths of Scripture distinguished evangelical Protestantism from Roman Catholicism. In rejection of papal authority, the former emphasized the individual's conscience in matters of biblical interpretation and communion with God. The concepts of freedom of speech and expression and the marketplace of ideas have their roots in this Protestant tradition. Consequently, the mainline Protestant denominations were leery of censorship boards and boycotts, considering them violations of constitutional rights. They preferred helping people make their own decisions according to individual conscience. One writer indicated that even reform groups had doubts about movie censorship, which, he wrote, "ran counter to one of the basic impulses of the Progressive reformer, who hoped to open up all the access routes to information about man's environment, about his culture and his past."[22]

The myriad Protestant groups, spanning the diversity of opinion from fundamentalism to liberalism, made it virtually impossible to create a unified effort to confront the film industry. In contrast, the Catholic Church had much greater unity, a tradition of ecclesiastical obedience and an extensive network throughout the world that made it an ominous threat to the film industry. During the 1920s, Protestant churches passed resolutions at their annual conferences, lobbied for censorship bills and crusaded in their journals. The Catholic Church introduced the boycott.

American bishops of the Roman Catholic Church formed the Legion of Decency in 1934. Using the extensive church network, the Legion called for members to sign a pledge in support of the organization and to participate in a national boycott of movies the church ruled indecent. The Legion's "campaign for scrubbing the screen," as one writer referred to it, had a wide base of support that reached beyond the Catholic community.[23] Protestant organizations like the Federal Council of Churches and even Jewish groups like the Central Conference of American Rabbis joined in the crusade, along with educational and fraternal organizations. The religious community was united, at least for the moment, in a campaign for decency in movies. That the Legion wielded enormous power became immediately apparent, as it was able to galvanize public attention on the issue of "cleaning" up the movies like no other previous attempt.

The Legion used the momentum generated by the Payne Studies and the studios' economic plight to turn the Production Code from a voluntary set of guidelines into an instrument for industry self-regulation. The Catholic Church commanded enough economic clout to force Hollywood moguls to agree to self-censorship by adhering to the guidelines of the Production Code. Almost immediately the Legion claimed two million members, and according to a report in *Time,* a Legion boycott that year cut Philadelphia exhibitors' business by 40 percent.[24] In 1933 it was estimated that there were over sixty million registered church members, with over twenty million on the Catholic rolls.[25] Some 310 Catholic newspapers and periodicals had a combined circulation of over seven million. Moreover, the Legion operated on Vatican approval, and the Catholic Church extended around the globe. Studio heads did not take lightly the Legion's request that bishops in Europe help "curb the moral menace of the lurid American film."[26] Between 30 and 40 percent of Hollywood's gross receipts came from overseas distribution.

In response Hays established the Production Code Administration (PCA) headed by Joseph I. Breen, a prominent Irish Catholic layperson, to enforce the tenets of the Code. Film companies that belonged to the MPPDA agreed not to distribute or exhibit any film without a seal of approval from the PCA. As long as the major film studios that made up the MPPDA owned and controlled the most important theaters, the Code could be kept in force. Fears of boycotts by religious and women's groups and additional censoring by local and state boards were enough to keep independent theater owners from showing films without a certificate of approval. This arrangement lasted until the early 1950s, when a Supreme Court ruling forced the studios to divest themselves of their theater chains. Although not the only factor, the dismantling of the studio system subsequently undermined the feasibility of the Code. Without studio enforcement there was no way the MPPDA, renamed the Motion Picture Association of America (MPAA) in 1945, could prevent independent theater owners from running films that did not have PCA approval.

At the same time that the Production Code was instituted as a means of contending with the mass communication of movies, another line of discourse existed suggesting that Hollywood could satisfy many of its critics by differentiating its product. Hollywood established a formulaic approach to filmmaking to increase the efficiency of production and make it easier to communicate with a mass audience, including immigrants with minimal fluency in English. By this time, however, the movies reached all segments of society, and Hollywood's mass approach seemed "out of focus" with its expanded and diverse audience. Instead of making homogenized movies for a sizable minority, why not be genuinely democratic and produce different kinds of movies for specific segments of the population?

In 1930, the same year the Production Code was written, Universal Pictures departed from its routine low-budget features to release *All Quiet on the Western Front*, a prestigious and realistic antiwar film that was both critically acclaimed and commercially successful. Laemmle said it "upset all of our oldest traditions." In a letter to the editor of *Outlook*, he suggested that the movie industry was at an "impasse" and wondered if *All Quiet on the Western Front* indicated "that the American public has grown more mature and more sophisticated in its taste than we have in motion picture production." Theater critic Creighton Peet used this as an opportunity to make a case for the production of a variety of movies that would appeal to a number of different audiences.

Peet understood the dynamics of mass culture—that a film company might "produce cheaply a bit of trash" that will become the year's most commercially successful film. But he encouraged film producers to take seriously their role as a creative artistic enterprise by aiming "certain types of stories at certain types of people," including "highbrow" films that could be exhibited at some of the smaller theaters, a situation strongly resembling the art-film circuit today. These films did not have to be "super films" with expensive budgets, but the more sophisticated audiences looked instead for solid direction, acting and story. As it was, by emphasizing common elements to attract everyone, Hollywood movies were "too complicated for the simplest of the simple-minded, and not entirely right for the slightly superior audiences of the present day," Peet wrote, referring to former legitimate theater patrons, those "millions of people throughout the country who were left without entertainment of any sort when the road shows and stock companies were driven away by the mob movie." In the past the film industry had "scorned these people as hopeless, useless 'highbrows' incapable of meaning anything at the boxoffice," but now they represented millions of potential customers who visited a movie theater only once or twice a year because there were too few films that appealed to their tastes.

In a sense Peet was suggesting a way through the dilemma Shaw described earlier regarding the "colossal proportions" of the movie audience that "make mediocrity compulsory." Unfortunately, Peet's prediction that "there will be a regular supply of films aimed at the now despised 'highbrow' " did not come true.[27] The prior censorship of the Production Code supported cultural conformity and ensured that movies were suitable for all age groups, and Hollywood continued to aim at the widest possible audience for each production. The dual effect was to maximize the potential audience for each movie while requiring filmmakers to affirm the accepted moral standards in order to avoid violating the code by offending anyone.

Hollywood and the American Dream

The stock-market crash in October 1929 brought the optimism of the "Roaring Twenties" to a screeching halt. During the 1930s unemployment and poverty rates soared while birth and marriage rates fell. Banks failed at an alarming rate, and farm prices fell to disastrous lows. America's system of relief from economic hardship proved inadequate. There was widespread fear of revolution, but despite the terrible suffering Americans experienced during the Great Depression, no revolt came. Instead a redefinition of America emerged.

According to Warren Susman, it was during the trauma of the 1930s that Americans first began to think of themselves as part of a distinctly "American" culture. By this time the stream of new immigrants entering America had been reduced to a trickle. The plurality of ethnic, racial and religious groups that characterized American life around the turn of the century was assimilated under the overarching umbrella of an "American way of life." Members of immigrant groups no longer identified themselves with their ethnic heritage, represented by language, religious and cultural heritage. Now, in America's "melting pot," they shed their "foreignness" to be remade in the image of the Anglo-American ideal in order to better fit in and take advantage of the mobility of mainstream American society. The phrase "the American dream" came into common use then as an individual pursuit and yet "something shared collectively by all Americans."[28]

American mythology crystallized around the notion of a classless society, values associated with personality and rugged individualism, material consumption and success, and the unquestioned superiority of the American way of life and Judeo-Christian morality. More than a new nationalism, the quest for the "true" America became a kind of secular religion and a new basis for conformity. This age of consensus was solidified as the new prosperity beginning in the late 1930s eased class tensions; the presence of a formidable enemy strengthened national unity.

More than ever before, mass entertainment media were crucial in the creation of a national culture (and especially during the crisis of the Depression).

The nineteenth-century epic novel had functioned this way, and indigenous cinemas served nation-building roles in other countries, including the Soviet Union and several Latin American countries.[29] On an unprecedented level now, radio and movies broke down cultural barriers by generating a body of myths and symbols that united people and helped define the American way of life. Even as entertainment served like art in transmitting the culture, the industry was guided by the pursuit of corporate profits and not a conscious effort at nation building. The trend among educators, clergy and civic leaders, however, was to make radio and the movies an instrument of consensus by ensuring that they affirmed middle-class values. Not unlike many of today's critics, they wanted the media to serve as vehicles for moral and social values in order to foster the growth of a national culture. The primary means to this end in the early 1930s was to force the entertainment industry to adopt and abide by self-censorship codes.

Based on the philosophy and directives of the Code, movies became a form of escape and a defender of the status quo during the studio era. Passing through the filter of the Production Code, Hollywood films paraded American mythology, showing "the rewards of social mobility—wealth, success and the girl for the hero; fellowship, happiness and trustworthy leaders for the rest of us," Sklar explains. "It was a religious faith in a secular social myth that found its embodiment in patriotism and American democracy."[30] Conflicts in love, life and society were always resolved in a glamorous and compelling way with people living happily ever after. In operation, the Code enforced a moral and social sterilization of life. While some of its strictures may be interpreted positively in our age of excessive sex and violence in the media, taken as a whole, they were obviously restrictive, limiting not only the manner of presentation but thematic possibilities and treatment as well.[31]

Adultery, illicit sex, childbirth, seduction and rape could only be suggested. Miscegenation, drug addiction and excessive drinking were expressly forbidden, as were the use of racial epithets and "obscenity in word, gesture, reference, song, joke, or by suggestion." Techniques of crime, murder, revenge or brutality could not be explicitly presented, and "the sympathy of the audience should never be thrown to the side of crime, wrong-doing, evil, or sin." The complexity and diversity of the American religious community was condensed to a nebulous "natural law . . . which is written in the hearts of all mankind, the great underlying principles of right and justice dictated by conscience." Further, the Code required an upbeat, optimistic ending regardless of whatever transpired throughout the film. The application of the Code did much more than scrub Hollywood movies morally clean. It made American films seem superficial, unrealistic and even dishonest, especially when compared with the realism of the European cinema after World War II.

As many film historians have shown, the practice of self-censorship actually went beyond "cleaning up" the moral content of movies and became an instrument of social control by requiring an idealized portrait of American life and democracy. Instead of becoming serious art, movies were regulated as the collective memory and transmitter of idealized middle-class culture. As symbolic representations, they were prohibited from doing social criticism and used instead to forge social and cultural unity.

As Bruno Bettelheim has explained, social consensus is based on a mythic vision that binds people together in common experiences that give purpose to life and make activities meaningful.[32] Myths offer shared ideas, dreams and fantasies that connect individuals with the larger group. They provide patterns for normal behavior and a means for individuals to examine their own lives by comparing them with commonly held expectations.

During the studio era, Hollywood's mythmaking powers were used to build a national cultural consensus. There are some critics today who think this should be the primary use of entertainment rather than the roles for art I described earlier. These critics advocate the making of movies for the general family audience, as was the practice during the studio era. But as the remainder of this chapter will show, this is really a means to control the content of films by having them cater to a white middle-class audience, the purpose being to use movies to re-create a mythical consensus in American life to obscure racial, cultural and class conflicts that exist in reality.

Forced to avoid social and political criticism during the golden era, American movies religiously affirmed the status quo. As film historian Terry Christensen has observed, "This reduces politics to a need for occasional individual action to regulate an essentially good, smoothly functioning process by pointing out flaws in the form of bad individuals and sometimes bad organizations like gangs, machines, and corporations."[33] The forces of power and privilege could not prevent right from always triumphing over wrong. And so the individual pursuit of truth and justice overcomes political corruption in Frank Capra's *Mr. Smith Goes to Washington* (1939), a film about a naive individual who exposes the corruption of a fellow senator. The real source of social and personal problems was not economic injustice, poverty or class conflict as demonstrated by *It's a Wonderful Life* (1946), but individual greed and malice. The common people rally behind the virtuous hero to save their town from graft and corruption. In gangster pictures like *Little Caesar* (1930) and *The Public Enemy* (1931), criminals who are enticed by the American dream of success but use illegal means to acquire it are punished in the end. Likewise, the greedy and malicious couple in *Double Indemnity* (1944) is destroyed by their own distrust and corruption.

Even today, Hollywood films rarely (if ever) treat serious problems with the American political system without reducing them to individual heroism. In *Clear and Present Danger,* for example, even the president of the United States is not beyond an abuse of power, but Jack Ryan (Harrison Ford) weeds the individual corruption out of an otherwise good system. Tom Cruise does the same for the legal profession in *The Firm* and the military in *A Few Good Men.*

Hollywood films promoted the myth that the world was divided into the forces of ultimate evil and righteousness, slavery and freedom. The United States was the superhero fighting for truth and justice, the cowboy in the white hat defending democracy. In countless westerns a lone hero rescued civilization from the forces of savagery. War was glorious, and an ethnically and racially mixed group of soldiers fought side by side in *Bataan* (1943), although the armed forces were not desegregated until 1948.[34] The good guys were reluctant soldiers who discover that war is necessary to eliminate villainy; the bad guys torture prisoners and kill innocent civilians. Though not unlike the propaganda of other nations, this simplistic mythology could not be sustained amidst the complexity and revelations of the Vietnam War, although some retrospective films about the war tried to do so.

The Hollywood mythology was perhaps most appealing in its idealization of romance and marriage. Continuing the tradition of the romance novel and melodrama, Hollywood produced an inordinately high proportion of movies emphasizing love as the theme with the greatest human appeal. According to one study, romance was one line of action in 95 percent of the movies produced in Hollywood between 1915 and 1960, and the principal one in 85 percent.[35]

As expected, Hollywood's treatment of its most popular subject was severely restricted by the Code's directives and notion of "pure love." The sanctity of marriage and family translated into a Victorian treatment of sexuality as something foreign to the basic procreative unit of society. Married couples slept (and did nothing else) in twin beds, a practice imitated by television shows in the 1950s. Nudity of all kinds and "scenes of passion" (which in the language of the Code meant "excessive and lustful kissing, lustful embraces, suggestive postures and gestures") were forbidden. Consequently, film portrayals made love seem trivial and without passion, and marriage as sexless; normal human reactions were not dealt with honestly. Divorce in the movies, for example, occurred for petty reasons (misunderstandings or personality quirks) and not for lust, unfaithfulness, sexual dysfunction, economic pressures or domestic abuse. This made it easy for divorced couples to be reunited, as they invariably were in Hollywood films.

There was a tendency in Hollywood films to affirm a Victorian mythic ideal. Women did not derive pleasure and fulfillment from sexual love. Love that was sensual was depicted as immoral and occurred between evil characters. This tended to divide portrayals of women into "good"—that is, sexless mothers and housewives—and "evil"—vamps or seductresses. PCA reviewers did permit subtle innuendo, double entendres and sexy subtexts in movies (such as *The Lady Eve*, 1941); this fostered the creation of clever and subtle dialogue that could actually be quite risqué. In the years just prior to the institution of the Code, characters played by Greta Garbo, Marlene Dietrich and Jean Harlow were "sensualists without guilt," as film critic Molly Haskell puts it. The Code suppressed the "salutory impulse of female sexality," she writes, but its prohibition against nudity took women out of negligees and the bedroom and put them in work clothes and professional careers, like Katharine Hepburn as the attorney in *Adam's Rib* (1949) and Rosalind Russell as the hyperactive news reporter in *His Girl Friday* (1940). These films, and others like them, explored real value tensions in the culture of the time and, however ambiguously, approved the entry of women into permanent work careers. But even cursory testing of established gender roles was restricted by the social and sexual framework the Code enforced. As Haskell observes, "A woman's work is almost always seen as provisional, and almost never as a lifelong commitment, or as part of her definition as a woman."[36]

There were no social or economic barriers in Hollywood's tunnel of love. Unlikely pairings became a solid comedic device in what one writer described as "sex comedies without sex."[37] In Frank Capra's *It Happened One Night* (1934), an ambitious poor reporter played by Clark Gable wins the love of a rich and beautiful young woman (Claudette Colbert). The zany and unpredictable niece of a millionaire (Katharine Hepburn) wreaks havoc on a preoccupied professor (Cary Grant) in the hope of securing a research grant in Howard Hawks's *Bringing Up Baby* (1938). Screwball comedies emphasized romantic love as the source of personal fulfillment and the basis for marriage. But there was no connection between the fairy-tale romance and the realities of married life. "And they lived happily ever after" summarized how the characters played by idyllic movie stars worked out issues associated with passion and sex, children, sacrifice, and social and psychological adjustments.[38]

By today's standards, some aspects of the Code seem not only remarkably quaint but also racist and sexist. Film historian David A. Cook goes so far as to write that in its reaction against the "new morality" of the 1920s, the Production Code was "awesomely repressive, and it prohibited the showing or mentioning of almost everything germane to the situation of normal human adults."[39] Films—and those made under the Code are not exceptions— are cultural documents that deal with a society's values, beliefs and assumptions, as well as social problems and tensions that beset a cultural system. Movies do not simply reflect the events they portray, but do so with a certain attitude toward them. In American movies that attitude is circumscribed by the Hollywood ideology, which in turn is based on dominant American myths that people use to guide their behavior and construe meaning for life. Movies, then, should be understood as reflecting a reality they help to create.

The Production Code kept American films morally safe, but also artistically immature. The Breen Office made sure that every Hollywood-produced film conformed to a lowest common denominator, and was suitable for viewing by the entire family. As late as 1959, a Chicago censor argued that "children should be allowed to see any movie that plays in Chicago. If a picture is objectionable for a child, it is objectionable period."[40] The intent was to offend no one in Hollywood's vast international audience, but the effect was to prohibit American movies from treating issues that might be controversial to some segment of the audience, adult or child, whether in Paris, France, or Peoria, Illinois. Ironically, this method of combining creativity and marketing works to produce the kinds of movies that draw the most criticism. Critics at the time were aware of this, as a remark by a writer in *The Nation* indicates. "The magnates of Hollywood are not emissaries of Satan seeking whom they may destroy," but "business men of rather limited imagination eagerly seeking for a common denominator, and so far unable to find anything except legs, questionable jokes, and bedroom stories which seem to possess the requiste universal appeal."[41] As this comment suggests, PCA reviewers allowed a certain amount of sexual intimation and suggestiveness on the screen in conversation, story and especially Busby Berkeley's female chorus lines, presumably because of producers' arguments for the box-office viability of these elements.

In other words, the Legion-enforced Production Code ensured an unlimited audience for Hollywood films, for which Hollywood executives were no doubt grateful. But the cinema's potentials as an art was sacrificed in the process. "If the movies were given the freedom now enjoyed by the play and the novel to treat serious things seriously; if the *ostensible* moral were not always required to be so completely conventional; then the very competition of serious themes might well reduce somewhat the number of merely salacious spectacles," *The Nation* proposed. "But even that would not solve the problem created by the fact that the industry as now organized must appeal to everybody everywhere."[42] Today's reformers are guilty of much the same. By limiting their efforts to negative criticism and a demand for morally safe entertainment suitable for the entire family, they fail to recognize other legitimate roles for the cinema and to acknowledge the need for artists to cultivate the potential of the medium and for people to understand its significance as a medium of cultural communication.

The Code severed film from treatment of the most significant social, moral, political and cultural issues of the time. The most telling illustration of this is Hollywood's treatment of the Depression. The Depression shook the foundations of American culture. Deferred gratification and the assurance of success for hard work were shattered by unemployment lines. Despite the economic calamity and the rising threat of Fascism in Europe, Lewis Jacobs observes, movies of the 1930s were largely "superficial" and "devoted to trivialities." Always looking to tout the movie industry, Will Hays claimed that while other countries were rocked by "revolutions, riot and political turmoil" during the Depression, the mission of Hollywood was "to reflect aspiration, achievement, optimism and kindly humor in its entertainment."[43]

The most celebrated images from the period expressed the confidence of the early New Deal. "We're in the Money . . . We've Got a Lot of What It Takes to Get Along" was a song and chorus-line dance from a Busby Berkeley musical, *Gold Diggers of 1933*. (A double entendre, the chorus affirmed individualism while also joking about what the voluptuous dancers would be compelled to do if the show failed.) The Disney cartoon *Three Little Pigs* also promoted values of self-reliance and hard work. Its theme song "Who's Afraid of the Big Bad Wolf?" set "the whole nation whistling to keep up its spirits," according to Jacobs. The song symbolically minimized the depth of the national crisis and "helped to turn the tide of pessimism toward optimism and strengthened the hope that co-ordinated action would pull the country out of its slump."[44] Hays said, "Historians of the future will not ignore the interesting and significant fact that the movies literally laughed the big bad wolf of depression out of the public."[45]

With the notable exceptions *I Am a Fugitive from a Chain Gang* (1932) and *Our Daily Bread* (1934), no serious film was made about the realities and hardships of the Depression until John Ford's *The Grapes of Wrath* in 1940, when the economic disaster was over. It was as if the Depression did not exist, or had little impact on most people's lives. Still, in the film version, John Steinbeck's novel *The Grapes of Wrath* was transformed from an indictment of the economic system to a story of enduring faith in individual survival despite the odds. There was nothing in the context of the film to justify the Joads' optimism at the end, except the Breen Office's requirement that the film conform to American cultural myths.

Conclusion

The "innocence" of Hollywood films during the studio era is largely due to the commercial pressures of the profit-driven film industry and the self-censorship imposed by the Production Code. Filmmakers were never entirely comfortable working under the Code's restrictions. Many of the most prominent directors did their best to maneuver around it but were often frustrated by the Breen Office's alterations of their creative works. This is not to say, however, that the Code completely stripped movies of any artistic excellence or the ability to seriously investigate issues. The Code was a hindrance but did allow for the production of many great films, as evidenced by the body of works from John Ford, Howard Hawks, Alfred Hitchcock and others. The manifold cinematic achievements of the period can be seen in films like *Gone with the Wind* (1939), *Stagecoach* (1939), *Citizen Kane* (1941), *The Maltese Falcon* (1941) and *Casablanca* (1943), to mention just a few of the most renowned. Still, these artistic achievements can be credited to the potential of the medium and the imagination of filmmakers rather than the succor of the Code's provisions. And they cannot entirely make up for Hollywood's failure to fulfill other roles for the cinema during this time.

According to one writer, "Censorship was a painful pill for Hollywood moguls to swallow." After studying letters from the Hays Office, he pictures the studio heads "thrashing about like hooked marlin, as the censors gutted the most dramatic ingredients from their most prized and profitable pictures."[46] It may seem strange that these autocratic Hollywood chiefs would institutionalize such a system of restraint, but a closer examination reveals a number of reasons that movie magnates accepted this state of affairs.

The Legion's threat to boycott any film the church hierarchy found objectionable was real and far-reaching during the worst years of the Depression. "To have Mammon desert them and then find God coming up on their flank was too horrid to contemplate," one writer said.[47] Hollywood could not afford to alienate so large a segment of the potential audience as the global Catholic community represented. Instead, abiding by the restraints of the Code, however restricting, promised acceptability for Hollywood films among all segments of American society, and especially the middle class. It was also a successful means to fend off outside regulation from local, state or federal government agencies. In terms of filmmaking, the code could be used like a "scriptwriter's blueprint," making production more efficient by minimizing problems of creativity in the process.

Finally, in the climate of open anti-Semitism of the Depression years, religious prejudice gave these first- and second-generation Jewish immigrants good reason to fear social, economic or political reprisals against the film industry. As discussed earlier, industry leaders were aware that religious antagonisms were often behind actions taken to censor film production. It was hoped that a code of ethics drawn up by Catholic bishops would reassure the predominantly Christian movie audience of the decency of Jewish film moguls. Joel Spring pointed out the irony that "as patriotic organizations beat the drum for 'Americanism' and the end to immigration, Hollywood, under the domination of Jewish immigrants and their children, was producing films that would shape the consciousness of Americans and create an image of Americanism for the rest of the world."[48]

Movie moguls seized the moment to legitimize the film industry by redirecting the energies of Hollywood. Instead of testing and raising questions about prevailing values, the film industry now joined the guardians of the middle class. According to Sklar, Hollywood now "directed its enormous powers of persuasion to preserving the basic moral, social and economic tenets of traditional American culture."[49] Themes associated with the schemes and problems of the urban world disappeared as studio heads realized greater profits could be reaped from films appealing to people's ideals, dreams and sentiments associated with middle-class culture during the renewed nationalism of the New Deal era. As Neal Gabler shows, the Jewish studio heads promulgated "a vast, compelling national fantasy," a fabrication of an idealized America that was invented out of their own desperate longing for security and acceptance in genteel America.[50]

Jack Cohn, vice president of Columbia Pictures, suggested that the attack on the movies in the early 1930s was much more than a moral cleansing as was proclaimed. "This violent burst of condemnation is directed against something greater than the motion picture," he said. "The motion picture reflects the thing against which the Crusaders inveigh—the tendencies of the times."[51] As Cohn noted, movies were being used as a scapegoat for social problems associated with the social transformation of which the amusements were visible symbols. Movies were particularly vulnerable to attacks by reformers and religious groups. They were not protected by the First Amendment, and because they were so open and accessible to a wide range of social groups, they were a constant target of any self-proclaimed guardian of American culture or crusader of righteousness.

The Production Code inaugurated an era of morally safe family entertainment. For the next two decades moviegoing was established as an important social ritual, a weekly family outing or dating activity that Americans enjoyed not only as a means of passing their leisure time but also as an important cultural experience and source of news and information, especially during the war years. Box-office figures rose steadily throughout the thirties. From sixty million in 1932, weekly admissions climbed to eighty-five million in 1942 and peaked at ninety million in 1946, according to U.S. Census Bureau figures.

The film industry's role as a provider of entertainment for the American middle-class family was reified during the "studio era." As John Izod put it, during the studio era "family-oriented features were celebrated for their power to entertain and amuse, not for their authority as significant documents."[52] Hollywood moguls were in the business of propagating a national culture; the payback was a large national audience, high profits and no federal censorship. But promoting American mythology according to the strictures of the Production Code was also a way to streamline the creative process, making American films appear more like an assembly-line production than imaginative art.

Despite the glory of Hollywood's productions in 1939, for example, movies were still looked upon as second-class commercial art. "East Coast intellectuals, who thought that the only real acting was done on Broadway, sneered at Hollywood's output," Gerald Clarke wrote in a *Time* retrospective on 1939. "But then, why shouldn't they have? The studio bosses, after all, liked to brag that they were just businessmen whose job it was to turn out movies—no one in those days called them films—the way General Electric did refrigerators and Ford did cars."[53] Movies served this way until after World War II, when a combination of factors, both internal and external, created a crisis for the American entertainment industry. The changes that followed affected every aspect of the film industry (and others as well), the composition of its audience and the role of entertainment in society.

8

· · · · ·

Somewhere
over the
Golden Era

In the popular imagination, the golden age of Hollywood is re-
membered for those memorable movies the major studios produced that
were distinguished for their production quality, emotional impact or box-
office success. The Civil War spectacle *Gone with the Wind* and the wonderful
fantasy *The Wizard of Oz* immediately come to mind. Both of these films
were released in 1939, considered by many to be Hollywood's greatest year.
There are maybe a dozen other movies released in this watershed year that
are considered "classics," but with the exception of *Gone with the Wind,* none
of these films was what we might call a "blockbuster" hit today.[1] Most people
are surprised to hear that *The Wizard of Oz,* often referred to as "the grandest
and most glorious of all fantasies," was actually panned by many critics in
1939 and was a major financial disappointment. MGM did not begin to see
a profit on its $2.7-million investment until the movie was shown on televi-
sion almost twenty years later.[2]

Studio era "classics" have been canonized today; you can read about them
in film books, see them on the *American Movie Classics* channel and rent or
buy them at local video stores. But these represent only a handful of the 483

films Hollywood studios produced that year.[3] Between 1930 and 1945, American film companies produced over 7,600 feature films. The vast majority of these did not withstand the test of time, but as a group they should not be forgotten, for they give us some intriguing insights into the golden years of Hollywood and shed some light on the extraordinary changes that occurred after World War II.

A confluence of events both within the film industry and in American life after the war shifted the tectonic plates on which the film industry rested throughout the studio era. A metamorphosis of the Hollywood cinema took place over the next two decades that recast the whole discussion about high and popular art. It began with a series of momentous Supreme Court decisions that transformed the role of film and entertainment in general. In 1948 the Court found the studios in violation of antitrust laws. This decision eliminated the distinction between the major and minor studios by forcing the majors to sell off their theater chains. Thereafter they contracted with independent producers, distributed films and expanded into television. In other rulings, the Supreme Court reversed its stance on the free-speech status of movies and distinguished obscenity from the representation of sexuality; film was no longer "a business pure and simple" but a constitutionally protected art.

The dismantling of the studio system and the new judicial freedoms granted by the court brought some unexpected results. Previously, the studio monopoly effectively kept independent and foreign films out of first-run American theaters. During the 1950s, independent distributors and exhibitors discovered that there was a large enough audience among educated young people to support European "art" films. Foreign productions, however, were not regulated by the Production Code Administration (PCA); many of these films challenged the prevailing ethos by introducing topics previously considered taboo in American movies. Movies were still considered a special public medium by virtue of their direct accessibility to a wide and diverse audience, but the artistic license the Supreme Court granted the cinema now complicated the issue of prerelease censorship. The Production Code and the pressure tactics of the Legion of Decency came under increasing attack as violations of free speech. The studio system and threat of boycott by the Legion, you will remember, were the two main conditions for the Code's existence. As the Code became unenforceable, the need for a classification system rose from public discourse. In 1968 the Production Code was replaced by the MPPA ratings system, which classified movies based on suitability for different age groups.

Changing population trends and new work and leisure patterns redefined life in postwar America. As people tried to get on with their lives after the disruptions of the war, the explosive postwar birth rate (the baby boom) and suburbanization changed the lifestyles of working- and middle-class Americans, Hollywood's regular audience. In addition, television expanded at a phenomenal rate, largely replacing movies as regular family entertainment. Just as movies had earlier changed the theater's economic position, now the film industry experienced increased costs and greater risk with each production in the competition with television.

The postwar period began a time of crisis for Hollywood. For the first time, the American film industry fell behind the rest of the world. For the two decades since 1934, the Production Code Administration monitored Hollywood productions. That box-office revenues reached new heights during this period seemed to confirm for film moguls the wisdom of providing good, clean entertainment for the whole family, particularly the white middle class. As they watched box-office receipts plunge throughout the 1950s, studio heads magnified their efforts to recapture this vanishing audience. They introduced new technologies like 3-D, color and wide screen projection, and they began making fewer movies, but more expensive ones. The reorientation of the Hollywood majors in the postwar era was marked by a shift to the production of "blockbusters," or what Robert Sklar has called "the motion-picture equivalent of a home run."[4]

The production of big-budget films aimed at a general "family" audience was one general trend in the American cinema during this time. Beginning in the 1950s, however, there was a growing awareness that a specialized segment of the potential moviegoing audience could financially support a movie. There was a shift in the regular moviegoing audience from a general, national audience to specific, demographic groups. Studio executives, however, were accustomed to providing entertainment for the whole family based on the general theory that all people had to like all films. Hollywood was slow to respond to the obvious demographic changes that were rocking the entire entertainment industry. Independent film companies, however, were happy to accommodate the more youthful audience. The combination of these events caused the near collapse of the Hollywood studio empire. It took until the early 1970s for the film industry to reorient itself to both these changes and the new audience of regular moviegoers. A new Hollywood emerged, creating popular art for the under-thirty generation. Some critics today argue the opposite, however: that the reason for Hollywood's financial straits was that filmmakers abandoned the general family audience in the late 1960s. This is a faulty explanation for the events that took place during this time and the great effect they had on the entertainment industry. Consequently, understanding this period is critical to discerning the controversy over entertainment and the movement to reform it today.

Revisiting Hollywood's Golden Age

During the worst years of the Depression, the moviegoing audience dropped by a third. Exhibitors had to resort to prizes and giveaways to lure patrons into the theaters. Eventually, they introduced air conditioning and confectionery sales (popcorn, candy and soft drinks) to help keep their businesses profitable. Most important, however, was the double feature. Exhibitors found that two films for the price of one was successful in boosting attendance during the Depression years. Hollywood studios responded by filling the second bill with "B" pictures—low-budget formulaic films that were produced quickly and without box-office stars. It was reported, for example, that while over five hundred films were produced in the United States in 1936, almost two-thirds were "B" movies, meant to fill the bottom half of the double bill.[5]

Generally, only about a quarter of Hollywood's total annual production were high-budget "A" films with well-known stars; the majority of Hollywood's output consisted of "routine bread-and-butter productions," their titles and stars long forgotten and omitted from the history books. Nevertheless, as popular culture historian Russel Nye has explained, the "B" pictures were the financial mainstay of the industry. "While some (but by no means all) of the 'big' pictures make money, steady, safe returns lie in the low budget pictures done for the drive-in, triple-feature trade, the films that titillate, enthrall, and amuse mass audiences at cheap prices just as the melodrama, vaudeville, farce, popular novel, and dime shocker always have," Nye writes.[6] Producers, critics and fans alike often complained about the quality of these films; most of the ire of social and religious groups was aimed at them as well.

Ironically, another aspect of this controversy was the lack of differentiation in Hollywood productions enforced by the Production Code. Unlike the legitimate stage, for example, which was understood historically as a sophisticated and adult medium, movies remained by the Code's definition a mass entertainment medium. Since film was capable of reaching a large, diverse audience, the Code ensured the suitability of every Hollywood release for adults and children alike. The film industry did not make movies aimed at specific segments of the public, especially based on age and maturity. Few attractions were intended solely for children; a 1933-1934 report classified 66 percent of the films produced during that period as suitable for adults only.[7] That children attended movies that were really "adult" fare was a major source of contention for parents, reformers and clergy.

For this reason the Catholic Church urged Hollywood to adopt a classification system that would identify adult films not suitable for children. Film producers resisted, preferring to tailor and market every film to reach the widest possible audience, with the obvious intent of maximizing the profits of each picture. Instead, Catholic and Protestant churches developed ways to help church members in their decisions of conscience. In 1936 the Legion created its own moral rating system for movies based on age. The Protestant Motion Picture Council began previewing films in 1944, and the following year the Film Board of National Organizations began publishing and distributing the *Green Sheet,* a rating of films based on suitability for age groups. Films were rated based on reviews submitted by organizational representatives and according to five age designations: adults, mature young people, young people, general audience and children. The *Green Sheet* was distributed to newspapers, schools, libraries and churches and was reportedly read by ten million Americans, although it apparently had little impact on movie attendance.[8]

Production Code procedures alone did not resolve these problems, which were only intensified by the preponderance of "B" (and "C") movies. Most of this criticism came from Protestant groups. The more conservative denominations continued their ban on movie attendance, but among the mainline groups the "menace of the movies" was the glut of low-budget "B" and "C" pictures playing at neighborhood theaters. As they saw it, the problem was Hollywood's domination of the exhibition business. In a confluence of morality and commercial interests, women's groups and Protestant leaders joined independent exhibitors in an effort to end the monopoly of the major studios. Their campaign centered on support for legislation to abolish "block-booking" and "blind-selling." *The Christian Century* urged its Protestant readers to support this legislation, declaring that "all the rotten pictures produced by the 'Big Eight' in the last thirty years have been marketed through the block-booking process."[9]

Block-booking and blind-selling were industry trade practices that forced exhibitors to lease a "block" of movies from a film company at a sum total price. To ensure an outlet for all of their releases, the studios tied films of lesser quality to desirable titles featuring a prominent star. The exhibitor, then, was forced to lease a package of high- and low-quality films ("A," "B" and "C" titles) from the production and distribution company, without preview and without regard to content (blind-selling). These practices were foundational to the studio system. The monopoly the major film companies had over first-run exhibition guaranteed a theatrical run for all of their movies, regardless of quality; buying in "blocks" reduced the exhibitor's cost of renting a single film. In this way, the studio system ensured profits and reduced the financial risk of film production. It also eliminated the competition by keeping independent productions out of the first-run movie houses.

Block-booking highlighted the dilemma of film as both art and commercial product. In one sense, this was a standard wholesale practice widely used in other commercial fields. But it became increasingly difficult to maintain the idea that movies were merely commodities along the lines of household cleaning products; the Payne Studies demonstrated the psychological impact of film on individuals and its potential to influence social and cultural life. Concerned groups protested these trade practices, blaming them for the problem communities had maintaining local standards. Even the federal government targeted block-booking as a major source of the problems associated with the movies. Basically, the argument was that block-booking thwarted local control over film exhibition because managers had to accept whatever the film studio offered in order to get a reasonable rental price. Independent exhibitors who operated neighborhood theaters were especially affected. While they constituted about 70 percent of the theaters in the United States in 1927, the major studios catered to the first-run downtown theaters they owned that captured a proportionately higher percentage of the total rental fees. These pictures did not always fit the needs of neighborhood theaters. It was thought that abolishing these practices would give more power in film selection to local exhibitors, who in turn would be more responsive to community tastes and pressures than Hollywood producers.

These reform efforts, however well-intended, brought about some unexpected results. The campaign to eliminate block-booking led to the dismantling of the studio monopoly which had been essential to the maintenance of the Production Code and became a key factor in the Code's termination. One has to wonder what unintended consequences may result from today's reform movement.

The End of the Studio System

In response to complaints, the U.S. Justice Department began an investigation and filed an antitrust suit against the major studios in July 1938. After a decade of on-and-off litigation, the Supreme Court ruled that the vertical integration of the major Hollywood studios constituted an illegal monopoly. The court ordered the major studios to divest themselves of one of the three operations: production, distribution or exhibition. The studios remained in production and distribution, and sold off their domestic theater chains during the 1950s. *United States* v. *Paramount et al.,* or the Paramount Decree, destroyed the studio system by ending block-booking and eliminating the guaranteed distribution and exhibition of studio productions.

As we shall see in chapter eleven, the formation of large media corporations in the 1980s and 1990s has reconstructed the old studio system, but now on a larger scale by including film, television and music along with new delivery systems like cable and video. Distributors are once again able to guarantee exhibition for their films through theater chains, cable channels or video stores owned by the parent company. Also, the Justice Department has relaxed its regulation of film distribution, and while independent exhibitors still bid for individuals titles, some companies have reinstated wholesale practices like leasing their entire summer output to an exhibitor.

Even though distribution has come full circle in many ways, the end of the studio system put in motion a number of changes in the 1950s that greatly affected the role of film in American life. Hollywood had to restructure its production and delivery system. Each film now had to be financed and marketed individually, theater by theater, irrespective of other films. Ticket prices rose as independent exhibitors had to bid for quality films. The price increase kept lower-income groups out of the theaters—the very audience Hollywood considered its reliable support base. Increased ticket prices also meant that studios could see greater profits from less films, and since a guaranteed market no longer existed, they reduced their output and started financing independent productions. The number of releases by the major studios dropped from 388 in 1939 to 252 in 1946 to a low of 142 in 1963.

As they scrambled for movies to show, some theater owners discovered there was a sizeable audience, especially among college and university students interested in the more sophisticated and realistic foreign productions. Prior to the *Paramount* decision, the major studios' control over exhibition and the restrictions of the Production Code effectively kept both independent and foreign films out of the U.S. market. Now, however, enterprising distributors began importing films for exhibition in the United States, including European "art" films like Federico Fellini's *La Strada* and Ingmar Bergman's *The Seventh Seal.*

Foreign cinemas produced their share of mediocre genre and exploitation movies, and not all imports were "art" films. But those that were introduced both American filmmakers and audiences to new thematic and stylistic possibilities for the cinema. These European productions "offered a striking alternative to Hollywood's slick products by revealing slices of life and dramatic elements that American films, following the strictures of the Production Code, had failed to develop," film industry analyst Thomas Guback explains. "Imported films, moreover, were often made more on an artisan and less on a factory basis, and consequently seemed to present more personalized statements than the sanitized and anonymous Hollywood product."[10] Also, many foreign films were more sexually explicit, revealing a markedly different attitude toward sex than those regulated by the Production Code. Exhibitors found that their notoriety alone could make them very profitable. *And God Created Woman,* which showed Brigitte Bardot in the nude, made as much money in the United States in 1957 as all the other French imports combined.

Foreign productions, however, were not regulated by the PCA, and were shown in the U.S. market even though they did not have a seal of approval. The matter came before the courts when the state of New York tried to prevent the exhibition of an award-winning Italian film, *The Miracle.* In *Burstyn Inc.* v. *Wilson* (1952) the Supreme Court reversed its decision on the free-speech status of movies, ruling unanimously that motion pictures were "a significant medium for communication of ideas. They may affect public attitudes and behavior in a variety of ways, ranging from direct espousal of a political or social doctrine to the subtle shaping of thought which characterizes all artistic expression." Motion pictures, the court now declared, served the same functions as other arts and communication media like newspapers and magazines. The Court's decision undercut censorship codes and brought entertainment forms under the protection of the First Amendment.

The Court's verdict did not occur in isolation. The power of Hollywood films to shape perceptions and attitudes about the war increased awareness of its potential as a communication medium, and especially as a propaganda tool. The director of the Office of War Information (OWI) wrote in 1943, "The easiest way to inject a propaganda idea into most people's minds is to let it go in through the medium of an entertainment picture when they do not realize that they are being propagandized."[11]

Perhaps to defend the industry against government interference after the war, MPAA president Eric Johnston explained the cinema's contribution to society as a "stimulus" to real "culture." He explained that movies were important, not for their exploration of the filmic medium or artistic purposes, but because those based on classic books and plays or those including classical music increased demand for the original texts by Shakespeare or Dickens, or for recordings of Chopin and Rachmaninoff. "The motion picture," he wrote, "could lack every one of the characteristics which distinguish it as a distinct and unique art unto itself and still rank as a powerful instrument of culture because of its ability to disseminate the knowledge upon which culture is based."[12] In other words, movies were to be valued as a vehicle for the dissemination of "culture," by which he meant "a conversance with, and a taste in, fine arts, the humanities, and the broad aspects of science." The influence of Matthew Arnold is clear as Johnston employed common cultural conceptions. "Culture, so defined, implies that education must have preceded it and then kept pace with it. Culture is not inborn; it is not instinctive. Knowledge is a prerequisite to appreciation," Johnston wrote. This elitist definition of culture excluded movies even though it was acknowledged that film exhibited specific properties making it a peculiar art distinct from literature and drama. Further, as was clear from Hollywood's contribution to the war effort, movies were capable of serving the functions of art, and potentially powerful weapons of propaganda.

Of course, the film industry was content to have its product considered harmless entertainment in order to maintain a large national audience and avoid outside censorship. After Hollywood's unequivocal role in the war effort, however, it was difficult to maintain this posture. One writer in *The Christian Century* rebuked the film industry for failing to instruct the American people about their responsibilities in the atomic age. "On account of its obsession with entertainment for profit, the motion picture industry is drugging the national consciousness into slumber at a time when it should be helping to prod the nation into an intense realization of our responsibility for the right use of atomic energy," the writer concluded, indicating a shift in public perception.[13] Another Protestant minister wrote that a child who watches movies "will suffer from an extra and cruel pressure to believe that to be happy it is essential to ride in expensive cars, wear beautiful clothes, be seen at overprivileged resorts, and otherwise live in a dream world where one can get everything through money and glamour." He too charged that movies shirked their social responsibility, because they rarely treated issues like monopoly, segregation, imperialism or the need for international coop-eration, and were doing nothing to stop the spread of totalitarianism. The "tragedy of Hollywood," he wrote, was the "almost complete failure to *at-tempt* to show us what kind of world it is we really live in today."[14]

The assumption that movies were primarily a commercial business was supplanted during the war years by the understanding of film as an important agent of education and social change. This same conviction undergirded the House Un-American Activities Committee (HUAC) investigations of Holly-wood personnel. In the climate of paranoia during the McCarthy era, movies were not treated as harmless entertainment but as an important mass medium that could affect the values, beliefs and political attitudes of American society. HUAC recognized the potential of movies as political propaganda, and the committee's allegations set the stage for the Supreme Court ruling about the free speech status of film.

The Court's free-speech ruling started a domino effect on subsequent de-cisions regarding motion pictures. Their impact on the role and possibilities for film cannot be underestimated. In a series of cases beginning in 1957, the Court judged that obscenity and the representation of sexuality were not the same thing and that "material dealing with sex in a manner that advocates ideas . . . or has literary or scientific or artistic value or any other forms of social importance may not be branded as obscenity and denied constitutional protection." This extended constitutional protection to an array of topics, including subject matter previously considered obscene. Ensuing court deci-sions continued to undermine the Production Code and limit the power of censorship groups; state boards collapsed during the 1960s as a trend toward a ratings system emerged.[15]

Trouble with the Production Code
Through World War II the film industry profited greatly by its adherence to

the Code. It served as a successful means to fend off government censorship and to generate regular industry profits. Its restrictions, designed to eliminate blatant sexuality and obscenity, ensured that motion pictures would be acceptable to the widest possible audience. Under these circumstances, however, the artistic development of film was wed to the threat of external censorship and healthy box-office returns, a system of prior restraint that was detrimental to the development of American film.

Regardless, the Production Code remained in force for MPAA productions after the *Paramount* decision; member studios continued to distribute only those movies that received a seal of approval. Despite the new legal freedoms the movies were winning in the courts, and shifting attitudes in their audience, Hollywood producers remained cautious and reluctant to change. When *The Miracle* was shown at the Paris Theatre in New York in 1950, the exhibitor received bomb threats, and the archbishop of New York called for a Catholic boycott of the film. Cries of religious sacrilege from some two hundred protesters were mixed now with anticommunist rhetoric. As long as the threat of government censorship and massive boycotts by the Legion of Decency existed, the Production Code remained a reliable shield. American filmmakers tolerated the Code, even though they realized it was embarrassingly outdated, especially in light of the Supreme Court's rulings and the possibilities demonstrated by foreign cinemas.

The relative success of foreign imports, however, demonstrated that there was a large enough audience to support American productions that were similar in theme, style and sophistication. As it became clear that audiences were interested in movies with controversial themes forbidden by the Code, some filmmakers began challenging the Code's restrictions. United Artists (which was an on-and-off member of the MPAA) released two films without a seal of approval. Otto Preminger's lighthearted sex comedy *The Moon Is Blue* (which used the forbidden words *virgin, seduce* and *pregnant*) topped three million dollars in earnings against production costs of $450,000. *The Man with the Golden Arm,* a film about heroin addiction, was also refused a seal, but MPAA representatives conceded that it should have been approved—a sentiment confirmed when the Legion of Decency did not condemn the movie.

These films (among others) forced changes in the Production Code Administration. A new review board was formed that now included representatives from the major film studios as well as independent producers and exhibitors.

The Code itself was revised in the late 1950s and early 1960s to permit representation of previously prohibited subjects like drug addiction, kidnapping, prostitution, abortion, homosexual and lesbian themes, and miscegenation. These revisions were intended to keep the Code relevant, but as one writer observes, even though "the new Code reflected the increasing sophistication in the tastes and sensibilities of the movie theater audience, it still fell far short of allowing artistic expression of the full range of human experience."[16] The new environment in which movies now existed in the fifties and sixties worked against the PCA's regulation of movie content and the Legion of Decency's boycotting tactics. Both were increasingly seen as a violation of the principle of free speech.

When the award-winning Italian film *The Bicycle Thief* was refused a seal of approval in 1950, *New York Times* film critic Bosley Crowther commented on the inconsistencies with which the Code was applied. He concluded, "One cannot help but wonder uneasily whether the code has not been used to support some parochial resentment toward aliens and adult artistry."[17] The religious rancor and cultural strife that marked the inception of the Code now seemed outmoded and senseless. Social and moral attitudes were changing; leisure and amusement were no longer threatening to values associated with work and productivity. The building of a national culture during the 1930s and 1940s had diminished ethnic discord. New battlefronts had been established; communism was a much more imminent threat now than religious apostasy.

The Supreme Court recast the discourse about prior restraint of movies. In 1961 the Court upheld the constitutionality of prior censorship but limited the scope of its ruling to ensure that it allowed "no unreasonable strictures on individual liberty." Again, Crowther wrote that "it is hard to grasp the reasoning of the court that motion pictures should be liable to pre-released censoring and other media of communication should not. . . . The effect is to continue the ancient stigma of motion pictures as a second-class, subordinate art."[18]

Many Hollywood movies produced during this time were based on critically acclaimed novels or Broadway plays that already had a level of financial success. Despite the artistic stature of these works, the PCA still demanded significant changes in the film versions. A statement by Elia Kazan, who directed the film version of Tennessee Williams's *A Streetcar Named Desire*, describes the struggle over art and business, audience and morality that existed during the production of a film.

> Warners just wanted a seal. They didn't give a damn about the beauty or artistic value of the picture. To them it was just a piece of entertainment. It was business, not art. They wanted to get the entire family to see the picture. They didn't want anything in the picture that might keep *anyone* away. At the same time they wanted it to be dirty enough to pull people in.[19]

The long-held justification for prior restraint was that movies reached a larger and more diverse mass audience than other art forms, and therefore had greater potential for harm. But this was no longer a convincing, let alone legitimate, argument for prior censorship now that movies were protected by the U.S. Constitution.

As Sklar observes, "The tendency in motion-picture production and exhibition had always been to get away with as much risqué and socially disreputable behavior as the vigilance of censors would allow and economic necessity dictated."[20] Historically, when Hollywood has pushed the boundaries of sensationalism, religious groups have been able to find initial common ground in their collective outrage. The unity of the religious community in the early 1930s was a major impetus behind the institution and enforcement of the Production Code. Unanimity about movie regulation did not last long, however, for as we saw earlier, there was much disparity among religious groups over issues regarding entertainment. The Production Code and the Legion's tactics came under increasing criticism from both within and outside the Catholic Church. An editorial in the Catholic publication *Commonweal,* for example, revealed changing attitudes:

> If a government, city or otherwise, can prevent the showing of "undesirable" movies, what is to stop them from moving into the fields of magazines and newspapers, and deciding that certain publications are "undesirable" on political, or even personal, grounds? Obscenity is evil. But for a free society, there is something a whole lot more evil—giving a government the right to silence ideas that are "undesirable" before they even have a chance to reach the public.[21]

The release of Elia Kazan's *Baby Doll* in 1956 proved a pivotal moment. The film is based on a Tennessee Williams play, a tragicomedy about the child bride of a southern cotton miller who is seduced by her husband's revenge-seeking rival. *Time* called it "just possibly the dirtiest American-made motion picture that has ever been legally exhibited" but added the qualification that "there is room for doubt that the carnality of the picture makes it unfit to be seen. The film was clearly intended . . . to arouse disgust; not disgust with the film itself, but with the kind of people and the way of life it describes."[22] Regardless of its artistic merits, when *Baby Doll's* tale of lust and moral decay set in the passing grandeur of the South received PCA approval under the revised Code, the Legion of Decency was stunned. In response, the Legion not only publicly condemned the picture but also placed six-month boycotts on theaters that showed the film. A national controversy ensued, and the Legion was soundly attacked by defenders of the First Amendment. An Episcopal priest said, "Those who do not want the sexual aspect of life included in the portrayal of real-life situations had better burn their Bibles as well as abstain from movies." A member of the American Civil Liberties Union (ACLU) called the Catholic ban "contrary to the spirit of free expression in the First Amendment. It can threaten a theater's existence, and may deny to other groups within the community a chance to see films of their choice."[23]

Friction between Catholics and Protestants had surfaced shortly after the Legion began its work. A 1936 article in *The Christian Century* began, "The guardianship of public morals is a task in which Protestants, Roman Catholics and Jews may properly unite their efforts," but concluded that non-Catholics "must form their own organization, embodying their own ideals, and bear their share of the responsibility for keeping America decent."[24] In a more serious charge, *The Christian Century* accused Catholics of playing into the hands of Hollywood. When the Legion opposed legislation to end block-booking, the *Century* noted that the organization had not condemned a single picture since 1936, even though Protestants continued to complain about the moral quality of Hollywood films. "The Big Eight, apparently, will produce nothing offensive to the Roman Catholic Church, provided the Roman Catholic Church keeps hands off the Big Eight's monopoly and its strangle hold upon the independent exhibitors," the paper reported. "What happens to the whole democratic principle of free enterprise and the right of community choice in the selection of its films seems of no consequence to the legion. But it matters a lot to some of the rest of us."[25] No doubt Catholic leaders realized the studio monopoly was essential to the effectiveness of the PCA and were reluctant to do anything that might change this structure as this could (and did) end PCA, and therefore Catholic influence over the content of movies.

Disagreements between Catholics and Protestants intensified after the war.

Protestant groups increasingly saw the Production Code as ineffective and accused the Catholic Church of wielding too much influence on the PCA and motion picture content. While Catholics protested the showing of *The Miracle,* for example, Protestants staged counterprotests against censorship. A 1960 report by the National Council of Churches attacked the movies for their "pathological preoccupation with sex and violence" and fundamental assumption "that man's end is material advantage, power and pleasure, to be achieved through competing with, manipulating and exploiting his fellow man." But members wanted to avoid the boycotting tactics of the Legion: "We want to draw attention to good film fare, while avoiding the error of certain groups of singling out bad pictures and therefore giving them particular attention."[26] There was still much conflict among different Protestant leaders about the merits or abuses of movies and the appropriate response for the church. But in general, Protestant groups objected to continuation of the Legion's strategies.

In the wake of the studio breakup and the court's decisions, the Legion of Decency reported a decline in the percentage of domestic films receiving its A-1 rating (nothing objectionable for a general audience) and a corresponding increase in those rated B (morally objectionable in part for all). One Catholic writer thought this presented an ominous threat to the nation. "Whatever may be said about B pictures, there can be no doubt that they are a degrading influence on movie audiences generally," he wrote. "They foster un-Christian views of life, and tend to sap the moral stamina of the nation." He called for "greater understanding and devotion to the full ideals of the Legion of Decency."[27] But this belief was not nearly as widespread or as compelling as it had been in the 1920s and 1930s.

As it became clear its power was waning, the Legion reworded its pledge, reflecting a more positive attitude toward approved movies, and revised its ratings system, adding a category allowing more sophisticated viewers to attend mature movies. These had little effect on public attitudes, however. Specific tenets, but also the very presence of the Code as a form of prior censorship, came under increasing attack. When rating films, the Legion said it gave no consideration to "artistic, technical or dramatic values. Only moral content is weighed."[28] That the Legion gave its A-1 rating to shoddy productions, simply because they were morally clean, brought some ridicule. The religion editor of *The New York Times* observed that churches "frequently stood by and witnessed the spectacle of churchly kudos being bestowed upon artistic and religious trash in the form of very bad movies that are dubbed 'religious' merely because they deal with Biblical subjects or sentimentally pseudo-religious themes."[29] This observation, which remains true of religious groups today, reveals the antagonism that exists between elite and moral critiques. The latter are shown here to suffer from a myopic disregard for artistic quality and other factors in particular works, leading to acceptance and even praise for schlock and a disregard (perhaps even blindness) for what is good and excellent. There are many high-quality films, for example, about grace and redemption, such as *Tender Mercies, Places in the Heart, The Fisher King, Babette's Feast* and *Dead Man Walking.*

Despite alterations in the Legion's rating system, some Catholic bishops pondered inconsistences and wondered about its effectiveness: condemned films and boycotts actually promised notoriety and increased public interest in the disputed picture. Protestants complained that the Legion's reviews reflected a Catholic bias, and they objected to their use of boycotts as hindering the exercise of free speech. Also, other pressure groups had concerns that went beyond moral issues. The NAACP and the American Jewish Committee, for example, lobbied for fair racial portrayals, while the American Legion monitored movies for elements of political radicalism. Movies were increasingly being judged not simply on a specific line or scene but on the overall treatment of a subject. This represented a shift in approach from censorship of movies to an evaluation of them as artistic products.

A general course emerged from these debates. Acknowledging the artistic freedom of film, the church sought ways to provide information about specific movies, allowing individuals to decide according to their own conscience whether seeing them would imperil their moral or spiritual well-being. Most religious groups adopted this approach, which represented a dissolution of many of the differences between Catholics and Protestants. Catholics abandoned boycotting and acknowledged that morality was but one factor in evaluating a film; Protestants accepted movie ratings as a decision-making guide for parents. Even some of the more conservative Protestant groups lifted bans and acknowledged that film was a legitimate art form to be used and evaluated as part of faithful Christian living.[30] Civic and religious groups that had previously supported the prior restraint of the Production Code now called for a classification system that would restrict certain films to adult audiences.

A Rating System Established

The nature of the protests against controversial movies showed that Hollywood was unsure about how to proceed with its new role. Filmmakers could explore a greater range of themes that included "adult" subject matter, deemed unsuitable for younger people. But Hollywood continued to make and market movies for a general audience regardless of age, race, sex and education. The new judicial freedom moved the lack of differentiation of motion pictures to the center of the public debate. During the controversy over *Baby Doll,* for example, a writer in *Commonweal* argued, "If Hollywood wants to make adult pictures and to be taken seriously as an artistic medium, movie advertising should not suggest that the industry is simply a highly organized scheme to merchandise French postcards that talk."[31] Hollywood studios wanted to have their proverbial cake and eat it too. They wanted to present "adult" subject matter that people could not see on TV, but still market it to a general audience to maximize profits on each film.

Many social and religious groups were uneasy about the continued accessibility of movies to a general audience regardless of topics that were deemed unsuitable for younger viewers. Furthermore, the lowest common denominator method of filmmaking drew critical fire for making Hollywood productions seem artificial, and even dishonest, especially in comparison to their foreign competitors. "As long as children and adults presumably see the same pictures, writers have to write scripts on two levels: one for the sophisticated and one for the unsophisticated," one scriptwriter said. "Shakespeare did it very neatly. He threw in slapstick to entertain half of his audience, while the other half got the meat."[32] This approach was effective during the studio era, when the enforcers of the Production Code ensured that every film was made acceptable for viewing by a twelve-year-old. But it was no longer workable in the free-speech environment of the postwar era. The challenge for the American film industry was to cultivate the possibilities for film in light of its new artistic freedom, while maintaining its position as a mass medium.

To relieve public criticism and appease the PCA, the studios began applying audience restrictions to some releases. United Artists promoted *Elmer Gantry* (1960) as for "adults only," and Warner Brothers promoted *Who's Afraid of Virginia Woolf?* as "suggested for mature audience." Then in 1968, the Supreme Court ruled in *Ginsberg* v. *New York* and *Interstate Circuit* v. *Dallas* that local and state authorities had the right to protect children from materials that would not be considered obscene for adults. These judgments differentiated standards of obscenity for adults and minors (those under seventeen) and allowed local and state authorities to establish their own classification systems for movies. Fearing a proliferation of capricious rating boards across the country, the MPAA moved quickly to create an industrywide rating system.

The MPAA had previously assisted voluntary groups that reviewed and classified movies, but in 1968 the United States was one of the few Western countries that did not have a national film classification system. Members of the MPAA and related organizations agreed to submit films prior to their commercial release for classification by the "rating board," the Code and Rating Administration (CARA).[33] The intent of the Motion Picture Rating System, which went into effect in November 1968, was to enable the development of a vital and creative cinema by classifying movies according to (im)moral content and suitability for different age groups. The rating system acknowledged the public's changing moral attitude, while also fending off government censorship. It differentiated films but put the burden on the audience to decide which movies were appropriate viewing.[34] In many respects, this represented the direction that church and civic groups saw as the means to secure free speech for film in a democratic society. A rating system alerted the audience to potentially offensive material but left viewers responsible to make their own decisions according to conscience.

The availability of the industry's classification system rendered other efforts minor and largely obsolete. The *Green Sheet* ceased publication in December 1969. The Legion of Decency changed its name to the National Catholic Office for Motion Pictures in 1966 and, along with the National Catholic Office for Radio and Television, was reorganized as the Office for Film and Broadcasting (OFB) in 1972.[35] Tension between the movie industry and concerned religious and civic groups were alleviated, at least temporarily. Movie attendance had dropped significantly; the cinema was not nearly as central to American life as it had been prior to World War II. The more conservative religious groups turned their attention to the television, the new "family" medium that was even more pervasive in that it brought Hollywood programming directly into the home.

After the institution of the ratings system, X-rated titles like *Midnight Cowboy* (1969) and *A Clockwork Orange* (1972), as well as pornographic films like *Deep Throat* (1972), were finding national distribution. Some have argued that since that time the American film industry has simply exploited its freedom to treat mature themes, constantly pushing the boundaries of acceptable portrayals of explicit sex and violence for commercial purposes. There is no question that the artistic liberty granted by the courts has been misused. Is there any system that is not without abuses? But judicial freedom and the replacement of the Production Code with a ratings system were necessary for the American cinema to progress and mature as an art. Under the prior circumstances, it would not have been possible to make films like *The Godfather, Nashville, One Flew over the Cuckoo's Nest, Platoon, Do the Right Thing* and more recently *Schindler's List* and *Unforgiven.*

Postwar Box-Office Decline

As we have seen, even though movies became an established social habit during the studio era with household attendance at around twice a week, the popularity of movies per se never assured regular attendance and steady profits. Surveys show that by the 1940s, people went to the movies regardless of what was showing. They wanted to be entertained, but also perhaps to find refuge from the heat on a hot summer evening. There were many reasons for the towering attendance figures during the war years. Unemployment fell from Depression highs, and many workers were receiving higher wages. People had few recreational possibilities; along with wartime shortages, night-clubs and restaurants closed. In the absence of competition, the movies benefited greatly. The wartime economy demanded longer hours and the workweek reached a high of forty-eight hours, increasing the need for recreation among industrial workers, many of whom were women. Movie theaters were open twenty-four hours to accommodate round-the-clock work shifts. Newsreels shown at theaters were an important source of "visual" news about the war; a war tax on tickets made moviegoing a patriotic act. Immediately after World War II, returning servicemen and the absence of alternate sources of entertainment boosted box-office attendance; two-thirds of the U.S. population went to the movies weekly.

Systematic audience studies in the 1940s gave Hollywood every reason to be optimistic about its prospects in the postwar period. Predictions for an enlarged domestic market were based on population growth, continued reduction in the workweek, wider distribution of national income and increased expenditures on recreation. But other indications, generally ignored by Hollywood, revealed that moviegoing patterns and the film audience were changing. Independent studies revealed that the most frequent moviegoers were among the young and more educated and were from higher socioeconomic groups. People who read books, magazines and newspapers also spent more time listening to the radio and were among the more frequent moviegoers. A startling 84 percent of the respondents in one survey indicated that given a choice between radio and movies, they would part with the later, a portent of the effect television would have on movie attendance.[36]

Instead of long lines at theaters, however, Hollywood was greeted by a devastating box office decline beginning in the immediate postwar years.[37] During the war, weekly box-office figures climbed to eighty-five million, rivaling the years following the introduction of sound. Box-office receipts doubled between 1941 and 1946, soaring from $809 to $1,692 million as weekly attendance reached its peak at ninety million during the years 1946-1948. But then attendance figures plummeted, falling to sixty million in 1950 and forty-six million in 1953. In a decade, the postwar high figure was cut in half at forty-five million paid admissions weekly in 1957. The decline eased up in the late 1950s, but the general trend continued downward to forty million in 1960. By 1962, box-office receipts had sunk to their lowest level at around $900 million, which was just over half of the postwar high. The profits of the major studios slipped from a high of $120 million in 1946 to a 1952 low of $20 million.[38]

The dramatic decline in box-office attendance and shift in moviegoing patterns can be traced to lifestyle changes among middle- and working-class Americans. Large numbers of people whose lives had been disrupted by the war now began to settle down and start families. The workweek dropped to forty hours, and employers began offering paid vacations. The availability of VA and FHA mortgages enabled young couples to purchase houses. Home ownership increased 50 percent between 1940 and 1950, and another 50 percent by 1960; for the first time in history, more Americans owned homes than rented them. Eighty-three percent of the population growth in the United States during the 1950s occurred in suburbs. Accumulated savings and increased earnings fed the postwar spending boom. But while couples were saving money for big-ticket items (cars, improved appliances and home mortgages), there was a general increase in prices due to an inflationary period. This created an economic pinch for families, further tightening discretionary spending.[39]

Movies captured around 25 percent of all the money spent on consumer recreation during the war years. Immediately after the war, that figure began to drop as the range of leisure opportunities expanded and competition from other sources of entertainment heated up. The cinema's share dropped to 12 percent in 1950, 5 percent in 1960 and 3 percent in 1970. The figure for 1990 was 1.3 percent. In comparison, the amount of money spent on radios, television and recordings increased from 6 percent in 1945 to about 19 percent in 1960. The percentage of money spent on video and audio products, computers and musical instruments doubled between 1970 and 1990, from 10 percent to 20 percent of total recreational expenditures.[40]

The peak years in box-office attendance (1946-1948) marked the beginning of the postwar baby boom, which also curtailed leisure expenditures among the prime movie patrons. Some seventy-six million babies were born between 1946 and 1964—over four million each year from 1954 to 1964. As most parents are aware, it is difficult to find the energy, let alone the time and money, to get out of the house during the early childrearing years. The decline in movie attendance parallels the extraordinary birth rate of the postwar baby boom. By January 1953, when a record fifty million people watched Lucy Ricardo have her baby on *I Love Lucy,* weekly movie attendance had been reduced to almost half its 1946 level.[41] As more and more people moved to the suburbs and purchased cars, they left the downtown movie theaters behind. Poor public transportation made it difficult to get into the cities and downtown parking was a problem. At the same time, going out to a movie became more expensive. Now parking and baby-sitting costs had to be added to increasing admission prices.[42] Television provided a "functional alternative"; it was much easier and cheaper to stay at home and watch TV programs or reruns of old movies.

In 1946, when two-thirds of the United States population went to the movies weekly, there were only about ten thousand television sets in use in the United States. The drop in movie attendance was in inverse proportion to the increase in TV households. From 1.5 million in 1948, the number of sets in use leaped to 15 million in 1952 to over 45 million in 1960. Television virtually saturated the U.S. market, with 90 percent of all American homes having at least one set by 1962.[43] Even without the television revolution, suburbanization and the baby boom would have affected moviegoing, but the arrival of television greatly enhanced changes in leisure patterns.

The unprecedented expansion of television sent social shock waves across American life, greatly affecting the leisure time and entertainment habits of the vast majority of Americans. Theaters, restaurants and nightclubs all felt the impact. Libraries experienced a drop in circulation, and some bookstores

Table 8.1. U.S. Television Audience, Summer 1995

In the American home . . .
  98% have television (95.4 million homes)

Of TV households . . .
  99% have color television
  38% have two TV sets
  28% have three or more TV sets
  81% have a VCR
  65% receive basic cable
  31% receive pay cable

Average daily viewing:
  4 hours 28 minutes (women 18 +)
  3 hours 52 minutes (men 18 +)
  2 hours 47 minutes (teens 12-17)
  2 hours 42 minutes (children 2-11)
  6 hours 59 minutes (daily home use)

Source: Nielsen Media Research as published in *Video Business,* September 1, 1995, p. 68. Reprinted with permission from *Video Business.* Copyright 1995 by Chilton Publications. All rights reserved.

reported a decrease in revenues. Jukebox receipts were down, as were radio listening and movie attendance in cities with television broadcasts. In 1951 alone, almost all television cities reported a 20-40 percent drop in movie admissions, accompanied by a wave of movie theater closings.[44]

Television became nothing less than "a passion, a craze, a social event, and a new focus for family life," as one historian put it.[45] As a household activity it altered, and sometimes even replaced, other means of communication in the family. Since television brought entertainment right into the home, programming was clearly aimed at the whole "family," much the same as recordings and radio. Along with quiz shows and soap operas, Milton Berle's *The Texaco Star Theatre* and Ed Sullivan's *Toast of the Town* (later renamed *The Ed Sullivan Show*) reworked the vaudeville variety format for television. With a dose of the visual humor of vaudeville, *I Love Lucy* and *The Honeymooners* established the family/neighbor sitcom. Family sitcoms offered portrayals of the ideal suburban family and lifestyle, showing emerging values, conventions, practices, accepted gender roles, and addressing (however superficially) problems of raising kids in the suburbs. In that sense, television served working- and middle-class families as they adjusted to suburban and corporate life during the 1950s, in much the same way movies aided in the assimilation of immigrant families at the beginning of the century. By the late 1950s, westerns *(Cheyenne, Gunsmoke, The Virginian)*, family sitcoms *(Father Knows Best, Leave It to Beaver, The Adventures of Ozzie and Harriet)* and crime-detective shows *(Dragnet, Highway Patrol, Perry Mason)* made up over 50 percent of prime-time programming.[46] Children's programming was launched with *Howdy Doody; Kukla, Fran and Ollie;* and *Mr. Wizard. Lassie* and *Rin Tin Tin,* while featuring animals and children, also had an appeal for the whole family. Hanna-Barbera's *The Flintstones* launched the animated cartoon series in 1960, followed by *The Jetsons* in 1962.

Television became the "electronic ballpark," continuing the important role of sports in providing leisure enjoyment for a mass audience. By 1963, television had replaced newspapers as the prime source of news for the majority of Americans. Television brought the outside world into the home in an unprecedented way. Nightly TV viewing quickly replaced weekly moviegoing as television became the new family medium in the 1950s. Going out to the movies became an occasional family outing, although it continued to be an important dating activity among the young.

Hollywood Strikes Back

In the meantime, the pending antitrust suit kept film companies out of television broadcasting.[47] By the mid-fifties it was obvious that Hollywood would have to be content as a program supplier. All the major companies released their pre-1948 titles and began producing and selling films and episodic series to television. By 1957, over a hundred television series were either on the air or in production—almost all Hollywood productions. People were still watching movies during the 1960s, but at home on television and not at movie theaters.

Realizing they were in direct competition with television for the same audience, Hollywood's strategy was to offer something different, however extraordinary, expensive or even controversial. This shows the degree to which executives perceived the new family medium as the source of their misfortunes. First they tried to accentuate the difference between the small black-and-white television and the movie screen by gambling on new technologies. After the surprising box-office success of *Bwana Devil* (1952) and *House of Wax* (1953), sixty-nine 3-D features were released between 1953 and 1954; thereafter public interest died, and Hollywood quickly abandoned the trend. Hollywood experimented with several wide-screen formats like

Cinerama, Panavision, Cinemascope and Todd-AO and made a rapid change from black-and-white to color films between 1952 and 1955.[48]

The steady rise of the blockbuster film, however, was the premier trend in mainstream Hollywood. The elimination of block-booking meant that Hollywood studios could no longer occupy screen time with their large numbers of grade-B films that were tied to higher-quality "A" ones. With falling attendance and competition from television, the average film could not be relied upon to recoup its costs, let alone generate a profit. It took extravagant productions to lure the family audience out of their homes and away from their televisions. Since the studio system no longer guaranteed profits, the majors reduced their output, concentrating instead on fewer pictures, but with excessive budgets. As Thomas Schatz notes, this marked "a significant departure from the classical era, when the studios turned out a few 'prestige' pictures each year and relished the occasional runaway box-office hit, but relied primarily on routine A-class features to generate revenues. The exceptional became the rule in postwar Hollywood, as the occasional hit gave way to the calculated blockbuster."[49]

The regular moviegoing audience had shrunk, but a small number of movies attracted larger numbers at the box office than ever before. Previously, only about a hundred films had grossed over five million dollars; in the first eighteen months of Cinemascope over thirty reached that mark, and most of them were wide-screen productions like *The Robe* (1953), *How to Marry a Millionaire* (1953) and *White Christmas* (1954). This success can be attributed in part to the novelty of wide-screen cinema, which allowed theaters to charge higher ticket prices, translating into greater profits for these films.

Even so, the wide-screen spectacles were among the most expensive films of period, when the average film was produced for about one million dollars. The wide-screen format favored lavish and lengthy epics and spectacles that were costly to produce. The most successful ones registered unprecedented box-office returns. *The Robe* (1953), which cost four million dollars, earned over seventeen million, making it the third largest-grossing film in history, behind *The Birth of a Nation* and *Gone with the Wind.* DeMille's remake of his own *The Ten Commandments* (1956) cost thirteen million and earned nearly forty-three million dollars. *Around the World in Eighty Days* (1956) earned twenty-two million dollars against six million in production costs. *Ben-Hur* (1959) was made for fifteen million and captured over thirty-seven million dollars at the box office.

Table 8.2. Sample of Big-Budget Hollywood Films, 1951-1970

	Estimated Negative Cost (in millions)	Domestic Rentals (in millions)
Quo Vadis? (1951)	7	12
The Robe (1953)	4	18
20,000 Leagues Under the Sea (1954)	9	11
Around the World in Eighty Days (1956)	6	22
Ten Commandments (1956)	13	43
Ben-Hur (1959)	15	38
Spartacus (1960)	12	10
El Cid (1961)	8	12
How the West Was Won (1962)	15	21
Lawrence of Arabia (1962)	12	19
Cleopatra (1963)	44	26
My Fair Lady (1964)	10	12
The Sound of Music (1965)	10	80
Dr. Zhivago (1965)	15	47
The Greatest Story Ever Told (1965)	20	7
The Bible (1966)	18	15
Camelot (1967)	15	14
Dr. Doolittle (1967)	20	6
Chitty Chitty Bang Bang (1968)	10	7
Star! (1968)	15	4
Oliver! (1968)	10	17
Paint Your Wagon (1969)	20	15
Hello, Dolly! (1969)	24	15
Darling Lili (1970)	22	3
Molly Maguires (1970)	11	1
Patton (1970)	13	28
Tora! Tora! Tora! (1970)	25	15

Sources: *Variety: 1990—the Year in Review* (Boston: Focal Press, 1991); Susan Sackett, *The "Hollywood Reporter" Book of Box Office Hits* (New York: Billboard Books, 1990); David A. Cook, *A History of Narrative Film*, 2nd ed. (New York: W. W. Norton, 1990).

But there were fewer such hits. Most blockbusters were unable to recover their production costs from theatrical rentals alone (see table 8.2). The most devastating failure was *Cleopatra* (1963), a lavish production that established a new high in both production costs and admission price. The picture garnered tabloid headlines and advance publicity because of the behind-the-scenes romance of stars Elizabeth Taylor and Richard Burton. It took four years to make, and it cost Twentieth Century-Fox over forty million dollars; the film lost almost as much, even though it was the top-grossing picture of the year.[50]

The following year, however, Disney's *Mary Poppins* became a box-office smash, reaping forty-five million dollars. In 1965 *Dr. Zhivago* earned forty-seven million and *The Sound of Music* surpassed *Gone with the Wind* as the industry's all-time highest-grossing film. The stunning success of the Rodgers and Hammerstein musical, which earned over seventy-nine million against ten million dollars in production costs, renewed Hollywood's faith in the big-budget musical and spawned a string of imitations in the following years aimed at the family market. *Camelot* (1967), *Dr. Doolittle* (1967), *Star!* (1968), *Chitty Chitty Bang Bang* (1968), *Oliver!* (1968) and *Hello, Dolly!* (1969) generated respectable box-office grosses, but when measured against their production costs they all failed to produce the "sound of money" the studios had hoped for.

As these titles indicate, mainstream Hollywood pursued the general family audience throughout the 1960s (see table 8.3), even though conservative critics today try to argue the opposite. The following list shows that the production of genre films in the stylistic conventions of the studio era continued, but now in color and a wide-screen format. The major Hollywood studios produced a host of westerns, from *High Noon* (1952) and *Shane* (which finished third at the box office in 1953) to *Bad Day at Black Rock* (1954), *The Searchers* (a hit at drive-ins in 1956), the Cinerama spectacle *How the West Was Won* (1962) and *Butch Cassidy and the Sundance Kid* (clearly aimed at the youth audience in 1969). *Bridge on the River Kwai* (1957), *The Guns of Navarone* (1961), *The Longest Day* (1962) and *The Dirty Dozen* (1967) were among the top-grossing war films. The religious epic began with *David and Bathsheba* in 1951 and lasted until the dismal failures of *The Greatest Story Ever Told* (1965) and *The Bible* (1966). The light comedies of Doris Day and Rock Hudson and those of Dean Martin and Jerry Lewis were consistent box-office attractions. Other comedies included *How to Marry a Millionaire* (1953), *Operation Petticoat* (1959), *It's a Mad Mad Mad Mad World* (1963), *Those Magnificent Men in Their Flying Machines* (1965) and *The Odd Couple* (1968). A host of musicals, aside from those already mentioned, included *Singin' in the Rain* (1952), *White Christmas* (1954), *South Pacific* (1958), *West Side Story* (1961), *My Fair Lady* (1964) and *Paint Your Wagon* (1969).[51] Some of Alfred Hitchcock's finest mystery-suspense films

Table 8.3. Sample of General Audience Movies, 1946-1970

Westerns

My Darling Clementine (1946)
High Noon (1952)
Shane (1953)
Bad Day at Black Rock (1954)
The Searchers (1956)

The Alamo (1960)
The Man Who Shot Liberty Valance (1962)
How the West Was Won (1962)
Butch Cassidy and the Sundance Kid (1969)

Religious Epics

David and Bathsheba (1951)
The Robe (1953)
The Ten Commandments (1956)
Ben-Hur (1956)

Spartacus (1960)
The Greatest Story Ever Told (1965)
The Bible (1966)

Comedies

How to Marry a Millionaire (1953)
The Girl Can't Help It (1956)
Will Success Spoil Rock Hunter? (1957)
Rock-a-Bye Baby (1958)
No Time for Sergeants (1958)

Operation Petticoat (1959)
It's a Mad Mad Mad Mad World (1963)
Those Magnificent Men in Their Flying Machines (1965)
The Odd Couple (1968)

Musicals

Annie Get Your Gun (1950)
An American in Paris (1951)
Showboat (1951)
Singin' in the Rain (1952)
The Bandwagon (1953)
White Christmas (1954)
A Star Is Born (1954)
Seven Brides for Seven Brothers (1954)
Oklahoma! (1955)
The King and I (1956)
Carousel (1956)
The Pajama Game (1957)
Funny Face (1957)
South Pacific (1958)
Damn Yankees (1958)

Porgy and Bess (1959)
West Side Story (1961)
The Music Man (1962)
Gigi (1962)
My Fair Lady (1964)
Mary Poppins (1964)
The Sound of Music (1965)
Camelot (1967)
Dr. Doolittle (1967)
Star! (1968)
Funny Girl (1968)
Chitty Chitty Bang Bang (1968)
Oliver! (1968)
Hello, Dolly! (1969)
Paint Your Wagon (1969)

War Films

Battle Cry (1955)
Bridge on the River Kwai (1957)
The Guns of Navarone (1961)
The Longest Day (1962)

The Dirty Dozen (1967)
The Green Berets (1968)
Patton (1970)
Tora! Tora! Tora! (1970)

Disney Films

Cinderella (1950)	*101 Dalmatians* (1961)
Alice in Wonderland (1951)	*The Absent-Minded Professor* (1961)
Peter Pan (1953)	*In Search of the Castaways* (1962)
20,000 Leagues Under the Sea (1954)	*The Sword in the Stone* (1963)
Lady and the Tramp (1955)	*Mary Poppins* (1964)
Old Yeller (1957)	*That Darn Cat* (1965)
Sleeping Beauty (1959)	*Lt. Robin Crusoe, USN* (1966)
The Shaggy Dog (1959)	*The Jungle Book* (1967)
Swiss Family Robinson (1960)	*The Love Bug* (1969)

---

were *Strangers on a Train* (1951), *Rear Window* (1954), *Vertigo* (1958), *North by Northwest* (1959) and *Psycho* (1960). Disney family films were among the top box-office attractions in their respective years, including *Cinderella* (1950), *Lady and the Tramp* (1955), *Sleeping Beauty* (1959), *The Absent-Minded Professor* (1961), *Mary Poppins* (1964), *The Jungle Book* (1967) and *The Love Bug* (1969).

Though clearly entertainment modeled after the "golden age" and aimed at the general audience, these pictures did not change Hollywood's fortune at the box office. As film historian David A. Cook notes, the primary reason for the dramatic decline of the American film industry was its "obstinate refusal to face a single fact: that the composition of the weekly American film audience was changing as rapidly as the culture itself."[52] Between the mid-1950s and mid-1960s, the moviegoing audience shifted from a predominantly middle-aged, modestly educated, middle- to lower-class group to a younger, better educated, more affluent and predominantly middle-class group. This shift occurred not only in America but all over the world. Hollywood's old audience was content to stay at home watching television and going out to the movie theater occasionally for some spectacular entertainment. The regular moviegoing public was now younger and smaller than the pre-World War II audience; its values were different, reflected in its openness toward the portrayal of controversial topics in movies.

Conclusion

Beginning in the 1950s was a growing awareness that only vestiges of Hollywood's former constituency remained and that a younger, better-educated and more diverse group of regular moviegoers had replaced it. But the general theory held over from the studio era was that all people had to like all movies. Studios were accustomed to providing entertainment for the whole family, and Hollywood was slow to respond to the demographic changes that were rocking the entire entertainment industry. Sklar writes that Hollywood moguls continued to think of the better educated part of their audience as highbrow antagonists and were not interested in making pictures for them.[53] Instead, the major companies continued to act as if their golden age audience could be lured back to the theaters with just the right motion picture. Regardless of the effect the European art cinema was having on film style and audience expectations, American companies continued to make movies for everyone, based on the assumption that the mind of the average moviegoer was that of a twelve-year-old. The old Hollywood formula for a profitable picture was no longer working, but Hollywood remained reluctant to produce films for specialized audiences.

By the mid-sixties, the studios were in dire straits. A 1966 report indicated that nearly 90 percent of Hollywood movies failed to recoup their costs in theatrical exhibition.[54] Skyrocketing production costs were cited as the most significant factor. According to one study, by the end of the 1960s the production expenses of American film companies were double the potential market return.[55] The seven major studios reportedly lost $500 million between 1969 to 1972.[56]

This led to the conclusion, however temporary, that there was no correlation between a film's production costs and its earnings. By cutting their investment in production, it was reasoned, studios could reduce the risk of investment. The surprising success of low-budget youth-culture films like *Easy Rider* (1969) seemed to verify this and for a brief time led film executives to believe they could make inexpensive movies that would score in the huge baby boom market. Eventually the blockbuster syndrome and European film styles would be synthesized into a strategic effort to make movies for the youth audience.

The decades after World War II were a time of crisis for Hollywood. It was a period of identity re-formation that centered on the new roles for film that were being forged by the profound changes taking place—the breakup of the studio monopoly, the constitutional protection of movies as free speech, the passing of the Production Code and institution of the MPAA ratings system— as well as changes in American life that affected the attitudes and leisure patterns of the moviegoing audience. The "new Hollywood" that emerged and eventually flourished in this changing social and media environment is the concern of chapter ten.

A key factor in the shift in Hollywood and the entertainment industry at large was the postwar baby boom generation. The unprecedented size and prosperity of the white sector of this group coincided with the emergence of a leisure-oriented youth culture located in suburbia. For the first time in American history, the majority of teens from all classes and racial groups were attending high schools, forming an identifiable social group and youth sub-culture based on leisure, consumption, cars, dating and entertainment. Before we consider the effect this had on Hollywood, however, it is worthwhile to examine the recording industry, for the cultural and religious forces discussed throughout this book exerted a great influence on the American music scene. And beginning in the postwar period, the tastes and preferences of youth dominated popular music.

9

. . . . .

From Bach
to Rock
to MTV

During the storm over rock music in the 1950s, a writer in *The New York Times Magazine* related an anecdote about an Englishman who, while watching Americans dancing the foxtrot and the shimmy in the 1910s, asked a friend, "I say, old boy, they get married afterwards, don't they?"[1] As this story suggests, new musical styles and dances have always created some controversy; ragtime, jazz and swing all drew sharp criticism along with accompanying dance crazes like the grizzly bear and jitterbug. Young people's fascination with new kinds of entertainment is equaled by parental suspicion of it; nineteenth-century women's novels and the dance crazes at the turn of the century, movies and jazz in the 1920s, rock'n'roll beginning in the 1950s, and later MTV and video games.

Audience demographics have played a key role in American entertainment, as we have seen in the theater, vaudeville and the movies. Even though young people have always been major participants, radio, movies and the recording industry remained family-oriented until after World War II, when dramatic changes in American life resulted in a profound shift in the audience for radio, records and movies. The culture and preoccupations of young people re-placed the tastes and values of the eroding audience of middle-class adults in mainstream entertainment. Though not an entirely new development, the magnitude of this transformation based on marketing demographics was un-precedented, and redirected the artistic roles and functions of contemporary popular art for the youth audience.

The burgeoning postwar youth culture became the locus of popular culture and entertainment, not only in America but in other industrialized countries around the world. The immediate reaction of middle-class adults was to denounce the youth culture as a delinquent subculture, a manifestation of "working-class sensuality, urban gangs, juvenile delinquency, and black cul-ture," as historian James B. Gilbert writes. But by the 1960s, critics recognized that the youth culture had become "a major force affecting not just youth, but all of American culture and much of the popular culture of the world."[2] The under-thirty generation continues to represent the largest percentage of the global audience for entertainment.

Beginning in the late nineteenth century, the pattern of high culture insti-tutions was to differentiate "serious," or what we commonly refer to as "clas-sical," music from popular music in terms of both musical elements and performance setting. Live orchestral performances became the exclusive do-main of the upper classes, even though radio networks continued to offer classical music shows primarily as a public service. Still, popular music styles were what audiences wanted most, and radio and record companies not only allocated the largest proportion of their resources to a variety of popular styles but also were engaged in intense competition for a share of the changing market.

As high culture became distanced from the lives of most people, the new electronic-based entertainment forms with distinctly contemporary features were appropriated as living and vital forms of art, especially by younger generations. In a history of modern art and culture, H. R. Rookmaaker begins with the high art tradition but then identifies blues and jazz, gospel, rock and folk music as important contemporary art representing a "new culture" strug-gling with the issues of twentieth-century life. "Beat groups, protest singers, folk singers, these are the people forming the new art still in the making," he wrote. "Their protest is in their music itself as well as in the words, for anyone who thinks that this is all cheap and no more than entertainment has never used his ears."[3]

Roll Over, Beethoven

The trend toward the divorce of classical and popular music in the United States was another manifestation of the disjunction between high and low culture. Until the late nineteenth century, business entrepreneurs published songs and promoted concerts that included a mixture of religious, classical and popular songs. By the turn of the century, however, classical and popular music were encountered far less frequently in the same settings as institutions of high culture were established.

Attempts to organize permanent professional orchestras were made as early as 1840, but they were unsuccessful. After the Civil War, however, the growth and concentration of the population in urban centers was accompanied by the postwar boom in railroads, textiles, mining, banking, and communication, which greatly increased the wealth of those families invested in these industrial ventures. The number of millionaires in Boston, for example, jumped from a handful in 1840 to four hundred by 1890.[4] The upper classes could now afford to support their own orchestra.

Between 1870 and 1900, nonprofit corporations were established throughout the United States that isolated high culture and differentiated it from popular culture. For example, in a study of Boston's cultural elite, the Brahmins, Paul DiMaggio shows how the Boston Symphony Orchestra was founded in the late nineteenth century as a permanent orchestra devoted to classical music. In the years that followed, "the programs became more highly classified, the boundaries between popular and high-art music and between artist and audience were more firmly drawn," he explains, developments that "sealed the Orchestra off from the community as a whole and ensured that it would become more fully a part of the culture of the elite and of middle-class aspirants to elite status."[5]

To achieve the exclusivity they desired as a dominant social group, the Brahmins created a strong classification system defining high culture as a "sacred" culture, removed from contact with profane or popular culture and purged as much as possible from commercial elements. This ensured the purity of high art and allowed the elite to monopolize it as their own while also legitimizing their hegemony over those they dominated. The concert experience was framed as a sacred ritual, and the distance between artist and audience was strengthened by avoiding the work of living artists, darkening the concert hall during performances and developing a proper concert etiquette. Some of these features obviously characterize the cinematic experience, enhancing the élan of larger-than-life stars on the screen. But contemporary rock artists have appropriated these same elements in addition to elaborate theatrical stage performances that give today's concerts the appearance of a kind of religious ritual for youth. And in a complete reversal, so have some Protestant evangelical churches.

A prototype of the separation of classical and popular music in America can be found in Europe in the late eighteenth century. Previously, while levels of appreciation may have varied, the different kinds of music—church, opera, symphony, chamber, dance and many others—were enjoyed by the upper and middle classes, and there was much interaction between the "serious" music tradition, the European tradition of popular music best represented by the waltz, and folk music. "Highbrow and lowbrow lived in the same world; quite often they were the same person," musicologist Peter Van Der Merwe notes.[6] Musical "stars" like Haydn, Mozart and Beethoven wrote both serious and popular compositions. At one point in his career, Mozart was criticized for composing music that was too difficult for the average listener. In England, John Gay's *The Beggar's Opera* (1728) drew both from the serious music of the day and from popular English ballads.

As musical life was gradually democratized in the late eighteenth and early nineteenth centuries, exclusive performances in the private aristocratic salons of Vienna gave way to greater participation of the upper-middle and middle classes and an increase in public concerts. Aristocrats were no longer the exclusive music patrons; the musical means of social distinction eroded as participation was opened in principle to anyone who could afford it. Discernment of "good taste" on the part of the aristocracy, however, increasingly emphasized the "greatness" of a few master composers who were sponsored by wealthy patrons. One sociologist has proposed that the adoption of this "serious-music ideology" was a means of social preservation for the imperiled cultural elite.

To praise Beethoven . . . was simultaneously, albeit implicitly, to praise his patrons who . . . were primarily aristocratic. Similarly, to praise the symphonic and chamber works of Mozart—many of which were deemed . . . too complex to be really "pleasing"—was to praise the concert hosts who programmed them, again Vienna's old aristocrats. Thus, through the pursuit of the "greatest" of composers (whose status was dependent on recognition by aristocratic, powerful patrons), Vienna's social aristocrats could themselves be identified as aristocrats of taste.[7]

Regardless of how conscious the Viennese elite were about reconstituting their cultural authority, the idea of the cultural supremacy of great composers of serious music, first articulated in Vienna, subsequently became the basis for other aristocratic and upper-middle-class groups "who elaborated and revised it as a vehicle for constituting a new elite."[8]

In the mirror of the upper class, composers began to see a reflection of themselves as superior human beings. "The nineteenth century made music into a kind of refined, cultural, almost pseudo-religious revelation of humanism, composed by the great heroes and prophets of mankind," Rookmaaker writes. "Everyday music became vulgar and coarse, low and without truly human qualities—with the exception of the waltzes of Strauss and other kinds of simple classical music for the uneducated."[9] The divorce between classical and popular music during the nineteenth century was advanced by composers who now employed certain elements (melodies, harmonies or rhythms) that became popular when they were writing for the general public, but avoided these when writing serious music in favor of more esoteric and ostentatious elements that were unmistakably nonpopular.

That the segregation of high and popular culture emerged as social distinctions were diminishing in America reveals how much the acceptance of these categories had to do with maintaining the status of the upper class and its exclusive control over the traditional means of cultural authority. DiMaggio's case study of Boston illustrates by extension how the American cultural elite, despite tensions between monopolization and hegemony, exclusivity and legitimation, institutionalized a vision of art that made high culture increasingly less accessible to the majority of people. "Serious" music increasingly became the "classical" music of the past; however, as it became the exclusive province of the elite, high-art music declined through its failure to maintain contact and communicate effectively with other groups in society.

The guardians of traditional culture regarded contemporary works, if not always as inferior to achievements of the past, then as expressions of modern life that conflicted with traditional values or moral and spiritual ideals. Indigenous African-American jazz is a good illustration. Jazz began as a folk music in the South in the late nineteenth century. By the 1930s, it not only had become a tremendously popular and influential style but also warranted serious analysis. Jazz was not only danced to and imitated by other musicians but also studied and collected, even though it was severely criticized by some as barbaric and uncivilized, and promoting sexual promiscuity.[10]

While concert venues segregated the music audience, however, records and radio broadcasts exposed a greater number of people than ever before to a wide diversity of music, from opera and concert music to brass bands and pop vocalists. Opera singer Enrico Caruso's "Vesti la Guibba," minstrel singer Alma Gluck's "Carry Me Back to Old Virginny" and Al Jolson's ragtime songs were all among the first million-selling records.

Companies produced opera and concert music recordings as early as 1903. These early recordings, and later radio broadcasts, continued to make classical music and opera available to everyone. The major record companies (Columbia, RCA Victor and Decca) all launched a line of classical recordings in the late 1930s. *The RCA Victor Hour,* which premiered in 1925, had its own staff orchestra and regularly featured some of the most celebrated concert and operatic artists of the time. The New York Philharmonic Sunday-afternoon concert was a staple in CBS programming in the 1930s; the NBC Symphony Orchestra was led by renowned conductor Arturo Toscanini from 1937 to 1954. According to one source, however, CBS aired the New York Philharmonic weekly as a public service "to win over the custodians of public taste and appease the Federal Communications Commission," and also to expose "the classical-music lover, hence prospective record buyer, to more music than he had ever heard before."[11]

Likewise, NBC created its orchestra primarily for commercial considerations and over the protests of commercial sponsors that "symphonic music has no place in a mass medium."[12] Rather than compete with CBS on Sunday afternoons, NBC aired its orchestral program at 10:00 EST on Saturday evenings, past the bedtime of children and in direct competition with live orchestral performances across the country. Saturday night was "America's night out." The better-educated and wealthy citizens who represented the primary market for classical music preferred the live orchestral sound over the poor-quality AM transmission and the social status associated with attending the symphony. The middle and lower classes went out to the movies on Saturday night, leaving the elderly and those with less disposable income at home listening to the radio—not the kind of consumer group that attracts advertisers. Although NBC appeared to be serving the public interest, the symphony filled vacant airtime during an unattractive slot for commercial sponsors, and besides, a long symphonic program left little room for commercial interruptions. NBC lost little in terms of potential advertising revenues. The program did, however, generate record sales for parent company RCA and averted congressional investigations of the content of commercial radio broadcasts.

An estimated ten million families listened to opera and symphonic music each weekend in 1938-1939. But the bestselling record was "The Beer Barrel Polka," and it was the commercial pop of Tin Pan Alley that consumed most of the industry's resources and reached the large Anglo-American audience through radio, recordings and movies. Radio programmers were committed to the bottom line and not the diffusion of cultural standards. It was the most lucrative markets that largely determined the content of commercial broadcasts and the direction of the industry. Consequently, as musical styles that were popular with postwar youth began breaking industry records, companies drastically reduced their output and programming of classical music.[13]

From Parlor Pianos to Phonographs and Radios

Prior to the advent of the phonograph and radio, the American popular music industry was based on the manufacture and sale of sheet music for popular songs with piano accompaniment. The wholesale value of printed music more than tripled from 1890 to 1909, when over twenty-five thousand songs were registered for copyright and piano sales reached a new high. Sales figures vary greatly, but according to one source, around 200 million copies of sheet music were sold annually during the 1910s, with songs like "Down by the Old Mill Stream," "Let Me Call You Sweetheart," "Over There" and "Till We Meet Again" each selling in the millions; Charles K. Harris's "After the Ball" is believed to have sold five million copies worldwide.[14]

The music publishing houses acquired the collective label "Tin Pan Alley," a reference to the strip in New York City where the companies were located. Tin Pan Alley provided songs for vaudeville, the musical revues, the Broadway theater and later movies, which were important avenues for exposure for new songs. But the greatest single market for sheet music sales was middle-class families that made an evening's entertainment out of singing songs around the parlor piano. For this reason the music was kept simple, and the lyrics could not offend Victorian sensibilities. David Ewen's description of Tin Pan Alley ballads resembles the Hays formula of "compensating values" for movies. These songs "reflected the era by sentimentalizing over home, virtue, parental and filial devotion, while lamenting over those who followed a life of sin or sold themselves for gold," Ewen writes. "In all these songs, virtue was ever its own reward, and vice always met its just punishment." Typical of melodramatic forms, a plethora of topics endured between vice and virtue:

"the constancy of fickleness of lovers; the pathos of misunderstandings and separations; the pathetic plight of abandoned wives or children; the tragedy of death."[15]

With the advent of the phonograph in the late nineteenth century, however, people spent less time playing music than listening to it. Sheet music sales began a rapid decline as dissemination of popular music shifted to radio and recordings. Fueled by the dance crazes, money spent on records exceeded all other leisure expenditures in the early years of silent movies, and in the absence of commercial radio. Record production quadrupled from 27 million discs in 1914 to 107 million in 1919. Retail sales continued to climb, reaching $106 million in 1921. The arrival and rapid growth of radio had an immediate impact on record sales, and the recording industry had to restructure its practices in order to take advantage of the new medium as a vehicle for exposure of music.[16]

In 1920 there was only one radio station with a regular broadcast schedule; two years later over five hundred stations were on the air. Radio sales jumped from $1 million in 1920 to $400 million in 1925 as the medium expanded beyond the affluent middle class. It was estimated in 1933 that there were over sixteen million radios in operation with a listening audience of over sixty million—almost half the nation's population. These figures were nearly double at the end of the decade, with some thirty-five million radios being used by over one hundred million people by 1940. Variety shows, dramas, comedies, action/adventure shows and soap operas filled the airwaves during the 1930s, turning America "into a vast auditorium, into all corners of which a single voice can carry with dramatic ease and clarity," according to a report at the time.[17]

Radio was especially appealing to children, and their constant listening disturbed many parents. Critics condemned it as a corrupting influence on the young, turning their minds toward sex and violence, and they were also concerned that advertisers were exploiting children as consumers. Action/ adventure shows *(Jungle Jim)*, detective series *(The Shadow* and *The Green Hornet)*, and other programs based on comic strips *(Dick Tracy* and *Buck Rogers in the Twenty-fifth Century)* drew critical fire. In 1935, the networks established their own policy code modeled after the film industry's, designed to prohibit certain themes, prescribe dramatic treatment and reduce the level of violence in programming aimed at children. The adventures of heroes were used to teach moral lessons like patriotism and lawful obedience, and as in the movies, good always triumphed over evil.[18]

As anticipated, the popularity of radio drew attention from the phonograph, confirming the record industry's fear that people would stop buying records if they could listen to "music by wireless" at home for free; between 60 and 70 percent of radio broadcast time was occupied with music. Record sales began to decline, and then plummeted after the stock market crash in 1929, bottoming out at $5.5 million in 1933. At the same time, however, record companies began to see the value of radio exposure when they discovered that once a song became a radio hit, people purchased the recording in order to hear their favorite singers when and as often as they liked. Within a month of the radio debut of Irving Berlin's "All Alone" (1925), there were orders for 250,000 records, a million copies of sheet music and 160,000 player-piano rolls. Radio had the potential to create a hit overnight, and the incredible popularity of the swing bands in the following decade demonstrated radio's potential to provide a huge national audience.[19]

The record business also benefited from the introduction of sound in movies. When the Warner brothers were debating the merits of "talking" pictures, Harry reportedly said, "Who the hell wants to hear actors talk? The music—that's the big plus about this."[20] Warner's first "talkie," *The Jazz Singer* (1927), was really a silent film with songs, but it broke the sound barrier in movies; a transformation of the American cinema quickly followed. Advertised as "all talking—all singing—all dancing," MGM's *The Broadway Melody* became the first real Hollywood musical in 1929. When Al Jolson's "Sonny Boy" from *The Singing Fool* unexpectedly sold over a million records, and as many copies of sheet music, it was clear that movies were an important musical showcase. As the demand for music increased, Hollywood studios formed their own record companies and began purchasing music publishing houses. The great talent of Broadway and Tin Pan Alley migrated to Hollywood as film producers ordered songs for musicals and nonmusicals alike. These are the early signs of synergism in the entertainment industry. Radio stations were eager to play the songs of the big screen stars; Hollywood saw radio exposure of movie songs as a means of attracting people to the theaters. All this activity in turn, boosted record sales.[21] For the time being, as they were regulated by the various industry production codes, radio, movies and the recording industry were all doing lucrative business by making their products appealing to the whole family.

The Hills Are Alive, but with the Sound of Rock'n'Roll

As we saw in the previous chapter, the advent of television had a dramatic effect on the entire entertainment business. Most television programming—comedies, variety shows and soap operas—was derived from radio, and therefore vaudeville, formats. Now, however, audiences could both hear and see former radio stars (an appeal that MTV would later have for the young rock music audience beginning in the early 1980s). Many ex-vaudevillians like Jack Benny and George Burns and Gracie Allen, who had earlier made the transition to radio, now signed with television networks. Radio programs were quickly turned into television series, and advertisers abandoned radio for the new national medium. As radio advertising revenues declined, television's skyrocketed from $2.5 million in 1948 to $172 million in 1952.[22] Faced with a serious decline in audience and advertising revenues, radio had no choice but to dramatically change its format, relying now on musical recordings, news and localized personalities.

Television was only partly responsible for the record industry's postwar slump. In 1947, the industry topped its previous annual sales mark at $214 million, but sluggish record sales lingered around $200 million from 1946 to 1954.[23] This was a lackluster period in mainstream commercial pop music; most records, like those of Frankie Lane, Patti Page, Tony Bennett and Perry Como, were still aimed at the middle-class family. The situation was ripe for change.

With television ruling as the premier family entertainment, radio and the record industry turned their attention to specialized audiences in order to survive, and ultimately prosper. The loss of dramatic material on radio left plenty of airtime that could easily be filled with music. There was an explosion of "Negro radio stations" between 1948 and 1952 as many stations turned their attention to the African-American market that was largely untouched by the "white" media.[24] These stations gave white suburban teenagers their first exposure to rhythm and blues (R&B) music. When entrepreneurs like Cleveland disc jockey Alan Freed became aware of the trend, they targeted the white teenage market with radio programs and live concerts featuring black R&B artists.

"If rock'n'roll as art and entertainment was the expression of a new generation," music analyst Charlie Gillett wrote, "as a commercial product it was the dynamite that blew apart the structure of an industry."[25] In the years just prior to the advent of rock, from 1948 to 1955, the four largest record companies (Columbia, RCA, Decca and Capitol) placed over 75 percent of the records on the *Billboard* pop charts, virtually all of them licensed with ASCAP

(American Society of Composers, Authors and Publishers). But the situation began to change as R&B records, or imitations known as "cover" versions, began appearing on the pop charts. The number of Top Ten hits released by independent record labels (and licensed with ASCAP competitor Broadcast Music, Inc. [BMI]) doubled in 1956 as record sales rose by $100 million, then doubled again in 1957. The major record labels saw their share of the most important records on the *Billboard* charts drop drastically, while the independents' share climbed to 76 percent.[26]

With rock songs dominating the trade charts, record sales almost tripled by the end of the decade, jumping from $213 million in 1954 to $277 million the following year, and climbing to $603 million in 1959. Rock historians note, "A realization was dawning that with Elvis Presley leading the way, Sam Cooke, the Everly Brothers, and the rest had become the Sinatras and Glenn Millers of a generation." Artists with family appeal like Doris Day, Tony Bennett, Frankie Laine, Vic Damone, Eddie Fisher, Kay Starr and Tony Martin each managed only one chart hit in 1956. In comparison, Elvis placed an unbelievable seventeen songs on the national charts and had six of RCA Victor's twenty-five top-selling singles.[27]

The record industry establishment panicked. Representing the interests of the major record companies, ASCAP urged a House subcommittee investigation of corrupt broadcasting practices known as the "payola" probes. The release of rock records by the independents glutted the market and increased competition for radio exposure gave disc jockeys—who had become radio's new stars—a new power to influence hit-making. Disc jockeys were charged with accepting bribes from record companies to plug certain records, the assumption being that songs released by independent companies and copyrighted with BMI would be revealed as having become hits fraudulently because of payola. DJs were being blamed for forcing rock music on teenagers; rock was attacked as a tool of godless communism and charged with destroying the morals of youth and encouraging miscegenation.

Radio programmers were caught in a bind. Despite petitions and letters from teenagers requesting that they play more rock music, station managers were aware that many adults opposed the music; thus they initially resisted changing their formats "for the good of the youngsters." One station manager thought rock was "the worst influence to ever hit the music business—a disgrace." Another said, "We do not consider rock and roll music." *Billboard* reported in 1956, however, that a significant number of radio stations were altering their programming to include more rock'n'roll: "When consumers buy rock and roll at the record store and slip coins into juke boxes to hear it in quantity, it is bound to get its due from radio stations."[28] As rock records began placing on industry trade charts, more radio stations were capturing the top ratings in their market by introducing rock music formats, and especially a rotation of the "Top Forty" hit songs.

Frank Sinatra, perhaps representing the opinion of other recording veterans whose careers were seriously threatened by the new music, condemned rock'n'roll as "a rancid-smelling aphrodisiac."[29] But radio and record executives realized that rock music was more than a passing fad and that the future of their industries depended on popular music styles aimed at young people. Tin Pan Alley was invaded by a crop of songwriters whose average age was under twenty-five, and even the most conservative record companies began establishing new labels and signing young artists with the contemporary sound. This led to the full-scale commercialization of rock music as executives sought to remove the unpredictability originally inherent in rock and to bring the phenomenon (or fad, as they considered it) more into line with their own standards and marketing expertise. The idea was to improve, that is, "clean up" rock'n'roll, in order to ease the fears of concerned middle-class parents. By the end of the decade, wholesome white teenagers were shown dancing to rock music on the nationwide television show *American Bandstand*.

Don't Knock the Rock

Rock'n'roll contrasted sharply with the static music style and vapid sentimentalism of Tin Pan Alley. While the lyrics of early rock songs were frequently shallow, the music itself was a hybrid. Rock was a derivative of two other popular music traditions in the rural South that existed alongside the Anglo-American one: the country or "hillbilly" music of rural southern whites (country blues and gospel, honky-tonk and bluegrass) and the African-American tradition (blues, rhythm and blues, jazz and gospel music). These musical styles were kept out of the mainstream market, or co-opted by white musicians, but as companies began exploiting the markets for country, blues and gospel songs, it fostered a "democratization" of American popular music. This crosscultural synthesis largely accounts for rock music's symbolic power, not only in terms of the lyrics but also the force of the music itself. By adopting the vernacular of African-American culture, rock music introduced white teenagers to the language, attitudes and feelings of a minority group struggling against an oppressive establishment. Conversely, the massification of African-American music contributed to a homogenizing of youth culture.

Rock music was a distinguishing feature of being young in postwar America; that adults were aggravated by the music affirmed it as a unique expression of youth culture and young people's dissatisfaction with traditional social norms. The association of rock music with rebellious youth can be attributed less to the harmless content of early rock lyrics than to the inclusion of the music in the movie *The Blackboard Jungle* (1955). As rock historian Carl Belz writes, the "combination of the image of rebellious youth with the raucous and driving sound of rock spelled out an interpretation which was already implicit in the popular imagination: This was rebellious music."[30] MGM publicized the film as a contribution to the nationwide struggle against juvenile delinquency. In the pre-*Star Wars* era, a scripted introduction scrolled up the screen:

We, in the United States, are fortunate to have a school system that is a tribute to our communities and to our faith in American youth. Today we are concerned with juvenile delinquency—its causes—and its effects. We are especially concerned when this delinquency boils over into our schools. The scenes and incidents depicted here are fictional. However, we believe that public awareness is a first step toward a remedy for any problem. It is in this spirit and with this faith that BLACKBOARD JUNGLE was produced.

"One, two, three o'clock, four o'clock rock," Bill Haley (and the Comets) sang as "Rock Around the Clock" played over the opening credits. "Rock Around the Clock" was only a mild hit when it was first released in 1954, but rereleased in conjunction with *Blackboard Jungle,* the single sold an astounding three million copies in just over a year and made history as the first rock'n'roll song to top the *Billboard* pop singles chart.

Young people congregated at movie theaters, and hearing the backbeat of rock music on a radio or phonograph could not compare with the high volume and intensity that a sound system in a movie theater produced. The late Frank Zappa recalled: "I didn't care if Billy Haley was white or sincere. . . . He was playing the Teenage National Anthem and it was so LOUD I was jumping up and down. *Blackboard Jungle* . . . represented a strange sort of 'endorsement' of the teenage cause: 'They made a movie about us, therefore, we exist.' "[31] Rock music solidified the group identity of the postwar baby boom. One writer observes that "at no time in the nation's history had such a unifying cultural identity spread so widely and so deeply among the young of every social class, region, and race."[32]

Rock artist Chuck Berry sang, "Roll over, Beethoven, dig these rhythm and blues," celebrating rock music as something novel and exclusive to youth and also distinct from classical music. More than any other rock star in the 1950s, Elvis Presley personified the meaning of rock'n'roll. He was a "white man with the Negro sound," whose singing and spontaneous dancing made him an icon of rebellious youth, sex, and the mingling of black and white cultures. Critics considered Presley's act "singularly distasteful" and "nauseating stuff," but the hysterical reaction Elvis evoked in teenagers suggested that they were responding to more than just his music, and for deeper social and emotional reasons than the urge to dance to a driving backbeat.

"What is it that makes teen-agers . . . throw off their inhibitions as though at a revivalist meeting?" a writer in *The New York Times Magazine* asked in 1958. "And is this generation of teenagers going to hell?" Adults were mystified by the intense emotional response that rock music awakened in adolescents; *Time* compared rock concerts to "Hitler mass meetings."[33] That parents of postwar teens had earlier swooned and screamed over Frank Sinatra and idolized Bing Crosby, Benny Goodman and Glenn Miller did not diminish criticism of rock music or relieve the fears of some that the music was responsible for the emotional frenzy and sexual promiscuity of teenagers.

In the social setting of the 1950s, promoters of the music argued that they were contributing to the social good by fighting delinquency and breaking down racial barriers. Bill Haley, for example, said, "Rock and roll does help to combat racial discrimination. We have performed to mixed groups all over the country and have watched the kids sit side by side just enjoying the music while being entertained by white and Negro performers sharing the same stage."[34] Haley's observations were accurate, but they only fueled parental fears and suspicions by some white southerners that rock music was part of a miscegenation campaign.

That rock music had strong and distinct roots in African-American culture was not missed by those opposed to it; critics frequently referred to it as savage "jungle" music with a voodoo beat that could summon demons. Asa E. Carter of the White Citizens Councils of Alabama accused the NAACP of corrupting people with "the basic heavy-beat music of Negroes. It appeals to the base in man, brings out animalism and vulgarity." Jazz, bebop and rock'n'roll were all part of a "plot to mongrelize America," he said, and force "Negro culture" on the South. The segregationist leader contended that the NAACP had "infiltrated" southern white teenagers with rock music, and he mounted a campaign to have "immoral" records "purged" from jukeboxes. NAACP president Roy Wilkins, though hardly a fan of rock music, considered Carter's statement absurd. "Some people in the South are blaming us for everything from measles to atomic fallouts," he said.[35]

Condemnation of rock music was not unique, especially as it continued to expose assumptions about racial and cultural distinctiveness and the equation of these with the preservation of Christian values and the moral health of the nation. Newspaper articles in the 1920s protesting jazz, for example, revealed Anglo fears of the sensualism of African-American culture: "Moral disaster is coming to hundreds of American girls through the pathological, nerve irritating, sex-exciting music of jazz orchestras, according to the Illinois Vigilance Association."[36] An article in *Ladies Home Journal* in 1921 claimed that "jazz originally was the accompaniment of the voodoo dancer, stimulating the half-crazed barbarian to the vilest deeds."[37] Even the maudlin and often inane songs of Tin Pan Alley were considered a moral and spiritual threat by at least some religious conservatives who associated spirituality with class and musical taste. "We believe that there are two kinds of music, radically different— the one inspired by the Spirit of God, the other by demons," one writer argued, identifying musical elements themselves with spirituality. "The former is truly melodious and harmonious reminding one of heavenly perfection; the latter, in its crazy rhythm, its sensual swing, and hideous tunes, reflects the spirit of hell." According to this writer, Beethoven, Bach and Mendelssohn were appropriate for Christian participation, but the popular music of the day threatened moral and spiritual purity. Further, only the unbelieving masses, he implied, could possibly find "pleasure in listening to the baby talk of the boop-a-doop girl, the utter inanity of the verse of 'Mairzy Doats,' or the crooning of Sinatra and his ilk."[38]

As this suggests, any spiritual branding of rock music as "of the devil" was easily intertwined with social and cultural factors. Anti-rock crusaders used pulpits and publications to denounce rock music as demon-inspired, devastating to the moral and spiritual development of youth, and part of a communist conspiracy to subvert American values (although former Soviets could make a persuasive counterclaim today).[39]

Renowned record-burners, Dan and Steve Peters, for example, claimed that "rock music appears to be one of Satan's grandest schemes." David Noebel, the president of Summit Ministries, wrote that popular music "is invigorating, vulgarizing and orgiastic. It is destroying our youth's ability to relax, reflect, study, pray, and even meditate, and is in fact preparing them for riot, civil disobedience and revolution." Noebel linked rock music with communist ideology and the 1960s counterculture. Given to hyperbole, he claimed the Beatles were part of a diabolic "assault on Western values," and said that this "undeclared battle to subvert the values of our youth is without parallel, so far as I know, in the history of the world." Apparently, he was unaware that reformers and clergy had said the same about jazz and movies in the first quarter of the century. Regardless, Noebel employed the same apocalyptic theme: "Western civilization, its institutions, its moral values, are under increasing attack. We are tottering on the brink of spiritual suicide and a return to barbarism." The solution was a retreat into high culture. "Any serious Christian young person can see that rock music in particular lures us from true Christian living," he wrote. "It should also be obvious to Christian young people that 'The Hallelujah Chorus' might indeed welcome us into God's presence."[40] Though these critics recognize that religious forces are at work in cultural formation, their understanding of the process is oversimplistic; rock music was an outgrowth of the continual interplay between religious and secular, black and white cultures in America. They perceived the music itself as such a force for evil that Christians could not engage it under any circumstances without falling into the abyss of sin.[41]

When young evangelical Christians began using rock music with religious lyrics as a means for evangelism beginning in the late 1960s, critics condemned it as "spiritual fornication." David Wilkerson charged that Christian rockers "recoiled from the music born of the Spirit," by which he meant psalms, hymns and spiritual songs, and "embraced the music of this world," referring to rock music born of a "satanic seed." Televangelist Jimmy Swaggart also thought Christian rock was "of Satanic origin."[42] The church frowned on Christian rock, and even though evangelical tastes are distinctly middlebrow, congregational debates continue today pitting traditional hymns and "classical" music against contemporary styles. Underlying these discussions are assumptions about what constitutes "sacred" culture and the validity of popular music styles in worship.[43]

Cultural guardians thought of rock music as an attack on sexual decency and the family, fostering a "generation gap" between young and old. There is little doubt that rock contributed to the generational discord in the 1950s and 1960s as a potent means of youthful expression; contemporary popular musical styles like rap and grunge continue to function this way in the youth culture. But rock was wrongly identified as the cause of social problems and used as a scapegoat for deeper cultural anxieties. That rock music was perceived as somehow different from earlier adolescent fads and therefore more dangerous revealed great fears about the lessening of parental control and the new independence of postwar "teenagers." When the Beatles arrived in America in the early 1960s, adolescent fixation with the British rock group created an emotional stir that even surpassed the Elvis phenomenon. A writer in *The New York Times Magazine* likened "Beatlemania" to a "religion of teenage culture" and noted that unlike any previous generation, postwar youth had "a self-identifying culture which they need not transcend in order to find the values that reflect their own aspirations." That young people sought heroes among their own age group, he wrote, was "ultimately the product of an affluent society which, for the first time in history, has made possible a leisure class of professional teenagers."[44]

Before World War II there were no teenagers; the term entered the postwar vocabulary to describe adolescents who inhabited a new age-segregated youth culture that in many ways caricatured consumptive and leisure-oriented aspects of adult life. Adolescence evolved as a transitional period between childhood and adult maturity, while advances in secondary education in the 1920s and the shortage of jobs during the Depression prolonged the period of youth, delaying adulthood. While the youthful rebellion during the 1920s centered among college students on campus removed from parents, the displacement of parental authority began with the high-school years in the postwar period, when for the first time in history the majority of teenagers, including those of the working and lower classes, were attending school.[45]

The time spent in the youth culture coincided with the courtship years. The postwar generation had more access to the media, cars and unchaperoned time on dates than previous generations. Dating was increasingly disassociated from marriage and family, reflecting instead social status, competition and popularity within the youth culture.[46] The social rituals associated with dating and adolescent needs to establish personal identity and understand intimacy were increasingly wed to entertainment. The fact that young people had more spending money and free time than previous generations made them an even more lucrative field for commerical exploitation; their separation from adults also made them more vulnerable as consumers and more susceptible to manipulation by the media.

The sheer size of the baby boom generation alone was enough motivation for the entertainment industry to target the under-thirty crowd, but the postwar generation became such a powerful consumer group that one business entrepreneur referred to the youth market as possibly the final "merchandising frontier." It was estimated that teenagers spent $9.5 million annually during the 1950s. By 1965 that figure had skyrocketed to $12 billion as young people spent $570 million on toiletries, $3.6 billion on women's clothes and $1.5 billion on entertainment each year. Teenagers accounted for 53 percent of all movie tickets and 43 percent of all records purchased. In 1995 it was estimated that the approximately twenty-nine million teenagers in the United States represented between $200 and $300 billion in annual spending, with most of their money spent on clothing, entertainment, personal-care products and food.[47]

Table 9.1. How Teens Spend Their Money

Clothing	36%
Entertainment	23%
Personal care products	16%
Food	16%
School-related supplies	11%
Music	7%
Sports equipment and apparel	7%
Reading material	4%

Source: Packaged Facts as published in *Video Business,* June 16, 1995, p. 52. Reprinted with permission from *Video Business.* Copyright 1995 by Chilton Publications. All rights reserved.

Conspicuous consumption and leisure pursuits have become hallmarks of the youth culture, but the value of entertainment among young people should not be limited to a means of diversion or backdrop for their social activities. Along with a wide-scale isolation from adults, each generation since World War II has experienced rapid change, technological advance and educational innovations. Contemporary entertainment has become an important source of guidance and nurture in a society where other social institutions no longer shape the youth culture as powerfully as they once did. A symbiotic or mutually beneficial relationship emerged between the entertainment industry and the youth culture beginning in the 1950s.[48] The role of entertainment as a "quasi-educational" institution reached an unprecedented scale for post-World War II generations. In turn, the under-thirty group became the financial backbone of the entertainment business as the popular music and film industries struggled to survive amidst the profound changes in the decades after World War II.

Folk, Soul and Rock'n'Roll

Most critics at the time wrongly judged rock music to be nothing more than an adolescent fad. The music had the cultural force of a significant art form that at once captured the spirit of the times for young people and suggested new possibilities for life and society. While faddish elements persisted in popular music, the adolescent alienation and teenage rebellion against middle-class norms in the 1950s expanded into a new vision for democratic ideals in the following decade. "With the proliferation of musical forms and social experimentation and the gradual politicization of leading sectors of popular culture, youth culture proposed a different vision of life," historian James Gilbert explains. "It assumed a moral imperative distinct from what had prevailed during the fifties. It affirmed a self-conscious desire to change society."[49] Rock, and other musical styles like folk and soul, matured as a form of youthful protest, initially against parental authority and sexual taboos, and later against racism, war, materialism and the ethos of American society. These musical styles were all cultivated in the soil of the 1960s—the increasing violence, the civil rights movement, the war in Vietnam and the youth rebellion. As the music evolved, it was amplified by the postwar generation's politics and moral imperative to seek change for the betterment of society. While the American cinema floundered during the 1960s, producing movies for the general audience, contemporary music forms moved to the vanguard of the social revolution. As the music matured during that decade, critics drew comparisons with "serious" contemporary artists and even classical composers, blurring the line between art and entertainment.

That musicians used contemporary music forms to address the deep problems of American society did not diminish the cultural power or audience acceptance of their work as art. A Brown University student in the mid-1960s, for example, explained the significance of folk singer Bob Dylan as an artist for his generation.

We don't give a damn about Moses Herzog's *angst* or Norman Mailer's

216

private fantasies. We're concerned with things like the threat of nuclear war, the civil-rights movement and the spreading blight of dishonesty, conformism and hypocrisy in the United States, especially in Washington, and Bob Dylan is the only American writer dealing with these subjects in a way that makes any sense to us. And, at the same time, as modern poetry, we feel that his songs have a high literary quality. As far as we're concerned, in fact, any one of his songs, like "A Hard Rain's A-Gonna Fall," is more interesting to us, both in a literary and a social sense, than an entire volume of Pulitzer Prize verse by someone like Robert Howell.[50]

Along with other musicians like Joan Baez and the trio Peter, Paul and Mary, Dylan reshaped the nature of American folk music from collective propaganda to an expression of fiercely individualistic discontent and protest against injustices and concern with the plight of the poor and oppressed. Dylan's synthesis of folk and rock music in the mid-1960s heightened popular music's penchant for social criticism by fusing the explicit political and social commentary in the lyrics of folk with the musical style of rock, which was itself identified as a form of protest.

In contrast to traditional Tin Pan Alley fare, popular music had become a "forum for serious messages far removed from the moon-June variety," as a spokesperson for the Presbyterian Church put it.[51] Scores of songs exposed the inequities and hypocrisies of American life, dealing with the problems of youth, sex, alienation, drug experiences, environmental protection, race relations, war, political protest and social change. Contemporary music also became a means for the postwar generation to explore alternative cultural patterns. "This complicated development came in part because of the growing recognition of the legitimacy of the black experience in America and its contributions to culture and politics," Gilbert writes. "Indeed, certain aspects of popular culture (particularly music), because they were identified with black liberation struggles or the antiwar movement, claimed to be the only authentic voice of the American masses."[52]

At the same time that R&B was spawning rock music, Ray Charles was modifying revered black gospel songs to suit a secular R&B style. While many critics considered it an act of religious apostasy, the hybrid he created became a powerful expression of the African-American concept of "soul." The music was ignited by sassy sounds and double entendres that symbolically infused the secular concerns of African-Americans during the civil rights struggle in the 1950s and 1960s with the jubilation and triumph of gospel. Soul also mirrored the sociological reality of the central role the black church played in the civil rights movement.

In contrast to blues songs that communicated the humiliation and loss of dignity and self-worth that African-Americans experienced under the segregationist Jim Crow laws, soul represented a people's discovery of self-pride and identity and was an expression of their hopes and rising expectations for equality of opportunity and life. "Blues songs tend to state the way things are and offer neither hope nor suggestions for improving the situation," Michael Haralambos wrote. "By comparison soul songs advocate the way things should be and are filled with advice for realizing this ideal."[53] As a cultural force advocating self-definition and social change, soul was an important psychological factor in the civil rights movement.

More than any other popular music group, the Beatles played a leading role in defining the vanguard of popular culture in the 1960s. Beyond their unprecedented commercial success and phenomenal popularity, the Beatles created a new situation in popular music. Like Dylan, the Beatles used contemporary music as a vibrant and living art form and means of communication. They explored the world as artists, creating music to reveal their discoveries about ethical and religious issues, social concerns, cultural values and the ultimate questions about life.

The "Fab Four" first captured the serious attention of critics and intellectuals with their cinematic debut in *A Hard Day's Night* (1964), considered a precursor of today's music videos. Director Richard Lester used a *cinéma vérité* style, employing many devices of the European art cinema (flashbacks, jump cuts and narrative displacement), and the film's madcap comedy and social satire drew comparisons with the Marx Brothers. *A Hard Day's Night* resisted high and low categorizing and brought a new level of respectability to youth-oriented films with rock music. *Village Voice* film critic Andrew Sarris called it "the *Citizen Kane* of juke box musicals." Historian Arthur Schlesinger Jr. referred to the film as "the astonishment of the month" and thought the group represented the "timeless adolescent effort to deal with the absurdities of an adult world."[54]

After *A Hard Day's Night,* critics began writing about modal progressions and lyrical metaphors in Lennon and McCartney songs, setting the stage for the release of what became the Beatles' watershed recording, *Sergeant Pepper's Lonely Hearts Club Band* (1967).[55] *Sgt. Pepper* was an innovative album in that as a single entity it integrated an eclectic mixture of musical styles and sounds, from English music hall and rock to Indian raga and classical, into a single concept album. The recording was not just a collection of songs. It was intended to be listened to as a single performance by the "Lonely Hearts Club Band." Thematically, the album covered the major motifs of the decade: drug-induced experiences, religious mysticism, existential despair, generational and social discord, the loneliness and anxieties of youth, the search for meaning. *Sgt. Pepper* summed up the youth cultural revolution at the time and became a symbol of generational solidarity. Rock critic Langdon Winner wrote: "The closest Western Civilization has come to unity since the Congress of Vienna in 1815 was the week the Sgt. Pepper album was released. . . . For a brief while the irreparably fragmented consciousness of the West was unified, at least in the minds of the young."[56]

For a contemporary work in popular music, *Sgt. Pepper* reaped extraordinary critical praise. *The New Yorker* compared the Beatles to Duke Ellington, noting that they both worked "in that special territory where entertainment slips over into art." *Time* writers thought the Beatles "moved on to a higher artistic plateau" with *Sgt. Pepper.* "They are leading an evolution in which the best of current post-rock sounds are becoming something that pop music has never been before: an art form. 'Serious musicians' are listening to them and marking their work as a historic departure in the progress of music—any music." Art song composer Ned Rorem thought the songs on *Sgt. Pepper* were "equal to any song that Schubert ever wrote," Leonard Bernstein likened the Beatles to Schumann, and a musicologist thought the Beatles' contribution to electronic music put them on the vanguard of "classical" contemporary music. *Newsweek*'s Jack Kroll called recent Beatle albums "volumes of aural poetry in the McLuhan age" and drew comparisons with British poet laureates. " 'Sgt. Pepper' is such an organic work . . . that it is like a pop 'Facade,' the suite of poems by Edith Sitwell musicalized by William Walton," he wrote. "Like 'Facade,' 'Sgt. Pepper' is a rollicking, probing language-and-sound vaudeville, which grafts skin from all three brows—high, middle and low—into a pulsating collage about mid-century manners and madness." Kroll praised the ambiguity, sarcasm and self-mockery that penetrated the work, comparing the Beatles' "loss of innocence" theme with that of "more 'serious' new art from the stories of Donald Barthelme to the plays of Harold Pinter." He called "A Day in the Life" the Beatles' " 'Waste Land,' a superb achievement of their brilliant and startlingly effective popular art." *Sgt. Pepper* sold 2.5 million copies in three months and topped the *Billboard* charts for fifteen weeks. The album went on to sell an estimated thirty million units worldwide and remains a musical and cultural milestone of that period.[57]

Writing in the late 1960s, Columbia University professor Albert Goldman observed, "By pushing toward higher levels of imaginative excellence, rock has begun to realize one of the most cherished dreams of mass culture: to cultivate from the vigorous but crude growth of the popular arts a new serious art that would combine the strength of native roots with the beauty flowering from the highest art."[58] The sudden serious critical attention lavished on the Beatles and other popular musicians seemed at times to turn popular music forms into a highbrow art. But as one writer proposed, "Since the exalted arts (to which the novel, about a century ago, was the last genre to be admitted) have all but surrendered the provision of fun and entertainment to the popular arts, criticism must turn to film and song if it is to remind itself that the arts really do not need to be boring."[59] It is better to understand the force of popular music in the 1960s not in terms of the conventions and expectations associated with high and low culture, but as the result of its fulfilling the functions of contemporary art while also being inventive and entertaining.

Still, the creativity in popular music at the end of the 1960s was crowded by market and financial pressures. While popular music has its share of musical inventiveness, lyrical creativity and gifted performers, the industry has also manufactured a host of lifeless imitators. The year of *Sgt. Pepper,* for example, the Monkees, a commercially packaged imitation of the Beatles, had three-million-selling albums and as many singles. Several outstanding artists had hits that year: Cream, the Doors, Aretha Franklin, Jefferson Airplane and Stevie Wonder. But just as many schlock groups like the Cowsills, the Happenings, the Troggs and the Soul Survivors ended up in the Top Forty. Most rock critics would agree that among the popular music of any period, some of it is excellent, some dreadful, and most of it indifferent.

The Advent of MTV and Generation X

The recording industry reached unprecedented heights after the emergence of rock music and other styles oriented to youth. The dissipation of the protest movement in the early 1970s, however, cut popular music adrift from the sociopolitical context it had acquired in the previous decade. The distance between popular music and the audience and cultural milieu that sparked its creativity and provided its original cultural significance continued to increase, even as the music mirrored trends in American culture. Disco, for example, epitomized Christopher Lasch's "culture of narcissism" in the late 1970s. The impersonal forces of commercialism and marketing demographics, however, drove some forms of popular music to more extreme expressions of youthful rebellion. Devoid of its original context, the imagery of adolescent rock seemed starkly hedonistic, valuing sensual pleasure as an ultimate value in the leisure-oriented youth culture of the 1980s and 1990s. Even earlier advocates of rock music now condemned MTV videos for their extreme violent and sexist imagery and unapologetic exploitation of young people for commercial purposes. Regardless, as the postwar generation aged beyond the prime record-buying years, the entertainment industry aimed its products at the next generation in the youth culture.

The steady 6 to 8 percent growth in the early 1960s increased to 17 or 18 percent toward the end of the decade, and in 1967 the record industry topped the billion-dollar mark in annual sales. By the mid-1970s record sales outpaced movie admissions; Americans spent $1.7 billion on movie tickets but $2.2 billion on records and tapes in 1974. Several records generated unprecedented sales: Carole King's *Tapestry* (1971) and Peter Frampton's *Frampton Comes Alive* (1976) each sold over twelve million copies; Fleetwood Mac's *Rumours* (1977) topped twenty million. In the second half of the decade, sales of recorded music in the United States almost doubled.[60] Fueled by the astounding success of the *Saturday Night Fever* and *Grease* soundtracks (both sold over twenty million copies), record company grosses peaked at $4.1 billion in 1978.

The following year, however, revenues dropped 10.2 percent, ending a twenty-five-year growth pattern in the recording industry. Between 1978 and 1982, estimated retail sales showed a four year decline of 13 percent. The best-selling records were no longer moving the quantities they used to. "There's more than a recession going on right now in the record business," an executive at Warners said. "There's a transition to something that we're not sure what it is."[61] There were many reasons for the economic slump. The country was in a recession, and there was increased competition for leisure dollars from cable television, the videocassette market and video games. The proliferation of musical styles during the 1970s—punk, new wave, reggae, jazz-rock, hard rock, soft rock, classic rock, heavy metal, disco, R&B, funk, country, contemporary gospel and Top Forty pop—fragmented the audience along taste lines, which translated into smaller sales for most recordings. After the boom years of *Saturday Night Fever* and *Grease*, one record executive said that aging baby boomers were "more concerned with mortgages and babies than pop music."[62] Both the record and film industries increasingly turned their attention to the post-baby boom youth audience. What the industry needed was a concentrated means of exposure to solidify the tastes of the emerging "Generation X." The president of Virgin Records said, "We were looking for a savior and it came in the form of MTV."[63]

Launched in August 1981, MTV: Music Television sent shock waves throughout the entertainment industry, revolutionizing not only the recording business but the entire media industry, from films and television shows to advertising. The music video channel became the ultimate means of synergism. A video tie-in on MTV was a way to cross-promote films and albums through free exposure to the primary market for movies and records; the music video promotes the movie, which helps sell the album, and vice versa. The MTV audience did not have to leave their living rooms to see the "trailers" for *Flashdance* (1983), *Footloose* (1984), *Purple Rain* (1984), *Top Gun* (1986), *Dirty Dancing* (1987) and a host of other teen-oriented films with rock soundtracks that helped reverse the sagging fortunes of the entertainment business.[64]

The video format, in turn, influenced filmmaking. Scripts were chosen that would appeal to the MTV demographic and edited to leave room for music interludes (like the dance scenes in *Flashdance* or the aerial ones in *Top Gun*). Likewise, videos utilized advertising techniques, and advertising quickly took on the style of music videos. Rock songs have been used as tie-ins to sell everything from cars and fast food to razor blades, running shoes, breakfast cereals and California raisins.

Like most advertising, music videos try to link a product with pleasurable feelings or a desired lifestyle. MTV's target audience is young adolescents, and especially males. The video world of MTV becomes an unmediated extension of male desire as it exploits the preoccupation with courtship and leisure in the youth culture. Music videos display an adolescent fantasy world of passion, energy and high sexual excitement in which men are aggressive pursuers and women the romantic prize. Women are constantly on display for voyeuristic men in videos that take this cultural stereotyping to an extreme, reducing women from multidimensional human beings to the status of nymphomaniacs, sexual toys along the lines of Madonna's "Boy Toy" belt.[65]

MTV is aimed at passive consumers. Its primary if not exclusive purpose, as executives see it, is to maximize its profits as a promotional tool for the entertainment industry. And in that regard the music channel has been very successful. The previously fragmented tastes of the youth culture quickly coalesced around this new entertainment medium. By 1983 MTV surpassed radio, concerts and commercial TV as the prime exposure vehicle for album purchases by twelve- to twenty-five-year-olds.[66]

MTV was successful at breaking a number of new artists (Men At Work, Duran Duran, Madonna), but it was Michael Jackson's *Thriller* LP that confirmed the correlation between MTV exposure and record sales. Jackson was the perfect artist for the new visual medium; his sound was inseparable from the excitement generated by his dancing. When the video for the first single, "Billy Jean," went into rotation on MTV, album sales soared to one million copies in two weeks. Only five days after the MTV premiere of "Thriller," album sales shot up from 200,000 copies a week to 600,000.[67] Seven of the nine songs on the album were released as singles; all hit the Top Ten, with two reaching number one. *Thriller* eventually sold a staggering forty-eight million copies internationally, replacing *Saturday Night Fever* as the largest-selling album of all time. In turn, the Michael Jackson phenomenon boosted the fledgling music channel.[68] The album also marked a turnabout in the recording industry, which reached a new high in sales in 1984 at $4.46 billion, according to RIAA figures. Sales of prerecorded music and music videos topped twelve billion dollars in 1994—a record 20 percent increase over the previous year—marking thirteen consecutive years of positive growth, according to the RIAA. In this regard, the effect of MTV on the music industry was the same as that of rock music in the mid-1950s.

Even though some producers envisioned rock video as an art form itself (the Museum of Modern Art has included videos in its permanent collection), the music video revolution was conceived of as a commercial force. As one Geffen Records executive said, "Rock video isn't the art form. Rock video markets the art form." Videos are advertisements used to sell records. But this reduction of music video to purely commercial purposes makes it too easy for producers to ignore other important functions. "When you ask are we supposed to be moral, are we supposed to be humanistic, are we supposed to titillate . . . we're *supposed* to be none of those things," video producer Ken Walz said. "What we are supposed to do is . . . sell records, concert tickets and artists."[69]

Critics compared MTV with radio, calling the new exposure medium "a marching band for materialism" and "the ultracommercial video arena." Despite its commercial trappings and marketing designs, however, the music video form has become, as one scholar observed, "the most recent manifestation of our society's orientation to visual communication."[70] Music videos drew much of their style from the European art cinema. MTV needed twenty-four hours of programming, but with extensive radio exposure in the U.S. market, most American bands did not make videos. Consequently, the production of promotional rock videos began in Europe, where strict regulations of government-controlled radio stations forced music groups to seek other avenues of exposure. One way around conservative radio was to produce videos to be played at dance clubs or used on television.[71] The initial shortage of videos made MTV happy to feature those by groups from the United Kingdom, Europe and Australia, which in turn gave the new channel an international flavor.

Many of these videos relied on strong visual images and the loose narrative structure characteristic of European art films. These pioneers in the form exerted a strong influence on the emerging style of communication for the new music video medium. MTV relies on mood and image over narrative and substance, as MTV executives are aware. "What we've introduced with MTV is a nonnarrative form," Bob Pittman explained. "As opposed to conventional television, where you rely on plot and continuity, we rely on *mood* and *emotion*. We make you feel a certain way as opposed to you walking away with any particular knowledge."[72] In that regard, it is easy to see the great popularity of MTV as a new entertainment format for the high-tech oriented youth today, who are intimately acquainted with video games, VCRs and computers. These technologies are identified with new modes of communication based not on linear forms like print but on nonlinear forms—visual images that restructure our notions of space and time. Previously, television was based on earlier entertainment forms like vaudeville and radio, but as a visual medium, one scholar asserts, "broadcast TV, approaching its half century, has just developed its only original art form—rock video or MTV."[73]

As such, music videos have been studied as artifacts of postmodern culture. With the erosion of traditional categories and distinctions, postmodernism "self-consciously splices genres, attitudes, styles. It relishes the blurring or juxtaposition of forms (fiction-nonfiction), stances (straight-ironic), moods (violent-comic), cultural levels (high-low)," sociologist Todd Gitlin explains. Reference or allusion to authentic expressions of the past has become in itself the style of postmodernism illustrated by the practices of intertextuality and pastiche.[74] In her music video "Papa Don't Preach," for example, Madonna entertains viewers with sexual and religious imagery that is riddled with ambiguity and contradictions between familial love and incest, maternal responsibility and female independence and choice. "Material Girl" makes direct reference to Marilyn Monroe's "Diamonds Are a Girl's Best Friend" number in *Gentlemen Prefer Blondes*. Likewise, Michael Jackson's "Thriller" video borrowed from the 1950s teen classic *I Was a Teenage Werewolf* and earlier horror films, to the extent of using a Vincent Price voiceover.

That postmodern works use cultural artifacts like movies, commercials and popular icons suggests that images of the past and history itself are inseparable for today's media-oriented generation. Part of the appeal and popularity of new entertainment media has always been their compatibility with contemporary ideas and changing cultural patterns. In that sense, new forms of technology are progressive by nature, even though they may be used to convey traditional ideas and values (something that evangelicals who employ entertainment media and formats do not seem to understand). Music video and the cable channel MTV are only the most recent illustrations of this phenomenon.

Conclusion

From records, movies and radio in the first quarter of the twentieth century to television, video games, virtual reality and the proliferation of cable channels including MTV, novel styles of communication are often first exhibited or achieve their greatest popularity in the form of entertainment. Thomas Edison initially conceived of his "talking machine" invention as a dictating machine, even though the early success of the phonograph was as an entertainment device. Likewise, Edison's assistant William K. L. Dickson envisioned the kinetoscope as an instrument for the democratization of knowledge and had no idea that moving pictures would be used as a form of entertainment or personal artistic expression. When video games first made their appearance in arcades in shopping malls, they were quickly condemned by many as another brick in the road to delinquency. But a decade later, a U.S. Defense Department official speaking on public radio during the Gulf War took pride in the aerial combat success of what he identified as America's first generation of video game pilots.

Over the course of the twentieth century, technological innovations magnified piecemeal the controversy over the pervasiveness of the media by bringing not only entertainment but also more news and information into the home. Vaudeville and the movies, the phonograph and radio, television, and now Sony Walkmans and cable television each intruded in the family circle with greater intensity than the previous medium. That this collusion of technology, demographics and market logic is an inevitable development and has been an entirely positive force remains questionable, for it has certainly had some negative results in its effect on families and the formation of adolescent identity.

MTV is yet another illustration of this trend, as it tapped into the youth market of the 1980 and 1990s by bringing rock music to the "family" medium in an entirely new way. As an amalgam of music and video, radio, movies, new technologies and marketing, MTV is, as one critic called it, "a one-stop entertainment center for teens."[75] Like other entertainment media, MTV plays a role in defining the culture of youth today—a twenty-four-hour CNN in the youth culture, keeping young people informed on the latest trends, fashions, dance steps, language, recording groups, movies and entertainment news.[76] Furthermore, as it is marketed to a very specific demographic group worldwide, MTV fosters the creation of a global youth culture but also fractures culture along generational lines, based on consumer status and exploitation. A CEO of MTV Europe remarked that "an 18-year-old in Denmark has more in common with an 18-year-old in France than either has with elders in their own country."[77]

Young people around the world represent the largest share of the audience for American entertainment today. The film industry, however, was much slower to respond to the demographic changes that were fueling the tremendous growth of radio and the recording industry in the 1950s and 1960s. The reasons for this and the American cinema's journey into the youth culture will be examined in the next chapter.

10

. . . . .

Accent
on Youth

As we saw with rock and other musical styles, the popular arts became the province of youth after World War II. In one sense this contributed to continued criticism of the popular arts as mere amusement. At the same time, however, combined with their new legal status as art, entertainment forms became dynamic expressions of contemporary culture, even though marketing demographics demanded that they be aimed at youth. The movies have always been a primary means of entertainment for the young, and as middle-class families vacated seats at movie theaters after World War II, film studios turned their attention to the postwar baby boom and the themes of the youth culture.

As we saw earlier, this shift did not occur immediately but took place over the course of two decades. Major Hollywood studios were primarily interested in the expensive blockbuster aimed at a general audience, rather than pictures for limited, specialized groups. For example, Hollywood ignored African-Americans, despite the fact that they represented a significant proportion of frequent moviegoers. The Code's prohibition of racial mixing on the screen was partly responsible, but Hollywood clearly missed an opportunity to ameliorate changing racial attitudes after the war.

The Hollywood majors did produce a number of films, however, that had youthful appeal. The "restless youth" films, MGM's *The Blackboard Jungle* and Warner Brothers' *Rebel Without a Cause* (starring James Dean), were both released in 1955, although they were still intended for a general audience. Twentieth Century-Fox gambled on a Cinemascope production, *The Girl Can't Help It,* starring Tom Ewell and Jayne Mansfield and featuring an all-star lineup of fifties rock groups. MGM aimed its sanitized version of the collegiate spring break in Florida, *Where the Boys Are* (1961), at the teenage and young adult crowd. *Splendor in the Grass* (1961), starring Warren Beatty and Natalie Wood, dealt with adolescent sexuality. After the successful debut of Elvis Presley in *Love Me Tender* (1956), Twentieth Century-Fox signed his clean-cut counterpart, Pat Boone, to appear in *Bernadine* the following year. But the market viability of the postwar baby boom went largely unrecognized by the film industry until the late 1960s.

Two important factors played significantly in Hollywood's shift to the production of films for the youth audience. First, small independent film companies formed in the 1950s were enormously successful at producing and marketing low-budget movies specifically for the youth market. Though resembling the films of the studio era, now teenagers and not adults were in the starring roles. Capitalizing on the rock'n'roll explosion, for example, filmmaker Sam Katzman and radio disc jockey Alan Freed produced a series of low-budget movies to showcase rock groups; *Rock Around the Clock* and *Don't Knock the Rock* demonstrated the box-office prowess of the youth audience. American International Pictures (AIP) thrived with pictures aimed at the limited youth audience. AIP proved an important training ground for many talented directors who came into prominence beginning in the early 1970s. They saw no sharp distinctions between film as art and entertainment. The youth-oriented genres and styles pioneered by AIP—beach and surfing films, horror and teen comedies, rock'n'roll and countercultural films—became the topical fare of mainstream Hollywood in the 1970s.

Second, some American filmmakers began assimilating elements of the European art cinema into Hollywood productions during the 1960s. Films by Stanley Kubrick *(Dr. Strangelove, Lolita, 2001: A Space Odyssey)*, Arthur Penn *(Bonnie and Clyde, Alice's Restaurant, Little Big Man)*, Dennis Hopper *(Easy Rider)* and Mike Nichols *(Who's Afraid of Virginia Woolf?, The Graduate)* had great appeal to the postwar baby boomers as they explored alternatives to the vacuity of American middle-class culture. The baby boomer generation was the first to grow up watching television. They had a tacit understanding of cinematic language and a value system that allowed for the presentation of topics formerly considered taboo. The success of *The Graduate* and these other pictures turned Hollywood's attention to the independents and the youth market. Social fragmentation and the disillusionment of youth became topical fare for the majors who saw youth and the issues of the protest movement as box-office salvation. The rift these movies opened among established film critics revealed the changes taking place in the American cinema. Reviewers drew battle lines over *Bonnie and Clyde* (1967) because of the film's unconventional treatment of sex and its graphic violence. *2001: A Space Odyssey* (1968) became a box-office hit despite critical disdain. One critic wrote that *The Graduate* "has taken aim, satirically, at the very establishment that produces most of our movies, mocked the morals and values it has long lived by. It is a final irony that it has thereby gained the large young audience it has been seeking and has been rewarded by a shower of gold."[1]

Young people continued to be a vital market in the decades that followed. As Thomas Doherty has shown, since the 1960s movies aimed at the youth audience "have been an industry staple, if not the dominant production strategy for theatrical movies. Once questionable economically and disreputable aesthetically, they have grown in budget, frequency, and even respectability as teenagers have grown in fortune, numbers and influence."[2] It was estimated that during the 1970s about three-quarters of the regular moviegoing audience was under thirty, with 50 percent between the ages of twelve and twenty.[3] As the baby boomers began passing the thirty-year-old mark, the film industry continued to court the under twenty-five demographic. Beginning with *Star Wars*, the film industry witnessed an unprecedented phenomenon in movie attendance. Teenagers were coming back to see the movie three or four and sometimes as many as twenty or thirty times. The repeated attendance pattern among the new members of the youth culture made up for the losses in the baby boom numbers. The significance of this should not be underestimated. For postwar generations raised on radio, recordings, television and movies, the entertainment media are "a natural and necessary part of life," sociologist Landon Jones writes. "Entertainment was joining, and even replacing, work and education as an expectation of every young person."[4]

As we have seen, the American cinema went through a major transformation in just over two decades after World War II. The Supreme Court undercut censorship codes and brought movies and the other popular media under the protective umbrella of the First Amendment. In effect, these rulings changed the status of the popular arts from regulated commodities to significant media for the communication of ideas and artistic expression. As the courts undermined censorship, the Production Code was altered, but it no longer wielded the power to enforce the nation-building role the cinema played during the 1930s and 1940s. By the late 1960s, a "New Hollywood" emerged from a confluence of factors at work in the postwar cinema, including shifting audience demographics and changing social conditions and cultural values. The unprecedented profits that film studios reaped from productions aimed at the youth audience greatly impacted the direction of Hollywood and the role of film in society.

Passion Pits and Foreign Flicks

During the most severe drop in movie admissions, from 1946 to 1956, over four thousand theaters in the United States were forced to close. They were replaced, however, by an almost equal number of drive-in theaters. There were fewer than five hundred drive-ins or "ozoners" in 1950; the number soared to peak at over four thousand in 1958. In retrospect, and to the keen observer at the time, the rise of the drive-in audience was indicative of larger trends in the American cinema. Seeing a movie at the drive-in theater had distinct advantages, especially for lower-income groups. For a single admission price, audiences could watch double, triple or "dusk to dawn" features. Small children could be taken along, eliminating the expense of a baby sitter and downtown parking. Some drive-ins had playgrounds for kids, and even laundromats for suburban housewives.

But teenagers would discover other uses for these "passion pits with pix," as *Variety* described them. Drive-ins, like shopping malls today, became youth culture havens and a cultural icon of the fifties. It was estimated that 20 percent of all U.S. film revenues came from drive-ins and that as much as 75 percent of the drive-in audience was under the age of twenty-five.[5] As radio and the recording industry had discovered, the new affluence of postwar teenagers made them an attractive and identifiable market for the movie industry.

The film industry was reluctant to court the youth market, even though postwar surveys identified this profound shift taking place in the moviegoing public. Seventy-two percent of the weekly audience was under thirty, with slightly over half under the age of twenty, even though this group constituted just over 50 percent of the total population. Especially as a means of entertainment for dating couples, the role of movies and other entertainment media was intensified in the postwar youth culture. Groups of two or more people represented 81 percent of weekly admissions. Furthermore, single people accounted for over half of all admissions, while representing only 27 percent of the total population.[6] A 1958 report predicted that film executives would have to take account of the large numbers of postwar baby boomers.

> The growth of the "teen market" is bound to make itself felt in many areas, but nowhere is it of greater significance than in the film field, both in terms of audience potential and a guide to motion picture content. Not only are these the future homemakers, but they represent the "restless" element of the population, the people who don't want to stay home and watch TV and who are still immune to any sophisticated disdain of run-of-the-mill screen offerings.[7]

A Daniel Yankelovich survey in 1968 confirmed the earlier predictions, reporting that "being young and single [wa]s the overriding demographic precondition for being a frequent and enthusiastic moviegoer."[8]

This shift in audience occurred around the world as the postwar generation came of age. It coincided with a resurgence in world cinema in the 1950s and 1960s that heightened expectations about the possibilities for film as a serious art form. *Time* predicted the emergence of a "great cinema culture" during the 1960s, resulting from a "free exploration of the full possibilities of cinema as an art." The unique capabilities of film were looked upon as more characteristic of twentieth-century life than the other arts. "No other art can so powerfully exploit the dimensions of time and space," *Time* proclaimed. "No other art has so many ways of involving a human being. It involves his eyes, ears, mind, heart, appetites all at once. It is drama, music, poetry, novel, painting at the same time. It is the whole of art in one art, and it demands the whole of man in every man."[9]

The praise lavished on the cinema, however, revealed the depth of the problems that plagued the American film industry. For the first time in its history, Hollywood had fallen behind the rest of the world, both commercially and artistically. American companies continued to grind out genre films in the classic Hollywood style and according to the tenets of the Production Code. Along with its failure to respond to changes in the composition of its regular audience, Hollywood's reluctance to engage the topical and filmic innovations inspired by foreign cinemas contributed to its decline. The French and Italian new wave filmmakers, for example, were experimenting with new ways to tell a story with a camera, developing a visual approach to storytelling in film that differed from the narrative-driven style of the classic Hollywood movie.

Most of the excitement about the artistic prowess of the cinema was attributed to foreign productions, and especially the European "art" cinema. The European "art" cinema provided a distinct alternative to Hollywood productions.[10] The Hollywood film is driven by the character's actions, which reveal clearly defined traits, characteristics and goals; all the problems are resolved by the film's end. In contrast, foreign art films employ a looser, more tenuous linkage of events than the linear, cause-and-effect narrative of a Hollywood film. The narrative of an art film is advanced by an exploration of the nature and sources of the character's psychological state. Characters are often confused, ambivalent, alienated; their goals and desires uncertain, and their actions inconsistent and often followed by self-doubt. To reveal a character's psychological state, filmmakers used dream sequences, fantasies, flashbacks or hallucinations, and cinematic devices like freeze frames, slow motion and jump cuts. Art films often ended without complete closure.

The art cinema was defined by a certain kind of realism and the filmmaker's artistic expression or statement. Foreign productions were shot on location, showing "real" settings and "real" eroticism and treating "real" contemporary problems, like alienation and barriers to communication. Ambiguity, unresolved issues and loose ends in a story mirrored the way things happen in real life. Binding a character's psychological motivation to the depiction of his or her actions emphasized the subjectivity of the narrator, life's general disarray and the particular filmmaker's vision.

These foreign, non-Hollywood films were shown at specialty "art" theaters. While there were only about a dozen such theaters in 1946, by 1953 there were more than two hundred around the country. Hundreds of film societies were formed in association with museums, colleges and universities, and local art theaters. As this suggests, the primary constituency was college-age people who looked upon the cinema as an important medium alongside the arts and literature.

The realistic ambiguity of theme and character motive and reaction was typical of the novel and theater, and it followed that film critics began applying the interpretive techniques of literature and the visual arts to European art films. Films were being viewed now as artistic vehicles for a director's personal vision of the world. Heralding the director as a creative artist or *auteur,* critics began analyzing a filmmaker's body of work for recurring themes and cinematic style. They also applied these methods to the study of the popular Hollywood cinema, examining the body of work by directors like Howard Hawks, Alfred Hitchcock, Vincent Minnelli, John Ford and others. As this suggests, in European art cinema and postwar film criticism, movies were valued as a creative art without reference to sharp distinctions between high and popular culture. During the 1960s, filmmakers synthesized principles of the art cinema with the conventions of the classic Hollywood film as the American cinema began to adapt to the changes in postwar society.

Television rapidly took over the market for low-budget and less sophisticated entertainment, replacing the movies as regular "family" entertainment. One FCC commissioner described television as "the literature of the illiterate; the culture of the low-brow; the wealthy of the poor; the privilege of the underprivileged; the exclusive club of the excluded masses . . . a golden goose that lays scrambled eggs."[11] Commercial television somewhat succeeded the movies as low culture, to be shaped by the combined forces of the industry's production process and code, government, advertisers and advocacy groups.

In competition with TV and foreign films, Hollywood loosened its censorship standards, but with much diffidence. Films like *The Moon Is Blue* (1953), *The Man with the Golden Arm* (1955) and *Baby Doll* (1956) may have forced changes in the Code, but they were not among the top box-office attractions in their respective years. Hollywood "would much prefer to coast along making the peaceful 'family entertainment' that was a staple in the days when business was good," a writer in *Look* observed in 1959. "Hollywood is becoming bolder only because it must do so to stay alive."[12]

A study published in the *Harvard Law Review* concluded that the Production Code presented "a major obstacle to attempts to convey controversial ideas effectively or present a realistic portrait of American life."[13] Also, when Hollywood did take on more daring themes, the interminable assumption that films had to adhere to the conventions of the classic Hollywood style restricted artistic experimentation and made them appear less "real" than foreign productions. These films may have generated some steam in the audience, but the Code's requirements limited story possibilities. Wholesome virgins remained so in the end, heroines suffered some fortuitous accident on the way to the abortion clinic, and transgressors were punished for their unchastity or infidelity.

Even so, the new level of judicial freedom the film industry was given allowed greater specialization for movies and the freedom to explore mature subject matter. A *Time* report listed formerly taboo subjects that were now at least suggested if not intimated in Hollywood films: fornication *(From the Terrace)*, adultery *(Portrait in Black)*, incest *(The Last Sunset)*, prostitution *(Let No Man Write My Epitaph)*, pimping *(Girl of the Night)*, nymphomania *(The Fugitive Kind)*, voyeurism *(The Bramble Bush)*, frigidity *(Two Loves)*, rape *(Sanctuary)*, homosexuality *(Tea and Sympathy)*, cannibalism *(Suddenly Last Summer)*, abortion *(The Best of Everything)* and necrophilia *(Psycho)*.[14]

As expected, some films treated controversial subjects with artistic dignity and merit; *The Apartment, Elmer Gantry, Cat on a Hot Tin Roof* and *Who's Afraid of Virginia Woolf?* (based on Edward Albee's award-winning play) were all critically acclaimed social satires. *Rebel Without a Cause* and *The Blackboard Jungle* (both 1955) probed juvenile delinquency, and *Guess Who's Coming to Dinner?* (1968) addressed miscegenation. But in a desperate attempt to recover its vanishing audience, many motion pictures simply exploited the new artistic freedom, flooding the screen with sexploitation films and new levels of violence. "Few regret the passing of the phony Hays ethics in which morality was supposedly satisfied as long as movies stuck to a long list of artificial don'ts (don't show a man and woman in bed, even if they are married, etc.)," *Time* observed. "But Hollywood's new freedom, while making more room for honest art, has also made more room for calculated smut, drawing a barrage of protests from parents, pastors and assorted pressure groups."[15]

In another sense, the major studios remained cautious. Films treating the most controversial social issues of the 1960s—drug use, sex, violence, race, the youthful rebellion against the conformity of the World War II generation—were largely relegated to the marginal status of cheap, exploitation films produced by independent companies and made for a limited market.

It Conquered the World

Prior to the Paramount decision, the major studios' control over exhibition and the restrictions of the Production Code effectively kept both independent and foreign films out of the U.S. market. But independent producers were able to thrive in the new environment after the dismantling of the studio system. Their number rose from about 70 in 1946 to 165 in 1957, and it was estimated that 65 percent of Hollywood's features were made by independent producers by 1958.[16] They were "truly independent," Suzanne May Donahue writes, "of content restrictions, quality restrictions, and restrictions of the spirit."[17] The new flexibility in the production system allowed the independents to adapt their films to the demands and desires of specialty markets, and especially young people, who worldwide were becoming the most frequent movie-goers.

The largest and most successful of the independents was American International Pictures (AIP), formed by Samuel Arkoff and Jack Nicholson (not the actor) in 1952. Arkoff and Nicholson recognized that while the major film studios were investing in long-range blockbusters, theater owners were clamoring for short double-bill features that could be changed frequently and would make their money in shorter runs. To make their movies more attractive to exhibitors, AIP rented them as packages of double-bills, charging a flat rate instead of a percentage of the box-office gross. The company's low-budget youth pictures reaped relatively high profits. AIP features were made quickly and cheaply; most films were shot in two weeks for under $200,000, with several grossing over $2 million. Between 1954 and 1967, AIP released over 130 low-budget movies aimed at the "passion pit" crowd and reportedly grossed some $250 million.[18] Many elements of AIP films were later incorporated in movies the major studios produced for the under-thirty audience.

"We'd like to make nice family pictures, but we're in this for the money," an AIP sales director explained, echoing Carl Laemmle's sentiment in 1916. "If the kids think it's a good picture and the adults don't, that's all right. Seventy-five percent of the drive-in audiences are under twenty-five, and 70% of our gross comes from drive-in theaters."[19] AIP producers conducted their audience research exclusively among young people in order to tap into the desires and fantasies of the youth culture. They discovered that to capture the greatest percentage of the youth market, films should appeal to the nineteen-year-old male.[20] This marketing strategy eventually became the rule of thumb in Hollywood as the major studios zeroed in on the youth audience. The blockbuster success of *Jaws* (1975), the Star Wars trilogy (1977, 1980, 1983) and *Raiders of the Lost Ark* (1981) solidified this formula, while also drawing Hollywood's attention to the post-baby boom youth audience. The unprecedented success of these and other films was attributed to young males under twenty-five, "who bring along dates or groups of friends, and consider repeat viewings as a kind of pubescent badge of honor," the *Los Angeles Times* reported.[21]

The typical AIP fare changed over the years to keep up with the latest fads, fashions and trends in the youth culture. Most of today's popular genres can be traced back to AIP productions. Initially AIP specialized in sensational horror and science fiction films, turning out in rapid fire *The Beast with 1,000,000 Eyes, The Day the World Ended, It Conquered the World, The Undead* and *The Brain Eaters*. The classic *I Was a Teenage Werewolf* was made for less than $125,000 but grossed $2 million and caused traffic jams at drive-in theaters. The pictures themselves hardly matched up to their lurid advertising campaigns; the monster in *It Conquered the World*, for example, is a laughably oversized turnip with crablike arms. But what these films lacked in plot, characterization and special effects they made up for in visual impact, featuring what were for the time trenchant sexual, violent and horrific images. AIP also released black-humor pictures, *A Bucket of Blood* (1959) and *Little Shop of Horrors* (1960), and a series based on Edgar Allan Poe stories. Gangster films like *Machine Gun Kelly* and *I Mobster* (both 1958) and *The St. Valentine's Day Massacre* (1967) predated the graphic violence of *Bonnie and Clyde*.

AIP films also introduced a kind of knowing, campy irony that would become a staple among more visually literate audiences with a sarcastic sensibility. In 1963 the company began a series of beach party movies featuring ex-Mouseketeer Annette Funicello and teen rock idol Frankie Avalon. *Beach Blanket Bingo, Beach Party* and *How to Stuff a Wild Bikini* were predictable and formulaic, epitomizing youthful innocence and young love. Again, AIP's suggestive advertising promised risqué entertainment: "BIKINI BEACH, WHERE BARE-AS-YOU-DARE IS THE RULE!" "WHAT HAPPENS WHEN 10,000 KIDS MEET ON 5,000 BEACH BLANKETS!" While the cast of beachniks and bikini-clad women gyrating and jiggling to the beat of rock music displayed a lot of flesh, there was never any nudity or sex. The message was decidedly conservative, resembling the adult romantic comedies, only now in a youth culture setting. But for the drive-in crowd, as critics observed, "the constant display of nubile flesh twisting and frugging to the big rock beat more than compensates for the erotic constraints of the script."[22]

In the late 1960s, AIP turned its attention to the youth rebellion and made a number of films "reflecting the exciting social changes, crises, rationalizations and adjustments of society in our time," as executives put it.[23] *The Wild Angels* (1966) was a graphically violent film depicting the biker culture. *Riot on Sunset Strip* (1967) and *Psych-Out* (1968) explored the hippie phenomenon; *The Trip* addressed LSD experimentation. The outrageous *Wild in the Streets* (1968) satirized the youth revolution and exploited adult hysteria by showing a rock star elected president of the United States. These films generated enormous controversy and solid box-office returns. One reviewer blasted *The Trip* as an "hour-and-half commercial for LSD," but *Variety* recognized its youthful appeal: "As a far-out, free-floating LSD freak-out, 'The Trip' should provide enough psychedelic jolts, sex-sational scenes and mind-blowing montages and optical effects to prove a boxoffice magnet for the youth market."[24] *The Wild Angels* was made for $360,000. It returned $7 million to AIP and was selected as the American entry at the Venice Film Festival that year. *The Trip* made $5.5 million. Both starred Peter Fonda, who later combined their subject matter in the Columbia release *Easy Rider* (1969).

AIP's most prolific and influential director, producer and screenwriter was Roger Corman. Corman pioneered the rapid production of low-budget features for the youth audience, directing many horror, monster, gangster and black-humor pictures. It was Corman who directed *The Wild Angels* and *The Trip,* the films that served as Peter Fonda's inspiration for *Easy Rider,* a film Corman almost directed. Virtually all of his films were commercially successful, even though some of his highest moments of imaginative filmmaking are mixed with others of pure cinematic schlock. Regardless, the Cormanesque formula became a staple in contemporary filmmaking: action, sex, humor and a "slight social statement," as director Jonathan Demme put it.[25]

Though virtually unknown to the general public, Corman played a key role in the American cinema. He ran what amounted to a quasi-film school at AIP and then New World Pictures, giving many young and talented filmmakers their initial opportunities. His understudies got involved in every aspect of filmmaking—budgeting, scheduling, editing, shooting and directing. They acquired invaluable experience working on the nonunion, low-budget features that Corman produced for the youth market; their inexpensive labor helped keep production budgets down.

A surprising number of Corman's protégés came to prominence in Hollywood in the 1970s and 1980s and exerted a tremendous influence on the cinema. Francis Ford Coppola, one of the most prestigious directors of his generation, directed his first feature for AIP, *Dementia 13* (1963). Coppola captured critical praise and stunning commercial success by advancing the gangster genre with *The Godfather* (1972) and the war film with *Apocalypse Now* (1979). Jonathan Demme's *Caged Heat* (New World, 1974), which dealt with psychosurgery, predated the award-winning *One Flew over the Cuckoo's Nest* (1975) starring Jack Nicholson, whose career began at AIP. Demme went on to make *Something Wild* (1986), the award-winning *The Silence of the Lambs* (1991) and *Philadelphia* (1993). Peter Bogdanovich made the cult classic *Targets* (1968) with Corman and later directed *The Last Picture Show* (1971), *What's Up, Doc?* (1972) and *Paper Moon* (1973). Martin Scorsese directed *Boxcar Bertha* (1972) for Corman. His illustrious film credits include *Mean Streets* (1973), *Taxi Driver* (1976), *Raging Bull* (1980), *Goodfellas* (1990), *Cape Fear* (1991), *Age of Innocence* (1993) and *Casino* (1995). Corman also gave Jonathan Kaplan (*The Accused* [1988]) and Ron Howard (*Night Shift* [1982], *Cocoon* [1985], *Backdraft* [1991], *Apollo 13* [1995]) their first directorial opportunities.

Unlike their predecessors, most of these young filmmakers of the 1970s and 1980s attended major university film programs; Coppola studied at UCLA, Scorsese at NYU, and George Lucas at USC. At the same time, many received their early practical experience working with Corman, the master of the exploitation film, or were at least influenced by his films. The "new Hollywood" filmmakers had a keen awareness of their relation to the "old Hollywood" and shared the sensibilities of the contemporary generation of moviegoers. While they grew up watching television and youth-oriented movies, they also had a very strong awareness of the classic Hollywood cinema and were familiar with popular American genres (westerns, comedies and film noir) and classics like *Citizen Kane* as well as the European art cinema.

This array of influences is evident in many contemporary productions. On one level, for example, George Lucas's *Star Wars* is simply a classic Hollywood western set in outer space. But the film paid homage to Warners' war films and the Flash Gordon and Buck Rogers serials. By borrowing heavily from the mythical tradition and fusing elements of the sci-fi, fantasy and adventure genres, Lucas created a synergism that raised the film series to a level of artistic accomplishment that could not be reduced to any one of its particular elements. Lucas's semi-autobiographical *American Graffiti* (1972) was influenced as much by the AIP beach party films as Fellini's *I Vitelloni*, a 1953 film that shows a young hero leaving behind the mundane activities of adolescence to pursue the challenges of the larger world.

Steven Spielberg, whose blatant sentimental style and amazing blockbuster successes have brought criticism and eschewed his status as an artist, frequently uses allusions to Hollywood classics to heighten the intertextual meaning of his films. *E.T., the Extraterrestrial* (1982) is filled with references to *The Wizard of Oz, Star Wars* and *Peter Pan,* effectively associating the meaning of *E.T.* with its popular cinematic ancestors by invoking their memory in the audience. The Lucas/Spielberg collaboration *Raiders of the Lost Ark* (1981) was in one sense a revival of the Saturday-matinee action-adventure film. The final scene, however, is an obvious parallel to the Orson Welles masterpiece *Citizen Kane,* suggesting that the power of the ark is as unfathomable as the meaning of "Rosebud."

Likewise, the runaway carriage down the steps in Brian DePalma's *The Untouchables* (1987) is an obvious intertextual reference to Soviet filmmaker Sergei Eisenstein's classic *Battleship Potemkin* (1925). Films like *Taxi Driver* and *American Gigolo, Nashville* and *The Godfather* reveal the use of art film elements within the boundaries of the classical film style and genres.[26] Coppola's *The Conversation* (1974) and DePalma's *Blow Out* (1981) were obvious remakes of Michelangelo Antonioni's European-styled *Blow-Up* (1966). As these films demonstrate, many of the most important filmmakers today show an indifference for any distinctions between high and low art in the contemporary cinema.

Discovering the Youth Culture

While the major studios were ailing, desperate for ways to reduce their production costs and increase box-office revenues, AIP's low-budget films were drawing significant numbers of baby boomers to the theaters. Several major releases that scored at the box office confirmed the viability of AIP's youth market strategy. These films clearly reflected the sensibilities of the postwar generation. Warner Brothers earned over twenty-two million dollars from Arthur Penn's *Bonnie and Clyde,* a 1967 film that turned Depression-era gangsters into young populist heroes waging a violent campaign against a corrupt society. Stanley Kubrick's science fiction film *2001: A Space Odyssey* (1968) explored the origin and evolution of humankind and captured twenty-five million dollars for MGM/UA. Mike Nichols's *The Graduate* (1968) unexpectedly became the third top-grossing film of all time, behind *The Sound of Music* and *Gone with the Wind.* The main character's personal confusion and disillusionment appealed to alienated baby boomers, who were themselves frustrated with the moral and spiritual emptiness of affluent America. United Artists' three-million-dollar investment paid off handsomely with earnings of forty-four million.

These films were clearly oriented to the under-thirty audience, the generation that came of age in the postwar period and grew up watching television and Hollywood movies. Their familiarity with the Hollywood tradition allowed filmmakers to use established film genres as a means to reexamine traditional American mythology with contemporary sensibilities. Simultaneously, these films revealed a strong influence of the European art cinema in characterization, narrative and filmic style.

Easy Rider is a good illustration. The film is about two countercultural bikers who set out "in search of America," only to encounter social bigotry and disillusionment. Allusions throughout the film position it as a reaction against themes in the traditional western genre. Director Dennis Hopper employed a number of art-film devices like slow-motion, freeze frames, flash-forwards and dream sequences; a contemporary rock soundtrack gave a running commentary on the action. Columbia scored unexpectedly with *Easy Rider,* earning $19 million against a minuscule investment of about $500,000. The film was a hit at the 1969 Cannes Film Festival and grossed over $60 million worldwide.

The overwhelming success of *Easy Rider* suggested a future of Hollywood movies that would involve a small risk yet would yield an enormous profit, that would be relevant and artistic and popular, that would revitalize Hollywood at the same time it acknowledged Hollywood tradition," film historians Seth Cagin and Philip Dray explain. "Countless newspaper and magazine articles dubbed it the New Hollywood, and dozens of low-budget youth cult movies were immediately put into production. The relationships between art and schlock, between B-movies and cinematic savvy, between Hollywood and its market—all came under renewed scrutiny, and all were permanently altered."[27] The chasm between major releases aimed at the general audience and low-budget independent productions for the youth culture had all but vanished. Trends that began over a decade before—new judicial freedoms, the influence of foreign film styles, the blockbuster and the orientation toward a younger audience—merged in the films that characterized the "New Hollywood" in the late 1960s.

Even though these movies verified marketing research that identified young people as the bulk of regular moviegoers, the industry remained apprehen-

sive about the youth audience. MPAA president Jack Valenti still urged exhibitors to support "quality" family-oriented pictures like *Dr. Doolittle* (1967). "I
truly don't believe that the entire young audience and surely not the old, are
all of a psychedelic breed, hunkered up over their pot and acid, and lurching
off on supernatural romps and trips," he said in a speech to Canadian film
exhibitors.[28] Exhibitors apparently agreed as they remained unsure about the
long-term viability of the youth market. "Emerging from the obvious confusion in the film trade as old values and indeed old established trade marks
falter and collapse is a realization that the industry cannot afford to put all
its eggs in one youth basket," the National Association of Theater Owners
reported at its annual meeting. "The idea was enunciated that youth itself is
unpredictable, swings wildly in taste and is subject to the attrition of its own
maturation."[29] These sentiments were affirmed when it proved difficult to
replicate the financial success of *Easy Rider; Getting Straight, The Strawberry
Statement, Zabriske Point* and other films dealing with drugs, student protest
and the generation gap had disappointing theatrical runs. Hollywood's pursuit
of countercultural themes was short-lived, lasting but a few years.

Nevertheless, Hollywood discovered that the new artistic freedom it had
won in the courts could be exercised with great success while courting its
new regular audience, the under-thirty crowd. Also, youth-oriented Hollywood releases that showed the topical and stylistic influence of the European
art cinema were generating solid box-office and critical acclaim. Television
had taken over the role of grinding out cheap entertainment for a mass
audience. The new moviegoing audience was willing to pay higher ticket
prices for films they selected, an effect that shifted filmmaking "away from
aimless mass production into a quasi-art or even a form of simplified social
commentary," as Garth Jowett puts it. "In the minds of their customers, the
movies were now quite clearly differentiated from television, and audiences
expected something more than the old Hollywood formulae, and even more
explicit visual thrills."[30] With the discovery of the baby boom audience,
"movies had once again become a homogeneous medium—but one now
geared unequivocally and unapologetically to the young," Doherty notes. "If
their elders came along to the theaters occasionally, so much the better. But
when in need of a reliable audience, no end of the motion picture business—
production, distribution, or exhibition—trusted anyone over thirty."[31] Hollywood turned its attention to exploiting the youth market; the artistic functions
of the cinema were focused on the culture of American youth.

The Sixties and the Cinema

The consensus in American life that was forged during the Depression and World War II was solidified as a secular religion in the postwar world based on a fusion of conservative and liberal traditions. Most conservatives accepted some of the economic and domestic policies of the New Deal, and many liberals adopted a foreign policy whose major premise was the kind of anti-communism that had once been the mark of conservatives. As historian Geoffrey Hodgson explains, there were two faces of the consensus: a complacency about the perfectibility of American society and a paranoia about the threat of communism. These were represented by the two most important issues of the 1960s, the civil rights movement and the war in Vietnam.[32]

The World War II victory healed the nation's wounds from the Depression and restored confidence in the American dream. In the postwar period the United States dominated the world. Americans thought of themselves as a chosen people and, in pursuit of their national destiny, began a conscious effort to become the greatest nation in the history of civilization. The quest for greatness was based on three objectives: to create abundance in a world of scarcity, liberty in a world of tyrannies, and peace in a world torn by wars.[33] The sense that America was in the vanguard of a new age permeated the American experience.

That all men and women were created equal with the right to life, liberty and the pursuit of happiness was more than a national ideal for the generation growing up in postwar America; it became a principle for justice and a program for social change. The world was safe for democracy, but there remained a host of problems to contend with in order to bring about the realization of these shared democratic ideals. The atomic bomb had brought an immediate end to the war but loosed the specter of nuclear destruction. The Cold War cast a shadow over international relations and created constant anxieties about the possibility of war. There were concerns about worldwide population growth and the spread of communism. Changing gender roles, the mass consumer society, suburbanization, the bureaucratization of work and a crisis in education, as well as deteriorating urban conditions and racial injustices, topped a long list of domestic issues.

The consensus began to unravel in 1963, when a series of shocks beginning with the Kennedy assassination tarnished the high ideals Americans shared, and spread fear. The civil rights movement erupted into racial riots, and rapid troop buildup in Vietnam was accompanied by increased student protest against the immorality of the war. The idealistic postwar generation became disillusioned youth rebelling against what they believed was their country's loss of human purpose. They saw the Vietnam War as a brutal attack on a small, harmless nation of peasant people, and not a matter of containing communism. The war drained resources from the more pressing needs of social and racial justice that America was failing to provide for all its citizens. The frustrations of the civil rights and women's movements and government deceptions about the Vietnam War led to a fragmentation of the American cultural consensus.

The cinema reached a new level of artistic maturity at a time when American society seemed to be coming apart at the seams. Over the course of the decade, Americans witnessed incidents of egregious violence that shocked, enraged and devitalized the country. Nightly news coverage brought the horrors of the Vietnam War into family living rooms. The political assassinations of President Kennedy and later his brother Robert stunned the nation. Violent resistance to the civil rights movement culminated in the murder of Martin Luther King Jr., which took away the movement's most dynamic leader. Television cameras captured Chicago police beating young protesters outside the National Democratic Convention. Just after the release of the movie *Woodstock* (1970), the filmed version of the counterculture's symbolic zenith of "peace and love," four students were killed and nine wounded by National Guardsmen during an antiwar demonstration at Kent State University. Ten days later two more were killed and twelve wounded at Jackson State.

These events gave a real-life context to Hollywood films that fulfilled the important functions of art during a tumultuous time in American history. Haskell Wexler's *Medium Cool* (1969) probed the detachment that media representations of violence fostered between the audience and real events taking place in American life. The violent imagery in the American cinema served as poignant metaphors for the political activism and deep social unrest and discord of the late 1960s.

Inside theaters, Penn's *Bonnie and Clyde* (1967) and Sam Peckinpah's *The Wild Bunch* (1969) reveled in slow-motion techniques that escalated graphic violence to new levels. But as David A. Cook argues, these filmmakers were confronting the "dark realities of contemporary American life" during the Vietnam War. Both directors, he wrote, "insisted for the first time in American cinema that the human body is made of real flesh and blood; that arterial blood spurts rather than drips demurely; that bullet wounds leave not trim little pinpricks but big, gaping holes; and, in general, that violence has painful, unpretty, humanly destructive consequences. . . . Penn and Peckinpah had overturned decades of polite filmic convention that the body has the resilience of rubber and that death is simply a state of terminal sleep."[34]

Likewise, the cinema's exploitation of sex reflected a larger cultural preoccupation with the sexuality of the American woman. After working for wages during the war, many women retreated into suburban domesticity; the occupation of housewife-mother was idealized as the epitome of feminine existence during the 1950s. But instead of finding ultimate fulfillment in the role of suburban housewife, an increasing number of women suffered from a lack of personal identity, dissatisfaction and unfulfillment. Betty Friedan identified this "problem that has no name" in her book *The Feminine Mystique*. She argued that the pursuit of sexual fulfillment was exaggerated "beyond the limits of possibility . . . to fill the vacuum created by denial of larger goals and purposes for American women."[35] The American media became obsessed with women's intimate lives and fantasies, reducing femininity to sexuality. Coupled with the new freedom brought by the availability of an oral contraceptive, the sexual frontier became a dominant theme in the cinema with portrayals of romance increasingly centering on depersonalized sex. Film critic Molly Haskell notes, "With the substitution of violence and sexuality (a poor second) for romance, there was less need for exciting and interesting women; any bouncing nymphet whose curves looked good in catsup would do."[36] In the cinematic mirror, as in reality, women were exploited by the sexual revolution, reduced from provocative characters to objects of male voyeurism.

In his annual review, *Variety* editor Abel Green emphasized that "the deplored plot violence on cinematic and television screen was matched in 1967 by violence in the streets and farflung warfronts"; he cited "dissent and civil disobedience, racial and sexual revolution" as contributing to social unrest. He also observed that test cases on freedom of the press and freedom of expression had created a new permissiveness in the entertainment and publishing media's treatment of these issues that was met with a wave of anti-obscenity bills introduced in Congress as part of what he termed a "moralistic backlash."[37] The artistic freedom the courts awarded the cinema and the institution of the rating system allowed a rash of films with new levels of explicit sex and graphic violence to reach the American screen, making it difficult even in the midst of the tumult of the 1960s to distinguish at times between artistic liberty and license, freedom and responsibility.

The collapse of moral and cultural consensus and freedom of expression combined to bring new and different perspectives to the American screen. This was an important step in the evolution of film as an art form. But there was a lag between the new possibilities for the cinema and a general social acceptance and understanding of its artistic role. The situation demanded now that people understand both how and what the entertainment media communicate and be able to evaluate and think critically about the moral, social or religious perspectives offered in the popular arts. On the other hand, producers still wanted to attract the widest possible audience, and the lowest-common-denominator approach tended to generalize treatment of subjects in order to appeal to everyone instead of rooting it in a specific moral perspective.

This has led to the contemporary practice of including elements of sex and violence for their visceral effect, with no moral context. Sometimes this is just a feature of a genre (action-adventure, for example), but the proliferation of these images can make sex and violence as unrealistic and romanticized in today's movies as in those made during the studio era. As an artistic enterprise, the cinema should feature different perspectives, but movies are made to make money, and artistic responsibility is all too often overshadowed by financial goals. The head of production at MGM said in 1969, "It's not our business to promote the culture of the country, or to make art films. It's to make money for the studio."[38]

Tide of Teenpics

Hollywood's refusal to acknowledge that the weekly moviegoing audience was changing ultimately threatened the future of the major film companies. The stability of the studios often rested on the success or flop of a multimillion-dollar picture. By the mid-1960s the situation had not improved. Because of their erratic earnings, the stock of film companies was undervalued, and they were vulnerable to corporate takeovers. Film companies became units within larger multimedia conglomerates, a trend that continues today.[39] One effect of these takeovers was the beginning of synergism in the industry as entertainment corporations initiated more projects involving film, record, cable television, video and retail divisions.

Transnational corporate heads were as profit-minded as the studio moguls whose companies they bought. The strategy of both was to reduce box-office risk and produce profitable films. According to one writer, they were "no more interested in films dealing with sociological and political investigations and reforms, or artistic experiments, than were the Old Hollywood auto-crats."[40] The late 1960s had the markings of a major cinematic renaissance in America, but the diversity and creativity of the period were conditioned by audience demographics and commercial factors. Despite its newfound judicial freedom and indications that audiences wanted more mature and sophisticated movies, Hollywood's prime motivation remained profitmaking. In effect, the industrialization of film was intensified under the rule of the conglomerates.

During the 1970s the studios were restabilized. They reduced their output and began to see profits on more films. While only one in ten films made a profit at the end of the 1960s, that figure had risen to three in ten by the end of the 1970s. During the sixties only five films topped forty million dollars in rentals; almost thirty reached that mark the following decade, even though attendance figures remained about the same.[41] Box-office grosses doubled from $1.4 billion in 1970 to $2.8 billion in 1979, primarily due to escalating ticket prices. According to MPAA figures, average ticket prices rose from $1.55 in 1970 to $2.05 in 1975 to $2.69 in 1980; the price of admission topped four dollars beginning in 1988.

By the mid-1970s Hollywood was making fewer films. "The habit of going to *the movies* is over," Paramount production head Robert Evans said, acknowledging the social effect of television on movie attendance. "But the desire to see *a* movie is bigger than ever. I would rather put more money into fewer films than less on a lot of them. If you're making just another picture, forget it. You can't even get your advertising costs back. But if you have one or two big captivating entertainments a year, it's oil rush time."[42] A major studio like Paramount or Twentieth Century-Fox might have all of its capital invested in a handful of pictures each year, all intended blockbusters. Columbia, for example, had most of its resources invested in *Close Encounters of the Third Kind* in 1977. Production and marketing budgets soared throughout the decade. Between 1972 and 1977, average production costs shot up 178 percent, almost four times the general rate of inflation.[43] By 1980, the average film cost nearly ten million dollars. Big-budget pictures in the first half of the decade like *Jaws* and *The Towering Inferno* were in the ten- to fifteen-million-dollar range. In the second half, many topped twenty million dollars; according to *Variety, Apocalypse Now* cost thirty-one million, *Star*

Trek forty-two million and *Superman* fifty-five million. Higher costs also meant greater financial risk, forcing studios to escalate distribution and marketing budgets, which now average about 50 percent of a film's negative costs.

Beginning in the 1970s, increasing costs made it too risky for the studios to make films for a specialized audience. There is less effort involved in making a few blockbusters that might generate huge profits by appealing to a wide audience than in producing a larger number of pictures that make smaller profits. A statement by Irwin Allen, king of the lucrative disaster films in the early 1970s (*Poseidon Adventure* [1972], *The Towering Inferno* [1974]), reveals the studio attitudes and the blockbuster strategy. "I believe in big-budget pictures. I believe fervently in the star system. I believe in the Walter Mitty syndrome. And I believe in the all-family picture," he told a *Newsweek* reporter in 1974. "I include enough elements so you can't keep anyone away who wants to come. 'Inferno' has five love stories. There's tremendous derring-do for kids, there are great philosophical overtones for the senior citizens, and there's all kinds of hope for the teen-agers and young marrieds."[44]

The Hollywood majors gambled on the production of blockbusters again. The hits of the 1970s—*The Godfather, The Exorcist, Jaws, Star Wars, Close Encounters of the Third Kind* and *Superman*—generated unbelievable profits and, with the single exception of *Gone with the Wind,* were unrivaled in Hollywood's history. But there were also many unprecedented flops: *Barry Lyndon, Lucky Lady, Sorcerer, The Wiz, Hurricane* and *Meteor,* culminating in the financial debacle of *Heaven's Gate* (1980), which led United Artists into bankruptcy. These conditions can inhibit the creativity of filmmakers. With more filmmakers trying to secure funding for a smaller number of pictures that are being made, the pressure to score big at the box office always seems to bring out conservative tendencies. Producers tend to rely on formulas and elements like sex and violence that have already been proven successful at the box office.

Hollywood continued the economics and production of the blockbuster, but now the primary audience was under-thirty baby boomers. Paramount's *Love Story,* the top-grossing film of 1970, is indicative of the change. The movie is about a young couple (Oliver and Jenny), two Ivy League students from different class backgrounds who love and respect each other through a series of struggles, the final one being Jenny's premature death of leukemia. It became Paramount's biggest hit, even though the amazing popularity of this sentimental and escapist tear-jerker surprised critics and industry people alike. The film seemed out of context, reaching theaters a year after Woodstock and just months after the Kent State incident. There was conflict between Oliver and his parents; he and Jenny disavowed religion and slept together before they were married. But the film stood in sharp contrast to other "New Hollywood" pictures aimed at the youth market. Cagin and Dray wrote, *"Love Story* offered adults a view of contemporary young people which denied cultural anxiety, and the film pointedly avoids such trappings of the counterculture as a rock music score (Bach, Handel and Mozart were used), disillusionment (beyond the usual resentment of one's own parents) or drugs, while providing youthful viewers with an infantile fantasy of their own fleeting innocence."[45] Paramount had released a conventional and formulaic Hollywood romance aimed at a wide demographic audience, but its foremost and direct appeal was to those under thirty.

Following *Love Story*'s box-office earnings were Universal's big-budget and star-studded disaster film *Airport,* and Twentieth Century-Fox's *M*A*S*H* (a Vietnam satire in a Korean War setting) and traditional war film *Patton.* By 1972, after the record revenues Paramount earned with *The Godfather,* Hollywood resumed its investment in big-budget blockbusters and the production of genre films, geared now to a younger audience. The ten top-grossing films of the 1970s—*Star Wars, Jaws, Grease, The Exorcist, The Godfather, Superman, Close Encounters of the Third Kind, The Sting, Saturday Night Fever, National Lampoon's Animal House*—illustrate this trend, which is perpetuated to this day by the high percentage of young moviegoers.

Historically, Hollywood has proved to be extremely adept at assimilating themes and cinematic styles from successful foreign producers into the classic American cinema. The AIP model for producing and marketing youth-oriented films was well-suited for major motion pictures designed to reach the same audience beginning in the 1970s. As research showed that most moviegoers were under thirty years old, Hollywood increasingly made big-budget productions out of exploitation genres that previously were exclusive to independents like AIP—youth pictures, science fiction, gangster, monster and horror films.

In comparison to the recording industry, Hollywood's courtship with the baby boom was abbreviated as the vanguard of the generation began turning thirty, and therefore moving past the prime moviegoing years, in the late 1970s. The striking success of *Saturday Night Fever* and *Grease* as multimedia events was largely attributed to the postwar generation. Even so, young people had been identified by the film industry as the most frequent moviegoers. The film industry continued to target the youth audience during the 1980s, but that audience became increasingly younger and had different cultural sensibilities from those of the baby boomers. The latter were being assimilated into the job market, getting married and starting families. As it had been for their parents before them, going out to the movies became a special outing, and aging baby boomers became less frequent moviegoers during the 1980s. The trend would change, however, in the 1990s as the boomers moved past the early childrearing years.

In 1975 *Jaws,* which *New York Times* critic Vincent Canby called "a big-budget Roger Corman movie," became the first major release to use the youth exploitation model developed by AIP.[46] A wide-release or saturation booking and advertising strategy propelled *Jaws* to an unprecedented $100 million in domestic rentals. The film was soon surpassed by other Spielberg films and Lucas's sci-fi fantasy-adventure Star Wars series, beginning in 1977.

The extraordinary success of Lucas and Spielberg, and widespread influence among their contemporaries, illustrates the film industry's continued emphasis on the under-thirty audience. With the Star Wars and Indiana Jones series, Lucas and Spielberg revisited the comic-book serials and Saturday-matinee genres of their youth while also rejuvenating the moral and cultural system of the 1940s and 1950s. This launched a new breed of American science fiction that emphasized high-tech special effects in the Star Trek series, *E.T., the Extraterrestrial* (1982), *Bladerunner* (1982), *The Last Starfighter* (1984), the Alien series and a host of others. Lucas and Spielberg teamed together to have Indiana Jones, a scientist and adventure hero, battle the forces of evil in *Raiders of the Lost Ark* (1981), *Indiana Jones and the Temple of Doom* (1984) and *Indiana Jones and the Last Crusade* (1989). Their use of comic-book fantasies inspired other films, including *Dick Tracy* and the Superman and Batman series.

Beginning in the mid-1970s, traditional Hollywood genres recycled for the youth audience generated unprecedented profits. The Rocky series, *E.T., the Extraterrestrial* (1982), *Edward Scissorhands* (1990) and *Home Alone* (1990), though also a comedy, continued the melodrama. *The Exorcist* (1973), *Carrie* (1977) and *Poltergeist* (1982) revived the horror film. Teen terrifiers or "slasher" films like *Halloween, Prom Night, Friday the 13th, Nightmare on Elm Street* and their many sequels and imitations are horror films made specifically for the youth market. *Variety* reported that slasher films accounted for nearly 60 percent of all domestic releases in 1981, with twenty-five ranking among the fifty top-grossing films that year.[47] Utilizing high-tech special effects, *Jaws,* *Alien* and *Terminator* brought new and terrifying monsters to the screen. *Beverly Hills Cop* (1984), *Lethal Weapon* and *Die Hard* put young detectives on the trail of vicious criminals. *Blazing Saddles* (1974), *Young Frankenstein* (1974), *Caddyshack* (1980), *Stripes* (1981), *Ghostbusters* (1984), *Back to School* (1986) and the Back to the Future series became the new comedies. The stunning success of *Platoon* (1986) jump-started the war film, and a host of pictures like Stanley Kubrick's *Full Metal Jacket* (1987), Barry Levinson's *Good Morning, Vietnam* (1988) and Brian DePalma's *Casualties of War* (1989) explored America's involvement in Vietnam. *Chinatown* (1974), *Body Heat* (1981) and *Fatal Attraction* (1987) revisited the film noir style. As we saw in the previous chapter, the marriage of movies and music on MTV launched a wave of musicals with rock soundtracks that were intended to appeal to the music video audience: *Flashdance, Footloose* and *Dirty Dancing.*[48]

Nothing demonstrated Hollywood's preoccupation with the youth market more than the flood of "teenpics" during the 1980s. Beginning with *National Lampoon's Animal House* (1979), an impertinent look at college fraternity life, a host of films explored the adolescent search for identity, intimacy and sexual maturation. Many of these low-budget films were enormously successful financially. *Animal House* was made for $2.9 million and grossed over $150 million. *Porky's* (1982) grossed over $180 million against $4.8 million in production costs. Their success unleashed a wave of imitations. Most, like *Porky's,* simply appealed to teenage hormonal drives. But many were notable for their exploration of adolescent emotions and problems. Amy Heckerling's *Fast Times at Ridgemont High* (1982) showed the pain and disillusionment of a high-school girl trying to experience real intimacy through imprudent sex. The lesson learned in the dark comedy *Risky Business* (1983) is that sex and free enterprise are the keys to a successful life. The John Hughes trilogy *Sixteen Candles* (1984), *The Breakfast Club* (1985) and *Pretty in Pink* (1986) treated sex, dating, peer relationships and social class with both humor and sensitivity. *Ferris Bueller's Day Off* (1986), *Say Anything* (1989) and *Pump Up the Volume* (1990) looked at the vulnerability of young people and their lack of communication with adults. *Teachers* (1984) probed adolescent (and adult) struggles in the educational system.

The frequent patronage of teenagers became a common denominator for Hollywood, a trend that culminated in the 1980s with blockbuster productions targeting the youth market with the hope of broadening their appeal to other audience segments. The youth audience stole the show during the 1980s, as the slew of teenpics and explosive popularity of MTV demonstrate. Youth remain a lucrative market. Escalating costs and corporate bottom lines meant that fewer films were made for a specific segment of the moviegoing audience, and with the unprecedented success of youth movies like *Jaws* and *Star Wars,* Hollywood concentrated its resources on the adolescent market to the exclusion of everyone else. Near the end of the decade, however, shifting audience demographics began to move Hollywood in other directions, as we will see in the next chapter.

Conclusion

American attitudes near the end of the 1960s were characterized by a sense of disillusionment and despair. As popular support for continued involvement in Vietnam waned, President Nixon began withdrawing troops in an effort to bring an end to America's most controversial war. The protest movement, stunned by the Kent State shootings, quickly lost its focus and splintered into smaller issue-oriented groups. After the social activism of the 1960s, Americans became absorbed in what sociologist Christopher Lasch called the "culture of narcissism." Historian James B. Gilbert proposes that the 1970s represented the third stage in the development of entertainment after World War II. "If the fifties was an era of transition from a family-oriented mass culture of middle-class ideals and the sixties was a decade when a small but significant element of popular culture reflected political and moral radicalism, then the seventies represented a time when the collapse of radicalism left benign tolerance in its wake," he writes. "Rapidly changing and always creative, popular culture in the seventies nonetheless reflected overtones of retrenchment, tinged by nostalgia, sometimes haunted by alienation, and often unconcerned with solving problems."[49] The lesson that society could not be changed in any of the ways that really mattered gave way to a strategy for self-improvement during the "Me Decade."

As film critic Richard Corliss notes, there was a change in the American cinema over the course of the 1970s from a "multiplex of minority cinemas" to a "one majority, melting-pot cinema." For better or worse, as Hollywood recognized that young people were its most reliable audience, movies were made to have their most direct appeal to those under thirty, and increasingly the lower end of this demographic group. "It's a foolish industry that doesn't provide product for its largest market," Corliss writes, "but it's a meager art indeed that must tailor its work to fit the 12-year-old spirit."[50]

Film scholars have identified the late 1960s as having the markings of a major cinematic renaissance in America. The diversity and creativity of the period, however, were conditioned by audience demographics and commercial factors. The experimental cinema that coincided with the social upheaval of the time gave way to the recycling of big-budget Hollywood genre films for the youth audience.

The transformation of the cinema after World War II did not resolve the complex issues regarding the role of the popular arts in society. What it did do was create the necessity for people to be able to understand and evaluate the media which is so pervasive and essential to our lives today. But social institutions have not kept pace with the changing role of the popular media. Instead, the entertainment industry acquired a level of autonomy from other institutions, like family, church and school, that were far more significant in the past in shaping, maintaining and developing the roles and functions of entertainment. This was partly an effect of the diminishing cultural influence of the church in general over the course of the twentieth century.

The Production Code, however superficial, combined with the vigilance of organized watchdog groups, had assured that movie portrayals contributed to the building of national consensus during the 1930s and 1940s. The decline of this moral and cultural consensus and the Production Code as a mechanism for censorship cut film loose from its nation-building role. That this was necessary for film to mature as an art there is no doubt. Clearly, regulation impeded the artistic development of the cinema. But while the changes in the decades after World War II gave the movies freedom of expression, the cinema was still regarded foremost as a commercial enterprise. The institution of the rating system as a consumer guide, then, was supposed to be sufficient to protect children from exposure to adult material; the invisible hand of the free market would ensure cinematic portrayals within the bounds of respectability. Today's controversy over the popular arts, insofar as it involves issues that have persisted over the course of the century, raises serious questions about the continued viability of this approach.

In the late 1960s film, as well as the other popular arts, was still thought about in the context of the cultural hierarchy. That filmmakers could now deal explicitly with topics previously forbidden was not balanced by aesthetic, moral, social and religious criticism from other institutions, at least not outside academia or in a way that affected most people. The assumptions that separated high and popular culture continue to distinguish our treatment of the artifacts and practices associated with each. The entertainment industry is left largely on its own to determine the content of its productions and shape its own direction, with consumer taste, demographics, marketing and profit margins as industry guidelines and standards for success. The hard and fast contention of producers is that they are simply "giving the audience what it wants." Critics, consumer and religious groups all have ideas about what they think audiences want, but there is little agreement, as has always been the case. Film producer David Puttman is probably right when he suggests that audiences do not know what they want until they see it. Box-office returns seem to verify this, making mainstream Hollywood film production more analogous to gambling and instincts than an exact science.

11

. . . . .

Blockbuster
Instincts

Throughout this book I have focused on pivotal mo-
ments, highlighting social and cultural forces and specific events that shaped
the nature and role of American entertainment. The final decade of the twentieth century has all the marks of yet another transition period: changes in the
power structure of the industry, a shifting marketplace, new technologies, as
well as a changing social and cultural environment that creates anxiety and
evokes from religious leaders, politicians and the press strong criticism of the
means of communication.

The entertainment industry is undergoing colossal changes as it is increasingly monopolized by large corporations formed through acquisitions and
mergers. This trend is both a result and cause of the globalization of the
business. Through these corporations, as industry analyst John Izod observes,
"the oligopoly the anti-trust action had split apart in the late 1940s was now
being put together again through openings particularly in cable and satellite."[1] The Time-Warner merger, for example, combined Warner's production
capabilities in film, television and music with Time's cable delivery systems.
Viacom now owns Paramount Pictures, National Amusements Inc.—which has

one thousand screens nationwide—and video giant Blockbuster Entertainment. MCA is the parent company of Universal Pictures and Universal Television, as well as the exhibition chain Cineplex Odeon.

For the past decade or more, the entertainment industry has delivered movies, television programming and music via broadcasting, cable, CDs and video cassettes. But technological innovation and the convergence of the media promises new formats and delivery systems. The shape of these conglomerates reflects the integration of various media—computer, telephone, satellite, TV screen—that is rapidly taking place. Studios are integrating their creative and technical resources, gearing up for expected growth in the international market and emerging cable and satellite technologies. Three powerhouses in the world of entertainment, Steven Spielberg, Jeffrey Katzenberg and David Geffen, formed a new entertainment studio, Dreamworks SKG, with interests in film, television, music, animation and interactive multimedia.

At the same time, profit margins declined through the 1980s and early 1990s, and domestic box-office attendance has leveled off. In the meantime, star salaries have escalated, average production budgets have doubled, and marketing costs have tripled. Some movies today have to gross as much as $100 million just to break even. Consequently, as many as 70 percent end up in the red. Sidney J. Sheinberg, president of Universal Studios' parent company, MCA, Inc., said, "The reality is that films are costing more and more, profit retention is less and less and the business is being perceived by more and more people as really not such a wonderful business."[2] To broaden its audience base, Hollywood seems most interested in expanding foreign and video markets and developing new technologies. But there are some signs that the film industry is trying to reach marginal filmgoers and niche groups by exploring possibilities for producing a variety of movies for a differentiated audience.

Beginning in the late 1980s, film studios rediscovered the "family" market composed of baby boomers and their children. Other demographic trends indicated that specialty groups like women, minorities and the over-forty baby boomers could financially support a picture made for a specific but limited audience. At the same time, the independent filmmaking community began courting the adult audience with more sophisticated films that did not have expensive budgets and incredible special effects. Instead, these pictures combined solid acting and directing with thoughtful themes, raising important questions about contemporary culture and life. A good many of these films achieved artistic and reasonable financial success by reaching a sizable audience through both theatrical distribution channels and the video market. These three major trends—the dynamics of the blockbuster production, the changing marketplace and independent filmmaking—are together exerting a powerful influence on the contemporary cinema. Understanding these shaping forces gives insight into the rapidly changing world of entertainment today and helps clarify the issues in the controversy about it.

Hollywood's Blockbuster Business

Steven Spielberg likes to include a metaphor in his films that reflects on the movie itself. The mine car chase scene in *Indiana Jones and the Temple of Doom,* for example, suggested that the action-adventure film was like a wild roller-coaster ride. Stocked full of logo-inscribed merchandise, *Jurassic Park* itself worked as a clever metaphor for blockbuster movies that are turned into tourist attractions at theme parks, and mined for millions of dollars in retailing. Insofar as *Jurassic Park* was about a mega-event gone out of control, the movie commented on its own mode of production—Hollywood's undaunted obsession with the blockbuster movie.

A blockbuster movie is a big-screen theatrical release with celebrity talent, huge production budget and promotional campaign, musical soundtrack, and commercial product tie-ins that can be synergized into a cultural "event." The cornerstone of the blockbuster is the "high concept" film, a standard Hollywood term that refers to a simple idea that can be easily communicated.[3] As a mode of production, the high concept principle integrates moviemaking with marketing, but it also heightens the tension between artistic and commercial considerations in filmmaking. High concept films are by definition intensely market-driven, designed to give audiences familiar points of reference with other movies, making it easier to sell the new picture. This is routinely done by linking a star's persona with a film's concept (Tom Cruise or Sylvester Stallone movies) or replicating or combining successful films. Steven Segal's *Under Siege* was *Die Hard* on a boat; Tom Cruise's *Days of Thunder* was *Top Gun* in racecars. One critic called *Flashdance* "a seemingly impossible combination of a feminist *Rocky,* a bar girl *Fame* and *Jane Fonda's Workout.*"[4] Studios also rely on movie sequels (five *Rockys,* four *Jaws,* three *Die Hards*) and screen adaptations of bestselling novelists like Tom Clancy *(Hunt for Red October, Patriot Games* and *Clear and Present Danger),* John

Grisham *(The Pelican Brief, The Firm* and *The Client)* and Michael Crichton *(Rising Sun* and *Jurassic Park).*

As all this suggests, Hollywood is a slave to trends. In part, an inability on the part of executive decision-makers to distinguish good from bad in art and entertainment manifests itself in a kind of insecurity that leads them to follow popular trends.[5] But it is also a matter of economics. Distribution contracts give the studios their biggest share of box-office receipts in a movie's first weeks, with the percentage declining during the length of its theatrical run. This means that studios make more money on pictures that open big and drop off quickly than those that start slow but with good word-of-mouth have longer runs. Young people tend to be less discriminating than adults about the movies they see and are more easily lured by star power and flashy advertising campaigns. Because they make up a large share of the opening-weekend audience, studios invest heavily in movies and advertising campaigns, hoping to draw adolescents to the local cineplex. In contrast, adults do not necessarily rush out to see the latest release on opening weekend, but are more inclined to wait and base their choices on critical reviews and personal recommendations.

In the entertainment industry, a small percentage of huge successes offset losses incurred by the greater number of failures. "It's the big hits that carry you," Rupert Murdoch, chairman of News Corporation, said. "The majority of pictures end up losing money."[6] In 1994, for example, only 29 films (6.4 percent) out of approximately 430 U.S. releases topped $50 million in domestic box-office returns, accounting for 53 percent of the total.[7] This is a key reason the major studios continue to concentrate on high-concept, big-budget "event movies" like *E.T., Batman* and *Jurassic Park.*[8] The single blockbuster film generates the most revenues by attracting a very large audience to the box office for a single production, and statistical research indicates that big-budgeted movies have a higher rate of return than less expensive ones. Warner Brothers, for example, made $50.5 million off the $7.5-million production *Driving Miss Daisy* (1989), which grossed a surprising $100 million at theaters. But Warner's $50-million investment in *Batman* that year was parlayed into a $251-million gross, with $150.5 million returned to the distributor. "Look at *Batman,* going millions beyond budget, dumping millions on cast and marketing, and becoming this huge cultural experience," one studio production executive said. "What people conclude is that if you build a big enough mousetrap, you will succeed."[9]

In 1995 Warner Brothers spent $95 million to make *Batman Forever* and another $30 million to market it. Universal supported its $51-million investment in *Apollo 13* with a marketing budget between $20 and $30 million. Disney spent $20 million to promote its $45-million production *Pocahontas*.[10] The sheer size of the investment in a blockbuster (and proportionate risk) galvanizes a studio's efforts to make the film a financial success.

The blockbuster strategy has a lowest common denominator element that works to create a sameness about movies by reducing filmmaking to basic formulaic elements and predictable story structures. Filmmakers tend to rely on director and star power to generate a sense of uniqueness about each film; creativity can be reduced to dazzling audiences with special effects and a reliance on visceral imagery. This has only been intensified since American-produced entertainment is no longer made for the domestic audience alone but is conceived in terms of a global strategy. To produce one product for a worldwide market is less costly, but these films must rely on basic, universal themes in order to communicate across national and cultural boundaries. This in turn marginalizes specific perspectives in the cinema, and especially religious ones. The global market, then, fuels the blockbuster mentality, for as one writer pointed out, "the very ingredients that seem to ensure a film's success in the foreign market—action-filled scripts and big stars—are expensive, and in courting overseas sales, producers push budgets ever higher."[11] Regardless of their domestic performance, big action-packed movies with stars and special effects are more likely to score overseas than comedies or dramas.

Escalating costs and corporate bottom lines over the previous two decades meant that fewer films were made for specific audience segments. It is more difficult to make "a profitable small picture than a profitable large one," industry analyst James Monaco explains. "The small picture has to be precisely tuned to its minority audience, costs have to be watched carefully, and even if it's a success, the profit margin is narrow. Blockbusters, on the other hand, made for a worldwide mass audience, costs be damned, often recoup their massive investments simply because of the size of the investment."[12] The sheer size of the investment (and proportionate risk) in a big-budget movie galvanizes the studio's effort to make it a success. Average production costs soared 265 percent from $9.4 million in 1980 to $34.3 million in 1994. Studios simultaneously increased marketing campaigns to provide greater exposure for these films, and average advertising costs grew an incredible 291 percent, from $3.5 million in 1980 to $13.9 million in 1994. As a result, a film had to

---

Table 11.1. What Generally Works Well in the International Marketplace

---

Animation
The Lion King, Beauty and the Beast, Aladdin

Big U.S. movies
Forrest Gump, Apollo 13, Jurassic Park, The Bodyguard

Star-driven
Arnold Schwarzenegger, Sylvester Stallone, Kevin Costner

Action/adventure
Speed, Die Hard, Waterworld, True Lies, Lethal Weapon 3

Sex/exploitation
Basic Instinct, Showgirls, Sliver

Sophisticated/art house
The Piano, Pulp Fiction, Muriel's Wedding, The Brothers McMullen

---

What Generally Does Not Work in the International Marketplace

---

Purely American themes
Hoffa, Driving Miss Daisy, A League of Their Own, A Few Good Men

"Ethnic"-oriented films
Poetic Justice, Menace II Society, Blood In Blood Out, Clockers

Westerns
Unforgiven, Tombstone, Bad Girls, Maverick

Light Comedies
City Slickers 2, Sleepless in Seattle, Honey, I Shrunk the Kids, The Addams Family

Sports
Mr. Baseball, Mighty Ducks, Blue Chips, Angels in the Outfield

---

draw a much larger audience and make proportionately more money in order to be profitable. To break even, the average-budgeted film in 1994 had to sell more than twice as many tickets as in 1980 and gross more than four times as much at the box office.

In the long view, however, according to MPAA figures, the domestic film audience has remained constant at roughly one billion admissions per year beginning in 1961 (with a 20 percent fluctuation either way), even though the size of the U.S. population has increased by about 30 percent since 1960.[13] This means that fewer tickets are actually being sold per capita each year. Mounting costs and a flat domestic market are counter trends that threaten the industry's profitability. To ensure expanding revenues, either the movie-going audience has to be enlarged rapidly, or production costs have to be reduced. Evidence of both trends exists today.

Table 11.2. Average Film Negative Costs (in Millions of Dollars)

1941	$ .4
1949	1.0
1961	1.5
1971	1.75
1974	2.5
1980	9.4
1984	14.4
1989	23.5
1990	26.8
1991	26.1
1992	28.9
1993	29.9
1994	34.3

Sources: Cobbett Steinberg, *Reel Facts: The Movies Book of Records* (New York: Vintage, 1978), pp. 365-66; MPAA, "1994: U.S. Economic Review." Used by permission.

A successful U.S. project is increasingly dependent on the growth of international and ancillary markets. Domestic revenues increased by 36 percent in the late 1980s, but foreign revenues doubled, reaching $1.3 billion by 1989 and surpassing domestic rentals in the early 1990s. Currently some films are more than doubling their gross earnings overseas, and studios can expect sometimes 50 to 70 percent of a film's theatrical revenues to come from foreign markets. The global market represents "almost 6 billion people," MCA's Tom Pollock said. "That's where growth is going to be. In this country, we're just stealing markets from each other."[14] According to a recent report, overseas film earnings are growing at twice the annual rate of the domestic market; Hollywood accounts for about half the movie market in Japan and two-thirds of all movie tickets sold in Germany, France and Italy.[15] Generally about 70 percent of films shown around the world are U.S. productions.

Overseas growth is facilitated by U.S. investment in foreign cinemas. American and foreign companies in many countries including Australia, West Germany, Spain, France, Sweden, the Netherlands, Russia and other Eastern European countries are joining to build modern theaters. These efforts have greatly expanded the international market. With the addition of about seventy multiplexes during the 1980s, for example, theater attendance more than doubled in the United Kingdom. Major releases, like *The Lion King,* enjoyed expanded screenings in Europe, and the number of prints for a standard release has almost doubled.[16] U.S. companies are also cofinancing foreign productions and even investing in non-English-language films.

American investment abroad ensures the continual opening of the U.S. market for films from other countries. So while the expanding global market fosters a homogenization of movies on the one hand, it can also lead to the development of a more varied and pluralistic cinema on the other. Filmmakers in other countries often employ alternative ways of storytelling that can enrich the American cinema. The "magical realism" of *Like Water for Chocolate,* for example, shows how the supernatural can be woven into a story without disrupting the believability of the narrative.

In conjunction with video delivery, the internationalization of Hollywood has provided more distribution channels for the international cinema in the United States. While foreign-language films accounted for only 0.8 percent of total box office in 1994, and non-U.S. English-language films 3.2 percent, in recent years American audiences outside of the major cities have been able to see films from around the world, some resulting from international coproductions. From Asia came *The Wedding Banquet, Eat Drink Man Woman, Farewell My Concubine* and renown director Zhang Yimou's *Raise the Red Lantern* and *Ju Dou* (both starring Asian screen star Gong Li). Krzysztof Kieslowski's (French/Polish/Swiss) color trilogy *Blue, White* and *Red* delighted the arthouse crowd playing in U.S. theaters and on video. The Mexican hit *Like Water for Chocolate* became the highest-grossing foreign-language film in U.S. history, topping $20 million. From Australia came *The Piano, Muriel's Wedding, Strictly Ballroom, Heavenly Creatures,* and *Sirens.* From France *The Lover* and *Indochine,* from Spain *Belle Epoque,* from Italy *Mediterraneo, Cinema Paradiso* and *The Postman (Il Postino),* and from Britain *A Room with a View, Enchanted April, Howard's End* and *Four Weddings and a Funeral.* Most of these films played on only a small number of U.S. screens (often fewer than one hundred), but the advent of the video market has made them economically viable products for distributors.[17]

In contrast to the early 1980s, when there were few real alternatives to seeing a film in a theater, today there is a proliferation of new ways for people to see movies, all of which have an effect on theatrical attendance. The advent of new technologies in cable television, home video and satellite transmission inaugurated a new wave of film viewing in homes in the United States and increasingly around the world, transforming the contemporary cinema and entertainment. According to MPAA figures, the number of households with basic cable services and a VCR grew from 1.85 million in 1980 to 72.8 million in 1994, reaching 77 percent of American TV households. In 1980 video represented only 15 percent of studio revenues. By 1986 video had become a distinct market, accounting for about half of the total. While Americans bought 1.2 billion movie tickets in 1991, they rented 4.1 billion videos. The following year Americans spent $12 billion to rent or buy videos and $4.9 billion at the movie box office. It was estimated that the average American household spent $165.75 on videos (rentals and purchases) that year.[18]

As a new delivery system, video is also a field for exploitation. Not all international films are award contenders; other countries produce their own share of mediocre movies and exploitation fare that could eventually flood the video distribution system. As an increasing number of films from other countries with different standards of morality for cinematic presentations find wider distribution in the United States, they will present greater challenges to the MPAA ratings board, as well as the vigilance of parents and watchdog groups.

The advent of the home video market also had a major impact on the pornography business. According to one report, while under 1 percent of American households had VCRs in 1978, more than 75 percent of the video-cassettes sold were pornographic.[19] At the same time, the number of porn theaters dropped from 700 in 1980 to about 250 in 1987, when the porn video business was estimated at one billion dollars. The Video Software Dealers Association reported that profits from X-rated videos rose more than any other category, from 10 percent of total revenues in 1985 to 12.7 percent in 1986.[20] Watching a video in the privacy of one's home replaced going out to a sleazy XXX theater; an adult could leave a video store with two Disney tapes and *Debbie Does Dallas* with no one noticing the difference. More recent video store surveys show that "adult" titles follow children's tapes and new releases in popularity.[21]

While the video business is still dominated by A-titles following their theatrical run, direct-to-video releases (DTVs) represent one of the fastest-growing segments of the business. Most of these films are made on minuscule budgets using high-concept titles and promotion to exploit an existing popular genre, but bypass—or, as in the case of *Red Rock West,* precede—a theatrical run. Along with science fiction and action-adventure, erotic thrillers are among the most popular genres; "Hot, Tan, Alien" *Beach Babes from Beyond* and "Spies, Thighs, Bikinis and Bullets" in *The Dallas Connection* are among the exploitation fare in video stores. "We have been able to fill a niche that the studios weren't attending to," said the president of Prism Pictures, producer of the Night Eyes series. "As major features have become more costly, and as society has become more voyeuristic, we've been able to come up with more of these erotic thrillers, what used to be called B-movies."[22] Companies will sometimes make two versions, one unrated.

The same is being done with theatrical features. The director's cuts of *Body of Evidence* and *Basic Instinct* were simply the NC-17-rated versions. What distinguished the exclusive director's cut of Richard Rush's *Color of Night* was "15 Extra Steamy Minutes!" More recently, MGM released both R and NC-17 rated versions of *Showgirls* on video with different box art. While the size of the erotic and pornography business has been interpreted by some as a sign of moral decline, it does illustrate the preferences of an active audience segment that has not been lost on Hollywood producers.

Theatrical release is now only one stage in the history of a film. After its theatrical run, a movie is sold to pay-TV and movie channels (HBO, Cinemax, the Movie Channel, Encore) for viewing on cable. It is distributed on video-cassette for sales and rentals and is sold to network and syndicated television. These ancillary markets have changed moviegoing habits by replacing the second-run theater. People will pay the full price of a theater admission only for some movie spectacle or critically acclaimed film. They wait for films of lesser quality to be released on video ("renters").

In 1980 worldwide theatrical box office accounted for 80 percent of the revenue of feature films; however, by 1992 only about 25 percent of a film's earnings came from theaters, as ancillary markets in cable, home video and pay TV expanded enormously.[23] The international video market had become the fastest-growing ancillary market for U.S. studios in 1994. Foreign theatrical revenues were $1.86 billion that year, compared with $3 billion from the video business; foreign video revenues increased 48 percent between 1990 and 1994.[24] For the past several years, domestic box-office grosses have been around $5 billion, but films generate another $5 billion in revenues in foreign markets and approximately $11 billion from ancillary sources, in addition to sales of related paraphernalia like toys and fashion products. Disney's *The Lion King*, for example, reached $289.9 million in domestic box office but made even more ($341.4 million) in foreign revenues. The video became the top-selling video of all time (twenty-six million sold), with almost a third of the nation's ninety-seven million TV households owning a copy. It was estimated that *The Lion King* would reach $2 billion in revenues from theatrical, video, soundtrack, cable, TV and merchandising sources.[25]

There is nothing wrong with the blockbuster strategy itself, as it has obviously produced some of the most popular and profitable movies in film history. Many blockbuster films are enjoyable and fun to watch. I was speaking once to a group of high-school students who loved *Jurassic Park*. The film had a skeleton of a plot, shallow characterization and half-baked philosophical speculation about chaos theory—but, as a student exclaimed, "Did you see those dinosaurs?" Blockbusters are intended for a general audience, and they fulfill basic social and mythological functions. For these reasons they can be extremely popular and, as we have seen, profitable in both domestic and foreign markets.

It is ironic, then, that the blockbuster mentality is the cause of much criticism of Hollywood films today. The dilemma begins when it is used to expand the market for movies that should be more restricted in audience. Instead of criticizing the use, or perhaps abuse, of this approach to filmmaking for the way it leads to the mass marketing of almost every film regardless of content, reformers have made sweeping and exaggerated condemnations of Hollywood productions. This makes good headlines but does little to help people understand industry rationales or encourage producers to be more astute in correlating budget, market and topical fare, which would address issues of social responsiblity. As Warren Susman observes, "Films are not only a mass medium, they also represent one of the major ways in which a mass society can examine itself as mass."[26] But the blockbuster's mass, mythic formula approach is not the only mode of filmmaking. The cinema can and should honor and explore the diversity of human beings, the variety of their experiences and the value of different perspectives.

The economics of the blockbuster are a powerful force in the film industry, greatly affecting the content and marketing of motion pictures. Short of a major transformation in the production and distribution of films, there is little expectation for significant change in the near future. International growth and the advent of home video and other ancillary outlets fuel the production of big-budget films aimed at a large, undifferentiated audience. There are signs, however, that the confluence of these developments with other trends taking shape could perhaps lead to a more consistent production of different kinds of movies for different audiences. This is something critics have for a long time advocated as a resolution to artistic problems within the industry and its volatile relationship with other social institutions. The remainder of this chapter will consider the relation between Hollywood economics and the MPAA rating system and then survey two important trends in the cinema today: changing audience demographics and independent filmmaking.

The Rating System Revisited

When combined with the MPAA rating system, the mass dynamics of the blockbuster foster a homogenization of Hollywood films that continues to be a source of contention among the industry's critics. While the MPAA has argued that there is no ostensible connection between rating and box-office performance, there is little doubt that the rating system has a great effect on the cinema, influencing scriptwriting, editing, contracts, advertising, distribution and ancillary markets. Film studios work for a specific rating to maximize the potential audience for each movie. The nexus of production, marketing and movie rating has become problematic for those concerned about the film industry's responsibility to its younger patrons. It also highlights the tension between film as art and commercial entertainment.

After the institution of the rating system, a general consensus emerged in the film industry about the relation between specific ratings and audience. Based on the assumption that a film had to reach the widest possible audience, the R and X categories were initially seen as problematic; G and PG (originally M for Mature) were perceived as "safe," if also "childish." The perception gradually changed, however, as G and X were frequently referred to as "box-office poison," while PG and R became the ratings film producers most preferred. Moviemaking gravitated toward the middle ratings, based on the perception that the extreme ones (G and now NC-17) marginalized a film in the market. A survey of films released between 1968 and 1994 shows that the majority were in the R (52.6 percent) and PG (27.8 percent) categories (see table 11.3).

Table 11.3. CARA Ratings (1968-1994)

Rating	No. of Films	Percentage
G	1,032	8.5%
PG	3,376	27.8%
PG-13	951	7.8%
R	6,388	52.6%
NC-17/X	407	3.3%
Total	12,154	100.0%

Source: MPAA, "1994 U.S. Economic Review." Used by permission.

Today films rated PG, PG-13 and R are the ones thought most likely to be successful at the box office because they have the most appeal to the most avid moviegoers. In the 1990s Gallup conducted a telephone poll for *Variety* to determine the relationship between movie attendance and film ratings.[27] If a film were available in all five rating versions, the largest segment of filmgoers (39 percent) said they would prefer to see the R version. PG-13 was second (27 percent) and PG a distant third (16 percent), with NC-17 (7 percent) and G (6 percent) coming in last. The R and PG-13 categories ranked even higher among the most frequent moviegoers. The R category was most appealing among eighteen- to twenty-four-year-olds, with preference for this rating declining with age.

This survey also raised questions about the effectiveness of the system. Thirty-seven percent of those between twelve and seventeen indicated they had seen an R-rated movie without a parent or guardian. These findings affirm the industry's general perceptions about the moviegoing public, even though they do not match up with box-office performance when correlated with film ratings. Nor do these preferences entirely explain the high number of R-rated films produced. One reason is that preference cannot be equated with actual behavior. Many twelve- to seventeen-year-olds might prefer an R film, but that does not mean their parents allow them to see them or that local exhibitors admit them. Also, what people say they disapprove of and what they actually see are often one and the same.

The current rating system divides viewers into three age groups—up to twelve years, thirteen to sixteen, and seventeen and older.[28] The MPAA uses the legal age of seventeen to distinguish between an adult and a minor;

moviegoers under seventeen must be accompanied by an adult to see an R-rated film and are prohibited from NC-17 pictures. In other words, an R rating does not necessarily eliminate the under-seventeen audience. Accompanied by an adult, or overlooked by a negligent theater employee, a minor can see the R-rated *Body of Evidence,* advertised as "the erotic thriller of the year." According to MPAA research, the most avid moviegoers are the under-thirty age group, which accounted for 45 percent of total admissions in 1994. More specifically, the most frequent moviegoers are the sixteen- to twenty-four-year-olds, who constituted 15 percent of the population that year but account-ed for 25 percent of movie admissions. As a demographic group, then, the most frequent moviegoers, and therefore Hollywood's target audience, strad-dle the seventeen-year-old mark that divides the audience into adults and minors.

As filmmaking has gravitated toward the middle ratings for commercial reasons, the effect was once again to foster a lack of differentiation in movies and audience. Some films *are* made for specific audiences, but with most releases the studios try to reach the widest market to increase potential earn-ings. "A crucial guideline is that if a film aims only for a narrow segment of the audience, it is unlikely to appeal to a broader audience," John Izod explains. "Conversely if a project broadens its appeal, the narrow audience will still be attracted."[29] Based on commonly held assumptions about the ratings, filmmakers add gratuitous profanity (or other elements) to avoid the stigma of a G rating, so adults and teens will not think a movie is just for kids. Twentieth Century-Fox reportedly added explicit "fantasy violence" scenes to ensure a PG rating for *Star Wars,* for example. More recently, films like *Maverick* and *The Flintstones* combined slapstick and subtle adult humor in a PG package in the hope of attracting both "baby boomlets" and their par-ents.

To attract the under-seventeen crowd, however, producers also try to secure a PG-13 rating for more adult-oriented fare. Initially rated R, *Desperately Seek-ing Susan* (1985) was edited to allow under-seventeen "wannabes" to see rock singer Madonna in her film debut. Universal's *Jurassic Park* (1993) managed a PG-13 despite its lifelike rampaging dinosaurs and their trail of human carnage.

On the other end of the ratings spectrum, the NC-17 category created a new line for filmmakers to walk, now between material prohibited to minors and that requiring adult supervision. *Body of Evidence, Damage* and *Basic Instinct* pushed the boundaries of the R rating and had to be edited to shed an NC-17 rating. These films illustrate how the ratings function as "censorship, capitalist style," as one writer puts it.[30] Filmmakers must make alterations or deletions in order for a film to receive the rating most likely to increase the film's market potential. In this respect at least, the ratings system can be viewed as a continuation, although in different form, of the precensorship philosophy of the Production Code.

The ratings system has had a Janus-headed effect on the cinema. On the one hand, it was intended to distinguish serious entertainment for adults from child-oriented fare. There is a general (however false) perception that the more restricted the rating, the more serious and sophisticated the movie. In practice, however, a more restricted rating for some films can also simply mean more explicit sex and violence. The reason for this is that CARA rates a film's treatment of theme based on the inclusion of violence, sexuality, nudity and profanity. Sex is sex, violence is violence according to the board's method of evaluation; regardless of how the filmmaker presents them, the inclusion of these elements necessitates a more restrictive rating. The differentiation of films that the ratings represent is based almost exclusively on (im)moral content.

In practice, however, there is no necessary correlation between the moral standards used to determine a rating and the sophistication or artistic merit of a film. Are films rated PG or PG-13 like *Driving Miss Daisy, Terms of Endearment, On Golden Pond, Dances with Wolves* or *A Few Good Men* somehow less serious and sophisticated as adult entertainment than R-rated films like *Rain Man, Platoon* or *The Godfather?* Using the ratings as a guide, how are these films to be compared with *Teenage Mutant Ninja Turtles* (PG), *Wayne's World* (PG-13) or *Animal House* (R), which hold out little, if any, artistic pretension?

To use a specific illustration, *Jurassic Park* (rated PG-13) had a straightforward narrative, and its scientific musing over the "humans versus nature" theme was eclipsed by the Industrial Light and Magic dinosaurs meant to amaze everyone thirteen and older. Released the same year, *The Fugitive* also received a PG-13 rating, even though it was an entirely different kind of movie aimed at a different audience segment. The film's opening extended-montage sequence, the psychology of the two main characters (one hunted by the other as both try to solve the murder), the medical terminology and eventual revelation of motive and conspiracy made for a more complex characterization, theme and narrative structure than *Jurassic Park's*. But these differences in purpose and level of sophistication are not reflected in their common rating.

Furthermore, simple information about profanity, nudity, sexual situations and violence is actually very superficial, revealing little if anything about the moral universe portrayed by a film. *Body of Evidence* and *Basic Instinct* both received an R rating despite explicit and violent sex scenes between unmarried people. In contrast, most of the lovemaking in *The Wide Sargasso Sea* occurs between a newly married couple exploring their uncontrollable passion for each other. But the art-circuit release was given an NC-17 because of a single shot of male frontal nudity (an edited R-version was released on video). Likewise, how are we to compare or judge the violence in a Lethal Weapon or Die Hard movie with the atrocities depicted in *Schindler's List*, based on their common R rating?

The wedding of art and business with the morality of the rating system produced a circuity that remains a source of discord and misunderstanding about the role of the cinema as art. Putting a rating on a movie also has the effect of putting a category on the audience. If a film receives a G or PG rating, the perception is that it somehow has to appeal to and be "appreciated" by children. In other words, the rating also reflects on the level of maturity and sophistication of theme, plot and characterization. A film suitable for the under-thirteen crowd is routinely deemed juvenile, lacking in sophistication, artistic and otherwise. But regardless of thematic seriousness or cinematic creativity, a film will be rated acceptable for a general audience unless it contains restrictive elements. For these reasons, filmmakers who want their work taken seriously spice up their treatment of a theme to get an R or at least a PG-13 rating.

Filmmakers who want to do meaningful work must also contend with the forces of marketing, audience appeal and the desire for escalating profits. In other words, they want the freedom of expression to create significant works of art, but they also want their pictures to be commercially successful. That means they have to be "appreciated" in some way by adolescents, who constitute a large percentage of the audience for box-office hits. Film producers try to have it both ways: to include profanity, sex and violence to maximize the box-office lure, but to receive the more general ratings in order to restrict the fewest potential viewers. Even if a film probes important social, moral and psychological issues in contemporary life—what filmmaker Paul Schrader calls "rips in the social fabric"—despite the level of complexity, depth of drama or humor, and sense of realism, the studio will still not want to limit the box office with a more restrictive rating. The perception is that an NC-17 rating, indicating that it is suitable only for mature audiences over seventeen, promises a box-office disaster.[31] But what would audience and industry perception be of a film with a serious treatment of a sophisticated theme, complicated narrative structure and complex characterization that was rated G? These problems will persist as long as profit-making maintains its hegemony over artistic, cultural and moral values in defining the role of entertainment in American life.

Who's Going to the Movies?

A noticeable shift in audience demographics today suggests the existence, and greater viability, of a more differentiated audience for movies than in previous decades. As I showed in the previous chapter, beginning in the early 1970s Hollywood revised its moviemaking strategy around the under-thirty moviegoing group, as evidenced by the large output of genre films popular with young people—action-adventure, science fiction, horror and comedies. Hollywood courted its bread-and-butter audience, the sixteen- to twenty-four-year-olds, with the hope that films would connect with other audience segments as well. This pattern was repeated for blockbuster successes from *Jaws, Star Wars* and *E.T.* to *Home Alone* and *Jurassic Park*—films that became megahits by drawing young repeaters as well as those people who seldom venture out to the theater except for some movie spectacle. With the exception of *E.T.,* the ten top-grossing films of the 1980s were all driven by the repeater business of teenagers, and especially adolescent males: the three Indiana Jones films and the Star Wars trilogy, *Batman, Beverly Hills Cop, Ghostbusters* and *Back to the Future.*[32] For this reason, *Los Angeles Times* film critic Jack Mathews referred to the 1980s as "a decade of demographic tunnel vision during which people out of the twelve to thirty-four age range were statistically irrelevant" to Hollywood.[33]

Moviegoing remains a popular activity in the youth culture. Despite a general "graying" of the American population in the 1990s, the under-thirty group accounted for 49 percent of total admissions in 1994, even though they constituted only 31 percent of the total population. But this actually represents a significant drop in admissions share, from 67 percent in 1984. That year MTV exposure launched Michael Jackson's *Thriller* album to record-breaking heights, and the five top-grossing films were all teen-oriented: *Ghostbusters, Indiana Jones and the Temple of Doom, Beverly Hills Cop, Gremlins* and *The Karate Kid.*

The declining presence of young people at movie theaters does not mean they are seeing fewer movies. In fact, the opposite case could be made. Teens reduced their movie attendance by 20 percent in 1985 but tripled their viewing of rented videos. *Variety* reported that "VCR dates" were quickly becoming a less expensive way to date or gather with friends, replacing going out to the movies as a teenage social and dating ritual.[34]

As the percentage of youth dropped, however, the over-forties share of movie admissions more than doubled, from 15 percent in 1984 to 36 percent in 1994. These box-office trends largely reflect the return of baby boomers to the theaters as they move past the early childrearing years. Between 1990 and 1994, as increasing numbers of boomers entered their thirties and forties, the under-thirties share dropped from 56 to 45 percent, while the thirty-and-over share increased from 44 to 54 percent of the domestic box office.[35]

The middle-aged adult crowd enjoys a greater variety of movies than teenagers and is less interested in pyrotechnics, buckets of blood and adolescent alienation. They are more selective, favoring more sophisticated films with adult themes that are both serious and entertaining. Although they are not the most frequent moviegoers (those who attend at least once a month), they are the prime viewers of movies on cable and videocassette purchasers. Now that these ancillary markets exceed theatrical exhibition in dollars, the industry has begun a foray into the marginal audience.

Several other identifiable audience segments surfaced in the late 1980s. In contrast to conventional Hollywood wisdom, surveys showed that teenage and young women accounted for the largest percentage of the audience for several films in the late 1980s: *Rain Man, Three Men and a Baby, Working Girl, Big* and *Cocktail.*[36] Women in the industry still struggle for significant roles on both sides of the camera, but the box-office presence of women does challenge prevailing assumptions about gender and moviegoing. Spike Lee's films—*She's Gotta Have It, Do the Right Thing, Jungle Fever, Malcolm X*— revealed the box-office presence of African-Americans and also crossed over into the mainstream. Lee broke important ground for other young black filmmakers and actors in the 1990s, and there have been a number of movies with rap soundtracks exploring racism and urban anguish. The success of these and several foreign-language films in turn fostered studio interested in low-budget

Table 11.4. Movie Admissions by Age Groups

	Percent of total yearly admissions					Percent of resident civilian population as of 1/94
	1994	1993	1992	1991	1990	
Age						
12-15 yrs	10%	9%	13%	12%	11%	7%
16-20	14	17	16	19	20	8
21-24	11	10	11	12	11	7
25-29	10	13	11	12	14	9
30-39	18	19	19	19	20	21
40-49	16	15	15	13	12	17
50-59	8	7	7	5	5	11
60 and over	12	11	8	8	7	20
	100%	100%	100%	100%	100%	100%
12-17	14%	15%	18%	17%	18%	10%
18 and over	88	86	84	83	82	90
12-29	45	49	51	55	56	31
12-39	63	68	70	74	76	52
16-39	53	59	57	62	65	45
40 and over	36	33	30	26	24	48

Source: MPAA, "1994 U.S. Economic Review." Used by permission.

Latin-themed pictures with broader appeal.

By concentrating their financial resources and creative energies on the youth audience, film studios largely ignored everyone else. But these observations about audience demographics suggest that a number of different markets exist today, based on age, gender, race and ethnicity, that could support specialty films. A recent survey affirmed that movies that elicit a positive response from any niche group can expect to generate at least twenty million dollars in domestic box-office returns.[37]

By the early 1990s Hollywood also rediscovered the "family" market. During the 1970s several independent companies distributed features for the family trade—*Benji* (1974), *The Life and Times of Grizzly Adams* (1975), *The Adventures of the Wilderness Family* (1976) and *Pete's Dragon* (1977), among others. These films required strategic marketing and intense promotion and still did not generate the blockbuster revenues of *Jaws, Star Wars* and *Close*

Encounters of the Third Kind that established the primacy of the youth market in the following decade. Studios could not duplicate the blockbuster success of teen-oriented fare with the family trade. Most family-oriented movies were disappointing or only modestly successful during the 1980s: *Annie,* Jim Henson's *The Dark Crystal* and *The Muppets Take Manhattan, An American Tail, Benji the Hunted, The Land Before Time.* Even Disney could not lure families out in a big way for its stock-in-trade animated features like *The Black Cauldron, Adventures of the Great Mouse Detective* or *Oliver and Company,* until late in the decade when *Who Framed Roger Rabbit?* and *The Little Mermaid* became bona fide hits.

After a lackluster period during the 1980s, however, Disney scored with *The Little Mermaid* in 1989, demonstrating that an animated feature aimed at the family market could by synergized into a blockbuster event. The film topped forty million dollars in domestic theatrical rentals, the sparkling soundtrack sold over 800,000 copies, and videocassettes sold almost ten million copies. According to one Disney executive, it was that possibility of synergy with the video market that fueled the industry's resurgent interest in the "family" trade. Disney began releasing a series of successful animated features. *Aladdin* (1992) reportedly earned a billion dollars from box office, video and soundtrack sales, and merchandising. The direct-to-video sequel, *Jafar's Revenge,* sold over eight million units and included a lengthy preview for Disney's next animated feature, *The Lion King* (1994).

"It's a case of the right company, the right technology and the right time in history," a media analyst for Paul Kagan Associates explained. "The baby boomers are having their kids. They all grew up on Disney classics. Disney has restarted and stepped up the production of new classics in a big way. And the VCR is making it possible for people to take these movies home and enjoy them."[38] Disney dominated the video market in the 1990s with new releases and a library of animated classics, movies that kids can watch over and over again at home.

The success of Disney's animated features and the Home Alone films motivated studios to test the broad-audience family market. Between 1991 and 1994, the number of G- and PG-rated movies rose from 100 (16.3 percent of all releases) to 139 (21.9 percent). With the exception of *Terminator 2* and *Batman Returns* (both 1980s sequels), the top-grossing films of the 1990s have all been aimed at the more general family audience or adults: *Jurassic Park, Home Alone, Forrest Gump, The Lion King, Mrs. Doubtfire, Ghost, Alad-*

din, Dances with Wolves, The Fugitive and *Pretty Woman*. This suggests the continued viability of the general market for spectacular big-screen events like *Jurassic Park* and *The Lion King.*

Still, the general audience could not displace the more specific sixteen-to-twenty-four age group as the primary and regular moviegoing audience.[39] It cannot be overlooked that recent blockbuster hits *Jurassic Park, Forrest Gump* and *The Lion King* all scored with the sixteen-to-twenty-four crowd while also connecting across age groups. *Gump* expanded its audience by luring over-forty baby boomers to the theaters, and *Lion King* drew baby boomer families; everyone wanted to see *Jurassic Park's* lifelike dinosaurs.

The performance of the general market in the 1990s was predictable. A small number of films captured most of the box office, while a host of family-oriented movies were only moderately successful or simply failed. Beyond those already mentioned, *Home Alone 2, The Flintstones* and *The Santa Clause* topped $100 million in domestic box-office earnings; *Angels in the Outfield, The Little Rascals, Dennis the Menace, Rookie of the Year* and *Free Willy* were among the successful offerings. But there were a host of disappointments, including *Jetsons: The Movie, Ducktales: The Movie, We're Back: A Dinosaur's Story, Thumbelina, The Swan Princess, The Pagemaster, Little Big League, Andre, Lassie, Ferngully: The Last Rainforest, Miracle on 34th Street* and *Getting Even with Dad. Searching for Bobby Fischer* and *Black Beauty* were complete duds. John Hughes could not replicate the success of his "home alone" formula with *Baby's Day Out* and *Richie Rich.* Even Disney struck out with *Newsies, Born Yesterday, The Adventures of Huck Finn, Life with Mikey, Super Mario Brothers* and *North.* Some of these films were simply uninteresting, featuring kids and/or animals to attract the family crowd. Many were cheaply made, but big-budget efforts like *North* (forty million dollars) and *Baby's Day Out* (fifty million) also failed to attract an audience.

The moviegoing habits of the general family audience (twelve to sixty) tend to be irregular and somewhat unpredictable. While young people go the movies regularly as a social outing with friends, families only go out to the movies as a special event several times a year. The sheer numbers of such a wide demographic, however, can expand the box office for spectacular event pictures, especially during the Christmas season (Thanksgiving through New Year's) and during the summer holidays. That a successful year for the movie industry can depend on the handful of big films offered during the peak box-office seasons verifies the continual significance of this market.

The impressive box office for *Home Alone, Hook, Honey I Shrunk the Kids, Mrs. Doubtfire* and the Disney animated features from *The Little Mermaid* to *The Lion King* can be attributed not only to repeat viewings by children but also to the inclusion of their baby boom parents.[40] Surveys show that parents with some college education and with children under eighteen living at home are the most likely adults to attend movies. They enjoy getting out of the house alone but also like taking their children to the theater, and have made the over-forties and the family viable markets for movies in the 1990s.

Broad-based family pictures have been joined by serious dramatic fare *(A River Runs Through It, Shadowlands, Philadelphia* and *Bridges of Madison County)* and sophisticated comedies *(Bull Durham, Sleepless in Seattle, Four Weddings and a Funeral)* aimed at older audiences. Some of the most creative and memorable recent films have been by independent film companies. "The people who are making quality movies for an adult audience are the specialized labels like Miramax and Gramercy," MCA Motion Picture Group chairman Tom Pollock said. "Those films are made for a price that reflects the true size of that audience."[41]

Cowboys and Indies

The recent growth of the independent filmmaking community is the one trend in the contemporary cinema that is at once the most promising and the most irresolute.[42] Independents in the specialty markets exist within a network of assorted production and distribution arrangements. These companies work with low production and promotional budgets, aim at specific audiences and anticipate modest profits. They will sometimes secure production financing for a single project from several sources in different countries and negotiate coproduction deals and foreign presales. Depending on the project, a company might finance films in production, distribute or lease them to another company for distribution, or secure video rights. *The Crying Game,* for example, was independently made by producer Stephen Wooley and writer-director Neil Jordan. They pulled together financing from British and Japanese sources and from presales of theatrical rights in several European markets. Miramax, the leading independent distributor, bought the theatrical rights but sold the video rights to LIVE Entertainment.

The emergence of video as a new delivery system had a direct and immediate effect on independent filmmaking. As the home video market began to take off in the 1980s, newly formed video companies were eager for product and bought the rights to independent films, sometimes a company's entire slate of future releases. Video, then, became a source of upfront production financing; presales competition drove acquisition prices up. For their end of the deal, the independent distributors were expected to advertise and promote the films during their theatrical run so the titles would be familiar by the time they were released on video.

The current independent trend began with several successful films during the 1980s. Video retailer Vestron's low-budget *Dirty Dancing* film, soundtrack albums, video, concert tour and spinoff television series were synergized into gross earnings of about $350 million. New Line Cinema struck gold with its teenage horror series Nightmare on Elm Street. Spike Lee's first feature film, *She's Gotta Have It,* was both a critical and a financial success, made for under $200,000 but grossing a surprising $8 million. Several other independent productions drew critical acclaim and sometimes notable box office beginning in the 1980s. The British *A Room with a View* grossed $20 million and won three of its eight Oscar nominations. Steven Soderbergh's *Sex, Lies and Videotape* was a benchmark for independent filmmaking; made for $1.1 million, it became the top-grossing independent feature at $24.7 million in 1989. That year *My Left Foot* received five Oscar nominations, with Daniel Day-Lewis and Brenda Fricker winning Best Actor and Actress. In a somewhat different category is Oliver Stone's *Platoon* (1986), which was independently financed by the British Hemdale Film Corporation but distributed by Orion Pictures. The film was made for a modest $6.5 million but returned an impressive $69.9 million and won four Academy Awards, including Best Picture and Director.

The success of these independent productions suggested the existence of an untapped market "where middle-ground films—more commercial, quality-oriented material—can work very well," as one independent producer put it.[43] These "quality films," as a writer in *Premiere* called them, were low-budget pictures driven by story and characters that "appealed to that leviathan of postwar consumer culture, the 25-to-45-year-old baby boomers, who also happened to be the very group that drove home video's spectacular growth in the early days."[44]

The independents demonstrated the viability of the adult market for "quality films" but for a number of reasons found it difficult to capitalize on the emerging trend. There was a glut of film releases in the late 1980s that crowded out independent features from exhibition, hurting their chances on video. As the video business took off, it was increasingly dominated by big-hit Hollywood films that first scored in theaters. Video retailers preferred one hundred copies of an A-title with some box-office prowess to the B- and C-films made by independents. The result was a leveling off of the video explosion. After their initial successes several indies tried to compete with the majors, but enlarged budgets increased financial risk while lowering creative gambles. An alarming number of independent companies, many that scored with hits during the 1980s, ended up in serious financial trouble late in the decade.

The tenacity and art-house quality of the independents moved this trend closer to the mainstream. A significant number of these low-budget, independently financed pictures in the 1990s captured critical acclaim and notable box office and were among the most memorable films in their respective years. Robert Redford's low-budget pictures *A River Runs Through It* and *Quiz Show* dealt with human values and were both critically and commercially successful. The British drama *Howard's End* returned nine million dollars and was nominated for Best Picture in 1992. With the best-kept plot twist secret in cinematic history, *The Crying Game* became a stunning success as a low-budget art-house movie that broke into the mainstream. The film, which was made for five million dollars, debuted on just six screens in the United States, but as word of mouth spread it moved up to 239 screens and then jumped to 1,093. The film surpassed the previous art-house champ, *Sex, Lies and Videotape,* by grossing $62.5 million and returning $26.6 million in U.S. rentals to Miramax. Australian director Jane Campion's *The Piano* (1993) grossed $128 million worldwide, with $40 million of that coming from the U.S. market. The film received eight Academy Award nominations, with Holly Hunter and Anna Paquin winning Best Actress and Supporting Actress, respectively. *The Remains of the Day* (1993) had a worldwide gross of $58.7 million; Anthony Hopkins picked up the Academy Award for Best Actor.

In 1994 two independent films broke into the mainstream in a big way. *Four Weddings and a Funeral* was launched with a promotional campaign that cost twice its five-million-dollar production costs. A low-budget British comedy with only American actress Andie McDowell among a cast of British unknowns, it went on to gross a surprising $250 million and was nominated for Best Picture.[45] Another contender in the Best Picture category that year was Quentin Tarantino's *Pulp Fiction. Time's* Richard Corliss described this award-winning film as "*Die Hard* with a brain," referring to the innovative narrative, complex characters and artistic edge in a popular work that "accommodates the high-octane and the highbrow." With a domestic gross of over $100 million (against $8.2 million in production costs), *Pulp Fiction* became Miramax's biggest hit and demonstrated "that small-budget, auteurish films directed and produced without big-studio interference have the potential to be not only good business, but publicity-generating, star-making motion-picture events," one writer observed.[46]

The indies had an important presence at the 1994 Oscars. Of the seventeen films that received more than one nomination, over a third were independents. Miramax set a record for an independent company with twenty-two nominations. After Oscar night, *Variety* reported that more specialized films were due for release in 1995 than ever before, an effect that when combined with an increase in the majors' output crowded the marketplace for art-house fare.[47]

Many of these independent films were too original to qualify as high-concept spectacles aimed at an undifferentiated audience. Combined with the growth of the international cinema and the video delivery system, a flourishing field of independent productions holds the prospect for a renewal of the mainstream cinema. These factors provide an environment for a more pluralistic cinema that reflects diverse perspectives for various audiences. The contemporary period of independent growth can be likened to other creative periods in film history like the prestudio era, and the late 1960s and early 1970s, before the high-concept film and blockbuster economics became predominant.

Successful independent productions and the rediscovery of the aging baby boom market brought the majors into territory that traditionally belonged to the small independents. The studios began taking on independent companies, providing them with financing for development, production and marketing, promising wider distribution for international and independent films with a specific market niche. Sony created a new company, Sony Classic Pictures, to acquire English and foreign-language films. Twentieth Century-Fox established a specialty division, Fox Searchlight. In a joint venture, Universal and the European-based PolyGram Filmed Entertainment formed Gramercy, a distributor of moderately budgeted independent films. Disney established a formal relationship with the prestigious independent producer-director team Ismail Merchant and James Ivory *(Howard's End, A Room With a View* and *Jefferson in Paris)* and acquired the independent Miramax Film Corporation; New Line Cinema and Fine Line Features were absorbed by

Turner Entertainment. At this writing, the Samuel Goldwyn Company is looking for a buyer.

These new companies and alignments represent attempts by both the studios and independents "to battle booming marketing and production costs, capture fragmented audiences and scramble for bigger market shares," according to a *Variety* report.[48] They also mark studio efforts at greater diversification now that video is an established delivery system and audience demographics are changing. The Miramax deal, for example, lets Disney reach beyond its animated and live-action mainstream product to include lower-budget art-house films for niche audiences.

Some industry veterans insist that the surge of the independents is just the latest fad and that the infusion of studio money will hamper the adventuresome and creative spirit of the indies. Others think this is the beginning of a long-lasting trend. "This is not a cyclical thing, like 'this year it's independents, next year will be studios,' " Gramercy president Russell Schwartz said. "The lines are blurred now, and everyone wants a piece of the action. So studios invest in boutiques."[49]

It remains to be seen, however, what effect these new entities that have redefined the independent landscape will have on the cinema. At present they seem a mixed blessing. While they offer financial stability for the independents, they also threaten to homogenize the film industry by virtue of the majors' control over the distribution channels. One-third of independent releases came from Turner's New Line and Disney's Miramax in 1993.[50] The success of small pictures depends on a high level of creativity and savvy marketing. The studios can oversupervise these projects, interfering with the creative risk-taking that characterizes the independents and moving them toward star-studded formulaic packages in order to widen the film's appeal. (If the Oscars are any indication, many independent productions have offered lucrative and challenging roles for actors.)

Furthermore, studio marketing departments are not accustomed to cultivating niche markets, and creativity often represents a huge marketing challenge regarding how to communicate the style and content of the movie to an audience. As one marketing executive put it, "The intention might be good and valid but the machine is really geared to handle very mainstream product with appeal that hits every age group, major and minor markets, and cuts across all ethnicities."[51] One can only speculate at this point on whether the mega-mergers that are consolidating the industry will create opportunities for independents or limit their growth.

Conclusion

Perhaps Steven Spielberg's two films of 1993 can be used to symbolize the state of the film industry today. *Schindler's List,* a film "whose commercial expectations did not drive the decision to make it," according to Pollock, became Spielberg's cinematic triumph, capturing seven Academy Awards, including Best Picture and Director.[52] Spielberg's other film that year, *Jurassic Park,* was not up for Best Picture, but with a worldwide gross of over $900 million it became the colossal blockbuster event of the year, finishing second to Spielberg's *E.T.* among the highest-grossing films of all time.

Over the course of the twentieth century, analysts have been critical of Hollywood's tendency to seek a single homogenous audience to support expensive blockbuster productions. This propensity not only has fostered a lack of creativity but also results in an exploitation of audience (especially children) that continues to fuel the controversy about entertainment. *Los Angeles Times* film critic Jack Mathews has echoed the opinion of many who argue for the differentiation of movies. "It seems obvious that to maximize its business, Hollywood should diversify its product, produce movies aimed at all segments of the population, and embrace rather than scorn originality," he writes. Noting the demographic shift in moviegoers in the 1990s, he suggests that "the industry stands a better chance of improving business by broadening its aim than it does in isolating one audience and squeezing it like a wet tea bag."[53]

Big-budget "event" movies aimed at Hollywood's main constituency, the under-twenty-five crowd, are the industry's bread and butter. Blockbusters promise extraordinary financial gain, but few are phenomenally successful. The ambivalence between commercialization and artistic roles arises again here: the commercial tendencies of the industry can limit its creative possibilities and social responsibilities by urging the exploitation of the most financially lucrative audience at any given time. As I have tried to show, this as much as anything fosters the problems and controversies surrounding the popular arts today.

Thinking about film not just as a commercial product, however, but as a living and vital art can recast questions and issues and change expectations. We would not expect a museum curator or symphony director to determine exhibits or orchestral programs based even primarily on audience preferences. By the same token, we should not be satisfed with executives or analysts whose bottom-line argument is that the entertainment industry exists only to make a profit for its shareholders. Many filmmakers and actors approach their work as artists, and there are movie executives (but not all) who regard it as art. And movies are radically diverse; some are very good, many are mediocre, others are bad. The same is true of the other arts. Films like *Schindler's List, Pulp Fiction, The Player, Amadeus, Sense and Sensibility, Dead Man Walking* and *Leaving Las Vegas* are both art and moneymaking commodities, demonstrating that while there is always a struggle between art and commerce, the two are not mutually exclusive.

In order to carry out the many functions film has acquired in American life, studios should cultivate a commitment to diversify their offerings, serving specific audience segments and allowing for the presentation of a variety of prespectives in the cinema. As I have shown, this is already occurring in degree. The advent of video and other new forms of delivery has opened possibilities for alternative filmmakers and the international cinema. In conjunction with changes in the makeup of the movie audience in the last years of the twentieth century, these innovations suggest not only a transformation in the production, distribution and exhibition of films but also that a redirection of purpose and resources is not entirely out of the question, despite the industry's bottom-line mentality. Big-budget pictures generate huge box-office grosses, but films with modest production costs can be very profitable in terms of return on investment.

Even this is not entirely satisfactory, for the industry and the audience must change together to establish a long-term redirection of entertainment as a social institution. Today entertainment forms are recognized as having the cultural import in our society and around the world that was previously the province of the traditional high arts. But too much of the analysis and critique continues to be based on their being low or commercial culture, leaving consumer boycotts, watchdog groups and threats by federal legislators as the proposed solutions to problems associated with the popular arts. These can have only a limited effect and offer a partial solution at best. For more lasting change, we need to acknowledge that the distinction between art and entertainment itself is fraught with difficulties, and to engage the popular arts with recognition of their potential and service as art.

12

. . . . .

Some
Like It
Hot

We are experiencing a profound shift today in the historical conditions that maintained the cultural consensus reached during the Depression and World War II; the breakup of that consensus has brought a return of cultural strife. Urbanization and industrialization have given way to suburbanization and the age of information and communication. Long-term economic growth has been interrupted by periods of recession and unemployment; our national economy and policy are increasingly shaped by global concerns and competition. Social institutions are under strain trying to keep pace with major changes in work and society brought about by economic dislocation and technological advance.

Current immigration trends are comparable with those at the beginning of the twentieth century. The assimilationist "melting pot," however, has been replaced with an emphasis on maintaining a distinct subcultural identity while still being an American; the integration goals of the 1950s and 1960s have shifted to the creation of a wholly multicultural society. This in turn has given rise to new cultural identities and political factions, mirrored in the intellectual force of postmodernism with its emphasis on the validity of diverse perspectives based on race and ethnicity, gender, sexuality, nationality and, to a lesser extent perhaps, religion.

In addition, there is great concern about the impact these forces might be having on today's youthful "Generation X," as they have been dubbed by the media. In unprecedented numbers, they are growing up experiencing the effects of the high divorce rates of recent decades, single-parent families, a more pronounced absence of parents and other adults in their lives, increased rates of child neglect and domestic abuse. The economics of the 1980s left a dearth of well-paying jobs for today's "twentysomethings," who find themselves stuck in meaningless "Mcjobs," facing a future of diminished opportunities. Unable to earn a living wage, they are postponing marriage and "boomeranging"—returning home to live with their parents in numbers comparable to the Depression years. Critics today are alarmed at this generation's disillusionment with American institutions, often expressed in an attitude of cynicism and blatant disregard for (or ignorance about) social issues, history and government. Reports indicate that they feel trapped in a spiral of disillusionment, futility and despair.[1]

These issues have made their way into contemporary entertainment. *Reality Bites, Boyz N the Hood* and the unrated and controversial *Kids* each offered different, and even provocative, portrayals of youth subcultures today. New images for women can be heard in the popular music of artists like Mary Chapin Carpenter—"Shut Up and Kiss Me"; films like *A League of Their Own, Thelma and Louise, Sleepless in Seattle, Something to Talk About* and others legitimize gender perspectives and the female audience. Spike Lee has pioneered a distinctly African-American perspective in his films, considering the impact of social forces on individual actions. Lee reverses commonly held stereotypes by individualizing blacks and using these portrayals to explore stereotypes and the society that produces them. Pictures by Lee and other black filmmakers have reached beyond the African-American market, allowing black directors to explore mainstream themes with even wider appeal, as in *Waiting to Exhale* (1995).[2] In addition, however limited the success of Michael Moore's *Roger and Me, Clerks* and *Hoop Dreams,* these films show that with meager funding and the availability of video technology, the cinema will continue, if not expand, as a viable artistic forum for a wide range of perspectives. Also, openings in cable and satellite television hold out the promise at least of greater pluralism in programming.

Oliver Stone's pictures have generated much publicity for representing a countervailing perspective in the cinema. Stone's *JFK* suggests that lone individuals are no match for government so thoroughly corrupted by power and deceit. In *Platoon,* it is not that America lacked the resolve to win in Vietnam, but the meaning of the war is best understood in terms of conflicts and contradictions within the American belief system. Stone's films stood in contrast to other mainstream films like *The Firm, The Pelican Brief* and *Clear and Present Danger* that continued the Capra tradition *(Mr. Smith Goes to Washington* and *It's a Wonderful Life)* showing an individual hero triumphing over the corruption in institutions in order to ensure the survival of the system.

Despite conservative charges that the American cinema is a leftist propaganda machine, one of the most significant trends in the mainstream cinema is what film analyst Andrew Britton called "Reaganite entertainment." These films reflect the conservative social, political and cultural climate of the period, embodying qualities associated with the political persona of former President Reagan himself. Film historian John Belton defined it as "a cinema of reassurance, optimism, and nostalgia."[3] The conservative magazine *National Review* itself marked the beginning of this "recovery" of the American cinema in the mid-1970s with the Star Wars films, "whose simple truths about heroism and the triumph of good over evil (not to mention space defense) were harbingers of the Reagan Eighties," a writer for the magazine maintained. "The Reagan years saw quite a number of conservative films—not to mention destruction of the real-life Evil Empire."[4]

Beyond the slew of anticommunist films in the 1980s *(Red Dawn, Red Heat* and *Hunt for Red October* among them), Stallone's Rocky and Rambo series, Arnold Schwarzenegger's Terminator films and *True Lies,* and Spielberg's Indiana Jones series all extolled the values of rugged individualism. The patriarchal family was resurrected as a haven from the outside, threatening world in *Ordinary People, Three Men and a Baby* and *Terms of Endearment.* The reaffirmation of the father, however, often came at the expense of the mother, as in *Kramer vs. Kramer,* which blamed the discontented woman for the breakdown of the family. Likewise, the threat to the family in *Fatal Attraction* was the single career woman, portrayed as both promiscuous and psychotic.

Reaganite entertainment restores faith in American institutions. The image of the military was revived in *An Officer and a Gentleman, The Right Stuff* and especially *Top Gun,* a film described by a Defense Department official as "an excellent opportunity to tell about the pride and professionalism that goes into becoming a Navy fighter pilot."[5] The Lethal Weapon series promoted law and order, interracial harmony and the family. Films like *Wall Street, Trading Places* and *Broadcast News* showed that despite problems, American institutions work. Finally, the Back to the Future series represented a nostalgic return to the Eisenhower America of the 1950s that Reagan symbolized in the 1980s. In a similar vein, the award-winning *Forrest Gump* epitomized the Reaganite cinema of reassurance, optimism and nostalgia; *National Review* named it "Best Picture Indicting the Sixties Counterculture."[6]

As we saw at the beginning of the twentieth century, because the entertainment media are among our most active and vital processes of communication, they are also considered powerful weapons along a cultural battlefront. The perspective employed here offers a particular way of looking at today's cultural conflict, at least as it pertains to entertainment and related issues. As we have seen, our ideas and assumptions about art and entertainment have a long history and have been complicated by social, cultural and religious forces that continue to affect today's dialogue.

Today's Reform Movement

The critique and proposals of Michael Medved and Ted Baehr are good avenues into the conservative movement to reform entertainment today. (Progressives are just as likely to find Hollywood to be too conservative as conservatives to find it too liberal.) As mentioned in the introduction, Medved, a film reviewer with PBS *Sneak Previews* and *The New York Post,* gave a critical assessment of the entertainment industry in a 1992 book, *Hollywood vs. America.* Baehr made news when he advocated industry adoption of his revised production code (and later for spreading false allegations about subliminal messages in Disney's *Aladdin*). His analysis is drawn from books and various issues of his *Movieguide* newsletter. Though they represent different social and religious groups, Medved and Baehr share a conservative ideology—both believe in the promise and deliverance of the marketplace—and demonize opposing perspectives. They also think of entertainment primarily (if not exclusively) as a commercial product and not art, and while both show a preference for what Dwight Macdonald called "midcult," they employ the cultural hierarchy in their model for reform. These four related issues are direct concerns of this study, and these critics are recent representatives of the religious and moralist critique.

According to these critics, what is wrong with Hollywood today can be traced back to the late 1960s, although they disagree over the importance of certain events. Baehr thinks the Legion of Decency and the Protestant Film Commission were Hollywood's "hotline to mainstream American values." With the closing of these offices in the 1960s and the MPAA adoption of a rating system, "the church abandoned Hollywood," Baehr maintains. Consequently, Baehr thinks of his Christian Film and Television Commission as a replacement for the Protestant Film Commission (whose records he inherited) and even lobbied the industry to adopt his updated version of the Production Code. Medved sees these events in the 1960s as symptomatic of a deeper problem in the entertainment industry that resulted from "the changing of the generational guard in Hollywood," he said in a magazine interview, and as Baehr so aptly put it in his review of Medved's book, the "cancer of leftist ideology that overcame popular culture in the mid-1960s."[7] Provocative theories, but without force. Despite the small differences of opinion that reflect each critic's own particular vantage point, they share a fundamental agreement that the problems with the entertainment industry stem from the dominance of a leftist ideology in Hollywood that began in the late 1960s.

Medved and Baehr, as well as others in today's reform movement, begin their critique with an ideological charge: Hollywood is a bastion of liberalism, and when filmmakers are "freed of all commercial considerations," as Medved wrote, they produce "malign propaganda."[8] Hollywood is not as monolithic a community as these critics contend; Ronald Reagan, Charlton Heston, Arnold Schwarzenegger and Bruce Willis represent a continual Republican presence. Further, that artists work in a risky occupation with scarce job opportunities fosters an inherent tension in their community. While there is intense competition, artists must also maintain collegial ties with each other to maintain the support of the art world that legitimizes their activities, providing validation and criticism. The competition, publicized personal and professional conflicts, and various hostilities between the independents, major studios, television networks, labor unions, producers, writers and so forth strain the idea of Hollywood as a concerted community.

Surveys do confirm, however, that the dominant social and political atttitudes in Hollywood are considerably more liberal than the rest of the American population. Film industry analyst David F. Prindle observed that Tinseltown may be "the only concentration of educated, wealthy, powerful economic liberals in the country."[9] This is not, as Medved and others seem to argue, a recent phenomenon in Hollywood history. According to historian Neal Gabler, the Jewish moguls who controlled Hollywood during the studio era "forsook the Democrats, for whom the overwhelming majority of their coreligionists voted, and swore fealty instead to the Republicans as American artistocrats did."[10] Their politics, like every other aspect of their lives, illustrated their desperate need for social acceptance among the wealthy and powerful in America and their deep and legitimate fear of anti-Semitism, a force they worried could lead to the loss of their studios, fortunes and social position.

Outside the top echelon, however, Hollywood was a "left-leaning artistic community," as Gabler writes, with some visible ties to the Communist Party in the 1930s and 1940s. Of course anticommunist witch-hunters at the end of World War II (many of whom were also anti-Semites) put even New Deal liberals under suspicion for subversion, and most studio employees supported liberal causes. One Hollywood writer in the mid-1930s estimated that "probably 70 percent of the writers, directors, actors, and so on were liberally minded."[11] That this was so during the film industry's "golden age" is revealing about the relation of politics and art in Hollywood. For example, Sidney Buchman, who penned the script for Frank Capra's *Mr. Smith Goes to Washington,* admitted to being a communist. Apparently his membership in the Communist Party from 1938 to 1945 had little effect on his writing, as the Capra film is generally viewed as a patriotic movie depicting faith in American institutions.[12]

Political differences in the film community had common roots in the Jewish experience. Gabler explains, "Hollywood was a community of utopians— genteel utopians on the right who envisioned a brave new world of decent, upright, upper-middle-class Americans; and starry-eyed utopians on the left who envisioned a world of compassionate, morally lathered comrades smiting injustice."[13] The left-wing politics of Hollywood were suppressed during the McCarthy years but resurfaced during the 1960s. In the nation's shift to the right in recent decades, Hollywood emerged as one of few remaining liberal communities.

But this creates a paradox. Surveys show that wealthy people tend to be economic conservatives, and it can be argued that it would be irrational for them to be anything else. Even though they have their wealth and power to defend, the "media elite" who control the structure and content of the entertainment and communications industries are overwhelmingly economic and social liberals. How is it that well-to-do and successful people in the entertainment industry endorse an ideology that normally belongs to the lower classes, the poor, the oppressed and outsiders?

In contrast to ideological conspiracy theories, Prindle argues persuasively that "the pattern of liberalism evident in Hollywood beliefs, values, and actions can better be explained by examining the forces *within* the Hollywood community rather than by hypothesizing an imagined conflict between people in the industry and institutions *outside* that community."[14] In his study of Hollywood as a whole social system, Prindle suggests that at least part of the explanation for the industry's liberal outlook on life and politics is that it is a natural outgrowth of an artistic colony. Hollywood's "artistic liberalism," as he calls it, tends to be directed at "symbolic" politics, with celebrities campaigning for environmental causes and gay and human rights around the world. Artists are perhaps more emotionally sensitive to matters of personal and social justice, Prindle explains, and in the course of their creative work cannot escape dealing with these issues in ways that most people do not. Also, executives seem to identify themselves with artists, as suggested by veteran entertainment executive Barry Diller's comment that "this creative process forces you to be somewhat humanistic. . . . It comes with the work."[15]

More important, since its earliest days Hollywood was forced to defend itself against continual threats from repressive forces in American society. This fostered attitudes of "frustration, resentment, and even paranoia," Prindle writes, with even the most successful in Hollywood adopting the perspective of outsiders. In addition, the economic uncertainty of many in the entertainment industry helps them identify with other groups who traditionally support liberal causes. Prindle also points out that there is a higher percentage of both homosexuals (though difficult to estimate) and Jews in Hollywood than in the rest of American society—and both groups tend to be more liberal than other groups in the United States. Prindle concludes:

> If unemployment were lower, if artists had more control over their work, if the market were more stable, if the audience were easier to predict, if the community were not so stress-ridden, if the place did not have so much glamour, then the people who lived there would have different lives, would see the world differently, and would possess different political values. As it is, Hollywood both attracts and produces an alienated citizenry, and such people tend to be liberal.[16]

That Hollywood is dominated by people on the liberal end of the spectrum does not mean, however, that entertainment necessarily affirms the ideological convictions of its producers. As we have seen, most American films, despite their iconoclastic portrayals, conclude with the triumph, or at least the survival, of American institutions and the values they represent. In this way the majority of American movies, however subversive in appearance, reaffirm the prevailing mythology. That they expose and probe the inconsistencies of life in the larger context of affirming the established value system enhances their persuasive power and meaning while also increasing their popular appeal.

Also, it is difficult to conclude just how audiences interpret particular films. Howard Hawks's *Gentlemen Prefer Blondes* (1953), for example, has been treated as both a feminist and an antifeminist film, Sylvester Stallone's *Rambo* and other films about Vietnam as both pro- and antimilitary, patriotic and unpatriotic.[17] Further, the movies made by Hollywood conservatives (Schwarzenegger and Willis, for example) show that liberal ideology alone cannot be blamed for all the graphic depictions of sex and violence on the screen.

People in the entertainment industry have the right to hold and express their views. Yet if the problems with entertainment are ideological, as some critics contend, it would follow that solutions ought to be ideological as well. Critics should demand fair media representation of voices other than the dominant one, a greater pluralism in the media that gives more access to social and religious minorities and perspectives.

That does not seem to be the intent of critics like Medved and Baehr. While they begin with an ideological charge, their methods of analysis and proposals for reform work from the premise that the entertainment industry is an ominous force, and we can hope to shield ourselves from its harmful influence only with either some kind of moral regulation or consumer attacks. The basic assumption is that entertainment is primarily, if not exclusively, a commercial product to be controlled by the marketplace, which becomes a kind of cultural democracy; record sales, box-office tickets and Nielsen ratings represent the "votes" of the majority of the people. In the quest for profits (and not ideological persuasion), they reason, the producers of entertainment will supply whatever audiences demand. As we saw earlier, this is a valid assumption to make about the popular arts, but only to a certain extent, for the degree of dominance and even exclusivity these critics attribute to the commercial aspect of entertainment obfuscates artistic functions and, ironically, does not guarantee the kind of moral programming they desire. Moreover, they are employing this approach with an ideological purpose and specific audience in mind that raises doubts about the validity of their argument.

According to Medved's theory about what went wrong with Hollywood, a liberal takeover in the late 1960s "prevented the entertainment industry from responding in a normal way to the forces of the marketplace."[18] He described films with offensive content as "the sort of art that leading filmmakers choose to create when they are freed of all commercial considerations."[19] (Of course the creation of high art institutions was based on the opposite conjecture, that commercial considerations have a negative influence on the quality of art.) In today's struggle, he said, "it's going to take an aroused public engaged in long-term struggle using boycotts occasionally, public shaming, stockholder meetings, using every kind of legal free enterprise—marketplace guerrilla warfare."[20]

Baehr confounds ideology and profiteering, suggesting that "sex, violence, and anti-Christian messages" are "ideological preferences" but that "producers in Hollywood are ultimately concerned with the bottom line."[21] Either way, these critics argue that Hollywood is out of touch with its audience and that in a truly free market, producers would provide the kind of "moral" entertainment that Medved and Baehr argue is what most Americans want.

But this line of reasoning and emphasis on consumer tactics actually weaken and cast doubt on the magnitude of their ideological charges, while also raising suspicions about their intent. If the entertainment industry is a leftist propaganda machine, as these critics assert, why would liberal producers suddenly abandon their ideological assault under consumer pressure and convert to profit-making? While Medved and Baehr claim that Hollywood is not giving the audience what it wants, they ironically base their proposal for change on the same market-driven premise. They are then compelled to argue for the existence of a lucrative "moral American marketplace," as Baehr called it, that represents an economic bonanza for the entertainment industry.[22]

This seems like a wholesome consumer tactic, and its advocates have demonstrated the existence of concerned groups who have an interest in the moral quality of entertainment. But as I noted earlier, this scheme fosters the worst commercial tendencies in the industry and greater consumer exploitation of youth and the family. The increase in family-oriented fare in recent years has meant more pictures with commerical product tie-ins and marketing campaigns exploiting children and building their identities as consumers. *Jurassic Park* had over one hundred corporate tie-ins, and Universal spent over sixty million dollars marketing the movie. A report in *Variety* pointed out that family movies can be parlayed into business ventures from theme parks to toys and clothing.[23] Ultimately this only makes the family more vulnerable to commercial exploitation, and we do not need to invite more influence of market forces into our homes.

But these moral guardians never criticize the entertainment industry for its unrelenting commercial exploitation of markets. In fact, they invite *more* marketing forces into the family as a solution to the problem with excessive profanity, violence and sexuality in the media, as though the consumer economy does no harm to families. In other words, the commercialization of the industry documented in previous chapters has produced the very situation Medved and Baehr purport solving with more commercialization. Armed with opinion polls and box-office figures, they set out to persuade entertainment executives of the financial viability of making movies for the general family audience. Baehr writes, for example, that "it is financially prudent for Hollywood executives to understand and target this vast audience if they want to survive and prosper."[24] How they perceive the makeup of that audience is clear from Medved's label "lifestyle conservatives" and Baehr's reference to "the biblical perspective shared by most moral Americans."[25]

As we saw earlier, Hollywood's renewed interest in the family trade had already begun before these critics became self-proclaimed champions of the American family, suggesting that they are riding a wave rather than creating one. And it did not take much "marketplace guerrilla warfare" to convert Hollywood. Shortly after Medved's book was published, he took credit for "some welcome signs of progress."[26] In an article in *U.S. News & World Report* entitled "Hollywood: Right Face," industry observers noticed a surge in "family friendly" movies in 1994. Medved was quoted as saying, "It's really extraordinary how fast the change has come about." Likewise, Baehr said, "I'm happy to report that 1994 was an extraordinary breakthrough for the good, the true and the beautiful in popular entertainment."[27] So much for ideological warfare in the movies.

Competition and Quality
The fact that the commercial aspect of entertainment establishes priorities for production and marketing decision-making can by no means be overlooked, of course. But a free market alone cannot resolve the dilemmas surrounding entertainment and its present role in our society, as if it does not create enough problems of its own. As one writer pointed out, the market may be giving people what it wants, but so does a Colombian cartel.[28]

Intense industry competition fosters the mentality, as Disney's Joe Roth put it, that "if I don't do it, someone else is going to do it and they'll make a profit and I won't." In the competition with television and other leisure activities, film producers "have to have some kind of an edge to our work in order to get people out of the house," Roth explained. "When you've got the First Amendment as wide as a house to protect you, even though your own values may be half as wide, you may step outside of how you feel in order to get that edge you're looking for."[29] The competitive market does not ensure personal or corporate responsibility, or even that the tastes and values of a majority will prevail.

Regulatory practices and the consumer tactics employed by various groups today, while effective at times, are at best only partial solutions to what is a larger institutional issue. Ultimately marketplace strategies cannot establish an appropriate role for entertainment, because the emphasis on the commercial obfuscates the artistic functions of entertainment forms. This has regrettably limited our engagement with the popular arts to the consumer process. Ironically, it is the artistic functions that provoke criticism, but the most outspoken critics continue to advance the workings of the consumer marketplace as a ready solution. Unfortunately, the leading proposals for reform share this common assumption.

Members of Congress criticize the entertainment media as means of communication and cultural transmission but then treat them as pure commerce, seeking solutions in the marketplace and new technologies like the V-chip. Despite charges of liberal bias in the media, for example, it was the Republican-led Congress in 1996 that deregulated the telecommunications industry that provides Americans with information and entertainment, while legislators who criticized the condition of American television opposed government mandates regarding children's programming or federal support for public broadcasting.[30]

Such proposals for reform resemble the Victorian "spheres" and are designed to protect institutions in the domestic sphere from any harmful effects of the public one: fierce competition in the business world or competing ideologies in the media. As discussed earlier, this social scheme creates a schism between private and public spheres, appealing to personal religion and morality as a means to harness the greed and exploitation that exists in the public world. Legislators then talk about the "shaming" of individual executives within the corporations that produce movies, music or television programming they find offensive or think is harmful to society.

The campaign to get Hollywood to clean up its act by producing more family movies is another market-based strategy. The assumption at work here is that the entertainment industry should simply cater to the most viable and financially lucrative market indicated by box-office and sales receipts. Should consumer power be the primary determinant of the content and quality of entertainment? If so, we can expect another wave of adolescent films when the children of the baby boom who are watching Disney videos today reach their teens. "Our audience is kids who continue to like what they've always liked: Horror movies and action movies," Universal's Tom Pollock said in a 1992 *Premiere* interview with several film producers.

There's a big bulge of them coming up—the baby boomlet, as it's called—who have been going to cartoons and family films, which is why you've been seeing a lot of them, but they're about to come into their teens, so we're going to be having a whole raft of coming-of-age movies again. Everybody's going to lose their virginity again. At the same time, there are the conservative boomers and their kids, who are too young yet to be into horror movies, still into the family stuff. The parents are into what they can take their kids to. *Beethoven* is our most profitable movie of the year. Family movies are cheap. You don't have to pay the dog, and you don't have to pay the mouse, and you don't have to pay the baby. All those children—other than Macaulay Culkin—you don't have to pay them anything!

If you wish to make money and you believe that your audience is turning more conservative, yes, be more conservative because it's profitable. You don't have to think you have a social obligation to do it because we are leading society or we set the values. You don't have to get into that kind of hypocrisy. You can simply say, "It's good business to do it."[31]

Pollock's remarks reveal the profit-oriented drive to cater to fickle and changing consumer tastes that permeates the industry. It is this attitude, and not a common social understanding of the role of art in mass society, that directs decision-makers. Hollywood should make films to be enjoyed by the whole family, as well as others that are of more specific interest to particular groups, including youth. But the cinema should not become a giant puberty rite just because adolescents are the most frequent moviegoers. Nor should its mandate be reduced to producing entertainment that can be viewed by every member of the family. All this amounts to is Hollywood exploiting one market over another with indistinguishable products.

As I have already shown, the family market has not turned out to be the consumer force that conservative critics portend; advocates of more family movies have not been able to galvanize the moviegoing public they claim to represent. This supports the assertion that the entertainment industry *is* mirroring public tastes and demands. To one degree or another this is undeniable and casts doubt on the viability of the free market as a salvific cure for the problems with entertainment. It also shows that the marketplace is fundamentally amoral, giving people what they want and not what they should see (from the moralist perspective).

The market is not homogeneous. As we have seen, there is an audience for family films, as there is for pornography and extreme violence. As I also noted earlier, what people disapprove of is often the same as what they pay to see. According to a survey conducted by John Evans's Texas-based Movie Morality Ministries, for example, three-fourths of single Christian adults polled thought that "movies containing vulgarities, explicit sex, nudity, and antibiblical messages had an adverse effect on their moral and spiritual condition." But at least half of the respondents approved of films that contained these elements. An appeal can be made for better films based on morality, but not on market forces as today's reformers do, treating films as pure commercial products.[32]

Furthermore, if my local Dove Association's "Family Film Spectacular" is any indication, acceptable family entertainment too easily translates into "kiddie" movies like *The Swan Princess, Rookie of the Year, The Pagemaster, Little Big League, Free Willy* and *The Little Rascals.* The Dove Association lists Medved as a board member, but his top pick for 1993, *Schindler's List,* was not awarded a Dove "seal of approval," even though this critically acclaimed film makes a valuable contribution to our collective memory about one of the most horrific events of the twentieth century. Beyond affirming consumer choice, how does such an approach help people, and especially young people, understand the cinema and develop a critical perspective regarding its role in our personal lives and society? Ultimately this consumer approach is too limited in scope and fails to address more significant issues about the role of the popular arts and the nature of the industry.

The reduction of entertainment to sheer commercialism does little to promote the industry's responsibility as an influential social institution. Nor does it create an environment for the cultivation of these contemporary art forms.

Ultimately this strategy does not call for a more responsible entertainment industry, but a more profitable one. Consumer tactics are short-term solutions that, in this case, promise nothing more than a brief surge of family-oriented entertainment. That these critics act on this assumption makes the whole affair seem more a matter of market perception than an ideological contest. But in a manner strangely reminiscent of the reform movement in the 1920s and 1930s, their family values rhetoric and consumer-based strategies are part of a determined effort to assert their life perspective. And so for them it is an ideological battle.

We have already seen the mythmaking power of the entertainment media and how important it was in the building of national consensus during the 1930s. Even more recently, a writer in *Time* noted, "a major [popular culture] phenomenon is comforting to Americans because it is spectacular evidence of consensus, a palpable national agreement that has nothing to do with quarrelsome issues of race or religion or class."[33] Like their predecessors, today's reformers employ the rhetoric of family and morality to mine a lowest common denominator in the public (not unlike Hollywood producers), and opinion surveys do support their concern about there being too much profanity, sex and violence in entertainment. There is a place for such criticism, but these moral guardians extend their critique beyond their family values rhetoric. This becomes evident, for example, in criticism of movies like *JFK*, *Dances with Wolves* and *Top Gun* (all box-office successes) that is based not on moral but on ideological issues. Medved and Baehr give little if any indication that they are interested in seeing a more pluralistic media. To the contrary, in consideration of their rhetoric and proposals, it is not difficult to conclude that their aim is for greater control over the content of entertainment in order to propagate a particular ideological perspective.

Ironically, as a basis for his reform strategy, Medved at least has taken a cue from Marxist ideas about how the ruling class maintains consensus in a mass society, especially Italian Marxist Antonio Gramsci's theory about cultural hegemony. As communication scholar Chris Jenks explained, "Contemporary Marxism has generated the 'dominant ideology thesis' which supposes that varieties of hegemonic strategies of mass media and political propaganda create a distorted illusion of shared concerns in the face of the real and contentious divisions that exist between classes, genders, ethnic groups, geographical regions and age groups."[34] The proposal for more family entertainment, which clearly has production and market limitations, is really a means of social control over the content of the popular arts.

A new production code is unconstitutional, but if producers were to shift the bulk of their output, tailoring it to "lifestyle conservatives," the effect would be the same. As we saw during the studio era, movies that adhered to a lowest common denominator formula based on accepted middle-class culture and values is itself a kind of propaganda, and one that excludes progressive ideas and minority and subcultural perspectives.

This gives us some insight into the nature of their critique and proposals for reform. Medved and Baehr both touted statistical studies showing that G- and PG-rated films do better at the box office than R-rated ones and that the percentage of G and PG films dropped in direct proportion to an increase in those rated R throughout the 1980s. They used these reports to support their assertion that the majority of Americans want more G and PG films but that today's movie producers (in contrast to those of the studio era) are out of touch with this vast audience and have sacrificed it (and potential profits) to their ideological pursuits.

"Recent history shows conclusively that whatever motivations pushed the motion picture business to its current obsessions, financial self-interest was not among them," Medved wrote. "How could an industry that radically changed its focus and thereby permanently sacrificed nearly two-thirds of its audience be described, in any serious sense, as 'following the money'?" Instead, he asserted, the industry is "following its own warped conceptions of artistic integrity, driven by some dark compulsion beyond simple greed," apparently referring to his charge that the "loony left" is determined to use the media to undermine "traditional" values.[35] This explanation for the state of entertainment today, which has been repeated in the press, warrants more careful consideration.

Medved is referring of course to the dramatic box-office decline in the decades after World War II. The many reasons for the drop in movie attendance treated in chapter eight show this statement to be not only a gross oversimplification but simply erroneous. And you will remember, the major film studios pursued the general family market like a holy grail until this course threatened their financial survival and they acknowledged the shift in the primary moviegoing audience to the under-thirty group.

Medved contends, however, that between 1965 and 1969 Hollywood lost 60 percent of its audience because "the values of the entertainment industry changed, and audiences fled from the theaters in horror and disgust."[36] As I noted earlier, this contention is based on erroneous box-office figures. Weekly attendance did not plummet from 44 million in 1965 to 17.5 million in 1969; according to the MPAA it dropped from 19.8 to 17.5 million (box-office gross actually rose from $1,041.8 million to $1,294.0 million due to admission price increases). These figures do not support Medved's ideological charges and claims regarding "the alienation of the audience" in the late 1960s; however, they do show the shift in the regular moviegoing audience that had already begun in the years after World War II and was solidified during the 1960s, and that Hollywood had finally begun to respond with movies aimed at the under-thirty group.

Even though these recent observations about movie ratings and box-office grosses are better explained by shifting audience demographics and the intent of maximizing the range of potential moviegoers for every film (as I showed in chapter eleven), Medved and similar critics attribute it to the ideology of Hollywood producers and not the drive for profits.

The reports on the success of G and PG films are misleading, for a direct comparison of box-office gross and film rating does not take into account other variables that affect a film's earning power. The study conducted by Paul Kagan Associates, for example, included 1,187 U.S. films released from 1984 to 1991 that played on at least one hundred screens. To compare the theatrical gross of one film that plays on one thousand screens with another playing on one hundred screens, regardless of its rating, would in all probability find the first to have a higher gross. Most films rated G and PG (indicated by their rating) are intended to reach a wider demographic group than those rated R and open on one thousand screens or more, while a higher percentage of R-rated pictures debut and run on a much smaller number of screens.

In addition, production and marketing budgets can be important factors in box-office success. As we saw in chapter eleven, big-budgeted films and wide releases get more publicity and exposure than modest ones. According to a representative at the Kagan consulting firm, their survey was a straight comparison of rating and box-office earnings that did not take into account these other variables. Also, as we have seen before, the relation between box-office gross and actual profits is an important industry factor in production and marketing decisions.

As all this indicates, consideration of variables such as production and marketing budgets, number of opening screens and the relation of profits to production costs reveals the direct correlation between MPAA ratings and box-office figures to be overly simplistic. Furthermore, the audience opinion survey conducted by *Variety* which was noted earlier did not confirm the assertion that the most ardent moviegoers prefer G- and PG-rated films.[37]

Once again, this does not mean that Hollywood studios should not make G and PG films, nor does it excuse the gratuitous inclusion of profanity, sex and violence in pictures aimed at young moviegoers. It does suggest, however, that Hollywood is reaching its regular bread-and-butter audience in a manner similar to the production of what were called A-, B- and C-films during the studio era.

As we saw in the previous chapter, demographic changes are once again affecting Hollywood productions, as indicated by the increase in both family-oriented fare beginning around 1990 and interest in specialized markets. "No one in Hollywood wants to be associated with the Michael Medved school of prudery, to be sure," *Variety's* Peter Bart observes. "The decision-makers in Hollywood, however, are trying to come to grips with demographic phenomena that reveal an oddly bifurcated marketplace." Here he refers to young people, who continue to be the most frequent filmgoers, and the increase in theater attendance in the over-forty group. Bart notes that at least one studio was "carefully aiming more films toward this [over-forty] market, without ignoring the Clearasil crowd."[38]

Although current staistics indicate a growing differentiation in the movie market (perhaps more than ever before) and that young people are the most reliable and frequent moviegoers, Medved and Baehr remain adamant that the general family audience is Hollywood's cash cow and that what is needed is more G- and PG-rated family-oriented movies. On the surface, it seems, the reason for their argument is that G-and PG-rated films are less likely to contain elements they consider offensive, and promoting them wins the support of other family values advocates. More important, however, their promotion of family-oriented pictures is based on the separation of high and low culture and the roles cultural products designated as such are assigned. These critics want the popular arts to serve as harmless amusement for the masses. That explains their longing for the "golden age" of Hollywood, as it is rooted in their desire for today's entertainment to affirm a cultural and moral consensus as it did during the studio era.

Medved likens the movies of the 1930s and 1940s to the classics of Western civilization. "We are now seeing the popular culture taken over by the same nihilistic mentality that has already wrecked classical music, the visual arts, and the world of poetry," he said in an interview in *Christianity Today.*

> Once upon a time, people had the vision—in the most general sense— that what made art worthwhile, lasting, and praiseworthy was that it was created for the greater glory of God, in one sense or another. That is what inspired Shakespeare and Tolstoy and Beethoven and Mozart and Dickens, even though there is obviously social protest in his work. And that was also true to a great extent in the so-called Golden Age of American movies.[39]

This statement is not only nebulous (vision "in the most general sense," God "in one sense or another"?) and unfounded but also a naive attempt to create an idyllic past (and what's wrong with social protest in art?). The underlying structure of Medved's film history is a mythic one: the "golden age" of Hollywood, when movie moguls profited by paying homage to family, religion and American institutions, is portrayed as a Garden of Eden that was infected by liberals in the late 1960s. But as we have seen, the golden age was fraught with problems, and there was intense quarreling and disagreement among industry leaders, educators, legislators, reformers and religious leaders about the condition and role of entertainment. And many conservative religious groups still forbade movie attendance during this period.

Constitutional issues regarding free speech make such an appeal to the past unrealistic, as the consensus exhibited by movies during the studio era depended on the prior censorship of the Motion Picture Production Code. You will remember that the era of prior censorship was brought to an end by the Supreme Court rulings that extended the free-speech protection of the First Amendment to the popular arts.

Regardless, Baehr advocated a return to industry self-censorship and wrote a fundamentalist version of the 1930 Production Code that he wanted the film industry to adopt. According to one report, Medved thought Baehr's code was "unrealistic and dated in parts," although on the matter of prior censorship he is not entirely clear or consistent.[40] While he claims that he is not in favor of censorship, the essence of his proposal is that film should serve as it did during the studio era, "respecting" the values of the conservative middle-class audience segment. He writes, "The essence of [his] argument [is] that the products of the popular culture should become *less* propagandistic, not more so," and follows with an appeal to the "eminently reasonable guidelines, violated so repeatedly and so gratuitously in recent years," of the "notorious Production Code of 1930."[41]

That Medved proposes industry adherence to the general principles out-lined in the preamble of the Code as "an informal and unofficial basis for handling religious material," however, seems not only uninformed but also quite unrealistic. As the Legion of Decency knew in the early 1930s, without an official means of enforcement an industry code is only token rhetoric. There are many media critics and politicians today who say they are opposed to censorship but still hold up this era of industry self-censorship as the ideal. It is not difficult to see why others react with alarm and invoke the First Amendment in response.

Progressives generally resist efforts to regulate the entertainment industry for fear of ideological management such as occurred in the past, even though neo-Marxist critics like Theodor Adorno argue that ideological management is built into the media industries.[42] Conservative critics have fueled these concerns, for they have not only censured contemporary art but also ques-tioned the artistic validity of works they find morally offensive, leaving open the consideration that these works are beyond the protection of the First Amendment.

Even though their criticism begins with the reality that entertainment is most effective at performing the functions of art, today's reformers regard entertainment as a commercial product and not as contemporary art. Baehr is clear on this. "Movies are *not* art," he wrote. "Rather, they are a form of *entertainment* which employs artistic and communicative elements."[43]

Medved once again is not always consistent on this point. His basic argu-ment reflects the distinction between high and low culture: entertainment forms should not serve as art, but primarily as wholesome amusement for the general family audience. He writes, for example, that the tendency of film critics to treat movies as "artistic statements" instead of just "pieces of popular entertainment" actually fuels the problem with movies by making a "subtle but significant contribution to Hollywood's increasingly contemptuous atti-tude toward the tastes and values of the mass audience."[44] Medved sarcasti-cally derides entertainment that does not affirm his moral or ideological perspective as "cutting-edge" art, suggesting not that it is just bad art (and some of the films he describes are just that) but that it is not art at all. The question remains unanswered about what should be done about it, however, leaving Medved vulnerable to charges that he is in favor of some form of censorship.

As a film critic, Medved does discuss basic cinematic quality when giving advice to consumers. In his book he limits discussion of movies as art to technical aspects (camerawork, editing, set design, acting). He writes, for example, that "these components of moviemaking have reached a level of consistent competence—even artistry—that would be the envy of Hollywood's vaunted Golden Age."[45] But in writing and lectures, the basis of his argument for what constitutes a "good" film is almost always box-office figures. These indicate popularity and, in his line of thinking, an affirmation of the values of most Americans. But any use of box-office attendance as a barometer of the values of the American public has to be done with much reservation.

Medved applauds those financially successful films that support his mythology and criticizes (or does not mention) other equally successful films that do not—thus exposing his own bias while also undermining his method. Some movies containing high levels of sex or violence like *Basic Instinct* and *Terminator 2* have been huge box-office successes. What does this indicate about public taste and values? Medved's contention that the "appalling" and "potentially offensive content" of *Silence of the Lambs* is not what American audiences want to see seems unfounded considering the film's success, both critical and financial. Respondents to an *Entertainment Weekly* poll indicated that it was the film for which they most wanted to see a sequel made.[46] Further, the equation of box-office success and quality production also contradicts the long-standing elitist assumption that the finest art cannot appeal to the general mass audience—another illustration of how Medved does not think of movies in the same way as art.

It is ironic that Medved employs a populist argument to defend what is really an elitist cultural perspective and social system. "Marketplace guerrilla warfare" is his means to preserve the separation between high and popular culture as the solution to the problems with entertainment today. He is disturbed, for example, that traditional high culture does not wield the force of popular culture today and would prefer that the American people emulate what the Victorians referred to as their "betters." "In every society," he writes, "ordinary folk have been able to cultivate a sense of style by aping the airs of the aristocracy; in this stubbornly democratic culture, the only aristocracy that counts for anything is the world of 'celebrities' who appear on the tube and in the tabloids."[47]

Medved continues a movement for social control, based on the assumption that economic pressures will keep not only obscene material from children but also ideas considered subversive, or even progressive, out of profit-oriented entertainment. The media, after all—and entertainment is a large programming component—is the most sustained means of communication in our society, especially with the lower classes, and like reformers at the beginning of the twentieth century, critics like Medved and Baehr want to use it to teach moral lessons and affirm the authority of traditional values.

As we have seen, however, alternatives exist to this kind of hegemonic control. Recognizing that the popular arts serve as art undercuts the elitist assumptions of the cultural hierarchy and supports a different analytical tradition, one that criticizes Hollywood's profit-minded tendencies to homogenize its product and exploit markets, regardless of age and perspective, while affirming the differentiation of movies and a pluralistic cinema as the appropriate role for the cinema in a democratic society. This leads to the consideration of alternative strategies for reform that involve not just consumer tactics but other social institutions.

Today's reformers have attacked the entertainment industry as a formidable threat to family, school and religious communities. "One of the reasons for the unparalleled potency of the media in shaping attitudes and values arises from the absence of countervailing forces," Medved writes, referring to family, school and alternative media. "More and more parents view the popular culture as a powerful enemy in an ongoing war for the souls of their children."[48] Despite such fiery rhetoric, however, reformers do not recommend engaging entertainment at an institutional level, but at the level of personal consumption, an approach that splinters vital social institutions like church and school into special interest consumer groups. This is predictable, based on their ideology, but disappointing. The inflammatory speeches and consumer boycotts employed over the course of the twentieth century ultimately have not brought about the kind of long-lasting change that matches the magnitude of society's concern about the effect of entertainment. With only consumer boycotts, watchdog organizations and a nostalgic return to a greater cultural consensus in the past to offer, it would not be difficult to conclude that these critics are merely exploiting the confusion of the changing social and cultural landscape in American life.

The Culture Wars Revisited

One aspect of the social and intellectual developments in the late twentieth century is the dissolution of the conceptual and social borders between high and low culture. Scholars have come to recognize that high and popular culture have much in common as human social practices, and have begun to trace their mutual influence, recognizing that the division between them has been social and political, rather than a defensible intellectual or aesthetic distinction. "The redefinition of popular culture studies has made problematic earlier views of mass culture as degraded and elite culture as elevating," the editors of a recent volume on this subject explained. "Instead, the new studies recognize the power of the ordinary, accept the commonplace as a legitimate object of inquiry, hammer away at the often arbitrary and ideological distinctions between popular, mass, and elite culture, and ask serious questions about the role of popular culture in political and social life."[49]

The erosion of the barriers between high and low culture, however, challenges the Anglo-American hegemony. At issue in today's culture wars, like those at the beginning of the century, is control over "the" national culture and the use of established institutions to maintain cultural consensus or express diversity. The current debate is extremely politicized, embroiled in battles between political parties and ideologies of the left and right, over freedom of expression for new ideas and perspectives against maintaining the authority of traditional values.

According to Hunter's configuration of today's conflict, evangelicalism has aligned itself with the orthodox or conservative side. Armed with its premillennial eschatology that has the country going to hell, evangelicalism has equated the culture and values of the Anglo-American tradition with moral righteousness and the Truth (with a capital *T*), as though a 1930s all-Americanism could repair the cultural cleavages in our divided and perplexed society that it helped to create, and reinvent a cultural consensus. Opposing cultural pluralism as an assault on the core values of Western civilization, evangelical leaders have joined social conservatives in their condemnation of contemporary art and entertainment as cultural decadence. In the conservative camp, maintaining the Anglo-American cultural hegemony is seen as the only means to preserve the American character and democratic society. In education, for example, Allan Bloom and his followers advocate an Arnoldian approach, arguing for a curriculum composed of the great books of Western civilization in order to teach proper middle-class values and behavior and raise the aesthetic and intellectual standards of the masses.

Medved is also representative of this position. His is a synthesis of elements of both the moralist and the elitist critiques that shows the relation of the conservative movement to reform the media with the larger cultural conflict today. Medved rejects the inclusion of the popular arts in school curricula, asserting the conservative line that students need to learn "the Great Tradition of Western Culture."[50] In a 1995 speech Medved criticized American schools, saying that "today's politically correct curricula convey the clear message that the older generation is comprised of a bunch of sexist, racist, homophobic, puritanical, Eurocentric, materialistic and generally benighted bozos." He went on, "Nothing contributes so powerfully to the present plague of pessimism [in the United States] than the despicable attempt—now firmly entrenched from elementary schools to elite universities—to smear the extraordinary and honorable history of the United States of America."

Such idealism and defense of Anglo-American culture may seem strange coming as it does from a Jew, but it affirms Medved's higher faith in an American religion. This is explicit in his hagiographic depiction of a national hero as a Christ-figure comparable to Abraham of the Bible:

George Washington, the justly beloved Father of Our Country, never had children of his own. One can almost see the hand of Providence in this, because its means that to this day, my children and your children are just as much Washington's descendants as anyone else. In effect, we have all been adopted into a noble family line. That is why it is so essential that we celebrate not the multicultural contributions of our various ancestors in Eastern Europe or West Africa or Asia, but the achievements of our common forefathers, our national ancestors. . . . Perhaps the most basic explanation for the epidemic of ingratitude in this country is that too many of us, especially among our academic and media elites, refuse to recognize the great Benefactor who most richly deserves our thanks.[51]

Here and elsewhere, Medved is clearly attempting to rejuvenate a 1930s Americanism—the nation's manifest destiny and the subordination of ethnic and religious identity to a homogeneous national one. God's chosen people are the descendants of George Washington, who deserves our gratitude. This explains why Medved's highest praise is for movies like *Forrest Gump* that lack a specific religious perspective and treat God ("in one sense or another") as some nebulous cosmic force of one's own choosing that helps those who help themselves. Religious convictions based on a specific faith are lost or at best take a back seat to the myths and values of American individualism: self-interest and materialism. Evangelical Christians might agree with this film critic that there is too much sex and violence in the media, but they should be very leery of his compromising civic faith.

On the other side in the culture wars, progressives generally view popular culture as an expression of democratic pluralism and argue that because the United States is a culturally diverse society, adequate institutional representation of minority groups is critical to the healthy development of their personal and social identity.[52] They propose a "multicultural" curriculum that does not focus exclusively on the dominant Anglo-American tradition but includes works by women, African-Americans, Native Americans, Asian-Americans, Latinos, gays and others. How the media represent these groups (for example, negative portrayals or exclusion) is largely the basis of the progressive critique.

The broadening of the canon of necessity advances the study of popular culture texts. Contemporary art and entertainment represent, both symbolically and practically, new ideas and perspectives, as well as the culture of marginal and less powerful groups whose artistic voice is the contemporary media and popular culture (despite the extent to which that voice is restricted in the media). For that reason conservative critics consider popular culture a threat to the core values of Western civilization and oppose the inclusion of multicultural courses and popular culture in the curriculum. Bloom, for example, proposed that young people take off their Walkmans and listen instead to the Greek and European sages. Media critics, as we have seen, advocate a nostalgic return to the mythological consensus of the studio era, "the Golden Age of Motion Pictures when Mr. Smith went to Washington and it was a wonderful life," as Baehr puts it.[53]

The approach that conservatives employ assumes that true knowledge and wisdom are the exclusive property of one group of people based on race and nationality, leading to the denigration of other cultures, even those that share a Christian tradition. For within the church worldwide there are many cultural perspectives that take shape along racial, class, theological and denominational lines. The pluralist view, however, still has to contend with the problem of order and the difficulty of maintaining cultural consensus within society. And in its more extreme versions, the progressive response to a history of hegemony has tended to overemphasize the relativity of culture, even denying critique of one culture based on the moral or cultural perspective of others.

Navigating a course through the landscape of premillennialism and postmodernism—that is, conservative evangelicalism's efforts to establish its own cultural hegemony versus a postmodern pluralism that either abandons the possibility of truth or pretends that all cultures more or less equally lead to truth—is a great challenge today.[54] As I explained earlier, however, a biblical idea of culture allows for cultural pluralism while affirming the existence of a world ordered by God.

Culture refers to the network or system of shared meaning in a society, a conceptual collection of ideals, beliefs and values, ideas and knowledge, attitudes and assumptions about life that is woven together over time and is widely shared among a people. It is a kind of invisible blueprint—a map of reality that people use to interpret their experience and guide their behavior. The term *culture* refers directly to this fabric of meaning that is a people's way of life, and in its general usage also describes the "texts" of everyday life and material works that are a manifestation of a cultural system.

To be human, as distinguished from all the other creatures, is to be created in God's image as an inherently cultural being.[55] The creation, fallen in sin and redeemed in Christ, is a world pregnant with potential and possibilities, and God gave humans the specific task to "do" culture, to explore and cultivate the creation (Genesis 1:28; 2:15; Psalm 8:6). The process of culture, then, is universal. Even the most primitive societies have their own peculiar culture—characteristic ideas, activities and material works. But cultures are formed, maintained and transformed by human beings in response to a wide range of environmental conditions peculiar to a time and place. It follows that the cultural characteristics of one society and period in history—its patterns of life, thought, art and institutions—will have a degree of uniqueness and can be differentiated from others. Also, although a culture has deep roots in the past, it is a living, dynamic process rather than a static legacy. Culture and society are unfinished entities, living traditions and conditions that change as we contribute to them.

The biblical directive to be "in the world but not of it" implies that Christians ought to be both forming and reforming, measuring cultural development against the principles of love, truth, justice and stewardship that follow from the command to love God with all one's heart, soul and mind, and one's neighbor as oneself (Matthew 22:37-40). Cultural activity reveals people's deep-seated beliefs and convictions about God, the meaning and purpose of life, and the nature of the universe. While these basic and fundamental questions can be divisive, they are also central to human existence and too important to be excluded from public life.

Human achievements, then, ought to be interpreted and evaluated with an understanding of the cultural context in which they belong. And vice versa, it must be acknowledged that any comparison or judgment of one culture always occurs from within the context of another. The aesthetic criteria for evaluation of eighteenth-century symphonic music, for example, should not be used to condemn African-American musical forms. But it does not follow that social, religious, moral or cultural perspectives have to be abandoned in public discourse if we are to truly appreciate the cultural expression of a different group or advocate diversity and pluralism.

A biblical perspective, then, is solid ground amidst the centrifugal tendencies in our postmodern world. Its view of creation allows openness to cultural diversity, while its understanding of fallenness allows for critical analysis of former and contemporary cultural endeavors as representing the myriad ways that humans have responded to the cultural mandate, resulting in both blessing and curse.

A specific interest of Christian critical approaches is the uncovering and disentangling of the dominant religious and cultural forces at work in our lives and society. And the products and practices associated with popular culture represent a powerful and effectual expression of the spirit of our age. Popular culture influences how people think about themselves, their relation to others and their place in society. The entertainment media in particular inform, explore controversial moral and social issues, help people navigate through the complexity of our rapidly changing world and offer visions of life. Music, movies, television and other aspects of popular culture are both wildly entertaining and instructive, and are a vital means to uncover the religious and cultural forces at work in our world, especially in the youth culture, where popular culture continues to play a crucial developmental role. Even Bloom, an elitist and champion of classicism, observed that the producers of entertainment "have the strongest motives for finding out the appetites of the young—so they are useful guides into the labyrinths of the spirit of the times."[56]

Appreciating how different cultural forms and practices coexist, relate to and influence each other and understanding the place of minority perspectives in the course of history and study of the contemporary world can serve as an integrating influence in our postmodern society. Seeing culture and society as a whole and yet complex interacting environment is a sign of a biblical vision—that the earth and everything in it belongs to God—granting religious pluralism and cultural diversity a capacity based on the belief in the centrality of religion to human existence in a fallen world.

Conclusion

As alarmist as some people are about the influence of entertainment, they do not take it seriously enough in my estimation. Based on the idea of entertainment as a consumer product, concern about the influence of the media has resulted in two distinct strategies: regulation and consumer pressure on producers or advertisers. The advance of some kind of production code cannot re-create the national consensus of an earlier time and is bound to be entangled in constitutional issues regarding free speech. Watchdog organizations and consumer boycotts may voice the concerns and opinions of special interest groups and have some short-term effect, but they do not promise long-term transformation. These strategies represent a protectionist attitude that people need to be shielded from any effects of the media, and a way of thinking that makes it easy to treat the entertainment media as an outside force, blaming it for the loss of an imaginary past or for impeding our progress to a desirable future.

The pervasiveness of the popular arts and their role in American life—especially the youth culture—undermine the assumptions and continued viability of the protectionist model. Further, this view prevents us from confronting the nature of entertainment and the interrelationship of the industry with other forces that form, maintain and transform our culture and society.

Even though the entertainment industry has acquired a niche in American life quite apart from other established institutions, it does not exist in a social vacuum. Films, recordings and television programs are created and experienced amidst the interaction of various social and cultural forces and institutions. Historically, family, school and faith community (we could add business, government and the art community as well) have been most immediately involved in the dialogue about entertainment. Beyond regulation and consumer advocacy groups, however, the popular arts do not benefit very much from the constructive force of analysis and criticism that these other institutions could provide.

There are many aspects to this, of course—theorizing, historical analysis and textual criticism—all of which now engage academics. But there is a need for general audience education today. As the next chapter will show, family, school and faith communities can reclaim their social responsibility in part and serve as important mitigating influences by helping people learn to think critically about the media. The profusion of ideas and information that people receive from the media, and therefore outside their formal educational experience, raises serious questions about the viability of our present social arrangement, and more specifically about school curriculum.

An alternative to putting our faith in the dynamics of the market is to emphasize the public sphere as a place for dialogue and action. As long as we think about entertainment primarily in terms of marketing and consumption, we will continue to allow people to venture alone into a marketplace that offers individual consumers an endless array of choices, but limited perspectives on matters that concern us most: sex and violence, race, gender and ethnicity, psychological and social problems, and cultural issues. Relegating entertainment to matters of personal taste and consumer choice prevents other influential social institutions from carrying out their mandates as they might relate to entertainment. In effect, they relinquish their influence and abdicate their role as social, cultural, aesthetic and moral critics, allowing their efforts to be reduced to the consumer tactics of self-interest groups.

Instead of using one aspect of entertainment—the commercial—as representing the whole and the basis for reform, if we begin to consider contemporary entertainment in light of the artistic and cultural functions that it serves, a third course of action emerges suggesting a transformation in our social arrangement. Social institutions with educational purposes can examine the different ways entertainment functions as contemporary art, evaluate it on that basis and work to see that the industry is responsible for fulfilling these functions. In effect, this brings entertainment into the public sphere of discourse where questions can be addressed about what kind of arts and media we want, and what is the best set of circumstances and institutional arrangement for contemporary art to flourish in a democratic society.

13

· · · · ·

Back
to the
Future

In his book on film history, David Cook makes an analogy between audiovisual media and verbal language: "Imagine that a new language form came into being at the turn of the twentieth century," and that "although public anxiety about the potentially corrupting influence of the new language was constant from its birth, it was *perceived* not as a language at all but as a medium of popular entertainment." Now at the end of the twentieth century, we discover that we have "become massively illiterate in a primary language form" that has "become so pervasive in our daily lives" that it "surround[s] us, sending us messages, taking positions, making statements, and constantly redefining our relationship to material reality." Even worse, when it comes to understanding this language we find ourselves "barely literate—able to assimilate the language form without fully comprehending it."[1]

Cook's scenario accurately describes our present situation. We live surrounded by the entertainment media but have little understanding of how these media communicate or how the industry operates; we do not take seriously the role of the entertainment media in our lives. We cannot assume that people simply know how to analyze a movie, television program or musical recording (or novel or painting, for that matter), any more than we can be assured that they know how to do geometry or understand the workings of government. Consequently, most people simply see what they want to see in the popular arts, with little basis for further discussion.

Without knowledge and critical skills, however, people are vulnerable. The media's potential to influence ideological and moral perspectives is the source of much of the fear and consternation about entertainment today.

At different times throughout the twentieth century, social and religious critics claimed that entertainment wielded such enormous influence that it threatened to overwhelm the combined impact of family, faith community and school in shaping children and the direction of our culture. Recently the entertainment industry has been charged particularly with contributing to aggressive and even violent behavior in individuals and fostering a collective cynicism about American life.

If the cinema and other entertainment forms are as powerful as these critics claim, why do we allow these ominous media to continue to function outside most people's arena of serious criticism and evaluation? Why are institutions responsible for people's enculturation and socialization not helping them think critically about the entertainment media? How is it that something perceived as such a powerful force in our world is excluded from serious discernment by the very institutions purportedly most threatened by it?

The entertainment media have become pervasive and are too important to ignore. Despite tremendous fears about the influence of the media (or perhaps because of them), however, many people remain opposed to the study of the entertainment media. They see current music, movies and television programming as conflicting with the values that other social institutions seek to promote. Some religious groups perceive our popular culture as a threat to religious authority and faith tradition. Churches argue over the appropriateness of using religious popular music in worship; sermons warn against the evil that is sure to follow if movies penetrate the sacred triangle of family, school and religious life. At home, parents often feel inadequate, lacking training and skills not only to perform their own evaluation but also to instruct their children. They tend to be passive consumers, relying on the rating system or advice from other uninformed parents. Schools try to ignore entertainment, while continuing to complain about the impact it has on young people. Because entertainment frequently tests established standards, it is deemed inappropriate material for classroom use.

Even so, to argue that the state of entertainment is so horrific that it belongs in the "secular" marketplace and not in the arena of criticism maintained by other institutions not only is fallacious thinking but also keeps these institutions from carrying out certain crucial nurturing tasks. A member of the Catholic clergy suggests, "If church leaders want to elevate the quality of the country's entertainment, they should forget about boycotts, production codes and censorship. They should work at educating their people in media literacy and at mobilizing them to support quality shows in huge numbers."[2] Media or "visual" literacy may not be the entire solution to the array of problems within the entertainment industry and the conflicts that have arisen. It is a necessary component of an education today, however, and a viable avenue along which to move in addressing the issues.

Unfortunately, educational institutions are out of sync with today's most popular and perhaps most influential cultural forms and social practices, as well as the sensibilities of current generations. That we do not include popular culture in the formal curriculum implies that we can get along without theorizing about it or paying it much serious critical attention. Outside the classroom, however, students are avid consumers of popular culture. In fact, the notion that young people must be protected from the culture industries is no longer realistic, let alone a viable assumption to use in constructing strategies for reform. This suggests the need for reform in our social arrangement to bring popular culture into the sphere of public discourse instead of leaving it to the forces of the marketplace.

The Complex Issue of Media Influence

We cannot ignore the reality that entertainment is a significant aspect of our total environment. Over the course of the twentieth century, entertainment has become an important social institution addressing our needs for both leisure and artistic interpretation of our lives and times. We go out to the movie theater, watch television programs with regular devotion, purchase recordings, rent and collect favorite movies on videocassette. Entertainment is an established and influential social institution that provides artistic experiences for most people. Movies, television and music not only entertain us but help us make sense of life, shaping our perceptions, understandings and ways of thinking. We learn about love, business and democracy from the entertainment media, and surveys show that these media play an important role in the development of adolescent identity, helping young people work through struggles regarding intimacy and other relationship issues.

As a pervasive means of communication, entertainment plays a significant role in our public discourse, both affirming and challenging prevailing attitudes and assumptions about things that matter. This is especially true for post-World War II generations, who look to the media for insights into living and an understanding of the world. For them, distinctions between high and low culture have little meaning, other than superficial associations with class and wealth. Going to the movies is as valid an artistic experience as going to the art museum. In other words, for better or worse, the contemporary popular arts, and not the symphony, museum and art gallery, serve the purposes of art for most people.

In the first quarter of the century, a way of thinking about the emerging entertainment forms developed, based in part on the division of American life and culture into high and popular categories. The confluence of this cultural hierarchy and the religious sacred-secular antithesis led to the restriction of the aesthetic experience to certain high art forms. In effect, the high arts were divorced from everyday life. The burgeoning entertainment industry re-created this relationship in its own way, offering varied but equally valid artistic experiences for people through the popular arts. The new entertainment forms, though not afforded the status of art, nevertheless fulfilled roles and functions associated with the traditional arts and institutions.

Today's discourse about art and entertainment exposes a cultural lag between our values and assumptions about art and entertainment and the social conditions in which they exist. As sociologists use the phrase, a "cultural lag" occurs when cultural ideals and patterns fail to keep pace with novel conditions created by rapid technological, social and material advances in society. William Fielding Ogburn first introduced this theory in 1922, showing how aspects of marriage, family, education and roles for men, women and children were slow to adapt to the changes that occurred as people moved from a rural, agricultural setting to an urban, industrial one.[3]

The expansion of entertainment provides another illustration. The popularity of the movie theater (and other urban amusements) affected family life as more people went out of the home during leisure hours. Movies were also a new source of information about life, along with parents, clergy and teachers. Television dramatically changed social, leisure and family habits. The role of entertainment in the youth culture redefined those of other social institutions.

Technological advances now promise not only the continued viability of electronic-based entertainment but indeed its expansion. New formats and delivery systems will intensify the entertainment experience while increasing access and availability. George Lucas's Industrial Light and Magic Corporation is at the vanguard of computer-generated graphics that have already expanded the possibilities for live-action special effects and animation. The possibilities of virtual reality (VR) represent a new frontier. For over a decade virtual reality has been used to train pilots, cure phobias and create three-dimensional models of molecular structures. Now the technology is being employed for entertainment purposes, with VR games appearing in arcades—the same place where movies began a century ago.[4]

Companies are investing in high-definition television (HDTV), the DVD (digital video disc) system, fiber-optic networks, consumer satellite services and interactive media. The new interactive technologies have the potential to link telephones, computers and televisions into a home entertainment network offering movies, sports, shopping and games. RCA's Digital Satellite System (DSS) already delivers more television programming than cable, and in digital-quality sound and pictures. Companies have begun experimenting with interactive cable TV services that include movies-on-demand, full VCR capability, home shopping and video games. As with most consumer technologies, a pattern of increasing quality and decreasing cost will eventually bring these products into the general market. And the explosive growth of the video market, sales of "home theater" systems and enthusiastic consumer response to DSS confirm people's desire for more programming options and enhanced audiovisual quality.

In conjunction with the greater accessibility to the popular arts allowed by advancing technology, fears that entertainment media would be used for ideological subversion or lead to moral decadence have been constant over the course of the century. As a society, we remain unsure of the media's effects, either positive or negative, and have difficulty discerning their real value or potential harm. While experts disagree over the impact of the media, several major conclusions drawn from social science research point to the need for increased media literacy.

There is a general consensus that the entertainment media do influence behavior, shape attitudes and opinions and inform perspectives. This is hardly surprising; all of the arts have power to persuade individuals and contribute to a community's collective self-image. But as I have already shown, the nature of the entertainment media, given their pervasiveness and undifferentiated audience, make them constant subjects of study for their effect on audiences. Seldom if ever are the same questions asked about a high art experience. Are patrons sexually aroused by Renoir's nude bathers and more inclined toward promiscuous behavior following a moment of voyeurism at the art museum? Do Shakespearean tragedies foster cynicism about political leaders and subversive attitudes about government? Does novel reading desensitize people to real-life pain and suffering? Art does have the power to influence, and the extensive and sustained communication offered by the media, while it arouses ample fears and anxieties, should also increase their value and significance for their role as art in the maintenance and transformation of society.

That the media have an influence there seems little doubt, but the nature of the media's impact is limited and circumscribed—and this has important implications for how we should respond to media issues. Television research, for example, shows that the medium makes violence seem more common than it is, minimizes the consequences of violent acts and implies that violence is a common way of solving disputes. One recent analysis of prime-time television shows concluded that sex is most often portrayed as a competition, a way to define masculinity and an "exciting amusement for people of all ages."[5] It is difficult to prove, however, that portrayals of sex and violence in the media have a direct effect on viewers. Instead, the effects of the media are better understood as indirect and mediated by a host of other variables. Furthermore, it is not an isolated movie, song or television program that has an effect on viewers, but it is the cumulative effect of repeated viewing of the world portrayed in the media over a period of time that wields the power to persuade.

The inclusion of specific elements in the media, like sex or violence, is less important, then, than the context in which they are presented—that is, the value and perspective the media gives to them. This supports the idea that people would be well served by learning how cinematic images are formed and structured to convey meaning and by learning to recognize perspectives in the media, as well as to evaluate and think critically about them.

Studies also show that younger children are the most vulnerable to media effects. Children through the age of three or four are particularly receptive, and while they are adept at imitating behavior, they are not discerning about what behavior ought and ought not to be imitated. Unlike adults, young children do not necessarily recognize portrayals in entertainment as fantastic representations. In one of the studies most frequently cited on the effects of media violence, Brandon S. Centerwall concluded,

The critical period of exposure to television is preadolescent childhood. Later variations in exposure, in adolescence and adulthood, *do not exert an additional effect.* However, the aggression-enhancing effect of exposure to television is chronic, extending into later adolescence and adulthood. *This implies that any interventions should be designed for children and their caregivers rather than for the general adult population.*[6]

Using longevity studies of the effects of television violence in the United States, Canada and South Africa, Centerwall concluded very specifically that long-term childhood exposure to television and television violence was *one among many contributing factors* to violent crime. It followed that his recommendations were centered on preadolescent children. Some critics, however, misused this and other studies to generalize about the media's influence across the entire population, and then indicted carte blanche the output of the entertainment industry.

It is important to realize that the effect of the media is not homogeneous but specific to individuals based on a number of variables. People are not autonomous individuals existing in an existential vacuum. The impact of the media is tempered by a host of mitigating factors, including age, personal temperament, viewing skills, gender, race and ethnicity, family and neighborhood, education, community standards, political perspective, and social and economic status.

In addition, cultural environment cannot be discounted. In the United States, for example, most people think there is too much sex and violence in the media, according to recent surveys. In comparison, a marketing research study in Britain showed that depictions of drug use, violence and profanity were generally more objectionable than sex, horror, blasphemy and nudity (which was at the bottom of the list). In Southeast Asia, graphic violence on the screen is accepted, but sex is forbidden. Japan is famous for its pornographic cartoons and gory, violent movies (even though Japan has a low violent crime rate). But while pornography can be bought at convenience stores and there is nudity on late-night television, kissing in public is taboo. All kinds of sexual materials are easily available in the Netherlands, a country whose teenage pregnancy rate is far below that of the United States. Pakistan, Malaysia and the Philippines have strict censors who ban violence, sex and religion.[7] All this highlights the circumscribed effect of the media and the difficulty of making direct correlations between media presentations and social behavior—and it underscores the importance of viewing skills.

Finally, the media are more influential when other social institutions are weak. While all social institutions have unique practices and mandates centering on a fundamental human need, activity or value, they also have a relationship with one another, and the interaction between healthy institutions is vital to the well-being of society. When one institution fails to fulfill its roles and functions, another institution can become more influential for individuals and in society at large. At a personal level, for example, someone living in a dysfunctional home might find her deep needs for love and care fulfilled by members of a local church congregation. At a societal level, political groups might extend their power in the absence of a prophetic voice from the religious community.

The increasing presence of the entertainment media over the course of the twentieth century has reconfigured our social arrangement and has redefined the roles of other institutions as a result. At the beginning of the century, when motion pictures were born, the most influential nurturing institution in American life was the family, followed by the church, school and finally the media; today the order is almost completely reversed. Aspects of marriage, family and church were slow to adapt to the changes that occurred in the transition from a rural, agricultural setting to an urban, industrial one. With the need for more extensive education in our technological society, schools have replaced families as the primary source of education. Also, the entertainment industry became a significant social institution, not only filling leisure time but also, as the Payne Studies showed, serving as a "quasi-educational institution." Today the entertainment media serve people in many ways that were formerly, and sometimes more appropriately, the domain of family, school or faith community. The media inform, offer visions of life, explore controversial moral and social issues and help people navigate the complexity of our rapidly changing world.

In sum, audience studies demonstrate the effectiveness of the entertainment media as contemporary art. The impact of the media is not universal, however, but particular to individuals and affected by a number of variables, including the force of other institutions. It follows that a viable avenue for reform is to influence audiences through involvement at the institutional level, rather than defaulting to matters of personal taste and consumption.

Media in Education

As early as 1914, a prominent educator argued that because of the "cheap-ening and vulgarizing of the motion picture, schools and other educational agencies have been loath to attach to it the importance which it deserves."[8] Even so, American educators began an association with Hollywood in the 1920s. In 1923 the National Education Association (NEA) inaugurated a study of the use of movies for classroom instruction, and during the 1920s and 1930s educators developed movie appreciation courses in high schools and universities. At least two of the Payne Studies contributors, Paul Cressey and W. W. Charters, urged cooperation between schools and the film industry and, in particular, that film be included in a child's education.

The NEA established a reviewing committee and developed study guides for movies. The purpose of film appreciation courses, however, was linked with character education; films were used to teach moral and social lessons and found a place in the curriculum insofar as they contributed to the larger goal of building a national culture. They were, as Will Hays said in a speech at the NEA meeting in 1939, "courses in discrimination, in good taste, and not of the photoplay art alone or of the literature on which it is based, but discrimination in matters of conduct and custom, morals and ethics."[9] Students were not examining the cinema as a culture-producing industry or first-run movies shown at local theaters. Film appreciation was located in the humanities, with specific units in English courses (a model that is still in use today). The film curriculum, paying homage to the cultural hierarchy, was based on literary classics like *Great Expectations, David Copperfield, Wuthering Heights, Romeo and Juliet, Beau Geste, The Scarlet Letter* and *Emperor Jones,* along with children's classics like *Little Women, Alice in Wonderland* and *Treasure Island.*

After World War II there was a protest against life adjustment courses and a return to foundational education. The realities of the Cold War, the launching of Sputnik and America's new international role as a world power demanded changes in school curriculum. A back-to-basics movement followed, with an emphasis on the "new math," science and foreign languages. Film appreciation was considered nonessential. Also, the costs of projectors and film rentals proved prohibitive to many schools operating on small budgets, and there was a shortage of "instructional" films for classroom use (such as those showing a bean plant grow or a cell divide, a "newsreel" clip of Roose-velt's declaration of war or a travelogue geography lesson).[10] There was also a lack of understanding of film, and a need for the development of curriculum and appropriate pedagogical methods. As early as 1947, a representative of the U.S. Office of Education observed, "It cannot be said that the use of motion pictures in the classroom is typical or that films are as yet an integral part of our educational system."[11]

Since then cinema studies have made inroads in the academy, but primarily at the collegiate level. Film was eventually included in the liberal arts curriculum at most colleges and universities beginning in the late 1960s. By 1978 over a thousand schools offered ten thousand courses in film and television, and graduate programs at major universities had become a training ground for filmmakers. During the same period, a number of film journals and magazines came into existence, helping to create a wider and more sophisticated film culture. Bowling Green State University in Ohio introduced undergraduate and graduate programs in popular culture studies around 1970.

Models for media education in primary and secondary schools were pioneered in Canada, Britain and Australia during the 1980s. Media literacy was recently mandated for grades seven through twelve in Ontario, Canada, and media education organizations lobbied to expand the program to other provinces. Germany has a voluntary "media competency" program. In Britain, the British Film Institute has spearheaded public debate about the role of media education. The discussion centered on a new English curriculum that virtually excluded audiovisual media. The principal education officer of the British Film Institute argued that "cinema and television are the most significant new communicative media since the printing press and that they deserve knowledgeable, critical audiences. To demand that schools ignore them is . . . to commit an act of cultural vandalism equivalent to demanding that they burn all their books."[12]

In the United States, however, the inclusion of media studies at the elementary and secondary levels is only beginning, although the movement for media literacy is gaining momentum. There are a number of individual projects already in existence. The National Catholic Educational Association and the Center for Media and Values produced *Catholic Connections to Media Literacy* in 1992. A media literacy primer for high schools called *Living in the Image Culture* is expected to reach a significant number of the eighteen thousand Catholic parishes and eight thousand Catholic schools in the United States. The *Catholic Family Media Guide* contains articles and reviews of movies, videos and television programs to help conscientious Catholics make informed choices. Christian Schools International (CSI), a service organization for Protestant-based Christian schools in the United States and Canada, publishes *Media Studies*, a quarterly newsletter that includes reviews, articles and industry information. Although CSI has not developed a media curriculum, I am aware of many individual teachers and schools that have developed units or elective courses on the media and popular culture.

The National Academy of Television Arts and Sciences (NATAS) and the Pacific Mountain Network (PMN), a public television network and nonprofit membership organization, produced a curriculum for public schools called *Creating Critical Viewers*. The National Council of Teachers of English (NCTE), which is the largest professional teachers' organization in the United States, developed a twelfth-grade English course, *Voices in Modern Cultures*, that broadens the idea of literacy by incorporating various media, including film. A similar approach can be employed at the collegiate level by including competency in visual literacy among general requirements in the arts and humanities.

A variety of organizations make up the growing movement for media literacy in the United States, the oldest being the National Telemedia Council in Madison, Wisconsin. According to one report, the purpose of the movement is "to expand notions of literacy to include the powerful post-print media that dominate our informational landscape" with the intent of helping "people understand, produce and negotiate meanings in a culture made up of powerful images, words and sounds."[13] 1992 was an important year. The same year that Dan Quayle's "Murphy Brown speech" opened the entertainment front in the culture wars, three major U.S. conferences on media education took place, although they received far less media coverage than the vice president's remarks. The purpose of these conferences was to bring artists and educators together to promote media education in the United States. In addition to these events, there were over five hundred participants at the second conference of Ontario's Association for Media Literacy (AML), eighty from the United States (compared to fewer than twenty at the previous conference two years earlier). The pioneering work of the AML is responsible for several media textbooks and much of the growing U.S. knowledge in the field.[14]

This is not the place to develop a media literacy curriculum, but an apologetic for such a curriculum is a natural outgrowth of the historical and cultural analysis presented here. I do want to offer a few suggestions for a curriculum. To start, let me be clear that the inclusion of popular culture in the curriculum does not mean that students play with Barbie dolls and watch MTV or reruns of *Beavis and Butthead* all day. Most students already have plenty of exposure to entertainment but do not think critically enough about it. Thus the purpose is to bring popular culture into our formal arena for analysis so that people learn to critically engage popular culture in association with their experience with other institutions that help shape their identities, basic convictions and perspective on life. This is not an easy task, because people do not experience popular culture in the abstract; it is woven into the fabric of life. Still, popular culture should be considered seriously in the study of the humanities and social sciences as part of the terrain of social, cultural, historical, political and religious life.

There are at least three general aspects to popular culture studies and a visual literacy component in the curriculum. First, addressing visual literacy involves the design of specific units or courses to help students understand both *how* the media communicate (filmic conventions, for example) and *what* is communicated (beliefs, values, ideological perspective). Students need to learn to think critically about these as well as the cult of hyperbole, sensation, consumption and mass identification that the culture industries propagate. The study of the media is valuable in this regard, for it encourages reflection and critical thinking on personal values, creativity and the beliefs and values implicit in the media. Students should reach an understanding of the nature of production and marketing, the reading, viewing or listening experience, and the role and influence of entertainment not only in the youth culture but in our society at large. Based on these elements, teachers and students can work toward the establishment of basic criteria for evaluation.

Second, popular culture "texts" (that is, cultural products like films, programs, literature) can be used in the study of other subjects. A film like *Schindler's List* can serve as a point of integration for studies in history, religion and literature, raising moral and ethical issues while also introducing aspects of filmmaking and difficult evaluative concerns regarding portrayals of sex and violence. A unit on Vietnam might include films, television programming, comic books and popular fiction as part of the cultural discourse about the meaning of the war. Examining these media can also help students understand the valuable contribution the arts make to our collective memory and how they can provide social unity, while also exploring ways that our culture is transmitted and social criticism is done.

As another illustration, movies, music and television programs can be valuable in a study of the youth culture itself. This examination can encourage students to analyze the subculture they inhabit and think critically about social practices (sex and dating, for example) and the values and assumptions that sustain them, as well as how growing up in an age-segregated subculture affects their sense of identity, relation to others and the development of a life perspective. It would also show social and cultural aspects of entertainment: its role in the youth culture and the market exploitation of youth. As this study of the youth culture itself implies, popular culture studies cannot simply be modeled on the canonized approach in traditional literature, music or art appreciation courses, but requires a different pedagogy in part because of its existential immediacy.

Finally, teaching about the media necessarily involves emerging technologies that are central to the workplace today. Computers, for example, are a means of media production, along with video cameras and VCRs. Students are already using these to produce their own music videos and programs, but as equipment becomes more affordable, young people will have greater access to production technologies. Media education is important not only for acquainting them with the technology but also for showing them how to be responsible in its use. Also, in the process of constructing their own music video, daily program about school news and events, sitcom or short movie, students learn about methods and decision-making in media communication. Just as literary studies consists of both textual analysis and composition, so the study of visual communication requires an understanding of the methods of production and decision-making in the construction of media images.

Other Institutional Considerations

The school is the most obvious place to begin equipping people to think critically about the media. I do not mean to suggest, however, that education alone is the solution to all our problems, but rather to acknowledge a way forward. Obviously, there are many other factors that must be taken into account including family dynamics, the creation of social policy, the role of faith communities, and industry cooperation. Nevertheless, enhancing the role of education and the interaction of social institutions brings issues about art and entertainment into the public sphere for discussion, instead of leaving them to the whims of the marketplace. In that regard, the school can play an important early role in transforming, or reconfiguring our social arrangement in consideration of the prevalent and artistic role of the entertainment media today.

The entertainment industry is in the business of maximizing audience size within a competitive market, to increase advertising, box-office or retail revenues. Issues concerning quality, artistic integrity and social responsibility are peripheral to the primary goal of profit-making. Consequently, there are limits to any changes we might expect from within the entertainment industry. This does not, however, excuse the industry from its social responsibility as a creator of culture, or give producers license to do whatever they please in order to maximize profits. Again we are confronted with the complexity of the cultural production process: the role of mass-produced art, issues of free speech and media access, the pervasiveness of the media, the undifferentiation of its audience. Entertainment companies have a responsibility to give media access to legitimate cultural voices, for example. But it not simple or easy to separate this important function from the commercial exploitation that often fosters more extreme versions of the original for the sake of continuing the viability of a market. In that regard, the industry should be responsive to criticism from audiences (including youth), social groups and other social institutions.

Rather than argue that Hollywood should simply redirect its commercial resources, it is better to promote its responsibility to fulfill its various functions as a producer of contemporary art. This could enhance the dialogue about the role of film in society and raise questions about moral, religious and social perspectives that could lead to the kind of differentiation that allows for diversity and pluralism in the cinema as a means of free expression in a democratic society.

In chapter eleven I joined other critics in proposing greater product differentiation as an avenue for the film industry to pursue, with films designed—in terms of content, production budget and marketing strategies—for specific and varied audiences, not only in terms of age but also with respect to race, gender and life perspectives. Although the advancement of this idea is limited by the economics of the blockbuster movie, the possibilities of independent filmmaking and the video market keep it open as a viable alternative.

Although film producers generally oppose anything that might limit potential audience, and especially the crucial teen market, utilizing the NC-17 rating is one way the industry can begin to diversify its product for specific audiences and also demonstrate that it can put social responsibility and artistic concerns ahead of profit-making.

The initiative for the NC-17 rating came from prominent U.S. filmmakers who petitioned the MPAA to introduce a new rating that would limit viewing to those over seventeen for certain films that contained strong adult themes or images. The intent of the new rating was to remove the stigma of pornography associated with an X-rated film and allow filmmakers to treat provocative adult themes in movies that would be prohibited from viewing by minors.[15]

While the NC-17 rating has been criticized for legitimizing films that were previously rated X, in principle the rating is a good idea, as it prohibits minors from seeing adult-oriented fare. The British rating system works this way, using U (Universal) and PG (Parental Guidance Suggested) categories and then restricting viewing at the ages of twelve, fifteen and eighteen. Germany restricts viewing at six, twelve, sixteen and eighteen, and in South Africa the lines are drawn at ages ten, thirteen, sixteen and nineteen.[16] The NC-17 rating may become more important as more films made in other countries with different screening standards are distributed in the United States. The rating could be used to delineate the audience for films that treat serious adult-oriented topics (and not just those with explicit sex or violence), limiting admission to adults who should be most able to understand and evaluate the filmmaker's treatment. It is expected that films rated NC-17 will play on a limited number of screens. This means that studios must differentiate their output, work with lower production budgets and carefully market these films to specific audiences in order for them to be financially successful.[17]

In practice, however, the new rating has not panned out as expected. Hoping for as big a return as possible, studios package movies as entertainment for large audiences and prefer not to cut off a large part of the projected market with the most restrictive rating. Regardless of thematic content, studios contract with filmmakers in advance to ensure a specific rating, obviously preferring R or PG-13 to an NC-17 that would limit potential customers. Consequently, a minuscule number of films (0.6 percent in 1994) have been released with an NC-17 rating. Instead the rating is used as a marketing lure. Richard Rush's *Color of the Night* and Oliver Stone's *Natural Born Killers,* for example, both exploited a potential NC-17 rating to secure advance publicity, even though the directors were obligated to deliver an R version to the studio.[18] The pattern that has emerged is for companies to produce an R-rated version for theatrical release and an unrated "director's cut" for release on video and in foreign markets that have more relaxed standards on cinematic content.

One part of the problem was that the criteria the MPAA used to determine X were applied to the new NC-17 rating. This meant that some films formerly rated X (and considered by many to be pornographic) could be rerated as NC-17 for release in the video market. Public association of pornography with X was simply transferred to NC-17 for the most part; the release of *Showgirls* (1995) only affirmed this attitude. That the rating board does not act on sophistication of theme but on level of (im)morality only enforces common perceptions about the more restricted ratings. On the other hand, it is hard to change the general perception in our society that anything rated "for adults only" is somehow dirty or immoral and to be avoided, rather than limited to adult audiences. American culture has not yet been delivered from Victorian taboos. We have not been able to rid ourselves of the association of pleasure with guilt, for example, while also rejecting excesses like separating sex from love and intimacy.

Prior to schooling, the family is responsible for exposing children to television, movies and music and teaching them how to understand and think about them. Adults need to supervise young children's media usage, just as they would other activities such as development of language and social skills, academics, music lessons and sports. Families should also broaden their idea of entertainment so that using the media is one activity among many others that families do together, beginning especially with preschool children. The American Academy of Pediatrics recommends that parents limit children's television viewing to one to two hours per day. Just as important, children should learn from parents not just to watch television or a movie but *how* to watch it. They learn by seeing its role and place in the family life and schedule, and also from adult commentary. Continuing education courses could help adults establish criteria for understanding and evaluating entertainment.[19]

Also, parents need to take time to read critical reviews or form groups to keep each other informed. Much of the criticism in the popular press is intended to serve as a consumer guide, indicating that a picture is simply a good value for the money (basically analogous to touting a well-priced car or laundry detergent). At one level, these critics are simply telling us what they like or don't like, and they frequently disagree about the value of a particular movie. Still, they are helpful insofar as they provide information about the quality of storytelling, directing and acting and warn parents about the inclusion of violence, sex or profanity. And there are plenty of reviews that offer a more in-depth judgment of current releases. Many critics explore the film's theme and the caliber of the work, making comparisons with related films and considering the movie as a cultural document of our time.

Furthermore, since studies show that it is children who are most vulnerable to the persuasive power of the media, it seems reasonable to argue for some government regulation regarding children's programming and support for noncommercial public broadcast programming. During the 1970s the FCC judged that the unregulated marketplace had caused "a serious basis for concern about overcommercialization on programs designed for children."[20] Supported by advocacy groups like Action for Children's Television (ACT) and the findings of a 1972 research report commissioned by the surgeon general, the commission called on broadcasters to clearly separate children's programming from commercial content and prohibited the use of program characters in commercials as well as the "program-length commercial"—a program based on a toy product. During the deregulation of the Reagan years, however, the FCC ignored its earlier findings and argued that there was no need for government intervention and that marketplace forces would protect the public interest. Restrictions were removed on the number of commercials aired during children's programming and the incorporation of products and program content. The number of programs designed to promote toy products increased dramatically following the success of *He-Man and the Masters of the Universe,* as did the use of program stars and celebrities in ads aimed at children.

Ironically, the FCC's rationale for retaining its deregulatory stance was based on the popularity of these shows among children and the assertion that potential for harm remained speculative. The first point obviously affirms the free-market adage that producers are giving the audience what it wants and therefore are serving the public good. The second seems absurd to maintain at a time when reformers and politicians continually appeal to "thousands of studies" that link media content and real-life behavior. The issue of government regulation and children's television programming shows the limitations of the free-market approach and undermines the consistency of critics who condemn the entertainment industry for "putting profit ahead of common decency" but allow producers and manufacturers to shamelessly exploit children as a consumer market.

President Clinton signed the 1996 Telecommunications Act requiring TV sets to be manufactured with "V-chips," technology that will allow parents to block out programming designated as high in violence, sex or other objectionable material. The major television networks agreed to adopt a MPAA-like rating system for TV programs rather than allowing the FCC to create one. The V-chip would give parents more control over what their children see on television, and there is public support for a violence rating system to help parents determine the level of violence in a program without having to preview it. At its annual meeting in 1994 the American Medical Association adopted recommendations for an overhaul of the current MPAA system that would target more age groups, include more descriptive movie ratings, extend the system to television, video and music recordings, and include future entertainment technologies.[21]

But these can be overly simplistic solutions to a complicated situation, raising perhaps as many issues as they purport to resolve. Who decides what is objectionable content? Would such technology limit access to diversity of content and opinion? While a violence rating system can be quantitative, indicating the amount of violence in a program, aesthetic and social judgments are more difficult to make. How will differentiations in violence be decided? How is the violence in *Die Hard*, for example, to be compared with that found in cartoons, an A&E special on the dropping of the atomic bomb on Hiroshima or the *Eyes on the Prize* series on civil rights? Will definitions of violence be extended to sporting events, news, documentaries and educational shows? Furthermore, producers are unfortunately likely to respond by increasing their output of cheap exploitation fare on the premise that parents can simply block it out if they so choose.[22] This may be the chief legacy and supreme irony of today's reform movement.

Regarding faith communities, while I have shown that the church has denigrated popular culture, it is also true, if equally ironic, that the church has always shown a preference for popular over high culture, and in particular a desire for sentimental schlock over higher-quality art. This is a generalization, of course, for there are religious groups that take a thoughtful approach to contemporary art. But among evangelicals, morality and spirituality are usually the primary determinants of the quality and acceptability of art, at the expense of aesthetic and cultural considerations. Pious themes, jejune lyrics, sweet-sounding music, didactic dialogue and Pollyannaish endings characterize much evangelical music, movies, fiction and television programming.

Too often Christians want entertainment to build some kind of a heaven on earth ahead of time, either by performing an evangelistic service or by depicting an idyllic world in which love conquers all and good triumphs over evil. These elements of melodrama have a direct emotional appeal and a moral simplicity that people find uplifting and satisfying. And Hollywood producers know that. The blockbuster hit *Pretty Woman,* for example, was originally a very dark story with a grim ending. Producer Laura Ziskin said that if they had left the film that way "it probably would be a *really* good movie," but "it wouldn't make the same kind of money."[23] As we saw earlier, the melodramatic format is a staple in American entertainment, and in this regard the tastes of the American religious community are comparable to those of the general population.

The popularity of melodrama in American entertainment is an issue that warrants further consideration. Certainly it reflects the American tendency to see all issues as plain and simple, black-and-white issues of morality. Within the church, however, this has contributed to a preference for whatever is nice, heartwarming and comforting over what is true, right and excellent. This in turn has largely reduced the church's critique of the arts to a protest against the inclusion of profanity, explicit sex and graphic violence and has limited acceptable thematic content. The most vocal religious critics argue for more "family" entertainment that is quaint, superficial and escapist and for PG versions of R-rated films. This approach may serve the desires of a particular constituency in the church. In the long run, however, it discourages analysis of both contemporary art and the prominent cultural values it displays, leading many to uncritically accept American attitudes toward life—self-interest and self-reliance, a lust for power, violent resolutions to problems, materialism, stereotypes based on race, gender or disability, and even a humanistic outlook—as if these were Christian.

The classical Hollywood film is a good illustration. As we saw earlier, the classical film is driven by a cause-and-effect narrative centered on the actions of the main characters. This narrative style, at least in its dominant usage, represents a very humanistic approach to life and storytelling. Neal Gabler notes, for example, that director Frank Capra, who was a master of the classical Hollywood style in the 1930s and 1940s, propounded

a theology of comedy—a secularized displacement of Christ's tale in which a common-man hero, blessed with goodness and sense, overcomes obstacles, temptations, and even betrayals to redeem his own life and triumph.

(In his most extraordinary film, *It's a Wonderful Life*, . . . the hero actually attempts suicide and is "resurrected" by divine intervention.) If he was occasionally sentimental and overidealized the virtues of small-town Americans, Capra also created a powerful myth for the nation—one that would help sustain and define Americans for decades. "The ecumenical church of humanism," he called it. Others called it simply "being an American."[24] It is most ironic that in their battle against the subversive effects of entertainment, many religious critics today celebrate plainly humanistic films from Hollywood's golden age as though they represented Christian values and culture.

In combination, the classic narrative style and Hollywood ideology work to downplay the role of external social, economic and cultural forces in shaping human beings and affecting the course of events and even history. Story is based on the exposition of clear character traits and motivations revealed in actions. Hollywood heroes are idealized and identified with certain traits, the most important being self-reliance and goal achievement. Consequently, it is difficult within the classic style to present a personal encounter with the transcendent or the intervention of God with credibility.[25]

In contrast to the dominant Hollywood paradigm, the evangelical Christian tradition emphasizes the sovereignty of God and human sinfulness and inadequacy, which demand dependence on God's grace alone and centering all of life on the goal of glorifying God. The heroes of Hebrew 11 are commended for their faithful living, not their self-reliance and rugged individualism. While they exhibited a variety of gifts, they were all weak, flawed and sinful, accomplishing whatever they did because of God's grace and handiwork. Hollywood films may affirm a national mythology that gives the appearance of consensus, and their melodramatic appeal makes them charming and seemingly harmless, but Christians have to adopt a critical posture toward them. This is critical to maintaining religious identity and resisting secularization.

It follows that faith communities should discuss perspectives in the media to enhance their awareness and understanding. They can begin their analysis of particular works with a basic element of art criticism, the distinction between subject and content in a work of art. *Subject* refers to the topic, or whatever is represented in a work of art—the who, what, when and where. *Content* refers to the next level of questions in understanding or experiencing art—interpretation of the larger, total meaning of the work. For example, prostitution is a subject considered in both *Pretty Woman* and *Leaving Las Vegas,* but these films offer starkly different portrayals of the meaning of this subject. The life of a prostitute is romanticized and glamorized in *Pretty Woman,* while *Leaving Las Vegas* shows it as cruel, despairing and dehumanizing. The American military and war are the subjects of *Sands of Iwo Jima* and *Full Metal Jacket,* but these films' content represents contrasting depictions—the former a patriotic glorification of war, the later a dark journey into the psychology of training men to kill.

This basic approach leads viewers into questions of intended meaning and perspective in art and puts the subject, however charming or disturbing, in an interpretive context. Viewers then can appreciate a film, recording or television program as an artistic reflection on matters that concern us all (even though the work may not affirm one's particular religious, moral or ideological perspective), while also evaluating the work based on one's life perspective.

At regional or national levels, church denominations could publish reviews; members of local congregations could write critiques reflecting their theological perspective for discussion in Sunday-school classes or other regular meetings. At my church we periodically plan Sunday-school sessions open to adults, college and high-school students for analysis of current movies. Our discussions include reviews by local and national critics as well as personal opinions and insights. We also discuss aspects of the production and content of movies, the nature of the industry and the cinema as a mass communication medium. Also, youth ministries can make an important contribution to helping young people learn to think critically about entertainment and popular culture.

Ministers should encourage members of their congregations to develop critical skills as they look not for works that stay as far away from sin as possible, but for those that plumb the meaning and complexity of sin while also treating themes of mercy and justice, faithfulness, forgiveness and redemption. It has become a popular practice, however, for ministers to draw on entertainment for sermon illustrations of human depravity and moral decline. This may affirm for some congregants that the entertainment industry is an insidious evil threatening their moral and spiritual well-being. But for those who appreciate contemporary films, television and music, such sermonizing can make the church seem irrelevant to their lives. Sermons should treat the entertainment media as the important venue of public discourse that they are.

The Blurring of High and Low

Conceptual and social borders between high and low culture are dissolving today; distinctions between forms previously identified with either art or entertainment have lost much of their meaning. This is occurring simultaneously in intellectual circles and within the culture industries. The Museum of Modern Art, for example, organized an exhibit called "High and Low: Modern Art and Popular Culture" to examine the relationship between "modern fine art—painting, sculpture and the graphic arts—and a wide variety of expressions of popular culture." The Massachusetts Institute of Technology sponsored a summer professional program entitled "Ninja Turtles, the Macho King and Madonna's Navel: Taking Popular Culture Seriously." The editor of a new political magazine, *George,* described it as "a lifestyle magazine with politics at its core, illuminating the points where politics converges with business, media, entertainment, fashion, art and science. Whether it's violence in the movies or free speech on the Internet, culture drives politics."[26]

No aspect of popular culture is beyond the purview of academic study—comic books, fashion, advertising, television, film, popular music and other forms of entertainment. Colleges and universities now include courses on film, television and popular music and culture in recognition of the significance of these cultural forms. Steven Spielberg, Ella Fitzgerald and George Lucas all received honorary doctorates from the University of Southern California in 1994.

"In the academic world, writing in Hollywood still has a little stigma to it," veteran composer John Williams has said. But in the age of MTV and marketing synergy, the compilation movie score is a constant on the *Billboard* charts. And some of today's most talented young composers are creating outstanding movie soundtracks. Most are classically trained but able to combine jazz, rock, classical and folk elements in the same score; James Horner's *Braveheart* and *Apollo 13,* Elliot Goldenthal's *Batman Forever* and *Interview with the Vampire,* and Jerry Goldsmith's *Basic Instinct* are just a few examples. Williams, who composed the scores for the Star Wars films, *Jaws* and *Close Encounters of the Third Kind,* compared today's movie scores with operatic incidental music of the nineteenth century and predicted, "Music and film is just starting, but it will be the entertainment medium of the next centuries."[27]

Artists today easily work in film, television and theater even though the cultural statuses of these media still differ. Matthew Broderick *(Ferris Bueller's Day Off* and *Glory)* picked up awards for his Broadway performance as the lead actor in *How to Succeed in Business Without Really Trying.* Ralph Fiennes *(Schindler's List)* won a Tony Award for the title role in *Hamlet,* Glenn Close for Norma Desmond in Andrew Lloyd Webber's *Sunset Boulevard.* John Goodman *(The Flintstones* and TV sitcom *Roseanne)* recently returned to live theater as Falstaff in *Henry IV, Parts 1 and 2.* Broadway lyricist Tim Webber teamed with rock legend Elton John to compose the music for Disney's *The Lion King.*

One of the most prominent illustrations of the erasure of high and low borders has occurred in the theater. Andrew Lloyd Webber and Cameron Mackintosh have successfully conflated high and low art to create a popular and yet sophisticated theater with their string of celebrated musicals—*Cats, The Phantom of the Opera, Evita, Les Misérables* and *Miss Saigon. Les Misérables,* which is based on the 1861 novel by Victor Hugo, is a moving combination of opera and popular music. A more recent Webber production, *Sunset Boulevard,* utilizes cinematic techniques and is based on the 1950 movie/screenplay by Hollywood director Billy Wilder.

The durability of these blockbuster musicals has spurred a steady increase in theatrical box office, forcing the legitimate theater "to address the growing pains of an industry in the midst of a full-fledged boom," according to one report.[28] Escalating ticket prices and a reorganization of the industry's touring side contributed to box-office growth, which topped one billion dollars for the first time ever in 1994. Fully 66 percent came from road receipts as touring companies logged performances across the United States and Canada. The number of new productions went up, and others, like *Joseph and the Amazing Technicolor Dreamcoat, Jesus Christ Superstar* and *Grease,* were revived as the theater increasingly became a more popular and accessible art.

In addition, surveys now show that taste is not inherited or traditional but is influenced by such factors as level of income, education and occupational prestige, and moreover, that the effects of income are diminished when the other two variables are controlled. In several studies, for example, the up-wardly mobile among working-class and minority groups with few ties to the elite developed "populist" attitudes toward high culture, becoming active participants themselves instead of thinking of traditional high culture as be-longing only to the social elite. Furthermore, in contrast to stereotypes, the tastes of people with more education and greater occupational prestige are not limited to high cultural activities. Instead, research shows that they par-ticipate in and enjoy more of everything, from the European high arts to movies, popular music and television.[29] Studies also suggest that "in modern capitalist societies cultural development is fostered not by tiny elites or by much inequality, but by a substantial middle class with relatively little socioeconomic inequality," according to sociologist Judith Blau. "In other words, while individuals may accrue social prestige by exhibiting cultural sophistication, the development of culture on a grand scale may depend on the widespread distribution of social, economic, and educational resources, not the concentration of them."[30]

That contemporary entertainment functions as art and should be regarded as such in our institutional arrangement is not to say, however, that the arts enjoy a prominent place in our society. It is difficult for many artists to make a living at their vocation. Art galleries, museums, theaters and orchestras continually struggle for financial survival. Even combined revenues from patronage, public funding and box office are sometimes not enough for them to keep their doors open. Contemporary gospel singer Amy Grant, for example, did a special Christmas concert with the Nashville Symphony, with proceeds going to relieve the orchestra's $350,000 debt. In the schools, the arts are given a marginal status, often viewed as "extracurricular."

Many issues raised in this study warrant additional examination, including reform of cultural institutions, funding for the arts and creating standards for evaluation. Rethinking our ideas about art and entertainment can increase our understanding of the importance of these activities in our lives and lead us to create places for the traditional arts in everyday life, while also affording entertainment forms their legitimate role as contemporary art.

Yet our cultural ideals, values and patterns identified with the high art tradition and embodied in educational institutions remain out of sync with the presence and role of entertainment in people's lives today. They are restrictive and have limited the range of possible and acceptable alternatives to address the realities and challenges of today's world. It is necessary to consider new ways of thinking about art and entertainment. As Warren Susman suggests, we should be thinking " 'ecologically,' in terms of a total interacting environment," an approach that leads to a new consideration of the functions and expectations for art and entertainment.[31]

Words like *distraction, diversion* and *escape* have been used in a pejorative sense to distinguish art from entertainment by denying the aesthetic or cultural qualities of the latter. Vice versa, the term *art* often disguises how enjoyable and even escapist something like opera or an art exhibit can be. Such

333

distinctions, however, are superficial. As we have seen, a Mozart or Beethoven concert in the late eighteenth century served both artistic and social functions for aristocratic patrons. The same can be said of both a symphony concert and a rock concert today. People were reportedly willing to pay as much as $1,000 for a ticket with face value of $350 (still an extravagant amount) to see Barbra Streisand perform live in 1994.[32]

Art has always been produced amidst the interaction of various social and cultural forces and made to appease a certain audience, whether royalty, the church, a wealthy patron or ticket buyers. Historically, it is true, as Erwin Panofsky explains, that

> if commercial art be defined as all art not primarily produced in order to gratify the creative urge of its maker but primarily intended to meet the requirements of a patron or a buying public, it must be said that noncommercial art is the exception rather than the rule, and a fairly recent and not always felicitous exception at that. While it is true that commercial art is always in danger of ending up as a prostitute, it is equally true that noncommercial art is always in danger of ending up as an old maid. Noncommercial art has given us Seurat's "Grande Jatte" and Shakespeare's sonnets, but also much that is esoteric to the point of incommunicability. Conversely, commercial art has given us much that is vulgar and snobbish (two aspects of the same thing) to the point of loathsomeness, but also Dürer's prints and Shakespeare's plays.[33]

High and popular culture are socially constructed systems of classification that evolved historically and change continually in substance and significance. As social constructions, they created firm boundaries that legitimized traditional elite art and separated it from middle- and lower-class forms of entertainment. High and popular culture are also separate systems of production and distribution that have different effects on the art that is created within them. The categories of art and entertainment create standards for production and evaluation, as well as expectations for creative works. We expect films to be entertaining, and Hollywood filmmakers are obliged to make them so, regardless of content. Likewise, we expect an oil painting or a novel to deal with history, psychology and society and explore the meaning of life, and an oil painter or novelist is obliged to produce such a work. These expectations are real enough, however transparent the line between them in practice.

Today we have come to recognize a variety of ways that art serves people, a community or nation, and that there are historical and social dimensions to delineating art according to certain forms and practices. I want to suggest a model for a new approach. This is not a complete model, for it indicates nothing about the quality of specific works, but it does consider the distinctions we tend to make between art and entertainment and ameliorates these differences by showing how different art forms and practices actually share these qualities.

I prefer to think of artistic works as existing in a three-dimensional space in the shape of an American football (see figure 13.1). At one pointed end is entertainment; at the other end is enlightenment. These are not polar opposites, suggesting that the more entertaining a work, the less enlightening it is, but two general categories referring to aspects and functions that all artworks have in varying degrees, as well as our experience with them. The four lines (others could be added) extending from one point to the other can represent the functions I have emphasized: cultural transmission, social criticism, collective memory and social unity.

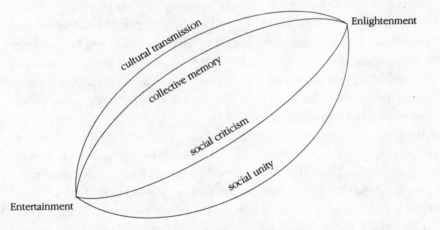

Figure 13.1. The Artworks "Football"

Inhabiting the space conforming to the outline of the ball are many art forms and associated practices with specific yet varied purposes and functions. Their significance and importance—that is, their value—may be understood differently by various groups and individuals at different times, and these can change under new circumstances. No function or purpose is exclusive of any one form in particular. Some forms may seem more favorable than others to carrying out a certain purpose, but that by no means limits them to that function or prohibits other forms from serving in that same way. The largest percentage of these activities—that is, the most popular ones—occupy the wide space in the middle, with their number narrowing toward the points. There is no hierarchy of form and practice here; paintings at art galleries and theatrical plays serve the same functions as movies and television programs.

Others have used similar terms and analogies to highlight characteristics of art. Cardinal Roger Mahoney's pastoral letter to the entertainment industry, for example, posits that entertainment and "enrichment" are complementary aspects of the artistic enterprise that presuppose each other. "Entertainment without enrichment is superficial and escapist," he writes. "Enrichment without entertainment is simply dull; it enriches no one. . . . To combine entertainment and enrichment is a creative challenge of the first magnitude."[34]

I prefer *enlighten* over *enrich,* because the latter connotes the Victorian notion of art for self-improvement or the idea of getting "cultured" by going to museums, concerts or theatrical plays. According to the dictionary, to enlighten means to illuminate, to furnish knowledge and to give insight—attributes associated with matters of perspective and functions of art like cultural transmission and criticism. I am using the term *entertainment* here to refer to the "entertainingness" of creative works—that is, the myriad responses, often emotional and associated with pleasure, that the arts elicit from people: the arts arouse, eroticize, shock, inspire, edify, disgust, horrify, thrill, excite, sadden, delight, amuse and so forth.

To illustrate, even a film as entertaining and seemingly innocent as *The Wizard of Oz* can be interpreted as a declaration of autonomous humanism. Dorothy and her friends have within themselves all that they need to secure their fate. They are better off without the Wizard, who as a God-figure is not only inept and insecure but a fake who does not really exist. The ribald comedy *Caddyshack* is also a comment on class differences, a cutting satire of the country-club set. The teen film *Dirty Dancing* explores issues of class, ethnic and gender identity, sexuality and pleasure, and the nature of democratic equality. Likewise, Herman Melville's creative novel *Moby Dick* explores the depths of human experience (and stomach gas) but is also gripping drama. Shakespeare's comedies provide both laughs and insight into the human condition, as do Chaucer's *Canterbury Tales* and Mozart's opera *The Marriage of Figaro* (based on the play by Beau Marchais).

Conclusion

The role of the popular arts, as they have been defined as low culture and by the interests of commercialism, has contributed to industry abuses of its artistic freedom, disregard for roles it serves other than appeasing corporate investors, and the exploitation of markets. These are good reasons for criticism; another is the industry's lack of inhibition, especially the liberal use of profanity and visceral sexual and violent imagery that can turn movie watching into a roller-coaster ride. When combined with cultural elitism and spiritual denigration, the industry's seemingly iconoclastic portrayals can make it difficult for some to even consider the possibility of a transforming presence in Hollywood. These critics, however, have confused the issue by identifying the potentials of the popular arts for service of God and neighbor with the forces of secularism at work in the culture industries.

This has contributed to a refusal on the part of some to acknowledge the importance of popular culture—an attitude that involves willful blindness and even hypocrisy. Entertainment is a crucial part of the world in which we all live. It plays a significant role in shaping how people think about themselves, their relation to others and their place in society. The media are a major source of ideas and knowledge, and young people especially appropriate the media as representing their voice and experiences. But popular culture is ignored in the school curriculum, condemned from the pulpit and blamed for society's ills. Except to denounce it as an enemy of the status quo or to assert the moral credentials of politicians, we too readily avoid engaging with entertainment. This conspicuous neglect of entertainment communicates that it is nothing more than harmless amusement, posing no serious personal or social threat, despite public anxiety to the contrary.

The purpose of education should not be limited to cultural transmission or socialization, for schools can and do serve an important role in equipping and challenging students not only to live in society but indeed to be able to transform it—to critique it, analyze its problems and suggest new directions to pursue in working toward solutions. Our culture and society are unfinished entities, living traditions and conditions that change as we contribute to them, and students need to understand that. T. S. Eliot wrote,

> Where that culture is regarded as final, that attempt is made to impose it on younger minds. Where it is viewed as a stage in development, younger minds are trained to receive it and to improve upon it. . . . We know now that the highest achievements of the past, in art, in wisdom, in holiness,

were but "stages in development" which we can teach our springalds to improve upon. We must not train them merely to receive the culture of the past, for that would be to regard the culture of the past as final.[35]

It follows that our educational curriculum should represent all that we deem important about knowledge, culture and society. We have to analyze our struggles and differences, hearing various perspectives and not simply the dominant ones. If students are to be transformers of culture, they must be equipped to deal with the world as it exists and be able to envision possibilities for its betterment. To that end, it is important that students be given the critical skills to access any cultural text, literature and audiovisual medium.

Family, schools and faith communities need to assert their presence in the cultural discourse about entertainment. Urging constituencies to join consumer boycotts or support watchdog groups, while these can be effective ways to deal with specific incidents, is not enough. What is needed is a better understanding of the issues and a sharper, more clearly articulated critique, accompanied by alternatives that can lead to a transformation of our social and cultural landscape.

Educational institutions can respond to concern about entertainment's influence on personal behavior, values and view of the world by shaping people's view of entertainment and its role in their lives. If we can help people enhance their understanding and appreciation of entertainment and develop a critical approach, we can become a society served by the potentials of the entertainment media, instead of one that is in constant fear of being possessed by them.

Notes

Chapter 1: Total Recall

[1]A recent article in the travel section of my local newspaper suggested that tourists visiting the "world-famous Philadelphia Museum of Art at 26th Street . . . run up the grand entrance of steps where Sylvester Stallone as 'Rocky' capped his workouts as he threw his arms up in the air. The view of the city at this spot is spectacular." See Gloria Hayes Kremer, "Tale of Two Cities," *Grand Rapids Press,* January 9, 1994, p. K8. Tom Muldoon, executive director of the Philadelphia Convention and Visitors Bureau, is quoted in Thomas Hines, "Putting Rocky on a Pedestal," *Philadelphia Inquirer,* March 4, 1990, p. 5J.

[2]Quoted in Bill Tonelli, "Movie Sculptor Hits a 'Rocky' Spot," *Welcomat,* March 4, 1981, p. 10. According to different accounts, the film company never intended to leave the statue in Philadelphia, but that as a "movie prop" it would be returned to Los Angeles. Schomberg reportedly suggested the "work of art" have a permanent residence at the top of the museum steps. Stallone was apparently less concerned about its location in the city. Nevertheless, the film producers enjoyed all the prerelease publicity the controversy over the statue generated. See Jack Smyth, " 'Rocky' Is the Underdog in Fight over Statue at Philadelphia Art Museum," *The Bulletin,* December 11, 1980, p. B2; Walter F. Naedele, " 'Rocky' Statue out of the Picture," *The Bulletin,* May 17, 1981, p. A11.

[3]This illustration is drawn from the author's personal experience and Paula Guzzetti, "Yo, Adrian! Is This Art?" *Newsweek,* June 18, 1990, pp. 6-7.

[4]Editorial, "The Art Museum Isn't for Hype," *The Bulletin,* May 12, 1981; Arthur Gorman, quoted in Gail Shister, "Rocky's Statue Finds Its Way Home at Last," *Philadelphia Inquirer,* May 24, 1982; Stallone, quoted in Fawn Vrazo, "Irked Rocky Says He'll Move Statue," *The Bulletin,* May 13, 1981, p. A1. These articles were found in the archives at the Free Library of Philadelphia.

[5]Mark Fazlollah, "Statue of Rocky to Leave the Art Museum—Again," *Philadelphia Inquirer,* February 25, 1990, p. 3B.

[6]Ruth Seltzer, "World Premiere of *Rocky III* Will Be Staged Here for PAL," *Philadelphia Inquirer,* May 11, 1982, p. 5E. *Rocky* won ten Oscar nominations and three Academy Awards (Best Picture, Best Director and Best Editing), and three of the five *Rocky* films remain on *Variety*'s "Top 100 All-Time Film Rental Champs" list.

[7]Clark DeLeon, "Rocky: Fanfare to the Common Man," *Philadelphia Inquirer,* February 16, 1990, p. B2; Sidney M. Steiger, "Put Rocky to Work for the Art Museum," *Philadelphia Inquirer,* February 22, 1990, p. 19A; Senator Vincent J. Fumo, quoted in Jodi Enda, "Fumo Strikes a Blow for 'True Art': Rocky," *Philadelphia Inquirer,* February 15, 1990, p. 1A. See also editorial, "Rocky in Bronze," *Philadelphia Inquirer,* February 17, 1990, p. A8; David R. Boldt, "Rocky Statue Is an Opportunity, Not a Problem," *Philadelphia Inquirer,* March 25, 1990, p. 7C.

[8]Guzzetti, "Yo, Adrian!" pp. 6-7. See Henry F. May, *The Enlightenment in America* (New York:

Oxford University Press, 1976), pp. 197-222; Dave Ivey, "Riots Between Catholics, Protestants Shook City 150 Years Ago," *Grand Rapids Press,* July 23, 1994, p. B4.

[9]Thomas Hines, "Putting Rocky on a Pedestal," *Philadelphia Inquirer,* March 4, 1990, pp. 1J, 5J.

[10]Kurt Anderson, "Pop Goes the Culture," *Time,* June 16, 1986, p. 68.

[11]See Thomas McCarroll, "New Star over Asia," *Time,* August 9, 1993, p. 53; John Huey, "America's Hottest Export: Pop Culture," *Fortune,* December 31, 1990, pp. 50-60. In 1990 alone, income from foreign theaters grew by 16 percent over the previous year, television revenues increased by about 29 percent and home video shot up 39 percent (David F. Prindle, *Risky Business: The Political Economy of Hollywood* [Boulder, Colo.: Westview, 1993], p. 24). The U.S. trade deficit topped $100 billion in 1993, but that figure omits the services category, which includes entertainment. There the United States is running a $50-billion global trade surplus. Kurt Andersen, "No Tariff on Tom Cruise," *Time,* July 19, 1993, p. 67. A study commissioned by *Music Business International* magazine predicted that the global music market would rise to $61 billion by the year 2001, with the Asian share alone increasing from 5 to 12 percent, or from $2 billion in 1994 to $7.09 billion in 2001 (Alice Rawsthorne, "China May Soon Lead Global Music Sales Growth," *Grand Rapids Press,* February 9, 1996, p. B2).

[12]Quoted in "Quayle Rips Media-Academia 'Cultural Elite,' " *Grand Rapids Press,* June 10, 1992, p. A2. For a sampling of the discussion that followed about defining today's cultural elite, see Jonathan Alter, "The Cultural Elite," *Newsweek,* October 5, 1992, pp. 30-34; Kenneth L. Woodward, "The New Class Warriors," *Newsweek,* October 5, 1992, pp. 40-41; Robert W. Welkos, "Is Hollywood Ruining America?" *Los Angeles Times/Calendar,* June 21, 1992, pp. 6-7, 66, 80. For a discussion of Quayle's assessment of the negative effect that divorce and out-of-wedlock births are having on children, see Barbara Dafoe Whitehead, "Dan Quayle Was Right," *The Atlantic Monthly,* April 1993, pp. 47-84.

[13]James C. Dobson, *Focus on the Family Newsletter,* June 1993, p. 1; Buchanan, quoted in Welkos, "Is Hollywood Ruining America?" p. 6; Michael Medved, *Hollywood vs. America: Popular Culture and the War on Traditional Values* (New York: HarperCollins/Zondervan, 1992), p. 3.

[14]Welkos, "Is Hollywood Ruining America?"; Alter, "Cultural Elite," p. 30; *Maclean's,* March 30, 1992; *Newsweek,* November 2, 1992; *Time,* May 7, 1990.

[15]"Churches and Clinton Criticize TV Sex and Violence," *Grand Rapids Press,* January 9, 1993, p. B3.

[16]"Southern Baptists Accuse Networks for the 'Moral Breakdown' of Society," *Grand Rapids Press,* June 12, 1992, p. C12.

[17]"Film Makers, Film Viewers—Their Challenges and Opportunities: A Pastoral Letter," September 30, 1992. Mahoney offered these criteria in the context of the social need for entertainment, while also defending the artistic freedom of film and television producers. Baehr claimed that Mahony was pressured by Hollywood executives not to endorse the code, even suggesting that the cardinal was paid off. See "Cardinal Mahoney Does 180 Degree Turnaround on Film Code," "On the Other Hand," and "Confused," in the "Short Takes" section of *Movieguide,* May 22, 1992, pp. 20-21; Paul Likoudia, "Fired Anti-porn Chairman Claims Cardinal Was Pressured to Abandon Call for Film Code," *Movieguide,* October 16, 1992, pp. 21-22.

[18]See Richard M. Clurman, "Pushing All the Hot Buttons," *The New York Times,* November 29, 1992, sec. 2, p. 1.

[19]By 1995, the critically acclaimed and award-winning show was aired in 99 percent of the country with advertisers paying market rates. My own local affiliate added it to the schedule because it was winning the time slot in the ratings.

[20]Quoted in Kim McAvoy, "Hundt's New Deal," *Broadcasting & Cable,* August 1, 1994, p. 6.

[21]Jim Impoco with Monika Guttman, "Hollywood: Right Face," *U.S. News & World Report,* May 15, 1995, pp. 66-72.

[22]"Survey Reveals That Americans Want to See More . . . ," *PRNewswire,* May 16, 1995. Curiously, another Gallup survey released that month reported that 52 percent of Americans thought

conservative Republican House Speaker Newt Gingrich did not share their values. See Peter A. Brown, "Gingrich's New Hampshire Visit Raises the Presidential Question," *Grand Rapids Press,* June 4, 1995, p. A10.

[23]Of note, Dole included *True Lies,* the high-tech, violent action-thriller starring GOP supporter Arnold Schwarzenegger, in his list of successful family films, while failing to mention excessively violent films by other party donors, Sylvester Stallone and Bruce Willis. Ironically, while Dole attacked violence in movies, in real life he opposed a ban on assault weapons. See Richard Lacayo, "Violent Reaction," and related stories in *Time,* June 12, 1995, pp. 25-39.

[24]Ellen Goodman, "Let's Ditch the Hypocrisy in This Tired Sequel," *Grand Rapids Press,* June 8, 1995, p. F1.

[25]Lawrence Levine, *Highbrow/Lowbrow: The Emergence of Cultural Hierarchy in America* (Cambridge, Mass.: Harvard University Press, 1988).

[26]Paul DiMaggio, "Cultural Entrepreneurship in Nineteenth-Century Boston, Part II: The Classification and Framing of American Art," *Media, Culture and Society* 4 (1982): 303.

[27]In a seminal essay on the historical emergence of art as such, Paul Oskar Kristeller showed that "ancient writers and thinkers, though confronted with excellent works of art and quite susceptible to their charm, were neither able nor eager to detach the aesthetic quality of these works of art from their intellectual, moral, religious and practical function or content, or to use such an aesthetic quality as a standard for grouping the fine arts together or for making them the subject of a comprehensive philosophical interpretation." See "The Modern System of the Arts," in *Renaissance Thought II: Papers on Humanism and the Arts* (New York: Harper & Row/Harper Torchbooks, 1965), p. 174.

[28]I am grateful to my colleague Lambert Zuidervaart for help in formulating these functions of art. The first three are clear enough. A general understanding of collective memory is commonly held representations that people in social communities give to past events, traditions, customs and social practices that form the content and context for future reminiscence. See David Middleton and Derek Edwards, eds., *Collective Remembering* (Newbury Park, Calif.: Sage, 1990), p. 3.

[29]Although in different form, the patronage system continues to function for high art supported by wealthy individuals, corporations or the government through tax revenues. Recent controversies over projects supported by grants from the National Endowment for the Arts (NEA) highlight these functions of the public patronage system and demonstrate the privileged position of the patron to give or withhold support. There is also a sense in which this same system operates in the entertainment industry. A filmmaker or musician is employed by a studio distributor or recording company, which in effect purchases a production for the purpose of making a profit by selling it to a market.

[30]Calvin G. Seerveld, *A Turnabout in Aesthetics to Understanding* (Toronto: Wedge, 1974), pp. 9-10. See also Kristeller, "Modern System of the Arts," pp. 163-227; Peter Burke, *Popular Culture in Early Modern Europe* (New York: New York University Press, 1978).

[31]Matthew Prichard, quoted in DiMaggio, "Cultural Entrepreneurship," p. 307.

[32]Nicholas Wolterstorff, *Art in Action: Toward a Christian Aesthetic* (Grand Rapids, Mich.: Eerdmans, 1980), pp. 24, 27.

[33]Warren I. Susman, *Culture as History: The Transformation of American Society in the Twentieth Century* (New York: Pantheon Books, 1984), pp. xx-xxi.

[34]Kathy Peiss, *Cheap Amusements: Working Women and Leisure in Turn-of-the-Century New York* (Philadelphia: Temple University Press, 1986), p. 6.

[35]Lewis Jacobs, *The Rise of the American Film: A Critical History* (New York: Harcourt, Brace, 1939), p. 12.

[36]Foster Rhea Dulles, *America Learns to Play: A History of Popular Recreation, 1607-1940* (Gloucester, Mass.: Peter Smith, 1959), p. 307.

[37]Robert Sklar, *Movie-Made America: A Cultural History of American Movies* (New York: Random

House/Vintage Books, 1976), p. 174.

[38]Susman, *Culture as History,* p. 154. See also Will Herberg, *Protestant, Catholic, Jew: An Essay in American Religious Sociology* (New York: Doubleday, 1955).

[39]*Synergy* is a term borrowed from biology that describes the cooperation of discrete components in such a way that the total effect is greater than the sum of the effects taken independently. The intent in practice is to increase the effectiveness of each component beyond its own capability in reaching a mutually desirable goal, an example being the cross-promotion of a movie and soundtrack to increase record sales and box-office revenues.

Chapter 2: Religion & "Worldly" Amusements

[1]James Davison Hunter, *Culture Wars: The Struggle to Define America* (New York: BasicBooks, 1991), p. 50.

[2]Maxwell S. Stewart, "Deflating the Movies," *The Christian Century,* August 13, 1930, p. 987.

[3]John Rankin quoted in Neal Gabler, *An Empire of Their Own: How the Jews Invented Hollywood* (New York: Crown, 1988), p. 356.

[4]The congressman's gender stereotypes aside, he asserted that "the real paying audience is made up of older people," a claim that proved to be absolutely wrong. As Gilbert Seldes pointed out, Hoffman's argument was unconvincing because "the background is out of perspective: the businessman does not go to the movies—the real paying audience is made up of younger people." Statistical research had already established that once people reached thirty, they became more selective and went out to the movies with much less frequency than in their youth. See Gilbert Seldes, *The Great Audience* (New York: Viking, 1950), pp. 11-12.

[5]Washington Gladden, "Christianity and Popular Amusements," *The Century Illustrated Monthly Magazine* 29, no. 3 (January 1885): 384.

[6]See Albert M. Wolters, *Creation Regained: Biblical Basics for a Reformational Worldview* (Grand Rapids, Mich.: Eerdmans, 1985). These concepts represent religious directions or orientations that are manifested in ways of life and thinking.

[7]Quoted in Os Guinness, *Fit Bodies, Fat Minds: Why Evangelicals Don't Think and What to Do About It* (Grand Rapids, Mich.: Baker Book House, 1994), p. 62.

[8]Mark A. Noll et al., eds., *Eerdmans Handbook to Christianity in America* (Grand Rapids, Mich.: Eerdmans, 1993), p. 312.

[9]This summary is based on George M. Marsden's *Fundamentalism and American Culture: The Shaping of Twentieth-Century Evangelicalism, 1870-1925* (New York: Oxford University Press, 1980); *Reforming Fundamentalism: Fuller Seminary and the New Evangelicalism* (Grand Rapids, Mich.: Eerdmans, 1987); and *Evangelicalism and Modern America,* for which he served as editor (Grand Rapids, Mich.: Eerdmans, 1984).

[10]Marsden, *Fundamentalism and American Culture,* p. 12. The decline of Victorianism has been associated with the failure of evangelicalism to sustain itself as a powerful force in the shaping of American culture.

[11]Quoted in Mendel Kohansky, *The Disreputable Profession: The Actor in Society* (Westport, Conn.: Greenwood, 1984), p. 139.

[12]Ibid., p. 9.

[13]Foster Rhea Dulles, *America Learns to Play: A History of Popular Recreation, 1607-1940* (Gloucester, Mass.: Peter Smith, 1959), p. 13.

[14]Gladden, "Christianity and Popular Amusements," pp. 385-86.

[15]Ibid., pp. 384-86.

[16]Claudia D. Johnson, "That Guilty Third Tier: Prostitution in Nineteenth-Century American Theaters," in *Victorian America,* ed. Daniel Walker Howe (Philadelphia: University of Pennsylvania Press, 1976), p. 118.

[17]Gladden, "Christianity and Popular Amusements," pp. 386-87.

[18]Albert F. McLean Jr., *American Vaudeville as Ritual* (Lexington: University of Kentucky Press,

1965), p. 82.

[19]"Christianity and Amusements," *Everybody's Magazine* 10, no. 5 (May 1904): 698.

[20]Ibid., pp. 669, 701.

[21]Quoted in Stephan Vaughn, "Morality and Entertainment: The Origins of the Motion Picture Production Code," *Journal of American History* 77, no. 1 (June 1990): 50-51.

[22]Will H. Hays, *The Memoirs of Will H. Hays* (New York: Doubleday, 1955), p. 370.

[23]D. De Beer, "Vaudettes," *The Banner,* September 30, 1909, pp. 636-37.

[24]"Report of the Committee on Worldly Amusements," in *Agenda: Synod of the Christian Reformed Church, 1928,* pp. 32-33.

[25]H. J. Kuiper, "The Movie Problem III," *The Banner,* March 26, 1937, p. 293. In contrast, Kuiper proposed that Christians should prefer lectures, sacred concerts and educational pictures to show that they were "distinctive even in their amusements and are developing refined and elegant tastes." H. J. Kuiper, "Protecting Our Children," *The Banner,* July 27, 1933, p. 77.

[26]Clifford G. Twombly, "Have the Movies Cleaned Up?" *The Christian Century,* April 13, 1932, p. 480.

[27]Quoted in Kathleen D. McCarthy, "Nickel Vice and Virtue: Movie Censorship in Chicago, 1907-1915," *Journal of Popular Film* 5, no. 1 (1976): 47.

[28]Lewis Jacobs, *The Rise of the American Film: A Critical History* (New York: Harcourt, Brace, 1939), p. 63.

[29]Warren I. Susman, *Culture as History: The Transformation of American Society in the Twentieth Century* (New York: Pantheon Books, 1984), p. 284.

[30]This quoted material is taken from an editorial by Henry Beets, *The Banner,* November 12, 1908, p. 724, and the following *Banner* articles by editor H. J. Kuiper: "Sodom and Gomorrah," December 12, 1947, p. 1380; "Moving Pictures," December 4, 1931, p. 1076. *The Banner* is the weekly publication of the Christian Reformed Church.

[31]H. J. Kuiper, "The Movie Problem I," *The Banner,* February 26, 1937, p. 196.

[32]Martin Quigley, "Importance of the Entertainment Film," *The Annals of the American Academy of Political and Social Science* 254 (November 1947): 67.

[33]Fred Eastman, "What Can We Do About the Movies?" *The Christian Century,* June 14, 1933, p. 779.

[34]Ibid., p. 781.

[35]Quoted in Joel Spring, *Images of American Life: A History of Ideological Management in Schools, Movies, Radio and Television* (New York: State University of New York Press, 1992), p. 52.

[36]Quoted in Terry Ramsaye, *A Million and One Nights: A History of the Motion Pictures Through 1925* (New York: Simon & Schuster, 1926; Touchstone ed., 1986), p. 483.

[37]Quoted in Spring, *Images of American Life,* p. 49.

[38]Quoted in Vaughn, "Morality and Entertainment," p. 46.

[39]Quoted in ibid., pp. 62-63.

[40]See Marsden, *Reforming Fundamentalism.*

[41]James C. Dobson, *Focus on the Family Newsletter,* January 1994, p. 6.

[42]Ted Baehr with Bruce W. Grimes, *The Christian Family Guide to Movies & Video* (Brentwood, Tenn.: Wolgemuth & Hyatt, 1989), 2:25.

[43]Michael Medved, *Hollywood vs. America: Popular Culture and the War on Traditional Values* (New York: HarperCollins/Zondervan, 1992), p. 280.

[44]Ibid., p. 291.

[45]Ibid., p. 281.

[46]For examples see Peter Biskind, "Kulturkampf," *Premiere,* December 1992, pp. 47, 112; Louis Menand, "Savonarola Comes to the Multiplex," *The New Yorker,* October 5, 1992, pp. 168-73; David Denby, "I Lost It at the Movies," *The New Republic,* November 2, 1992, pp. 29-36; M. Faust, "Hollywood Versus America?" *The Humanist,* January/February 1993, pp. 5-8; Brian Siano, "Michael Medved Drowns by Numbers," *The Humanist,* January/February 1993, pp. 9-12; Chris-

topher Lehmann-Haupt, "What Happened to the Capra Spirit?" *The New York Times,* October 5, 1992, p. B2. For my own reviews see "Hollywood-Style Scholarship Backfires on Critic Medved," *Grand Rapids Press,* October 25, 1992, p. B11; "Hollywood's Purported War on Values," *Perspectives,* May 1993, pp. 19-21.

[47]Medved, *Hollywood vs. America,* p. 3.

[48]Guinness, *Fit Bodies, Fat Minds,* p. 14.

Chapter 3: High & Low Culture Wars

[1]See Russell Lynes, "Highbrow, Lowbrow, Middlebrow," *Harper's Magazine,* February 1949, p. 20.

[2]Guy P. Griggs Jr. and Perry McCandless, *The Course of American History* (New York: Franklin Watts, 1983), p. 308; Lary May, *Screening Out the Past: The Birth of Mass Culture and the Motion Picture Industry* (New York: Oxford University Press, 1980), p. 29.

[3]One way of understanding the periodic revival of Victorian cultural values as a conservative force in American life is that a substantive alternative did not emerge from the cultural conflict that accompanied the social changes of modernism. Consider that "the powerful assaults upon Victorianism launched by intellectuals and other minority groups failed to replace crucial aspects of that culture with durable values, concepts, and institutions derived from their critiques," as Stanley Coben has observed. "Perhaps the greatest contribution scholars in American studies can make to this topic is to explain why viable new cultural syntheses eluded those who participated in the ferocious and considerably successful assault on Victorian culture." See Coben, "The Assault on Victorianism in the Twentieth Century," in *Victorian America,* ed. Daniel Walker Howe (Philadelphia: University of Pennsylvania Press, 1976), pp. 180-81.

[4]Daniel Walker Howe, "Victorian Culture in America," in *Victorian America,* ed. Daniel Walker Howe (Philadelphia: University of Pennsylvania Press, 1976), p. 16.

[5]May, *Screening Out the Past,* p. 18.

[6]Frederic Jackson Turner, *The Turner Thesis: Concerning the Role of the Frontier in American History,* rev. ed., ed. George Rogers Taylor (Boston: D. C. Heath, 1956), p. 2.

[7]Coben, "Assault on Victorianism," p. 176.

[8]May, *Screening Out the Past,* p. 27.

[9]Griggs and McCandless, *Course of American History,* p. 309.

[10]Frank Julian Warne, *The Immigrant Invasion* (New York: Dodd, Mead, 1913), p. 296. This writer is actually referring to Dr. Frankenstein's creation.

[11]Kathy Peiss, *Cheap Amusements: Working Women and Leisure in Turn-of-the-Century New York* (Philadelphia: Temple University Press, 1986), pp. 12, 34. The general trend from 1880 to 1920 was toward shorter workdays for women, from between ten to seventeen hours in 1885 to under ten hours a day for most wage-earners by the 1910s. The shortened workday for women was the result of middle-class reformers' efforts to safeguard their health and reproductive capacities, in response to the obvious rise in women working outside the home. Between 1900 and 1910 the proportion of all women who worked outside the home rose from 20.4 percent to 25.2 percent; this remained nearly constant until World War II, when the size of the female labor force increased by over 50 percent. See Peiss, *Cheap Amusements,* p. 42, and William H. Chafe, *The American Woman: Her Changing Social, Economic and Political Roles, 1920-1970* (New York: Oxford University Press, 1972), p. 55.

[12]Peiss, *Cheap Amusements,* pp. 35, 45.

[13]Ibid., p. 109; David Nasaw, *Going Out: The Rise and Fall of Public Amusements* (New York: BasicBooks, 1993), p. 90.

[14]Peiss, *Cheap Amusements,* p. 163.

[15]Ibid., pp. 148, 150; Nasaw, *Going Out,* pp. 27, 233.

[16]Elizabeth Ewen, "City Lights: Immigrant Women and the Rise of the Movies," *Signs: Journal of Women in Culture and Society* 5, no. 3, supp. (Spring 1980): S58.

[17]Peiss, *Cheap Amusements,* p. 180.

[18]Ibid., pp. 180-81.

[19]Quoted in Kathleen D. McCarthy, "Nickel Vice and Virtue: Movie Censorship in Chicago, 1907-1915," *Journal of Popular Film* 5, no. 1 (1976): 43.

[20]May, *Screening Out the Past,* pp. 14-15.

[21]Robert A. Divine, *American Immigration Policy, 1924-1952* (New Haven, Conn.: Yale University Press, 1957), p. 7.

[22]The president of Middlebury College (Vermont), quoted in *Education in the United States: A Documentary History,* ed. Sol Cohen (New York: Random House, n.d.), 2:995.

[23]William Miller, *A New History of the United States* (New York: George Braziller, 1958), p. 153.

[24]Warne, *Immigrant Invasion,* pp. 19-20. See also Maldwyn A. Jones, *American Immigration* (Chicago: University of Chicago Press, 1960); Philip Taylor, *The Distant Magnet: European Emigration to the U.S.A.* (New York: Harper & Row, 1971).

[25]Between 1912 and 1930, scientific rationales for racism had been disproved. Almost half the recruits tested for intelligence by the military during World War I, for example, rated as feeble-minded. In other tests, northern blacks scored higher than southern whites. These results ran counter to theories about genetic superiority. For a fuller discussion see Coben, "Assault on Victorianism," pp. 166-70; Ted Howard and Jeremy Rifkin, *Who Should Play God?* (New York: Dell, 1977), pp. 64-66.

[26]Warne, *Immigrant Invasion,* p. 311; Divine, *American Immigration Policy,* pp. 6-7.

[27]Quoted in Howard and Rifkin, *Who Should Play God?* p. 69.

[28]Divine, *American Immigration Policy,* p. 18.

[29]Charles Benedict Davenport, *Heredity in Relation to Eugenics,* ed. Charles E. Rosenberg (New York: Arno, 1972), pp. 216, 219. (Original edition appeared in 1911, published by Henry Holt.) See also John Higham's *Strangers in the Land: Patterns of American Nativism, 1860-1925* (New Brunswick, N.J.: Rutgers University Press, 1955) and *Send These to Me: Jews and Other Immigrants in Urban America* (New York: Atheneum, 1975).

[30]See Howard and Rifkin, *Who Should Play God?* pp. 59-73.

[31]See Lawrence Levine, *Highbrow/Lowbrow: The Emergence of Cultural Hierarchy in America* (Cambridge, Mass.: Harvard University Press, 1988).

[32]Louis Reeves Harrison, "Violence and Bloodshed," *The Moving Picture World,* April 22, 1911, in *American Film Criticism: From the Beginnings to "Citizen Kane,"* ed. Stanley Kauffmann with Bruce Henstell (New York: Liveright, 1972), p. 48.

[33]Henry Seidel Canby, *The Age of Confidence* (New York: Farrar & Rinehart, 1934), p. 184.

[34]Paul DiMaggio, "Cultural Entrepreneurship in Nineteenth-Century Boston, Part II: The Classification and Framing of American Art," *Media, Culture and Society* 4 (1982): 318.

[35]Howard Mumford Jones, *The Age of Energy: Varieties of American Experience, 1865-1915* (New York: Viking, 1970), p. 207.

[36]Quoted in Howard Mumford Jones, "Arnold, Aristocracy and America," *American Historical Review* 49, no. 3 (April 1944): 395.

[37]Matthew Arnold, *Culture and Anarchy,* ed. J. Dover Wilson (Cambridge: Cambridge University Press, 1932; reprint ed. 1988), pp. 6, 47, 76, 95. *Culture and Anarchy* was first published in 1869, with revised editions appearing in 1875 and 1882.

[38]Ibid., pp. 83-84.

[39]Quoted in Jones, "Arnold, Aristocracy and America," p. 398.

[40]Arnold had his share of critics in the United States, including Walt Whitman. Newspapers across the country criticized and even ridiculed his lectures (for which Arnold received $150 each) as boring and a rehash of earlier published material. One writer said, "As a reader he is a sad failure. He cannot be heard. It must be that he has come to fill his pensioned pockets." Quoted in ibid., p. 402.

[41]Quotes taken from Arnold, *Culture and Anarchy,* pp. 162, 130. For a Reformed Christian critique

of Arnold, see Henry R. Van Til, *The Calvinistic Concept of Culture* (Grand Rapids, Mich.: Baker Book House, 1959), pp. 26-27.

[42]Arnold, *Culture and Anarchy,* pp. 204, 212, 70, 69.

[43]Levine, *Highbrow/Lowbrow,* p. 206.

[44]In the Victorian world, Howe explains, "the specialized 'expert' had not yet become prominent. College professors taught what seems to us a bewildering variety of subjects; ladies and gentlemen of letters felt free to pontificate on all topics." See Howe, "Victorian Culture in America," p. 14.

[45]Allan Bloom, *The Closing of the American Mind* (New York: Simon & Schuster, 1987), pp. 185, 187, 322, 69, 75. For Levine's critique of Bloom, see epilogue in *Highbrow/Lowbrow,* pp. 249-53.

[46]See Warren I. Susman, *Culture as History: The Transformation of American Society in the Twentieth Century* (New York: Pantheon Books, 1984), pp. 118-19.

[47]D. L. Roper, *Wanted: A New Song unto the Lord* (Wellington, N.Z.: Foundation for Christian Studies, 1975, 1981), p. 19. See also Calvin Seerveld, *Rainbows for the Fallen World: Aesthetic Life and Artistic Task* (Toronto: Tuppence, 1980), pp. 184-90. The description of mass culture as feminine beginning in the 1920s also worked to designate women's culture as popular and therefore justify its exclusion from institutions of high culture. See Richard Maltby, ed., *Passing Parade: A History of Popular Culture in the Twentieth Century* (New York: Oxford University Press, 1989), p. 13.

[48]Orlando Patterson, "The Paradox of Integration," *The New Republic,* November 6, 1995, p. 24.

Chapter 4: To Be or Not to Be

[1]Washington Gladden, "Christianity and Popular Amusements," *The Century Illustrated Monthly Magazine* 29, no. 3 (January 1885): 387.

[2]Ibid., p. 388.

[3]James Silk Buckingham, quoted in Foster Rhea Dulles, *America Learns to Play: A History of Popular Recreation, 1607-1940* (Gloucester, Mass.: Peter Smith, 1959), p. 104; David Grimsted, *Melodrama Unveiled: American Theater and Culture, 1800-1850* (Chicago: University of Chicago Press, 1968), p. 52. The idea of theater as a microcosm of society is advanced by Lawrence Levine in *Highbrow/Lowbrow: The Emergence of Cultural Hierarchy in America* (Cambridge, Mass.: Harvard University Press, 1988).

[4]Washington Irving, quoted in Mendel Kohansky, *The Disreputable Profession: The Actor in Society* (Westport, Conn.: Greenwood, 1984), p. 142. See also Richard Butsch, "Bowery B'hoys and Matinee Ladies: The Re-gendering of Nineteenth-Century American Theater Audiences," *American Quarterly* 46, no. 3 (September 1994): 374-405.

[5]Quoted in Claudia D. Johnson, "That Guilty Third Tier: Prostitution in Nineteenth-Century American Theaters," in *Victorian America,* ed. Daniel Walker Howe (Philadelphia: University of Pennsylvania Press, 1976), p. 115.

[6]Grimsted, *Melodrama Unveiled,* p. 35.

[7]Quoted in ibid., pp. 45, 47.

[8]Ibid., p. 56.

[9]Oscar G. Brockett, *History of the Theatre,* 5th ed. (Boston: Allyn and Bacon, 1987), p. 444.

[10]Quoted in John Belton, *American Cinema/American Culture* (New York: McGraw-Hill, 1994), pp. 120-21.

[11]Grimsted, *Melodrama Unveiled,* p. 248.

[12]This summary of Shakespeare and the Elizabethan theater is drawn from Brockett, *History of the Theatre,* pp. 191-200, and James H. Forse, *Art Imitates Business: Commercial and Political Influences in Elizabethan Theatre* (Bowling Green, Ohio: Bowling Green State University Popular Press, 1993); the quotation is from Forse, p. 47. See also George McMichael and Edgar M. Glenn, *Shakespeare and His Rivals: A Casebook on the Authorship Controversy* (New York:

Odyssey, 1962).

[13] Robert Weiman, *Shakespeare and the Popular Tradition in the Theater: Studies in the Social Dimension of Dramatic Form and Function,* ed. Robert Schwartz (Baltimore: Johns Hopkins University Press, 1978), p. 208.

[14] Brockett, *History of the Theatre,* p. 196.

[15] Forse, *Art Imitates Business,* p. 47.

[16] Levine explained that while these adaptations made Shakespeare more understandable to the American audience, they did so not "by vulgarizing him to the point of utter distortion but rather by heightening those qualities in Shakespeare that American audiences were particularly drawn to." See Levine, *Highbrow/Lowbrow.*

[17] See Russel Nye, *The Unembarrassed Muse: The Popular Arts in America* (New York: Dial, 1970), pp. 154-56. Stowe's own religious convictions disallowed theater attendance; she refused to sanction dramatic versions and received no money from them. Apparently, she did see a production "hidden under a shawl." See Grimsted, *Melodrama Unveiled,* p. 24.

[18] William L. Slout, "*Uncle Tom's Cabin* in American Film History," *Journal of Popular Film* 2, no. 2 (Spring 1973): 140. A valuable source on nineteenth-century popular culture is Carl Bode, *The Anatomy of American Popular Culture, 1840-1861* (Berkeley: University of California Press, 1959).

[19] Grimsted, *Melodrama Unveiled,* p. 71.

[20] Quoted in ibid., p. 73.

[21] Ibid., p. 75.

[22] Levine, *Highbrow/Lowbrow,* p. 136.

[23] Quoted in ibid., pp. 134-35.

[24] Theodore Thomas, *Theodore Thomas: A Musical Autobiography,* ed. George P. Upton (New York: Da Capo, 1964), p. 278.

[25] Quoted in J. H. Mueller, *The American Symphony Orchestra: A Social History of Musical Taste* (Bloomington: Indiana University Press, 1951), p. 30.

[26] Susan Sontag, *Against Interpretation and Other Essays* (New York: Farrar, Straus & Giroux, 1966), p. 297.

[27] Walter Benjamin, "The Work of Art in the Age of Mechanical Reproduction," in *Film Theory and Criticism,* 4th ed., ed. Gerald Mast, Marshall Cohen and Leo Braudy (New York: Oxford University Press, 1992), p. 668. Art analyst John Berger suggested that in the age of reproduction "the uniqueness of the original [work of art] now lies in it being *the original of a reproduction.* It is no longer what its image shows that strikes one as unique; its first meaning is no longer to be found in what it says, but in what it is." The unique existence of a work of art is now determined by its rarity, which is gauged by its market value (John Berger, *Ways of Seeing* [London: British Broadcasting Company/Penguin, 1972], p. 21). There is evidence today of a change in values regarding mass-produced art. People replaced their collections of LPs when the new CD technology became available in the 1980s, for example, and now purchase their own copy of favorite films and television programs on videocassette and laser disc. (Disney's practice of limiting the run of animated classics on video has increased both the cost and the value of titles like *The Little Mermaid.*)

[28] Quoted in Richard Maltby, ed., *Passing Parade: A History of Popular Culture in the Twentieth Century* (New York: Oxford University Press, 1989), p. 13.

[29] Quoted in Joli Jensen, *Redeeming Modernity: Contradictions in Media Criticism* (Newbury Park, Calif.: Sage, 1990), pp. 24, 26. Judith Blau has pointed out that research has also demonstrated "a connection between classical music and discordant social conditions and so raises questions about the assumption that it is only the banal or inferior qualities of popular culture that reflect or contribute to social pathology" (Judith R. Blau, "Study of the Arts: A Reappraisal," *Annual Review of Sociology* 14 [1988]: 278). See also Karen A. Cerulo, "Social Disruption and Its Effects on Music: An Empirical Analysis," *Social Forces* 62, no. 4 (June 1984): 885-904; David Burrows,

"Music and the 'Nausea Delle Cose Cotidiane,' " The Musical Quarterly 62, no. 2 (April 1971): 230-40. Burrows's discussion of music in seventeenth-century Italy makes for an interesting comparison with African-American and popular music styles, and especially rock in the 1960s.

[30]Jensen, Redeeming Modernity, p. 27. Jensen shows how four media critics (Dwight Macdonald, Daniel Boorstin, Stuart Ewen and Neil Postman), despite differences in their central charges, share common assumptions and a basic structure to their criticism, namely that the purity of some aspect of life—art, perception of reality, true consciousness or public discourse—must be protected from the corruptive influence of the media. Jensen's analysis forms the basis of the observations that follow.

[31]Maltby, Passing Parade, p. 13.

[32]See Judith R. Blau, "High Culture as Mass Culture," Culture and Society, May/June 1986, p. 65.

[33]Reuel Denney, The Astonished Muse (Chicago: University of Chicago Press, 1957, 1974). See also Leo Lowenthal, Literature, Popular Culture and Society (Englewood Cliffs, N.J.: Prentice-Hall, 1961); Herbert Gans, Popular Culture and High Culture (New York: Basic Books, 1975); Richard A. Peterson, ed., The Production of Culture (Beverly Hills, Calif.: Sage, 1976); Janet Wolff, The Social Production of Art (New York: St. Martin's, 1981).

[34]Howard S. Becker, Art Worlds (Berkeley: University of California Press, 1982). Becker's approach dispels the Romantic myth of art as the product of a specially gifted artist working in isolation by showing how the production of artworks depends on the activities of many people and accepted conventions.

[35]For a fuller discussion see Raymond Williams, The Sociology of Culture (New York: Schocken Books, 1982).

[36]Jack Poggi, Theater in America: The Impact of Economic Forces, 1870-1967 (Ithaca, N.Y.: Cornell University Press, 1968), p. 13.

[37]Ibid., p. 17.

[38]Boston's metropolitan population was estimated at 625,000 at the time. The city's vaudeville, burlesque and movie houses combined could accommodate an audience of over 608,234 people weekly; movie theaters alone had a weekly seating capacity of 402,428. The legitimate theaters could accommodate only 151,135 and opera 13,590. See Garth Jowett, Film: The Democratic Art (Boston: Focal, 1976), pp. 36-37; Levine, Highbrow/Lowbrow, p. 79.

[39]Levine, Highbrow/Lowbrow, p. 79. There were a number of factors that contributed to the decline of Shakespeare in the latter part of the nineteenth century. As the moral reputation of the theater improved, Shakespeare was not needed to make it legitimate. Shakespeare was less familiar and less accessible to non-English-speaking immigrants, a fact that increased the competition from the new visual entertainments like baseball, boxing, vaudeville and movies. Also, the Victorian idealism of the nineteenth century was on the decline, along with the melodramatic acting style that accompanied it.

[40]Walter Prichard Eaton, "Class-Consciousness and the 'Movies,' " The Atlantic Monthly, January 1915, p. 51.

[41]Ibid., pp. 50-51.

[42]Levine, Highbrow/Lowbrow, p. 116.

Chapter 5: Highbrow Stuff Never Pays

[1]Richard Maltby, ed., Passing Parade: A History of Popular Culture in the Twentieth Century (New York: Oxford University Press, 1989), p. 13.

[2]Albert F. McLean Jr., American Vaudeville as Ritual (Lexington: University of Kentucky Press, 1965), p. 40.

[3]Alexander Bakshy, Mary Cass Canfield and Edward Reed, "Vaudeville Must Be Saved," The Nation, July 24, 1929, in American Vaudeville As Seen by Its Contemporaries, ed. Charles W. Stein (New York: Alfred A. Knopf, 1984), p. 371.

[4]Robert C. Allen, Vaudeville and Film, 1895-1915: A Study in Media Interaction (New York:

Arno, 1980), p. 39.

[5]Charles W. Stein, ed., *American Vaudeville As Seen by Its Contemporaries* (New York: Alfred A. Knopf, 1984), p. 23.

[6]Anonymous, "The Decay of Vaudeville," *American Magazine* 69 (April 1910): 840-48; quoted in Stein, *American Vaudeville,* p. 61.

[7]Stein, *American Vaudeville,* p. xiii.

[8]Caroline Caffin, *Vaudeville* (New York: Mitchell Kennerley, 1914), p. 15.

[9]Marian Spitzer, "Morals in the Two-a-Day," *American Mercury,* September 1924, p. 35.

[10]Russel Nye, *The Unembarrassed Muse: The Popular Arts in America* (New York: Dial, 1970), p. 171.

[11]Allen, *Vaudeville and Film,* p. 153.

[12]McLean, *American Vaudeville as Ritual,* p. 46.

[13]Stein, *American Vaudeville,* p. 25.

[14]Douglas Gilbert, *American Vaudeville: Its Life and Times* (New York: Dover, 1940), p. 206; quoted in Allen, *Vaudeville and Film,* p. 27.

[15]Caffin, *Vaudeville,* p. 15.

[16]McLean, *American Vaudeville as Ritual,* p. 48.

[17]Ibid., p. 15.

[18]Ibid., p. 11.

[19]Nye, *Unmbarrassed Muse,* p. 171.

[20]Caffin, *Vaudeville,* pp. 19, 115.

[21]Ibid., pp. 96-97.

[22]Ibid., pp. 132-33.

[23]Walter Prichard Eaton, "Class-Consciousness and the 'Movies,' " *The Atlantic Monthly,* January 1915, pp. 50, 53.

[24]Nye, *Unembarrassed Muse,* p. 170.

[25]"Edison's Vitascope Cheered," *The New York Times,* April 24, 1896, in *American Film Criticism: From the Beginnings to "Citizen Kane,"* ed. Stanley Kauffmann with Bruce Henstell (New York: Liveright, 1972), p. 4.

[26]Quoted in Allen, *Vaudeville and Film,* pp. 108-09.

[27]Ibid., p. 201.

[28]Russell Merritt, "Nickelodeon Theaters, 1905-1914: Building an Audience for the Movies," in *The American Film Industry,* ed. Tino Balio (Madison: University of Wisconsin Press, 1976), p. 62.

[29]David Nasaw, *Going Out: The Rise and Fall of Public Amusements* (New York: BasicBooks, 1993), p. 164.

[30]Kathy Peiss, *Cheap Amusements: Working Women and Leisure in Turn-of-the-Century New York* (Philadelphia: Temple University Press, 1986), p. 149.

[31]Merritt, "Nickelodeon Theaters," p. 63.

[32]Allen, *Vaudeville and Film,* p. 298.

[33]Merritt, "Nickelodeon Theaters," p. 63.

[34]Tino Balio, ed., *The American Film Industry* (Madison: University of Wisconsin Press, 1976), p. 107.

[35]Robert McLaughlin, *Broadway and Hollywood: A History of Economic Interaction* (New York: Arno, 1974), p. 7.

[36]Arthur Mann, "The American Theatre Goes Broke," *American Mercury* 28, no. 112 (April 1933): 420.

[37]Walter Prichard Eaton, "The Menace of the Movies," *American Magazine,* September 1913, p. 56.

[38]Mann, "American Theatre Goes Broke," p. 419.

[39]Ibid. Also, beginning in the late 1920s, brokers purchased blocks of tickets of the best seats for hit productions and sold them with a fifty-cent surcharge per ticket, further increasing the

cost of the better seats at the legitimate theaters. With only two or three sell-out productions during the 1932-33 season, Mann said "there were more ticket agencies on Broadway than legitimate productions!" ("American Theatre Goes Broke").

40The phrase is taken from Eaton, "Menace of the Movies," p. 56. Also, in keeping with the discussion about the cultural hierarchy in chapter three, it is important to point out that "high" class was understood to be a matter not only of education, social status and wealth but also race. A promotion in 1907 for a vaudeville theater in Lexington, Kentucky, applauded the "strictly high class" acts and the "fashionable and high-class" audiences that attended the theatre. Despite the fact that the black community in Lexington included "colored professional people of intelligence, ministers, teachers, doctors, and lawyers," the ad emphasized that "no colored people are admitted." See Gregory A. Waller, "Another Audience: Black Moviegoing, 1907-16," *Cinema Journal* 31, no. 2 (Winter 1992): 3-25. These quotes are taken from pp. 6, 8.

41"A Democratic Art," *The Nation,* August 28, 1913, p. 193.

42McLaughlin, *Broadway and Hollywood,* p. 2.

43Jack Poggi, *Theater in America: The Impact of Economic Forces, 1870-1967* (Ithaca, N.Y.: Cornell University Press, 1968), p. 29. See also Oscar G. Brockett, *History of the Theatre,* 5th ed. (Boston: Allyn and Bacon, 1987), p. 589.

44McLaughlin, *Broadway and Hollywood,* p. 100. See also Brockett, *History of the Theatre,* p. 589.

45McLaughlin, *Broadway and Hollywood,* pp. 95-97.

46Mann, "American Theatre Goes Broke," p. 422.

47See ibid., pp. 417-18.

48There was great competition for film rights to successful Broadway plays in the teens and twenties. The screen rights for *Ben-Hur,* for example, which was one of the most successful plays at the time, reportedly sold for one million dollars in 1921. The play was first produced in 1899 and grossed over ten million dollars from its legitimate theater run. Film companies, most notably Adolph Zukor's Famous Players-Lasky and the Fox Film Corporation, began financing legitimate stage productions in order to secure the film rights. This practice was quickly outlawed, however, by a royalty and options agreement between playwrights and producers. See McLaughlin, *Broadway and Hollywood,* pp. 56, 73-84.

49Tibor and Anne Scitovsky, "What Price Economic Progress?" *The Yale Review* 49, no. 1 (Autumn 1959): 105.

50Ibid.

51Brockett, *History of the Theatre,* p. 584.

52This was in part a competitive move against B. F. Keith's formation of the United Booking Offices of America, a clear attempt to monopolize the vaudeville business. Within a matter of months, however, and for reasons that remain unclear, they were persuaded by Albee (apparently to the tune of several hundred thousand dollars) to remain in the legitimate stage business. See Stein, *American Vaudeville,* pp. xii, 110; Allen, *Vaudeville and Film,* pp. 236-37; Merritt, "Nickelodeon Theaters," p. 68.

53McLaughlin, *Broadway and Hollywood,* p. 103.

54Eaton, "Menace of the Movies," p. 52.

55Quoted in Maltby, *Passing Parade,* p. 86.

Chapter 6: The Not-So-Silent Moving Picture World

1Erwin Panofsky, "Style and Medium in the Motion Pictures," in *Film Theory and Criticism,* 4th ed., ed. Gerald Mast, Marshall Cohen and Leo Braudy (New York: Oxford University Press, 1992), pp. 234-35.

2Foster Rhea Dulles, *America Learns to Play: A History of Popular Recreation, 1607-1940* (Gloucester, Mass.: Peter Smith, 1959), p. 292.

3Douglas Gomery, *Movie History: A Survey* (Belmont, Calif.: Wadsworth, 1991), p. 101. The

European *film d'art* movement begun in 1908, for example, brought prestigious stage plays, adaptations of classical novels and famous performers to the screen to enhance the aesthetic and intellectual appeal of movies to attract middle-class theatergoers. Though a dubious success, if not in some ways a negative model, the *film d'art* movement convinced many (including D. W. Griffith) of the possibility of a unique style of film acting, and that there existed a vast audience for longer screen stories (five reels and more). See David A. Cook, *A History of Narrative Film,* 2nd ed. (New York: W. W. Norton, 1990), pp. 54-56.

4Lewis Jacobs, *The Rise of the American Film: A Critical History* (New York: Harcourt, Brace, 1939), p. 59.

5Cook, *History of Narrative Film,* p. 34.

6Quoted in ibid., p. 77.

7See "The Drama, the Theater and the Films," *Harper's Magazine,* September 1924, pp. 425-35. Shaw also espoused the Romantic notion of the artist as gifted genius, arguing that a dramatist could not be trained: "Unless Nature has done ninety-nine per cent of the work, the one per cent which can be taught or learned is not worth studying." There is a suggestion that Shaw was bothered by competition from the popular media. He proclaimed, "I *am* a world dramatist," because his "currency [was] as universal as that of Sherlock Holmes or Charlie's Aunt or Mary Pickford or Bill Hart or Charlie Chaplin."

8Walter Prichard Eaton, "The Menace of the Movies," *American Magazine,* September 1913, p. 55.

9Jacobs, *Rise of the American Film,* p. 271.

10*The World Today,* October 1908, quoted in Kevin Brownlow, *Behind the Mask of Innocence* (Berkeley: University of California Press, 1990), p. xvii.

11Cook, *History of Narrative Film,* p. 207.

12Quoted in Edward Wagenknecht, *The Movies in the Age of Innocence* (Norman: University of Oklahoma Press, 1962), p. 41.

13Kathy Peiss, *Cheap Amusements: Working Women and Leisure in Turn-of-the-Century New York* (Philadelphia: Temple University Press, 1986), p. 154.

14Lary May, *Screening Out the Past: The Birth of Mass Culture and the Motion Picture Industry* (New York: Oxford University Press, 1980), p. 124. In reality such activity was not without its own potential dangers. Pickford embedded the new morality in the safety of marriage and the rebelliousness of eternal youth, reflecting the leisure pursuits of the emerging youth culture. Both, however, betrayed an underlying subordination of women. See May, *Screening Out the Past,* pp. 124-26, 142.

15Dulles, *America Learns to Play,* p. 299.

16The Reverend Charles Goodell, quoted in Peiss, *Cheap Amusements,* p. 159.

17Garth Jowett, *Film: The Democratic Art* (Boston: Focal, 1976), pp. 111, 115-16.

18Quoted in ibid., p. 113.

19Quoted in Jacobs, *Rise of the American Film,* pp. 64-65; Terry Ramsay, *A Million and One Nights: A History of the Motion Picture Through 1925* (New York: Simon & Schuster, 1926; Touchstone ed., 1986), p. 477.

20Quoted in May, *Screening Out the Past,* p. 44.

21See Jowett, *Film,* p. 112.

22Russell Merritt, "Nickelodeon Theaters, 1905-1914: Building an Audience for the Movies," in *The American Film Industry,* ed. Tino Balio (Madison: University of Wisconsin Press, 1976), p. 66.

23Quoted in Peiss, *Cheap Amusements,* p. 160.

24Quoted in Kathleen D. McCarthy, "Nickel Vice and Virtue: Movie Censorship in Chicago, 1907-1915," *Journal of Popular Film* 5, no. 1 (1976): 49.

25Ibid., p. 51.

26Richard Maltby, ed., *Passing Parade: A History of Popular Culture in the Twentieth Century* (New York: Oxford University Press, 1989), p. 13.

[27]Merritt, "Nickelodeon Theaters," p. 78.

[28]Ibid., p. 75.

[29]The National Board of Censorship of Motion Pictures had its precedents in theatrical watchdog organizations like the Drama Society of Boston and the Chicago Drama Committee. These were formed to review and, it was hoped, elevate the tastes of audiences and the quality of performances. Eventually a national organization, the Drama League of America, was established for the same purpose. See Albert F. McLean Jr., *American Vaudeville as Ritual* (Lexington: University of Kentucky Press, 1965), pp. 78-79.

[30]Merritt, "Nickelodeon Theaters," pp. 78-79.

[31]Quoted in Jacobs, *Rise of the American Film,* p. 175.

[32]May writes that in Griffith's films "Anglo-Saxon culture was portrayed as eternal truth" (*Screening Out the Past,* p. 80). Griffith's Civil War saga quickly became an enormous financial and critical success and was the most popular film ever until *Gone with the Wind* replaced it in 1939. It ran for almost a year at an admission price of two dollars. Film critics consider *The Birth of a Nation* the most influential silent film ever made.

[33]Robert Sklar, *Movie-Made America: A Cultural History of American Movies* (New York: Random House/Vintage Books, 1976), p. 32.

[34]May, *Screening Out the Past,* p. 59.

[35]Louis Reeves Harrison, "How to Improve the Business," *The Moving Picture World,* December 24, 1910, in *American Film Criticism: From the Beginnings to "Citizen Kane,"* ed. Stanley Kauffmann with Bruce Henstell (New York: Liveright, 1972), p. 46.

[36]Arthur Knight, *The Liveliest Art: A Panoramic History of the Movies* (New York: New American Library/Mentor Books, 1957), p. 115.

[37]Elizabeth Ewen, "City Lights: Immigrant Women and the Rise of the Movies," *Signs: Journal of Women in Culture and Society* 5, no. 3, supp. (Spring 1980): S61.

[38]Ibid., p. S63.

[39]These quotes are taken from "*Mutual Film Corp. vs. Industrial Commission of Ohio* (1915), United States Supreme Court," in *The Movies in Our Midst: Documents in the Cultural History of Film in America,* ed. Gerald Mast (Chicago: University of Chicago Press, 1982), pp. 141-42. Jowett makes the same observations, but with different context and intent; see Jowett, *Film,* pp. 120-21.

Chapter 7: The Yellow Brick Road to Respectability

[1]Robert Sklar, *Movie-Made America: A Cultural History of American Movies* (New York: Random House/Vintage Books, 1976), p. 130.

[2]"A Democratic Art," *The Nation,* August 28, 1913, p. 193; Lewis Jacobs, *The Rise of the American Film: A Critical History* (New York: Harcourt, Brace, 1939), p. 271.

[3]This summary is based on Arthur Kellogg, "Minds Made by the Movies," *Survey Graphic,* May 1933, pp. 245-46. Kellogg's information came from one of the Payne Studies by Edgar Dale, *The Content of Motion Pictures* (New York: Macmillan, 1935). Dale divided films into ten categories: crime, sex, love, mystery, war, children, history, travel, comedy and social propaganda.

[4]Joel Spring, *Images of American Life: A History of Ideological Management in Schools, Movies, Radio and Television* (New York: State University of New York Press, 1992), p. 50.

[5]Quoted in Arthur R. Jarvis Jr., "The Payne Fund Reports: A Discussion of Their Content, Public Reaction and Effect on the Motion Picture Industry, 1930-1940," *Journal of Popular Culture* 25, no. 2 (Fall 1991): 128. Hays solicited help from national women's organizations like the International Federation of Catholic Alumnae, the National Society of Daughters of the American Revolution and the General Federation of Women's Clubs. These groups functioned like review boards, previewing films and making suggestions to producers (who apparently listened), and also published lists of recommended films.

[6]Laemmle noted that "one after another [exhibitor] said that it would be wise to listen to the

public demand for vampire pictures" and that Universal was not the "guardian of public morals." Quoted in Kathy Peiss, *Cheap Amusements: Working Women and Leisure in Turn-of-the-Century New York* (Philadelphia: Temple University Press, 1986), p. 161.

[7]Arthur Knight, *The Liveliest Art: A Panoramic History of the Movies* (New York: New American Library/Mentor Books, 1957), p. 113.

[8]David A. Cook, *A History of Narrative Film*, 2nd ed. (New York: W. W. Norton, 1990), p. 298.

[9]Attendance figures vary from 50-60 million in 1927 to 90-110 million in 1929. See Robert McLaughlin, *Broadway and Hollywood: A History of Economic Interaction* (New York: Arno, 1974), p. 91. See also Russel Nye, *The Unembarrassed Muse: The Popular Arts in America* (New York: Dial, 1970), p. 379; Cook, *History of Narrative Film*, p. 264; Jack Poggi, *Theater in America: The Impact of Economic Forces, 1870-1967* (Ithaca, N.Y.: Cornell University Press, 1968), p. 81.

[10]Quoted in Kimball Young, "Review of the Payne Fund Studies," *American Journal of Sociology*, September 1935, p. 253.

[11]Quoted in ibid., p. 254. In one study, for example, the authors concluded, "That the movies exert an influence there can be no doubt. But it is our opinion that this influence is specific for a given child and a given movie. The same picture may influence different children in distinctly opposite directions. Thus, in a general survey such as we have made, the net effect appears small" (Ruth C. Peterson and L. L. Thurstone, *Motion Pictures and the Social Attitudes of Children* [New York: Macmillan, 1933], pp. 92-93).

[12]Herbert Blumer and Philip M. Hauser, *Movies, Delinquency and Crime* (New York: Macmillan, 1933), p. 202; quoted in Garth Jowett, *Film: The Democratic Art* (Boston: Focal, 1976), p. 224.

[13]Paul G. Cressey, "The Motion Picture as Informal Education," *The Journal of Educational Sociology* 7 (1934): 505.

[14]Ibid., pp. 512, 513.

[15]Ibid., pp. 508, 514-15.

[16]Henry James Forman, *Our Movie Made Children* (New York: Macmillan, 1933), pp. 64-65.

[17]Young, "Review of the Payne Fund Studies," p. 255. Beyond their procensorship bias, the studies suffered from a complete lack of context. The researchers isolated the movies and did not compare effects on people they observed with effects of other similar experiences. To paraphrase Robert Sklar, would they also have recorded an increase in heartbeat when the same subject was reading a romantic novel? Did nineteenth-century melodramas capture a young person's imagination the way movies did their twentieth-century counterpart? Could magazine articles have the same influence on cultural attitudes as seeing a movie on the same subject? Singling out the movies, however, dramatized the level of their influence. For a discussion of the Payne reports see Jowett, *Film*, pp. 220-29; Sklar, *Movie-Made America*, pp. 135-40; Jarvis, "Payne Fund Reports," pp. 127-140.

[18]Cook, *History of Narrative Film*, p. 317. *The Christian Century* blamed the box-office decline in 1931 on the lack of creativity in the movies and not the economic depression. People were "tired of stereotyped plots, . . . the cheap allurements of synthetic film-sin . . . [and] the everlasting sameness of the programs." That the cinema was regarded as something different from the traditional arts is clear in this writer's qualification: "This may not be to judge the movies by those standards of serious art, of moral responsibility and of social contribution" but was "a judgment rendered at the point where Hollywood has asked for judgment—at the box-office." "The Movies Are Brought to Judgment," *The Christian Century*, December 30, 1931, p. 1648.

[19]Quoted in Stephen Vaughn, "Morality and Entertainment: The Orgins of the Motion Picture Production Code," *Journal of American History* 77, no. 1 (June 1990): 60.

[20]Ibid., p. 51. Elsewhere Martin Quigley wrote that the "primary and substantially exclusive purpose" of film was "to entertain," although viewing movies entailed "certain educative effects" (Martin Quigley, "Importance of the Entertainment Film," *The Annals of the American*

Academy of Political and Social Science 254 [November 1947]: 65). This is not to imply that literature and other arts were not under censorship at that time. Probably the most notorious illustration is D. H. Lawrence's *Lady Chatterley's Lover,* which was banned as obscene in 1928 and published in an abridged form until 1959.

21Alexander Walker, *Sex in the Movies: The Celluloid Sacrifice* (Baltimore: Penguin, 1966), p. 76.

22Myron Lounsbury, " 'Flashes of Lightning': The Moving Pictures in the Progressive Era," *Journal of Popular Culture* 3, no. 4 (Spring 1970): 776-77.

23Edward Angly, "Boycott Threat Is Forcing Movie Clean-Up," *Literary Digest,* July 7, 1934, p. 7.

24"Legion of Decency," *Time,* July 2, 1934, p. 18.

25Jowett, *Film,* p. 250.

26Angly, "Boycott Threat," p. 7.

27The quoted material is taken from Creighton Peet, "A Letter to Hollywood," *Outlook and Independent,* December 17, 1930, pp. 612-13, 632. Gilbert Seldes made the same argument in *The Great Audience* (New York: Viking, 1950).

28Warren I. Susman, *Culture as History: The Transformation of American Society in the Twentieth Century* (New York: Pantheon Books, 1984), p. 154. For an important discussion of immigration and American religion see Will Herberg, *Protestant, Catholic, Jew* (Garden City, N.Y.: Doubleday, 1955).

29Communications scholar Frederick Wasser explains that "a vertically integrated American film industry played a role more similar to the popular cinema of Latin America than it did to European filmmaking. Both north and south American cinemas appealed to the masses flocking to the urban centers and seeking new national identities to replace the traditional ones of the village or the old world. By contrast, European films addressed audiences more secure in their national identity and more wary of massification" ("Is Hollywood American?: The Transnationalization of the American Film Industry," *Critical Studies in Mass Communication* 12, no. 4 [December 1995]: 428).

30Sklar, *Movie-Made America,* p. 212. For a discussion of the ideology of the classical Hollywood film see Robin Wood, "Ideology, Genre and Auteur," *Film Comment* 13, no. 1 (January-February 1977): 46-51.

31Even a partial list of films in recent memory that could not have been produced under the Production Code in any form remotely resembling the prints that reached the screen is striking: the Godfather series (1972, 1974, 1990), *Apocalypse Now* (1979), *Terms of Endearment* (1983), *Platoon* (1986), *The Mission* (1986), *Fatal Attraction* (1987), *When Harry Met Sally* (1989), *Dances with Wolves* (1990), *The Silence of the Lambs* (1991), *Unforgiven* (1992), *Schindler's List* (1993), *Pretty Woman* (1990), *The Bodyguard* (1992), *A Few Good Men* (1992) and countless others. What footage from *Jaws* (1975), *Jurassic Park* (1993) or the Indiana Jones series (1981, 1984 1989) might have ended up on the cutting-room floor of the Breen Office we can only imagine. And yet all of these films are either critically acclaimed or among the top moneymakers, with some qualifying as both.

32Bruno Bettelheim, "The Art of the Moving Picture," *Harper's,* October 1981, pp. 80-83.

33Terry Christensen, *Reel Politics: American Political Movies from "Birth of a Nation" to "Platoon"* (New York: Basil Blackwell, 1987), p. 212.

34According to World War II movies, the United States achieved victory single-handedly, with our allies playing only minor roles. Movies presented a home front of racial harmony and equality, even though about half of the African-Americans in a 1942 survey thought their lives would not be significantly changed if Japan won the war. See Spring, *Images of American Life,* p. 151.

35David Bordwell, Janet Staiger and Kristin Thompson, *The Classical Hollywood Cinema: Film Style and Mode of Production to 1960* (New York: Columbia University Press, 1985), p. 16.

36Ironically, this occurred while government, labor and media all encouraged women to stay at home as wives and mothers, leaving for men the jobs available during the Depression. Molly Haskell, *From Reverence to Rape: The Treatment of Women in the Movies,* 2nd ed. (Chicago:

University of Chicago Press, 1987), pp. 91-92, 142.

[37]Andrew Sarris, "The Sex Comedy Without Sex," *American Film* 3, no. 5 (March 1978): 8-15.

[38]For a more complete discussion see my essay " 'Take Your Girlie to the Movies': Cultural Dynamics of Dating and Entertainment in the Twentieth Century," in *Religion, Feminism and the Family,* ed. Mary Stewart Van Leeuwen and Ann Carr (Philadelphia: Westminster/John Knox Press, 1996); Virginia Wright Wexman, *Creating the Couple: Love, Marriage and Hollywood Performance* (Princeton, N.J.: Princeton University Press, 1993).

[39]Cook, *History of Narrative Film,* p. 299.

[40]Quoted in Murray Schumach, *The Face on the Cutting Room Floor* (New York: William Morrow, 1964), p. 205.

[41]"The Movie Boycott," *The Nation,* July 11, 1934, p. 34.

[42]Ibid., p. 34.

[43]Jacobs, *Rise of the American Film,* p. 507. The Hays quote appears on p. 517.

[44]Ibid., p. 517.

[45]Ibid.

[46]Gerald Gardner, *The Censorship Papers: Movie Censorship Letters from the Hayes Office, 1934 to 1968* (New York: Dodd, Mead, 1987), p. xvi. This book is an interesting account of the interaction of Hollywood producers and the Hays Office, revealing in detail the effects of the Code on moviemaking.

[47]Walker, *Sex in the Movies,* p. 77.

[48]Spring, *Images of American Life,* p. 49.

[49]Sklar, *Movie-Made America,* p. 175. For a discussion of American culture during this period see Susman, "The Culture of the Thirties," in his *Culture as History,* pp. 150-83.

[50]Neal Gabler, *An Empire of Their Own: How the Jews Invented Hollywood* (New York: Crown, 1988), p. 119.

[51]Quoted in "Cardinal's Campaign," *Time,* July 16, 1934, p. 28.

[52]John Izod, *Hollywood and the Box Office, 1895-1986* (New York: Columbia University Press, 1988), p. 183.

[53]Gerald Clarke, "1939: Twelve Months of Magic," *Time,* March 13, 1939, p. 73.

Chapter 8: Somewhere over the Golden Era

[1]Theaters were also showing *The Hunchback of Notre Dame* with Charles Laughton and Maureen O'Hara, *Babes in Arms* with Mickey Rooney and Judy Garland, *Wuthering Heights* with Laurence Olivier and Merle Oberon, *Goodbye, Mr. Chips* with Robert Donat and Greer Garson, *Only Angels Have Wings* with Cary Grant, Jean Arthur and Rita Hayworth, and the star-studded comedy *The Women* with Norma Shearer, Joan Crawford and Rosalind Russell. Bette Davis appeared in *Dark Victory,* Greta Garbo in *Ninotchka,* Henry Fonda and Claudette Colbert in *Drums Along the Mohawk,* and Jimmy Stewart in *Mr. Smith Goes to Washington* and with Marlene Dietrich in *Destry Rides Again.* John Ford's outstanding western *Stagecoach,* though not among the top box-office draws, also reached theaters that year.

[2]Apparently this was partly due to the fact that the initial audience for the fantasy film was children, who paid half-price or less for a ticket. The movie was first seen on television in 1956. See Susan Sackett, *The "Hollywood Reporter" Book of Box Office Hits* (New York: Billboard Books, 1990), p. 18. The quote is from Gerald Clarke, "1939: Twelve Months of Magic," *Time,* March 13, 1989, p. 72.

[3]For comparison, the MPAA companies released 168 new films in 1994; the total number of releases by all companies that year was 420. Sources for these figures are *Film Daily Yearbook of Motion Pictures* and "1994: U.S. Economic Review," provided by the Motion Picture Association of America.

[4]Robert Sklar, *Movie-Made America: A Cultural History of American Movies* (New York: Random House/Vintage Books, 1976), p. 289. The studios employed a conservative formula, seeking to

increase prerelease publicity. The proportion of original screenplays, for example, dropped from about two-thirds prior to the *Paramount* decision to less than 30 percent of Hollywood's output as more films were produced based on already successful stage plays, novels and even television plays. Increasingly the names of stars and directors were used to make each film unique, and more emphasis was put on marketing and advertising. John Izod, *Hollywood and the Box Office, 1895-1986* (New York: Columbia University Press, 1988), p. 154.

[5]"Screen Fans Organize to Bite Hand That Feeds Them Double Features," *Newsweek,* October 4, 1937, p. 25; Samuel Goldwyn, "Hollywood Is Sick," *Saturday Evening Post,* July 13, 1940, pp. 18-19, 44, 48-49. These film categories were distinguished by budget, time and talent. "A" films featured well-known stars and cost from $400,000 to $1.5 million to produce. "B" films fell in the range of $40,000 to $400,000, and "C" pictures were made for under $40,000. See "Three Classes of Motion Pictures," *The Christian Century,* May 27, 1936, p. 757.

[6]Russel Nye, *The Unembarrassed Muse: The Popular Arts in America* (New York: Dial, 1970), p. 387. See Nye for specific film titles. The percentage of big-budget pictures remains about the same today, with each year yielding its share of successes and failures. The video market (which has largely replaced the second-run theater) has become a way to recoup costs on box-office flops, as well as another venue for distribution of low-budget titles.

[7]Garth Jowett, *Film: The Democratic Art* (Boston: Focal, 1976), pp. 206-7.

[8]There were four categories in the Legion's rating system. Class A-1 was for films deemed morally unobjectionable for a general audience; Class A-2 restricted the film to adults; Class B films were morally objectionable in part for all; Class C films were condemned. The Film Board of National Organizations was funded by the Motion Picture Association of America (MPAA). Its board was composed of representatives from ten organizations: the American Jewish Committee, the American Library Association, the Daughters of the American Revolution, the Federation of Motion Picture Councils, the General Federation of Women's Clubs, the National Congress of Parents and Teachers, the National Council of Women of the United States of America, the National Federation of Music Clubs, the Protestant Motion Picture Council and the School Motion Picture Committee. Other publications that classified movies by audience suitability were *Consumer Reports, Parents' Magazine, Seventeen* and *The Christian Science Monitor.* See Jowett, *Film,* p. 421; Robert Henry Stanley, *Mediavisions: The Art and Industry of Mass Communication* (New York: Praeger, 1987), p. 118.

[9]"Big Eight" refers to the major American studios ("The Legion of Decency and the Big Eight," *The Christian Century,* March 20, 1940, p. 373). See these other articles in *The Christian Century:* "Give the Movie Exhibitor a Chance!" June 19, 1935, pp. 819-21; "Free the Movies Now!" March 25, 1936, pp. 454-55; "A Fateful Hour for the Movies" and "Three Classes of Motion Pictures," May 27, 1936, pp. 757-58; "Pass the Neely Bill!" February 21, 1940, pp. 240-41; "Why We Need a Neely Bill," April 10, 1940, p. 468.

[10]Thomas H. Guback, "Hollywood's International Market," in *The American Film Industry,* ed. Tino Balio (Madison: University of Wisconsin Press, 1976), pp. 398-99. The French and Italian new wave filmmakers showed that low-budget "art" films could be financially profitable. Furthermore, because of lucrative subsidization agreements with foreign countries, American film companies were investing in foreign productions—all the more reason to bring them back into the U.S. market. During the 1960s American films financed abroad increased from 35 percent to 60 percent of the total output of American producers. Because of rising salaries overseas and devaluation of the dollar, the trend declined in the five years before 1972, when only about 45 percent of the features produced by U.S. companies were made abroad. See Guback, "Hollywood's International Market," p. 401. According to *Film Daily Yearbook,* the number of imports dropped severely during the war but quickly rebounded afterward. The numbers increased until between 1956 and 1967 over two hundred imports were released in the United States, the number topping three hundred in 1961 and 1964.

[11]Elmer Davis, quoted in Clayton R. Koppes and Gregory D. Black, *Hollywood Goes to War: How*

Politics, Profits and Propaganda Shaped World War II Movies (New York: Free Press, 1987), p. 64.

[12]Eric Johnston, "The Motion Picture as a Stimulus to Culture," *The Annals of the American Academy of Political and Social Science* 254 (November 1954): 98-102.

[13]"Are Movies the Opium of the People?" *The Christian Century,* January 8, 1947, p. 36.

[14]Allan A. Hunter, "A Clergyman Looks at the Movies," *The Annals of the American Academy of Political and Social Science* 254 (November 1954): 95-97.

[15]Quoted in Stanley, *Mediavisions,* pp. 114-15. The Court defined obscene as material "utterly without redeeming social value," appealing only to a prurient interest in sex, and an affront to community standards relating to the representation of sexual matters. Revisions during the 1970s shifted the burden of proof regarding a work's value from the prosecution to the defense. In *Miller* v. *California* (1973) the Court's criteria for determining obscenity were "(1) whether the average person, applying contemporary community standards, would find that the work taken as a whole appeals to the prurient interest; (2) whether the work depicts or describes in a patently offensive way, sexual conduct specifically defined by the applicable state law; (3) whether the work taken as a whole lacks serious literary, artistic, political or scientific value." See Stanley, *Mediavisions,* p. 124.

[16]Ibid., p. 118.

[17]Bosley Crowther, "Unkindest Cut," *The New York Times,* April 2, 1950, sec. 2, p. 1. The film was voted best foreign-language film of 1949 by the New York Film Critics and the National Board of Review and received the Academy Award.

[18]Bosley Crowther, "A Hurtful Decision," *The New York Times,* January 29, 1961, sec. 2, p. 1.

[19]Quoted in Murray Schumach, *The Face on the Cutting Room Floor: The Story of Movie and Television Censorship* (New York: William Morrow, 1964), p. 78.

[20]Sklar, *Movie-Made America,* p. 294.

[21]"Censoring Movies," *Commonweal,* March 31, 1961, p. 17.

[22]"Cinema: New Picture," *Time,* December 24, 1956, p. 61. See also "Cardinal Scores *Baby Doll* Film," *The New York Times,* December 17, 1956, p. 28; "Theatre in Albany Is Banned to Catholics for Six Months for Scheduling *Baby Doll,*" *New York Times,* December 30, 1956, p. 24. The film was successful at the box office and was nominated for four Academy Awards.

[23]Quoted in Stanley, *Mediavisions,* p. 111.

[24]"Decency and Censorhip," *The Christian Century,* July 29, 1936, pp. 1030-32.

[25]"The Legion of Decency and the Big Eight," *The Christian Century,* March 20, 1940, p. 373. See also "Decency and Censorship," pp. 1030-32.

[26]Quoted in John Wicklein, "Sex and Crime on Screen Assailed in Church Report," *The New York Times,* June 2, 1960, pp. 1, 23. See also "Excerpts of Church Study of Mass Media," *The New York Times,* June 2, 1960, p. 23.

[27]Avery Dulles, "The Legion of Decency," *America,* June 2, 1956, pp. 240-42.

[28]Quoted in Schumach, *Face on the Cutting Room Floor,* p. 88.

[29]Ibid., p. 97.

[30]After a nearly forty-year ban on movie attendance, the Christian Reformed Church, for example, now argued that the church could not "be so unenlightened and so unbiblical as to put a blanket condemnation on one of the most influential and significant of modern art forms" in the twentieth century. The denomination reversed its position of "total abstinence" in 1967. Film and television were no longer regarded as merely "worldly amusements." Instead the church accepted "the film arts as a legitimate cultural medium to be used by the Christian in the same way that every cultural medium is to be used, whether that be the literature of the ages, the daily newspaper, news magazines, radio, television, the media in the field of music or whatever such media might be listed," the denomination's decision-making body wrote. "The fact that cultural media in general are largely under secular control has in no sense made them illegitimate to discriminating Christian use." These quotations are taken from Henry Stob,

"Are Movies Contraband?" *The Reformed Journal,* May-June 1964, p. 5; Henry C. Van Deelen et al., *The Church and the Film Arts* (Grand Rapids, Mich.: Christian Reformed Publishing House, 1967), p. 27. For a full treatment of the Christian Reformed Church's response to entertainment, see my essay "John Calvin Meets the Creature from the Black Lagoon: The Christian Reformed Church and the Movies, 1928-1966," *Christian Scholar's Review* 25 (September 1995): 47-62.

[31]"Baby Doll," *Commonweal,* January 11, 1957, p. 372.

[32]Jack Hamilton, "Hollywood Bypasses the Production Code," *Look,* September 29, 1959, p. 84.

[33]The original categories were G for general audiences, M for mature audiences, R for restricted, no one under sixteen admitted unless accompanied by an adult. X prohibited anyone under sixteen from admittance. In 1970 the M rating was changed to GP and then PG for "general audience, parental guidance suggested," at the same time that the R and X age restrictions were raised to seventeen. In the summer of 1984 the controversy over Steven Spielberg's *Indiana Jones and the Temple of Doom* prompted the addition of PG-13: "Parents are strongly cautioned to give special guidance for attendance of children under 13. Some material may be inappropriate for young children." Most recently the NC-17 category was added, restricting viewing to people over seventeen.

[34]The rating system is not meant to serve as a surrogate parent but to provide prescreening information and cautionary warnings to help parents decide which films are suitable for viewing by their children. To this end, the MPAA began including explanatory notes in 1992 to explain a rating decision: R for "strong violence and sensuality" or "drug use and language," for example, or PG for "sci-fi cartoon violence." Surveys show that the majority of parents do find the ratings system useful.

[35]The OFB publishes SHARE, a twice-monthly packet of film and broadcasting information, and the twice-monthly *Film and Broadcasting Review,* which presents critical reviews and moral classifications for motion pictures and commercial and public broadcasting television programs, as well as information and recommendations for educators. In 1995 the OFB established a toll-free telephone number that gives callers brief reviews of current movies. Felician A. Foy, ed., *1979 Catholic Alamanac* (Huntington, Ind.: Our Sunday Visitor, 1979), p. 685; "The Changing Legion of Decency," *Time,* December 3, 1965, pp. 77-78, 80; Gustav Niebuhr, "Movie Reviews Come with a Special Feature: Moral Authority," *The New York Times,* November 24, 1995, p. A22.

[36]Leo A. Handel, *Hollywood Looks at Its Audience* (Urbana: University of Illinois Press, 1950), pp. 97, 99, 159, 163. Also, a greater number of people indicated they were more likely to see a movie that had difficulties with censors than those who said they were less likely to see it—evidence that attitudes were changing. Even those people who thought censorship was not strict enough did not necessarily stay away from movies that had censorship struggles (Handel, *Hollywood Looks,* p. 129).

[37]The most frequently used statistics on box-office revenues and admissions are taken from *Statistical Abstracts of the United States,* the original source being various annual issues of the *Film Daily Yearbook of Motion Pictures. Film Daily Yearbook,* however, stopped providing admission figures after 1965. Using MPAA figures compiled from trade reports, average weekly admissions fell from 78.2 million in 1946 to 25.1 in 1960, leveling off at around one billion admissions a year, or roughly twenty million weekly admissions, beginning in the early 1960s and continuing to the present. Cobbett Steinberg erroneously combines these two different sources into one chart in *Reel Facts: The Movie Book of Records* (New York: Vintage Books, 1978), p. 371. A number of film historians (including Medved and Baehr) have misinterpreted box-office trends in the late 1960s because of this error.

[38]Robert McLaughlin, *Broadway and Hollywood: A History of Economic Interaction* (New York: Arno, 1974), p. 182. The curtailment of potential profits from European markets reopened after the war also cut into the revenues of Hollywood studios.

[39]See Landon Y. Jones, *Great Expectations: America and the Baby Boom* (New York: Ballantine

Books, 1980), pp. 43-45. Many couples found it impossible to keep up with rising consumer demands on one income alone; "economic need" was cited most frequently as the reason women continued or began to work outside the home. See William H. Chafe, *The American Woman: Her Changing Social, Economic and Political Roles, 1920-1970* (New York: Oxford University Press, 1972), pp. 190-95.

[40]According to one magazine survey, in the postwar era some thirty million Americans took up gardening. Americans spent $175 million annually on golf green fees, $21 million for hunting and fishing licenses, $800 million for sporting goods and $200 million for musical instruments. There was also a 700 percent increase in sales of power tools as people increasingly invested their time and money in home repairs and improvements. As a percentage of amusement expenditures, the cinema fell from 85 percent during the war to 51 percent in 1970 and 30 percent in 1990. See U.S. Bureau of the Census, *Statistical Abstract of the United States: 1970,* 91st ed. (Washington, D.C.: Government Printing Office, 1970), no. 307, p. 204; U.S. Bureau of the Census, *Statistical Abstract of the United States: 1992,* 112th ed. (Washington, D.C.: Government Printing Office, 1992), no. 383, p. 234; John Belton, *American Cinema/American Culture* (New York: McGraw-Hill, 1994), pp. 258-59; Izod, *Hollywood and the Box Office,* p. 134.

[41]Jones, *Great Expectations,* p. 48.

[42]The general cost of living rose 53.9 percent between 1956 and 1972, but theater admission prices increased 160 percent (David A. Cook, *A History of Narrative Film,* 2nd ed. [New York: W. W. Norton, 1990], p. 874).

[43]Television programming actually began in 1939, but the war interrupted expansion of the industry. Afterward television's exponential growth outpaced that of any other technological innovation, including the telephone, radio and automobile. The Federal Communications Commission (FCC) put a freeze on allocations for new stations from 1948 to 1952 in order to develop a comprehensive plan for the industry, solve technical problems and study competing color systems. During that time 108 licensed stations went on the air, and the number of American households with television topped fifteen million. Television now reached one-third of American homes. When the FCC lifted the freeze, television quickly became a viable entertainment medium. By 1955 there were 439 stations on the air, and network profits increased from $300 million in 1952 to $1.3 billion in 1960. See Cobbett S. Steinberg, *TV Facts* (New York: Facts on File, 1980), p. 142; Ray Eldon Hiebert, Donald F. Ungurait and Thomas W. Bohn, *Mass Media VI: An Introduction to Modern Communication* (New York: Longman, 1991), p. 254; Stan Le Roy Wilson, *Mass Media/Mass Culture: An Introduction* (New York: Random House, 1989), pp. 216-17.

[44]In contrast, movie attendance in nontelevision cities remained high or even increased. Erik Barnouw, *The Golden Web: A History of Broadcasting in the United States, Volume 2—1933-53* (New York: Oxford University Press, 1968), p. 286.

[45]Geoffrey Perrett, *A Dream of Greatness: The American People, 1945-1963* (New York: Coward, McCann & Geoghegan, 1979), p. 229.

[46]By 1959 there were thirty prime-time westerns. A television consultant at the time argued that people felt a hopelessness about the world's problems; in westerns, he wrote, "the good people are rewarded and the bad people are punished. There are no loose ends left. . . . The orderly completion of a Western gives the viewer a feeling of security that life itself cannot offer." Quoted in Erik Barnouw, *The Image Empire: A History of Broadcasting in the United States, Volume 3—From 1953* (New York: Oxford University Press, 1970), p. 81. The popular radio show *Amos 'n' Andy* brought African-Americans to television, a medium that was in 1951 "explicitly and glaringly white," Barnouw wrote. Much to the astonishment of white Americans at the time, the NAACP protested the show as an insult (Barnouw, *Golden Web,* p. 297).

[47]FCC regulations prohibited granting broadcast licenses to corporations convicted of monopolistic practices. The FCC, which oversees American broadcasting, postponed its decision on the

major studios' applications until the antitrust case was settled, and then refused to grant television broadcasting licenses to the Hollywood studios.

[48]Disney cartoons, *Gone with the Wind* and *The Wizard of Oz* are exceptional instances of the use of color in films before World War II. By 1955 over half of all movies were made in color, as compared to only 5 percent in the late 1930s and 12 percent in 1947. Color production actually dropped to about 25 percent of feature films in 1958, as studios tried to cut costs and began selling movies to television as a second market. After the television networks switched to color in 1965-1966, however, Hollywood reversed its course. In 1967, 75 percent of feature films were shot in color, and 94 percent by 1970 (Izod, *Hollywood and the Box Office,* p. 139).

[49]Thomas Schatz, "The New Hollywood," in *Film Theory Goes to the Movies,* ed. Jim Collins, Hilary Radner and Ava Preacher Collins (New York: Routledge, 1993), p. 9.

[50]Actually very few films after the war (perhaps one in ten) returned their costs in the domestic market alone, as compared with eight out of ten before the war. As Hollywood dependence on foreign markets increased, studios began releasing films that had a more universal appeal, starring actors with international reputations. Also, television became an important ancillary market; films were made that would not be controversial in order not to alienate potential advertisers. See Izod, *Hollywood and the Box Office,* p. 158.

[51]See "H'wood Poppin' to Sound of Music with Sixteen Film Tuners Set by Majors," *Variety,* February 1, 1967, pp. 1, 78. Probably the most important reason the traditional musical did not survive in the television era was the shifting demographic for movies and the youth audience's taste for rock music.

[52]Cook, *History of Narrative Film,* p. 874.

[53]Sklar, *Movie-Made America,* p. 271.

[54]See McLaughlin, *Broadway and Hollywood,* p. 183.

[55]See Izod, *Hollywood and the Box Office,* pp. 173-74.

[56]Suzanne May Donahue, *American Film Distribution: The Changing Marketplace* (Ann Arbor, Mich.: UMI Research Press, 1985), p. 31. According to *Variety,* the combined losses reported by the major film companies for the three-year period ending in 1971 came close to six hundred million dollars. See William Fadiman, *Hollywood Now* (New York: Liveright, 1972), p. 7.

Chapter 9: From Bach to Rock to MTV

[1]Gertrude Samuel, "Why They Rock'n'Roll—and Should They?" *The New York Times Magazine,* January 12, 1958, p. 20.

[2]James B. Gilbert, "Popular Culture," *American Quarterly* 35 (1983): 146.

[3]H. R. Rookmaaker, *Modern Art and the Death of a Culture* (Downers Grove, Ill.: InterVarsity Press, 1970), p. 190.

[4]Paul DiMaggio, "Cultural Entrepreneurship in Nineteenth-Century Boston: The Creation of an Organizational Base for High Culture in America," *Media, Culture and Society* 4 (1982): 39.

[5]Ibid., p. 308.

[6]Peter Van Der Merwe, *Origins of the Popular Style: The Antecedents of Twentieth-Century Popular Music* (Oxford: Clarendon, 1989), p. 3.

[7]Tia DeNora, "Musical Patronage and Social Change in Beethoven's Vienna," *American Journal of Sociology* 97, no. 2 (September 1991): 337. See also Mary Sue Morrow, *Concert Life in Haydn's Vienna: Aspects of a Developing Musical and Social Institution* (Stuyvesant, N.Y.: Pendragon, 1989); Joan Peyser, ed., *The Orchestra: Origins and Transformations* (New York: Scribner's, 1986).

[8]DeNora, "Musical Patronage," p. 343.

[9]Rookmaaker, *Modern Art,* p. 186.

[10]While visiting the United States in 1925, the celebrated composer Igor Stravinsky observed that "the music of the future will have to take [jazz] into account, no matter what the tendency of the composer. . . . In jazz you have something that sneaked in on us from an out-on-the-corner

cabaret. . . . We don't like to admit it, but real music *has* such simple origins." As one historian noted, "The monopoly that Victorians had granted to Western symphonic forms and orchestral concerts as the highest artistic accomplishments in music thus was broken by a music with deep and distinctly black roots." See Stanley Coben, "The Assault on Victorianism in the Twentieth Century," in *Victorian America,* ed. Daniel Walker Howe (Philadelphia: University of Pennsylvania Press, 1976), p. 174; Lawrence Levine, *Highbrow/Lowbrow: The Emergence of Cultural Hierarchy in America* (Cambridge, Mass.: Harvard University Press, 1988), p. 144.

[11]Russell Sanjek and David Sanjek, *American Popular Music Business in the Twentieth Century* (New York: Oxford University Press, 1991), p. 55.

[12]George Washington Hill of American Tobacco, NBC's largest commercial sponsor, quoted in Kenneth Bilby, *The General: David Sarnoff and the Rise of the Communications Industry* (New York: Harper & Row, 1986), p. 241. The NBC Orchestra illustration is drawn from G. Marcille Frederick, "The Founding of the NBC Symphony and the Cultural Context for Classical Music on the Radio," paper presented at the Arts, Community and Cultural Democracy Conference, Calvin College, Grand Rapids, Mich., August 1995.

[13]Sanjek and Sanjek, *American Popular Music Business,* pp. 56, 88. CBS classical records reached an all-time high of 35 percent of total industry volume in 1952, just before the birth of rock'n'roll. According to RIAA statistics, classical music accounts for less than 4 percent of record sales, compared with rock and country, which were the dominant formats in 1994, with 35.1 percent and 16.3 percent of the market respectively.

[14]In 1904, forty-five major companies were in the sheet-music business, which was valued at $2.2 million. Maltby has 200 million copies annually during the 1910s; Ewen has over two billion copies sold in 1910 alone. According to Sanjek and Sanjek, 30 million copies of sheet music were sold in 1910. See Sanjek and Sanjek, *American Popular Music Business,* pp. 7, 12, 16; David Ewen, *The Life and Death of Tin Pan Alley: The Golden Age of American Popular Music* (New York: Funk and Wagnalls, 1964), pp. 18, 122; Richard Maltby, ed., *Passing Parade: A History of Popular Culture in the Twentieth Century* (New York: Oxford University Press, 1989), p. 42.

[15]Ewen, *Life and Death of Tin Pan Alley,* pp. 39-40. See also David Horowitz, "The Perils of Commodity Fetishism: Tin Pan Alley's Portrait of the Romantic Marketplace, 1920-1942," *Popular Music and Society* 17, no. 1 (Spring 1993): 37-53.

[16]John Vivian, *The Media of Mass Communication* (Boston: Allyn and Bacon, 1991), p. 100; Sanjek and Sanjek, *American Popular Music Business,* p. 20. Record companies retaliated in the courts; radio stations were forced to pay a licensing fee for playing copyrighted songs. Broadcasters acquired a blanket license from the music licensing organization, ASCAP (American Society of Composers, Authors and Publishers), in return for a percentage of the station's gross income from advertising sales.

[17]Quoted in Gary Dean Best, *The Nickel and Dime Decade: American Popular Culture During the 1930s* (Westport, Conn.: Praeger, 1993), p. 62. See also Geoffrey Perrett, *America in the Twenties: A History* (New York: Simon & Schuster, 1982), p. 231; Robert McLaughlin, *Broadway and Hollywood: A History of Economic Interaction* (New York: Arno, 1974), p. 136.

[18]A parallel development occurred in the comic-book industry, although it did not adopt a code until the 1950s. Likewise, in response to threats of federal censorship, in 1951 the National Association of Broadcasters adopted a television code that strongly resembled those of the movie and radio industries. See Joel Spring, *Images of American Life: A History of Ideological Management in Schools, Movies, Radio and Television* (New York: State University of New York Press, 1992), p. 118. For an interesting discussion of comic books see Leslie A. Fiedler, "The Middle Against Both Ends," *Encounter* 5, no. 2 (August 1955): 16-23.

[19]The success of swing was attributed to young people, who accounted for as much as 40 percent of record sales by the mid-1930s. See Sanjek and Sanjek, *American Popular Music Business,* pp. 22, 26, 28, 50; Maltby, *Passing Parade,* p. 102.

[20]Quoted in William R. Meyer, *Warner Brothers Directors: The Hard-Boiled, the Comic and the*

Weepers (New Rochelle, N.Y.: Arlington House, 1978), p. 69.

[21]Record sales rebounded during the late 1930s. The use of records in jukeboxes gave the industry a needed boost and stimulated consumer sales as well. It was estimated that around 300,000 jukeboxes were in operation by the end of the decade, generating nearly ten million dolllars in record sales annually. Decca (which became the third major record label during the Depression) slashed RCA Victor and Columbia's price of seventy-five cents a record to thirty-five cents, or three for a dollar. RCA and CBS followed suit, making records an entertainment bargain. The improving economy and Decca-led price slash revived the record industry, with sales of phonograph records climbing to forty-four million dollars by the end of the decade. See Best, *Nickel and Dime Decade*, p. 78; Steve Chapple and Reebee Garofalo, *Rock'n'Roll Is Here to Pay* (Chicago: Nelson-Hall, 1977), p. 7.

[22]Peter Fornatale and Joshua E. Mills, *Radio in the Television Age* (New York: Overlook, 1984), p. 4.

[23]Sanjek and Sanjek, *American Popular Music Business*, p. 83.

[24]Erik Barnouw, *The Golden Web: A History of Broadcasting in the United States, Volume 2— 1933-1953* (New York: Oxford University Press, 1968), p. 288. Previously industry practices had isolated African-American music. The major companies with national distribution systems serviced the white pop market, while "race" records, or R&B, were marketed by indies with regional distributors. Trade publications, like *Billboard* and *Cashbox*, maintained segregated chart listings for pop, country and R&B. Black artists had little exposure on mainstream radio, television and movies, and were effectively excluded from the mainstream concert circuit because of audience and promoter racism and fear of disturbances. As the music began making inroads with white teenagers, however, sales of R&B records began to climb in the mid-1950s.

[25]Charlie Gillett, *The Sound of the City: The Rise of Rock and Roll*, rev. ed. (New York: Pantheon Books, 1983), p. 39.

[26]Licensing organizations collected fees from broadcasters for the rights to play copyrighted music and passed these royalty monies along to music publishers and songwriters. For a while the major companies exploited the popularity of rhythm and blues by releasing white "cover" versions of songs that were originally hits by black artists in the R&B market. This kept the black version out of the mainstream pop market and also denied the original singer the royalties generated by a crossover hit. Some crossover songs, like Elvis's rendition of Willie Mae Thornton's R&B hit "Hound Dog," were stylistically legitimate in their own right. But most were simply white sanitized versions of black R&B songs, like Pat Boone's "Ain't That a Shame," and "Tuitti Fruitti." For a while teenagers (and their parents) were happy to buy covers, but as young people were exposed to R&B artists, they began purchasing the original versions. See Ed Ward, Geoffrey Stokes and Ken Tucker, *Rock of Ages: The "Rolling Stone" History of Rock & Roll* (New York: Rolling Stone Press/Summit Books, 1986), pp. 86-87, 100; Sanjek and Sanjek, *American Popular Music Business*, pp. 125, 137; Gillett, *Sound of the City*, p. 39; "Indies Hit '57 Tape with 70% of Pop Single Hits," *Billboard*, January 13, 1958, p. 17.

[27]Gillett, *Sound of the City*, p. 39; Ward, Stokes and Tucker, *Rock of Ages*, p. 210. Within months after joining the company, Presley accounted for a phenomenal two-thirds of RCA Victor's singles output and fully one-half of the company's popular record business. Gary Kramer, "Record Firm Rule of Thumb Slips from Fickle Public Pulse," *Billboard*, December 22, 1956, pp. 1, 22; Sanjek and Sanjek, *American Popular Music Business*, p. 132.

[28]Gary Kramer, "R. & R. a Teen-Age Must," *Billboard*, November 10, 1956, p. 21. For a full discussion of the payola probes, see R. Serge Denisoff with William L. Schurk, *Tarnished Gold: The Record Industry Revisited* (New Brunswick, N.J.: Transaction Books, 1986).

[29]Quoted in Arnold Shaw, *The Rock Revolution* (New York: Crowell-Collier, 1969), p. 1.

[30]Carl Belz, *The Story of Rock* (New York: Oxford University Press, 1969), p. 36.

[31]Frank Zappa, "The Oracle Has It All Psyched Out," *Life*, June 28, 1968, p. 85.

[32]Philip H. Ennis, *The Seventh Stream: The Emergence of Rocknroll in American Popular Music*

(Hanover, N.H.: Wesleyan University Press, 1992), p. 17.

33Samuel, "Why They Rock'n'Roll—And Should They?" p. 16; "Yeh-Heh-Heh-Hehs, Baby," *Time,* June 18, 1956, p. 54.

34Quoted in Edith Schonberg, "You Can't Fool Public, Says Haley," *Downbeat,* May 30, 1956, p. 10.

35Quotes taken from "White Council vs. Rock and Roll," *Newsweek,* April 23, 1956, p. 32; "Segregationist Wants Ban on 'Rock and Roll,' " *The New York Times,* March 30, 1956, p. 39.

36Quoted in Stan Le Roy Wilson, *Mass Media/Mass Culture: An Introduction* (New York: McGraw-Hill, 1994), p. 280.

37Quoted in Maltby, *Passing Parade,* p. 72.

38H. J. Kuiper, "Foolish Song" (editorial), *The Banner,* May 5, 1944, p. 412.

39Among the antirock publications are Bob Larson, *Rock & the Church* (Carol Stream, Ill.: Creation House, 1971), and *Rock: For Those Who Listen to the Words and Don't Like What They Hear* (Wheaton, Ill.: Tyndale House/Living Books, 1982); David Wilkerson, *Set the Trumpet to Thy Mouth* (Lindale, Tex.: World Challenge, 1985); Dan Peters and Steve Peters with Cher Merrill, *Why Knock Rock?* (Minneapolis: Bethany House, 1984).

40Peters, Peters and Merrill, *Why Knock Rock?* p. 59; David A. Noebel, *The Legacy of John Lennon: Charming or Harming a Generation?* (Nashville: Thomas Nelson, 1982), pp. 14, 117; *The Marxist Minstrels: A Handbook on Communist Subversion of Music* (Tulsa, Okla.: American Christian College Press, 1974), pp. 5, 218.

41Even rock pianist Jerry Lee Lewis had a personal conflict trying to reconcile his southern Pentecostal background with his performance of what he called "*worldly* music, rock'n'roll." See Ward, Stokes and Tucker, *Rock of Ages,* p. 147. For a fuller discussion of rock and religion see Stephen R. Tucker, "Pentecostalism and Popular Culture in the South: A Study of Four Musicians," *Journal of Popular Culture* 16 (Winter 1982): 68-80; Davin Seay with Mary Neely, *Stairway to Heaven: The Spiritual Roots of Rock'n'Roll—From the King and Little Richard to Prince and Amy Grant* (New York: Ballantine Books, 1986).

42This quoted material is taken from "Can Religion Rock?" *Contemporary Christian Music,* October 1981, 21; David Wilkerson, *Set the Trumpet,* pp. 93, 104; John Styll, "Swaggart: One Man's Opinion," *Contemporary Christian Music,* September 1980, p. 5.

43The contemporary Christian music (CCM) industry itself is plagued by this tension, which is manifested in a perennial struggle between evangelical rock as "ministry" and as "business." Artists and audiences alike substitute an "artistic" experience with a "spiritual" one, with songs "ministering" to individuals. See William D. Romanowski, "Roll Over Beethoven, Tell Martin Luther the News: Evangelicals and Rock Music," *Journal of American Culture* 15, no. 3 (Fall 1992): 79-88, and "Contemporary Christian Music: The Business of Music Ministry," in *American Evangelicals and the Mass Media,* ed. Quentin J. Schultze (Grand Rapids, Mich.: Zondervan/Academie, 1990), pp. 143-69.

44David Dempsey, "Why the Girls Scream, Weep, Flip," *The New York Times Magazine,* February 23, 1964, p. 70.

45While in 1900 only 10 percent of American children ages fourteen to seventeen were in school, by midcentury 75 percent were attending high schools. Glen Elder Jr., "Adolescence in Historical Perspective," in *Growing Up in America: Historical Experiences,* ed. Harvey J. Graff (Detroit: Wayne State University Press, 1987), p. 15. See also Joseph Kett, *Rites of Passage: Adolescence in America, 1790 to the Present* (New York: Basic Books, 1977).

46As the age of puberty dropped, postwar teens reached physical maturity earlier, but they were strongly admonished not to let their sexual arousal lead to its logical end. The practice of "going steady," a kind of adolescent version of playing house, intensified dating relationships. For a full discussion see Beth Bailey, *From Front Porch to Back Seat: Courtship in Twentieth-Century America* (Baltimore: Johns Hopkins University Press, 1988).

47Dwight MacDonald, "Profiles: A Caste, a Culture, a Market-1," *The New Yorker,* November 22,

1958, p. 58; "Today's Teenagers," *Time,* January 29, 1965, p. 57; Landon Y. Jones, *Great Expectations: America and the Baby Boom Generation* (New York: Ballantine Books, 1980), pp. 84-85; "Fact Sheet," *Video Business,* June 16, 1995, p. 52. According to this source, "about 70 percent of the U.S. teen population works at least part time, and the median income among 15-to-19-year-olds is estimated at $11,000 annually, of which $40 to $80 a week is spent on discretionary items."

[48]For a full treatment see Quentin J. Schultze et al., *Dancing in the Dark: Youth, Popular Culture and the Electronic Media* (Grand Rapids, Mich.: Eerdmans, 1991).

[49]Gilbert, "Popular Culture," p. 147.

[50]Quoted in Thomas Meehan, "Public Writer No. 1?" *The New York Times Magazine,* December 12, 1965, p. 44.

[51]Benjamin DeMott, "Rock as Salvation," *The New York Times Magazine,* August 25, 1968, p. 30.

[52]Gilbert, "Popular Culture," p. 147.

[53]Michael Haralambos, *Right On: From Blues to Soul in Black America* (New York: Drake, 1975), p. 115. For example, Luther Ingram's "You Can Depend on Me" celebrated healthy and reliable relationships, associating the theme of togetherness with the larger cause of the civil rights movement. The call-and-response refrain of James Brown's "Say It Loud, I'm Black and Proud" encouraged audience participation and a sense of communal identity and self-pride. Aretha Franklin's call for "R-E-S-P-E-C-T" had as much to do with personal relationships as it did with the politics of black power. Sam Cooke's "A Change Is Gonna Come" had personal, religious and political connotations. The evolution of soul roughly corresponded to the stages of the civil rights movement and the emergence of the Black Power movement in the late 1960s. See also Arnold Shaw, *The World of Soul: Black America's Contribution to the Pop Music Scene* (New York: Cowled, 1970).

[54]Andrew Sarris, "Bravo Beatles!" *The Village Voice,* August 27, 1967, p. 13; Schlesinger is quoted in David P. Szatmary, *Rockin' in Time: A Social History of Rock-and-Roll,* 2nd ed. (Englewood Cliffs, N.J.: Prentice-Hall, 1991), p. 119.

[55]Richard Corliss, for example, described "Penny Lane" as "a Brueghelesque word-portrait of English suburban life" and compared "Strawberry Fields Forever" with Michelangelo Antonioni's film *Blow-Up.* He also noted, however, that the Beatles' music could not be completely understood as merely "musical cryptograms" for disinterested contemplation but were also "a delight to listen to, fine for dancing to." See Richard Corliss, "A Beatle Metaphysic," *Commonweal,* May 12, 1967, pp. 234-36.

[56]Quoted in Greil Marcus, "The Beatles," in *The "Rolling Stone" Illustrated History of Rock & Roll,* ed. Jim Miller (New York: Random House/Rolling Stone Press, 1980), p. 183.

[57]"Sgt. Pepper," *The New Yorker,* June 24, 1967, p. 23; Jesse Birnbaum and Christopher Porterfield, "Pop Music: The Messengers," *Time,* September 22, 1967, pp. 60-61, 68; Jack Kroll, "It's Getting Better . . . ," *Newsweek,* June 26, 1967, p. 70. By the time *Sgt. Pepper* was released in June 1967, the group had earned twenty-two RIAA Gold Records and sold an estimated 180 million units worldwide (Sanjek and Sanjek, *American Popular Music Business,* p. 204). Critical acclaim and commercial success aside, many fans and worried parents were disturbed by the Beatles' flirtation with drugs and the existential attitude of the album. In England the BBC banned radio broadcasts of songs thought to contain subversive drug references. In America some even believed that the Beatles were incapable of composing such excellent music and that they had to be part of a larger communist plot.

[58]Quoted in DeMott, "Rock as Salvation," p. 31.

[59]Richard Poirier, "Learning from the Beatles," *Partisan Review* 34, no. 4 (Fall 1967): 528.

[60]Sanjek and Sanjek, *American Popular Music Business,* pp. 220, 231; Vivian, *Media of Mass Communication,* p. 101.

[61]Stan Cornyn, quoted in Jean Callahan, "WB's Cornyn Tells Tribunal of Cost Fears," *Billboard,* July 12, 1980, p. 4. There was a 40-percent drop in gold and platinum records, and 1982 marked

the lowest number of singles to go gold since 1966; only three albums sold over two million units that year. In 1983 only six albums topped *Billboard*'s pop charts, and only three stayed there for more than two weeks—the fewest since 1979. Five albums topped unit sales of four million, selling a combined 28.5 million units. See Jay Cocks, "Sing a Song of Seeing," *Time*, December 26, 1983, p. 55; Alexander L. Taylor, "New Discs Click with TV Flicks," *Time*, May 23, 1983, p. 42; Sanjek and Sanjek, *American Popular Music Business*, p. 253.

[62]Gregg Geller, Epic Records, quoted in Jim Miller et al., "Is Rock on the Rocks?" *Newsweek*, April 19, 1982, p. 105.

[63]Jeff Ayeroff, quoted in Howard Polskin, "MTV at Ten: The Beat Goes On," *TV Guide*, August 3, 1991, p. 4.

[64]Panned by critics, *Flashdance* unexpectedly became the year's surprise success. Two hit singles, "Flashdance (What a Feeling)" and "Maniac," with energetic dance videos in rotation on MTV, were credited with drawing the under-thirty crowd out to theaters. The filmed earned ninety-three million, finishing second only to *Return of the Jedi;* the soundtrack sold seventeen million copies, and videocassette sales reached eight million dollars. The next year, ten movie sound-tracks topped sales of one million, doubling the number from any previous year. Television is following the same course, releasing soundtracks for hit shows like *Beverly Hills 90210*, *Melrose Place* and *Friends* "as a way cross-promoting both the show and the musicians whose work is featuring on it," according to one report (Ginia Bellafante, "Prime-Time Tunes," *Time*, October 30, 1995, p. 91). For a full discussion of films with rock soundtracks, see R. Serge Denisoff and William D. Romanowski, *Risky Business: Rock in Film* (New Brunswick, N.J.: Transaction, 1991).

[65]See Sut Jhally, *Dreamworlds: Desire/Sex/Power in Rock Video* (Amherst: University of Massachusetts Department of Communication, 1990), videocassette. For a discussion of music video, see the essays published in *Journal of Communication* 36, no. 1 (Winter 1986).

[66]Stephen Levy, "Ad Nauseum: How MTV Sells Out Rock and Roll," *Rolling Stone*, December 8, 1983, p. 34; J. Hoberman, "Video Radio," *Film Comment* 19, no. 4 (July-August 1983): 35.

[67]Cocks, "Sing a Song of Seeing," p. 56. MTV initially rejected the video for "Billie Jean" on the grounds that it did not fit the channel's rock format designed to appeal to white, middle-class suburban youth. Of the first 750 videos played on MTV, fewer than twenty-five were by black artists, even though albums by black artists were among the bestsellers on *Billboard*'s charts. Walter Yentikoff, then president of CBS Records, allegedly threatened to stop providing MTV with video clips of other Columbia artists if Jackson's was not added to its rotation. MTV executives acquiesced, although by that time there was nothing to lose. "Billie Jean" was already established as a smash crossover hit, scoring on the pop, R&B and dance charts, and it was estimated that 80 percent of Michael Jackson's record buyers were white. See R. Serge Denisoff, *Inside MTV* (New Brunswick, N.J.: Transaction Books, 1988), pp. 98-104; Levy, "Ad Nauseam," p. 37. After Jackson's "breakthrough" success with MTV's audience, the music channel redefined its format to include black artists and musical styles to the extent of including a specialty show, *Yo! MTV Raps*. This change is largely credited with the commercial explosion of rap music in the white suburbs, which has in turn again contributed to the continued popularity of MTV.

[68]Just prior to MTV, only twenty-three of the top one hundred singles had videos, but by 1986, eighty-two singles were accompanied by videos as record companies acknowledged the importance of the new medium. After recording losses of almost thirty-four million dollars after its first three years in operation, MTV turned a profit in 1984, with revenues exceeding sixty million. See "MTV's Garland Sez Video Business Is Healthy, Growing," *Variety*, May 14, 1986, p. 89; Sanjek and Sanjek, *American Popular Music Business*, p. 257.

[69]John Kalodner, quoted in Cocks, "Sing a Song of Seeing," p. 61; Walz, quoted in Eric Gelman et al., "MTV's Message," *Newsweek*, December 30, 1985, p. 55.

[70]Cocks, "Sing a Song of Seeing," p. 63; Levy, "Ad Nauseam," p. 33; Steve Jones, "Cohesive but Not Coherent: Music Videos, Narrative and Culture," *Popular Music and Society*, Winter 1988,

p. 15.

[71]See Bill Barol, "The Sight of Music," *Newsweek on Campus,* special issue, November 1982, p. 12.

[72]Quoted in Denisoff, *Inside MTV,* p. 241.

[73]J. Fiske, "MTV: Post-structural Post-modern," *Journal of Communication Inquiry* 10, no. 1: 74.

[74]Todd Gitlin, "Postmodernism Defined, at Last!" *Utne Reader,* July-August 1989, p. 52. Intertextuality refers to the way artists use references or allusions from past works to create the existence of several "texts" in a single contemporary work. This nostalgic appropriation of earlier works is related to pastiche, "a form of imitation of the unique style or content of earlier works that lacks any trace of the satire or parody that characterizes traditional forms of imitation" (John Belton, *American Cinema/American Culture* [New York: McGraw-Hill, 1994], p. 308). See also John Hare, "Jackie Kennedy and the Seven Dwarfs: Postmodernism and Its Roots," *Dialogue* 23, no. 6 (April-May 1991): 21-31. *Dialogue* is a journal of commentary and the arts published by the Calvin College Communications Board.

[75]Mary Billard, "MTV's Super Market," *Film Comment* 19, no. 4 (July-August 1983): 48.

[76]MTV has expanded its programming in recent years to include news, special "MTV Unplugged" concerts, cartoons, games and comedy shows, and even a documentary/soap series, *The Real World,* about a group of twentysomethings. Like its Canadian counterpart, Much Music, MTV got into politics with a "Rock the Vote" campaign that urged young people to vote during the 1992 presidential election. The Democratic candidates (Bill Clinton and Al Gore) participated in an MTV forum, but incumbent George Bush and independent candidate Ross Perot declined invitations to appear on the "teenybopper" channel. "I'm not going to have people 'jiving' behind me when I answer questions, am I?" Perot asked (quoted in Steve Appleford, "MTV Expands Political Platform," *Billboard,* September 5, 1992, p. 41; Joshua Hammer with Adam Wolfberg, "Not Just Hit Videos Anymore," *Newsweek,* November 2, 1992, p. 93).

[77]Bill Roedy, quoted in John Huey, "America's Hottest Export: Pop Culture," *Fortune,* December 31, 1990, p. 52.

Chapter 10: Accent on Youth

[1]Hollis Alpert, "*The Graduate* Makes Out," *Saturday Review,* July 6, 1968, p. 32.

[2]Thomas Doherty, *Teenagers and Teenpics: The Juvenilization of American Movies in the 1950s* (Boston: Unwin Hyman, 1988), pp. 231-32.

[3]John Belton, *American Cinema/American Culture* (New York: McGraw-Hill, 1994), pp. 303-4.

[4]Landon Y. Jones, *Great Expectations: America and the Baby Boom Generation* (New York: Ballantine, 1980), p. 139.

[5]The *Variety* quote appears in Lynn Langway with Susan Agrest, "The Disappearing Drive-In," *Newsweek,* August 9, 1982, p. 65; John Izod, *Hollywood and the Box Office, 1895-1986* (New York: Columbia University Press, 1988), p. 144; "Z as in Zzzz, or Zowie," *Time,* May 5, 1967, p. 61.

[6]See Garth Jowett, *Film: The Democratic Art* (Boston: Focal, 1976), pp. 375-76.

[7]"Film Future: GI Baby Boom," *Variety,* March 5, 1958, p. 1.

[8]"Pic Must 'Broaden Market,' " *Variety,* March 20, 1968, pp. 1, 78.

[9]"A Religion of Film," *Time,* September 20, 1963, p. 82.

[10]This summary is based on David Bordwell, Janet Staiger and Kristin Thompson, *The Classical Hollywood Cinema: Film Style and Mode of Production to 1960* (New York: Columbia University Press, 1985), pp. 373-75. Akira Kurosawa's *Roshomon* (Japan), Ingmar Bergman's *The Seventh Seal* and *Wild Strawberries* (Sweden), Alain Resnais's *Hiroshima, Mon Amour* (France), François Truffaut's *The Four Hundred Blows* (France), Federico Fellini's *La Dolce Vita* (Italy) and Michelangelo Antonioni's *L'Avventura* and *L'Eclisse* (Italy) are a representative sampling of European art films.

[11]Lee Loevinger, quoted in Joel Spring, *Images of American Life: A History of Ideological Man-*

agement in Schools, Movies, Radio and Television (New York: State University of New York Press, 1992), p. 232. Spring noted that at least part of the impetus behind the establishment of the Corporation for Public Broadcasting was to "save American culture from the vulgarity of commercial television" (p. 235).

[12]Jack Hamilton, "Hollywood Bypasses the Production Code," *Look*, September 29, 1959, p. 83.

[13]Ibid., p. 84. In retrospect, film historians agree that ultimately the Production Code was, as Jowett wrote, "detrimental to the natural development of the American motion picture" (*Film*, p. 396).

[14]"The Big Leer," *Time*, June 9, 1961, p. 55.

[15]Ibid.

[16]*The American Film Industry*, ed. Tino Balio (Madison: University of Wisconsin Press, 1976), p. 318; Michael Conant, "The Impact of the *Paramount* Decrees," in *The American Film Industry*, ed. Tino Balio (Madison: University of Wisconsin Press, 1976), p. 349.

[17]Suzanne May Donahue, *American Film Distribution: The Changing Marketplace* (Ann Arbor, Mich.: UMI Research Press, 1987), p. 35.

[18]"Z as in Zzzz," p. 61.

[19]Quoted in ibid.

[20]See Alan Levy, "Peekaboo Sex, or How to Fill a Drive-In," *Life*, July 16, 1965, p. 82.

[21]Nina J. Easton, "What's Driving *Rain Man?* Women," *Los Angeles Times/Calendar*, February 10, 1989, Home Edition, pt. 6, p. 1.

[22]David Ehrenstein and Bill Reed, *Rock on Films* (New York: Deliah Books, 1982), p. 48.

[23]Quoted in "Z as in Zzzz," p. 61.

[24]Judith Crist's comment can be found in Ed Naha, *The Films of Roger Corman: Brillance on a Budget* (New York: Arco, 1982), p. 188; *Variety*, August 16, 1967, p. 6.

[25]Quoted in *Roger Corman: Hollywood's Wild Angel*, produced and directed by Christian Blackwood (MPI Home Video, 1985), videocassette. After several disputes with AIP, Corman left in 1970 and formed his own company, New World Pictures, which became the largest independent producer/distributor in the United States. New World distributed some of the most important foreign films during the 1970s, including Ingmar Bergman's *Cries and Whispers* and Federico Fellini's *Amarcord*. Corman easily applied his production and distribution strategy to the new delivery systems in the 1990s. "The cable and direct-to-video markets are a natural outgrowth of what I've been doing for 40 years," he said after agreeing to produce a series of films for the cable channel Showtime. "These pictures are going to continue the tradition I set in the '60s and '70s. They will be fast-moving, exciting films with a little sex, some action, and solid special effects." Corman also established a family-oriented home video line to accompany his trademark genres. Quoted in Glenn Kenny, "It's Showtime for Corman," *TV Guide*, June 10, 1995, p. 50; Adam Sandler, "Corman Bows Family Vids," *Variety*, April 25-May 1, 1994, p. 14.

[26]See Bordwell, Staiger and Thompson, *Classical Hollywood Cinema*, pp. 374-77.

[27]Seth Cagin and Philip Dray, *Hollywood Films of the Seventies: Sex, Drugs, Violence, Rock'n'Roll and Politics* (New York: Harper & Row, 1984), p. 66.

[28]Quoted in ibid., p. 61.

[29]Quoted in David M. Considine, *The Cinema of Adolescence* (Jefferson, N.C.: McFarland, 1985), p. 7.

[30]Jowett, *Film*, pp. 435-36.

[31]Doherty, *Teenagers and Teenpics*, p. 233.

[32]For a discussion of the ideology of the liberal consensus in postwar America, see Geoffrey Hodgson, *America in Our Time* (New York: Doubleday, 1976).

[33]Geoffrey Perrett, *A Dream of Greatness: The American People 1945-1963* (New York: Coward, McCann & Geoghegan, 1979), p. 13.

[34]David A. Cook, *A History of Narrative Film*, 2nd ed. (New York: W. W. Norton, 1990), p. 884.

[35]Betty Friedan, *The Feminine Mystique* (New York: Dell, 1963), p. 249.

[36]Molly Haskell, *From Reverence to Rape: The Treatment of Women in the Movies*, 2nd ed.

(Chicago: University of Chicago Press, 1987), pp. 323-24. Historically, filmmakers have always been able to rely on eroticism to attract a crowd. Beginning in the mid-1950s, however, eroticism permeated the American screen as attitudes about acceptable sexual behavior changed. There was greater sexual explicitness in both foreign and domestic films, like *And God Created Woman* and *La Dolce Vita,* the continuing James Bond series (remember Pussy Galore in *Goldfinger?*), and films like *Kiss Me, Stupid, Lolita, Cleopatra, Irma La Douce* and *Barbarella.* In the late 1960s films like *The Graduate, I Am Curious—Yellow, Midnight Cowboy* and *Carnal Knowledge* dealt explicitly with sexuality and were all popular among young people.

[37]Abel Green, "Year of Violence and Mergers: Diversify Biz, Defy Morality," *Variety,* January 3, 1968, p. 1.

[38]Quoted in Russel Nye, *The Unembarrassed Muse: The Popular Arts in America* (New York: Dial, 1970), p. 389.

[39]In 1962 Music Corporation of America (MCA) acquired Universal Pictures from Decca Records, which had controlled it since 1952. In 1966 Gulf & Western bought Paramount, and Trans-America acquired United Artists. Warner Brothers went to Seven Arts in 1968, and then in 1969 to Kinney National Services, which changed the parent company's name to Warner Communications. Avco bought Embassy, and Coca-Cola bought Columbia Pictures Industries. Avco finally sold Embassy, and TransAmerica released United Artists to Metro-Goldwyn-Mayer. Donahue, *American Film Distribution,* p. 31.

[40]William Fadiman, *Hollywood Now* (New York: Liveright, 1972), p. 22.

[41]Izod, *Hollywood and the Box Office, 1895-1986,* p. 180.

[42]Quoted in Charles Michener, "The New Hollywood," *Newsweek,* November 25, 1974, p. 72.

[43]Cook, *History of Narrative Film,* pp. 887-88.

[44]Quoted in Michener, "New Hollywood," p. 72.

[45]Cagin and Dray, *Hollywood Films of the Seventies,* p. 99.

[46]Quoted in Roger Corman with Jim Jerome, *How I Made a Hundred Movies in Hollywood and Never Lost a Dime* (New York: Dell/Delta, 1991), p. xi.

[47]Cook, *History of Narrative Film,* p. 896.

[48]The changes in audience demographics and musical tastes experienced in the recording industry simultaneously contributed to the decline of the Hollywood musicals based on Broadway productions. By the mid-1960s people under twenty-five not only dominated record sales but were also the most frequent moviegoers. Early success with movie soundtracks from *Oklahoma! Carousel, The King and I, South Pacific* and others sparked industry interest in movies with Broadway show music, but the results were disappointing. From 1955 to 1965 only *Fiddler on the Roof* was an acknowledged Broadway musical hit. Film versions did not fare much better. Hollywood musicals with Broadway-styled scores had little appeal to young people, whose preference for rock and soul allowed these styles to dominate industry trade charts.

[49]James B. Gilbert, "Popular Culture," *American Quarterly* 35 (1983): 149. Christopher Lasch, *The Culture of Narcissism: American Life in An Age of Diminishing Expectations* (New York: W. W. Norton, 1978).

[50]Richard Corliss, "We Lost It at the Movies," *Film Comment* 16, no. 1 (January-February 1980): 34, 37.

Chapter 11: Blockbuster Instincts

[1]John Izod, *Hollywood and the Box Office, 1895-1986* (New York: Columbia University Press, 1988), p. 179; John Brodie, "Call of the Kerietsu," *Variety,* August 7-13, 1995, pp. 1, 47. In the late 1980s SONY purchased CBS Records and Columbia Pictures. The international newspaper baron Rupert Murdoch (Australian News Corporation) merged Twentieth Century-Fox with the Metromedia Television group to form Fox, Inc., and its subsidiary Fox Broadcasting Company, which became the fourth major television network in 1986. Warner Communications, Inc. (WCI), merged with Time, Inc., owner of HBO, Cinemax and many other holdings, to form

Time Warner, Inc. (TWI), the largest communications firm in the world; TWI later purchased the Turner Broadcasting System. The buyouts continued in the 1990s. The Italian-controlled Pathe Communications bought MGM/UA in 1990. In one of the most dramatic restructurings in corporate America, Gulf & Western divested itself of its nonmedia industries, which had generated almost half of the corporation's revenues, in order to become a communications powerhouse in publishing and entertainment, Paramount Communications. Paramount was eventually bought by Viacom. In 1990 the Japanese firm Matsushita bought MCA/Universal, which was sold to the Canadian Seagram Company in 1995, the same year that Disney acquired Capital Cities/ABC.

[2]Quoted in Bernard Weinraub, "Shaken Hollywood Is Relieved to See 1994 Reel to 'The End,' " *The New York Times,* December 29, 1994, p. B1.

[3]Former Disney and now DreamWorks SKG executive Jeffrey Katzenberg described high concept as "a unique idea whose originality could be conveyed briefly." Katzenberg stressed that the emphasis was supposed to be on originality, although more often it is the simplicity of an easily communicated narrative that informs industry practices. This quote is from an internal Disney memo written by Jeffrey Katzenberg that was reprinted in *Variety,* January 31, 1991, pp. 18-24. For a full discussion of high concept, see Justin Wyatt, *High Concept: Movies and Marketing in Hollywood* (Austin: University of Texas Press, 1994).

[4]Jay Cocks, "Sing a Song of Seeing," *Time,* December 26, 1983, p. 63.

[5]For an interesting discussion of these problems in Hollywood, see John H. Richardson, "Dumb and Dumber," *The New Republic,* April 10, 1995, pp. 20-29.

[6]Quoted in Weinraub, "Shaken Hollywood," p. B4.

[7]Leonard Klady, "Disney Takes 'Lion's' Share of '94 Boffo B.O.," *Variety,* January 9-15, 1995, p. 13. For comparison, a 1977 survey showed that of the 119 films that grossed over one million dollars that year, only 28 (23 percent) grossed more than ten million, accounting for three-quarters of the total box-office receipts. The top six films (5 percent) accounted for one-third of the rentals received by distributors, and the top thirteen films (11 percent) accounted for half. Of the 152 films that grossed over one million dollars in 1992, 57 (38 percent) topped ten million, accounting for 80 percent of total box-office receipts. The top eleven films (7 percent) accounted for almost one-third of the rentals received by distributors, and the top twenty-two films (14 percent) accounted for half. Izod, *Hollywood and the Box Office,* p. 180; David Gordon, "The Movie Majors," *Sight and Sound* 48, no. 3 (Summer 1979): 152. The 1992 figures are based on the data reported in "Top Rental Films for 1992," *Variety,* January 11, 1993, pp. 22, 24.

[8]A general Hollywood rule of thumb is that in order to break even, a film must gross between two and a half and three times its "negative" costs (all costs necessary to produce the final cut of the master negative). Film grosses are the amount of money generated by box-office ticket sales. That money is divided by varying formulas between the film companies and theater owners. The break-even figure represents the remainder of the box-office gross, returned to the producer-distributor (roughly 45 percent) after exhibitors have taken their cut. This figure allows for the cost of studio overhead and "marketing," which includes advertising and prints for distribution. In 1974, for example, the average film cost $2.5 million to produce and $1 million to market. Using the upper end of the formula, the break-even point was a box-office gross of $7.5 million from about four million admissions at an average ticket price of $1.89. Ten years later, the average picture cost about $14.4 million to make and $6.65 million to market. To break even, the film had to reach a box-office gross of $43 million from 12.8 million admissions at an average ticket price of $3.36. The average film made in 1994 for $34.3 million with $16 million in marketing and print costs had to gross $102.9 million from 24.6 million admissions at an average ticket price of $4.18. If the average budgeted film is to be financially successful today, it must attract *six times the audience* as in the early 1970s and earn almost *fourteen times* as much in theatrical box-office gross. See Cook, *History of Narrative Film,* p.

888; Donahue, *American Film Distribution,* p. 33; Aljean Harmetz, "Where Movie Ticket Income Goes," *The New York Times,* January 28, 1987, p. C19. The magnitude of profit returns from blockbuster films was also needed to appease conglomerate shareholders who would otherwise seek investments with a better return rate or enhanced capital value. The inexpensive film, then, even if it made a substantial profit against low production costs, was not enough to raise secure capital investments.

[9]Quoted in Andrew Marton, "Up, Up and Away," *Premiere,* October 1990, p. 41. For additional comparison, *Boyz N the Hood* (1991) cost only $7 million but grossed $49 million, seven times its costs, returning $26.7 million to Columbia. But that same year *Terminator 2,* which cost $95 million, grossed over $200 million, returning $112.5 million to distributor Tri-Star. A film is considered big-budget these days if the production budget is in the $40-to-$60-million range, although many films like *Jurassic Park* ($70 million) go beyond that range, with others approaching $100 million *(Terminator 2)* or exceeding that mark—most recently *Waterworld,* estimated at between $175 and $200 million.

[10]Geraldine Fabrikant, "Why Studios Bet on the Summer Blockbuster," *The New York Times,* July 3, 1995, pp. 21, 28.

[11]Marton, "Up, Up and Away," p. 42. Columbia's *Last Action Hero* (a $150-million investment) was a sensationalized domestic flop in 1993 but was still expected to at least break even because of the appeal of Schwarzenegger and the action-adventure genre outside the United States. Columbia's low-budgeted *Lost in Yonkers* (a $40-million investment) also flopped that summer but registered a significant loss for the studios because the drama could generate little in overseas and ancillary revenues. See Leonard Klady and Don Groves, " 'Hero': Slightly Less than Zero?" *Variety,* September 13, 1993, pp. 1, 46-47; Leonard Klady, "Foreign B.O. Beckons: Comedies, Dramas Get More of the Action," *Variety,* August 28-September 3, 1995, pp. 1, 79.

[12]James Monaco, *American Film Now* (New York: New American Library/Plume, 1984), p. 20. See also Tom Charity, "Hell and High Water," *Time Out,* July 26-August 2, 1995, pp. 20-23; John Horn, "*Waterworld* Strikes It Rich as Theme Park Show," *Grand Rapids Press,* November 28, 1995, p. C8.

[13]Box-office gross topped one billion dollars in 1965 and reached two billion in 1975, four billion in 1984 and five billion in 1989, due mostly to inflated admission costs. Average ticket prices rose from $1.01 in 1965 to $2.04 in 1975, $3.36 in 1984, $3.99 in 1989 and $4.18 in 1994. Higher ticket prices mean that movies have to deliver more spectacular entertainment. Recent years have produced record box-office attendance exceeding the 20 percent fluctuation: 1989 was 1.26 billion, 1993 was 1.24, and 1994 was 1.29. See Richard Natale, "Hollywood's Got the Billion-Ticket Blahs," *Variety,* March 20, 1992, p. 5.

[14]Quoted in Greg Evans, "Disney Stays at Arm's Length from *Priest,*" *Variety,* April 10-16, 1995, p. 61. See also Marton, "Up, Up and Away," pp. 41-42.

[15]Rex Weiner, "Filmers Set Sale on Overseas B.O. Tide," *Variety,* April 17-23, 1995, pp. 1, 51.

[16]See Geraldine Fabrikant, "When World Raves, Studios Jump," *The New York Times,* March 7, 1990, pp. D1, D8; "Time Warner to Help Build Theaters in Soviet Union," *The New York Times,* March 7, 1990, p. D8; Adam Dawtrey, "Euros Go on Screen-Building Spree," *Variety,* February 6-12, 1995, pp. 1, 15; Leonard Klady, "Earth to H'wood: You Win," *Variety,* February 13-19, 1995, pp. 1, 63.

[17]Video stores reported brisk average rental rates per copy for *White* and *Belle Epoque,* though not near the total turns of theatrical blockbuster hits like *True Lies* or *Blown Away.* "Video Sleepers," *Variety,* May 29-June 4, 1995, p. 6.

[18]Richard Corliss, "Backing into the Future," *Time,* February 3, 1986, p. 65, and "Binge and Purge at the B.O.," *Time,* January 20, 1992, p. 59; Peter M. Nichols, "Home Video," *The New York Times,* July 30, 1993, p. B8. After ten years of spectacular growth the video business seemed to level off in the early 1990s at about fifteen billion dollars, but analysts speculate that video sales represent an area for continued growth as more people think of videos like books to

collect and view repeatedly.

[19]Andy Marx, "Technology Is Sexy Biz," *Variety,* September 12-18, 1994, p. 33. In other words, sex largely drove the home video business in the early 1980s; apparently a parallel can be made with CD-ROM technology and the Internet today.

[20]Richard Corliss, "Turned On? Turn It Off," *Time,* July 6, 1987, p. 72; Jefferson Graham, "A Hot Market for X-Rated Videos," *USA Today,* June 22, 1987, p. 1D.

[21]A nationwide poll by the National Opinion Research Center at the University of Chicago in 1990 showed increases in the percentage of both men and women who had seen an X-rated movie compared to 1980. The percentage of men increased from 20 to 31 percent, women from 13 to 17 percent. See Nick Ravo, "A Fact of Life: Sex-Video Rentals Gain in Unabashed Popularity," *The New York Times,* May 16, 1990, pp. B1, B8. Elsewhere it was estimated that women accounted for 40 percent of the 100 million X-rated videos rented each year. John Leo, "Romantic Porn in the Boudoir," *Time,* March 30, 1987, p. 63.

[22]Barbara Javitz and Lance Robbins, quoted in Michele Willens, "Bypassing the Big Picture," *Los Angeles Times/Calendar,* November 29, 1993, p. 25. Direct-to-video movies *Almost Pregnant* and *Husbands and Lovers,* for example, sold thirty thousand tapes, with the unrated versions accounting for 90 percent of the total. Unrated versions of *Wild Orchard 2* and *Sexual Response* outsold others by eight to one. The unrated versions were the same as the theatrical release in Europe. See Earl Paige, "Unrated Vids Rate Highly in Stores," *Billboard,* August 29, 1992, p. 53.

[23]See Richard Corliss, "Return of the Grownups," *Time,* August 23, 1993, p. 60. It was estimated that by 1990, 70 percent of the American music business's twenty billion dollars in annual revenues came from foreign markets, and six major record labels—PolyGram, CBS, WEA, EMI, BMG and MCA—controlled 93 percent of all record sales. Sanjek and Sanjek, *American Popular Music Business,* p. 268; John Huey, "America's Hottest Export: Pop Culture," *Fortune,* December 31, 1990, p. 50.

[24]Rex Weiner, "Filmers Set Sale on Overseas B.O. Tide," *Variety,* April 17-23, 1995, pp. 1, 51.

[25]Peter Biskind, "Win, Lose—but Draw," *Premiere,* July 1995, p. 80; "The Year in Review," *Video Business,* December 22, 1995, p. 36.

[26]Warren I. Susman, *Culture as History: The Transformation of American Society in the Twentieth Century* (New York: Pantheon Books, 1984), p. 282.

[27]Thirty-nine percent of the respondents preferred R films, and only 7 percent would take someone under seventeen to see one. The NC-17 and G ratings had the least appeal; 33 percent would not consider an NC-17, 26 percent a G picture. The R rating was a lure among younger patrons, the twelve- to thirty-four-year-old group. See Adam Sandler, "H'wood: 'R' Kind of Town," *Variety,* September 12-18, 1994, pp. 1, 71.

[28]These groupings are somewhat arbitrary, and as the American Medical Association observed, they do not take into account mental and emotional stages in children: "Movies that are rated 'G' or 'PG' are deemed appropriate for any child under 13, without recognizing that a 5-year-old, for example, is likely to respond quite differently than a 12-year-old to a portrayal of violence." See "Movie Standards Overrated, Need Reform, AMA Says," *Grand Rapids Press,* June 15, 1994, p. A3.

[29]Izod, *Hollywood and the Box Office,* p. 183.

[30]Paul Attanasio, "The Ratings Game," *The New Republic,* June 17, 1985, p. 17. Working the rating system does not guarantee an enlarged box-office take. Columbia scaled down the violence in Arnold Schwarzenegger's *Last Action Hero* (1993) to get a PG-13 rating, hoping to expand the audience even more among under-seventeen adolescent males. Instead, the eighty-three-million-dollar production was one of the year's biggest and most widely publicized flops. Schwarzenegger returned to the R-rated action-adventure genre the next year and scored a hit with *True Lies.*

[31]*Showgirls* was supposed to be a groundbreaker. From the writer-director team of *Basic Instinct,*

Showgirls trailers promised, "Last time they took you to the edge; this time, they're taking you all the way." The film had the widest screening ever for an NC-17 picture (thirteen hundred screens) and a healthy $8.3-million opening weekend, but scathing reviews and negative word-of-mouth followed, and grosses dropped 60 percent. In other words, the box-office disappointment of *Showgirls* had nothing to do with the rating. See Andrew Hindes, *"Showgirls* Aside, Erotica Grinds On," *Variety,* October 30-November 6, 1995, p. M26; Gary Levin, "Ads' Basic Instinct: Show-It-All and Sell," *Variety,* September 11-17, 1995, p. 7.

[32]Hollywood's unparalleled success with the adolescent market drove studio decision-making. Of *Variety's* "Top 100 All-Time Domestic Grossing Films," only two—*Gone with the Wind* (1939) and *Snow White and the Seven Dwarfs* (1938)—were made before World War II, and another four—*The Sound of Music* (1965), *101 Dalmatians* (1961), *The Jungle Book* (1968) and *Dr. Zhivago* (1965)—before 1970. *Entertainment Weekly* combined box-office attendance and video sales and rental figures to compile a list of the "100 Most Popular Movies of All Time." Six pre-1945 films (three Disney) made the popularity listing, with another eleven made before 1970 (six Disney). See "Top 100 All-Time Domestic Grossers," *Variety,* October 17-23, 1994, p. M-60; "The Big Pictures: America's 100 All-Time Favorite Films," *Entertainment Weekly,* April 29, 1994, pp. 22-41.

[33]Jack Mathews, "Mark Canton's Wrongheaded Chant," *Los Angeles Times/Calendar,* April 18, 1993, p. 24.

[34]See Morry Roth, "Teens Leaving Theaters for Homevid," *Variety,* February 26, 1986, pp. 3, 34.

[35]It appears that movies continue to be a primary social activity for single people. In 1994, 36 percent of single adults were frequent moviegoers, seeing at least one film in a theater each month, compared to 22 percent of married adults. Also, 34 percent of frequent moviegoers had at least some college education, compared to 23 percent who completed high school and 12 percent with less than a high-school education. MPAA, "Incidence of Motion Picture Attendance Among the Adult and Teenage Public, July 1994." See also Alexander Cockburn, "Rituals in the Dark," *American Film,* August 1991, p. 27. The record industry is experiencing the same demographic changes. See Adam Sandler, "Do Platters Still Matter to Old Ears?" *Variety,* November 29, 1993, pp. 1, 74.

[36]Nina J. Easton, "What's Driving *Rain Man?* Women," *Los Angeles Times/Calendar,* February 10, 1989, Home Edition, pt. 6, p. 1. Hollywood began courting the female audience, however modestly, with films like *Beaches* (1988) and *Steel Magnolias* (1989), *Pretty Woman* (1990), *Ghost* (1990), the self-reflexive romantic comedy *Sleepless in Seattle* (1993) and other story-driven films like *When Harry Met Sally* (1989), *The Prince of Tides* (1991), *Fried Green Tomatoes* (1991), *A League of Their Own* (1992), *Sommersby* (1993) and *Something to Talk About* (1995).

[37]See Leonard Klady, "B.O. Bets on Youth Despite a Solid Spread," *Variety,* April 10-16, 1995, pp. 13-14.

[38]Quoted in Daniel Cerone, "The Mouse That Soars," *Los Angeles Times,* October 28, 1991, p. F10. Prior to the video age, Disney rereleased its animated features every seven years or so to a new generation of children. The tradition continues, only now a Disney theatrical rerelease like *101 Dalmatians* is followed up with video sales for a limited time afterward. In the early 1990s Disney's Buena Vista Home Video division generated more revenues than any major studio did theatrically, including Disney. Buena Vista has several direct-to-video projects planned, including a sequel to *The Lion King,* a third chapter in the Aladdin trilogy, a Winnie the Pooh feature film and a third installment in the Honey, I Shrunk the Kids series, *Honey, We Shrunk Ourselves.* Paramount is following suit with a family action-adventure series, Josh Kirby . . . Time Warrior! See "More Direct-to-Video Sequels from Disney," *Video Business,* June 2, 1995, p. 51; "Paramount to Debut Josh Kirby, Rental-Priced Moonbeam Series," *Video Business,* June 2, 1995, p. 52.

[39]See Klady, "B.O. Bets on Youth," pp. 13-14.

[40]See Fred Pampel, Dan Fost and Sharon O'Malley, "Marketing Movies," *American Demographic,* March 1994, p. 52. Salaries for actors, directors and scriptwriters have skyrocketed because of the pressing need for talent who can "open" a picture. See Marton, "Up, Up and Away," pp. 41-43.

[41]Quoted in Klady, "B.O. Bets on Youth," p. 14.

[42]By the late 1980s independent production companies actually accounted for as much as 69 percent of annual releases. But there is a distinction between autonomous production companies that deliver films under contract to studio distributors and those produced independently and bought in the open market by distributors. Steven Spielberg's Amblin Entertainment made *Jurassic Park* and *Schindler's List* for distributor Universal and *Hook* for TriStar. James Cameron's production company, Lightstorm Entertainment, made *Terminator 2* for distribution by Tri-Star and *True Lies* for Twentieth Century-Fox. In contrast, *Fried Green Tomatoes* was made by the independent Electric Shadows and then picked up for theatrical distribution by Universal. For a discussion of the independents, see David Rosen with Peter Hamilton, *Off-Hollywood: The Making and Marketing of Independent Films* (New York: Grove Weidenfeld, 1990), p. 263.

[43]Amir Malin of Cinecom, quoted in Debra Goldman, "Indie Boom Turns Bust," *Premiere,* May 1989, p. 33.

[44]Goldman, "Indie Boom." A 1992 survey by the Video Software Dealers Association, for example, showed that the average video renter was thirty-nine years old and married with children, and not part of a trendier younger audience. See Marc Berman, "Studios Miss Boat on Vid Demographics," *Variety,* September 14, 1992, p. 15.

[45]Weinraub, "Shaken Hollywood," p. B4; Anne Thompson, "Isn't It Romantic," *Entertainment Weekly,* May 6, 1994, p. 34.

[46]Richard Corliss, "Saturday Night Fever," *Time,* June 6, 1994, p. 73; "A Blast to the Heart," *Time,* October 10, 1994, p. 76; Lucy Kaylin, "Independent's Day," *GQ,* October 1995, p. 180. Buena Vista Home Video set a record for a rental title, shipping 715,000 units of *Pulp Fiction* in the United States.

[47]See Leonard Klady, "Niche Pix Fight for Summers Spots," *Variety,* April 17-23, 1995, pp. 9, 16. See also Leonard Klady, "Summertime B.O. Biz Limps to New Record," *Variety,* September 4-10, 1995, pp. 9, 14; John Brodie, "Summer's Niche Pix Nip at Blockbusters," *Variety,* September 4-10, 1995, pp. 1, 80; Leonard Klady, "Paucity of Pix Leaves Arthouse in Outhouse," *Variety,* October 30-November 5, 1995, pp. 17, 24.

[48]Claudia Eller and John Evan Frook, "Disney Munches on Miramax," *Variety,* May 3, 1993, p. 1.

[49]Quoted in Greg Evans, "Oscar Rings in New Era of Indie Chic," *Variety,* February 20-26, 1995, p. 191. See also Leonard Klady, "Where Have All the Independents Gone?" *Variety,* January 23-29, 1995, p. 16.

[50]Leonard Klady, "Studio Deals Spark Indie Identity Crisis," *Variety,* December 13, 1993, p. 91.

[51]Quoted in Kathleen O'Steen, "H'wood Tries to Think Small," *Variety,* January 16-22, 1995, p. 107.

[52]Quoted in Anne Thompson, "Why Oscar Matters," *Entertainment Weekly,* April 15, 1994, p. 13.

[53]Jack Mathews, "Mark Canton's Wrongheaded Chant," *Los Angeles Times/Calendar,* April 18, 1993, p. 24.

Chapter 12: Some Like It Hot

[1]For a discussion of Generation X, see David Lipsky and Alexander Abrams, *Late Bloomers* (New York: Random House/Times Books, 1994); Neil Howe and Bill Straus, *13th Gen: Abort, Retry, Ignore, Fail?* (New York: Random House/Vintage Books, 1993).

[2]See Bernard Weinraub, "Black Film Makers Are Looking Beyond Ghetto Violence," *The New York Times,* September 11, 1995, pp. B1, B4.

[3]Andrew Britton, "Blissing Out: The Politics of Reaganite Entertainment," *Movie* 31/32 (1984):

1-43; John Belton, *American Cinema/American Culture* (New York: McGraw-Hill, 1994), p. 322. See also Robin Wood, "Eighties Hollywood: Dominant Tendencies," *CineAction,* Spring 1985, pp. 2-5.

[4]Spencer Warren, "The One Hundred Best Conservative Movies," *National Review,* October 24, 1994, p. 53.

[5]Capt. Nancy LaLuntas, USMC, DOD, quoted on ABC News, *20/20,* Stone Phillips, "The Battle to Make *Platoon,"* March 26, 1987.

[6]Warren, "One Hundred Best," p. 54.

[7]Quotes taken from Joe Maxwell, "The New Hollywood Watchdogs," *Christianity Today,* April 27, 1992, pp. 39-40; "Interview: The Thorn in Hollywood's Side," *Christianity Today,* April 27, 1992, p. 40; Ted Baehr, review of *Hollywood vs. America* by Michael Medved, *Movieguide,* October 2, 1992, p. 23. As I noted earlier, the Legion did not actually close in 1966 but only underwent a name change. The report on Baehr's faux pas with the Disney film can be found in Lisa Bannon, "How a Rumor Spread About Subliminal Sex in Disney's *Aladdin,"* *The Wall Street Journal,* October 24, 1995, pp. A1, A6.

[8]Michael Medved, *Hollywood vs. America: Popular Culture and the War on Traditional Values* (New York: HarperCollins/Zondervan, 1992), pp. 29, 34.

[9]David Prindle, *Risky Business: The Political Economy of Hollywood* (Boulder, Colo.: Westview, 1993), p. 93. Prindle conducted his own survey of influential people in the movie and television industries for comparison with a massive one conducted by the Times Mirror Company in cooperation with the Gallup Organization. He received thirty-five responses from top executives, including "two of the three men generally regarded as the most powerful in the industry." See his "Methodological Appendix," pp. 102-3. According to the Times Mirror poll he cites, a large number of Americans are liberal on economic issues and conservative on social ones (*Risky Business,* p. 93).

[10]Neal Gabler, *An Empire of Their Own: How the Jews Invented Hollywood* (New York: Crown, 1988), p. 6. Prindle reaches a more qualified conclusion. He reports that with the exception of Louis B. Mayer, "to judge by the rather spotty records available on campaign contributions, the other moguls tended to support Democrats, at least at the presidential level," during the 1930s and 1940s (Prindle, *Risky Business,* p. 89).

[11]Philip Dunne, quoted in Gabler, *Empire of Their Own,* p. 328. According to Gabler, estimates put the number of people in the film community who were members of the Communist Party as high as three hundred during the period from 1936 to 1946, with almost half of them writers (p. 330). For figures on Hollywood contributions to the presidential campaigns see Louise Overacker, "American Government and Politics," *American Political Science Review* 31, no. 3 (June 1937): 473-98, and "American Government and Politics: Presidential Campaign Funds, 1944," *American Political Science Review* 39, no. 5 (October 1945): 899-925. According to the latter report, "local movie proprietors and amusement houses, as well as the big motion picture producers, were well represented, and without Hollywood's substantial support the [Democratic] party would have been in a sad financial plight. . . . In his fourth-term campaign, Hollywood's heart was with Roosevelt" (pp. 917-18).

[12]See Edward Buscombe, "Notes on Columbia Pictures Corporation, 1926-41," in *The Studio System,* ed. Janet Staiger (New Brunswick, N.J.: Rutgers University Press, 1995), p. 32.

[13]Gabler, *Empire of Their Own,* p. 386.

[14]Prindle, *Risky Business,* p. 97.

[15]Quoted in ibid., p. 95.

[16]Ibid., p. 100.

[17]See Maureen Turim, "Gentlemen Consume Blondes," and Lucie Arbuthnot and Gail Seneca, "Pre-text and Text in *Gentlemen Prefer Blondes,"* in *Issues in Feminist Film Criticism,* ed. Patricia Erens (Bloomington: Indiana University Press, 1990), pp. 101-11, 112-25; Stephen P. Powers, Stanley Rothman and David J. Rothman, "Hollywood Views the Military," *Society* 28 (November/

December 1990): 79-84; Peter Goldman et al., "Rocky and Rambo," *Newsweek,* December 23, 1985, pp. 58-62; Thomas Doherty, review of *Rambo: First Blood Part II, Film Quarterly* 39 (Spring 1986): 50-54; Claude J. Smith Jr., "The Rehabilitation of the U.S. Military in Films Since 1978," *Journal of Popular Film and Television* 11, no. 4 (Winter 1984): 145-51.

[18]Medved, *Hollywood vs. America,* p. 284.

[19]Ibid., p. 29.

[20]Quoted in "A 'Message' for Hollywood," *Newsweek,* October 5, 1992, p. 35.

[21]Ted Baehr with Bruce W. Grimes and Lisa Ann Rice, *The Christian Family Guide to Movies and Video* (Brentwood, Tenn.: Wolgemuth & Hyatt, 1989), 1:10.

[22]Ted Baehr, "The Word Is Out, But . . . ," *Movieguide,* April 1993, p. 5.

[23]Christian Mork, "Product Placement Gets Kick out of PG Pix," *Variety,* May 25, 1993, pp. 5, 18.

[24]Ted Baehr, "1993: First Fruits," *Movieguide,* February 1994, p. 7.

[25]Medved, quoted in Marc Silver, "Sex and Violence on TV," *U.S. News & World Report,* September 11, 1995, p. 64; Baehr, "1993: First Fruits," p. 6.

[26]Michael Medved, "And What About Hollywood Films These Days?" *Focus on the Family,* March 1993, p. 4.

[27]Quoted in Jim Impoco with Monika Guttman, "Hollywood: Right Face," *U.S. News & World Report,* May 15, 1995, p. 68.

[28]Pete Hamil, "Crack and the Box," *Esquire,* May 1990, pp. 63-66.

[29]Quoted in Peter Biskind, "Drawing the Line," *Premiere,* November 1992, p. 86.

[30]Ironically, as Congress was slashing federal support for the Public Broadcasting Corporation, a national poll conducted for PBS by Opinion Research Corporation revealed that fully 84 percent of Americans wanted the funding maintained or increased; 82 percent thought PBS programming was "neither too conservative nor too liberal" (Robert Hughes, "Pulling the Fuse on Culture," *Time,* August 7, 1995, p. 63). See also Richard Zoglin, "We're All Connected," *Time,* February 12, 1996, p. 52; Martin Peers and Dennis Wharton, "D.C. Greenlights Goliaths," *Variety,* February 5-11, 1996, pp. 1, 75.

[31]Quoted in Biskind, "Drawing the Line," p. 86.

[32]Quoted in Maxwell, "New Hollywood Watchdogs," p. 39.

[33]Kurt Anderson, "Pop Goes the Culture," *Time,* June 16, 1986, p. 69.

[34]Chris Jenks, *Culture* (London: Routledge, 1993), p. 11. Medved's analysis is apparently influenced by Richard Grenier, whose book he calls "indispensable." Referring to Antonio Gramsci, Grenier wrote that "those who want to change society must change man's consciousness, and that in order to accomplish this they must first control the institutions by which that consciousness is formed: schools, universities, churches, and perhaps above all, art and the communications industry." See *Capturing the Culture: Film, Art and Politics* (Washington, D.C.: Ethics and Policy Center, 1991), p. xliv. Baehr reprinted a favorable review of *Capturing the Culture* in *Movieguide,* June 5, 1992, pp. 14-15.

[35]Medved, *Hollywood vs. America,* p. 286.

[36]Ibid., p. 279. See also Ted Baehr, "Called to Be Salt and Light," *Religious Broadcasting,* February 1993, pp. 64-69.

[37]See Medved, *Hollywood vs. America,* pp. 286-91; " 'PG' Films More Profitable, Report Says," *Movieguide,* December 28, 1992, p. 15; Adam Sandler, "H'wood: 'R' Kind of Town," *Variety,* September 12-18, 1994, pp. 1, 71; Lawrence Cohn, "Profit's the Thing, Not the Box Office Tally," *Variety,* October 5, 1992, pp. 5, 8. Film critic Roger Ebert called Medved's figures on ratings and box-office success "erroneous." In a speech before the National Press Club, Ebert said it is "absolutely untrue . . . that R-rated movies lose money and family movies make money. The fact is, unfortunately, to the contrary" (Gene Siskel and Roger Ebert, National Press Club Luncheon, June 8, 1995, transcribed by Federal News Service, Washington, D.C.).

[38]Peter Bart, "Reeling in 'R' Pic," *Variety,* March 22, 1992, p. 7.

[39]"Interview: The Thorn in Hollywood's Side," p. 40.

[40]Quoted in Maxwell, "New Hollywood Watchdogs," p. 39. In his book Medved recognizes the difficulty of enforcing a production code without the centralization of the studio system. He also suggests that words like *evil* and *sin,* both of which appear in the 1930 code as well as Baehr's, are outdated, presumably because of their "unmistakably religious overtones," and would have to be replaced with terminology like "self-destructive and anti-social behavior." See Medved, *Hollywood vs. America,* pp. 323-25.

[41]Ibid., pp. 90-91, 324-25.

[42]See Max Horkheimer and Theodor W. Adorno, "The Culture Industry: Enlightenment as Mass Deception," in *Dialectic of Enlightenment,* trans. John Cumming (New York: Seabury, 1972), pp. 120-67.

[43]Theodore Baehr, *Hollywood's Reel of Fortune: A Winning Strategy to Redeem the Entertainment Industry* (Ft. Lauderdale, Fla.: Coral Ridge Ministries, n.d.), p. 5. Baehr enjoys pointing out the disparity between the annual top picks by film critics (including Medved) and their box-office performance—another indication that he has not the least concern for the artistic value of movies and measures the quality of a film (that is, moral and religious portrayal) by its box-office earnings. *Movieguide* choices do better at the box office, he wrote, because "we share the values of the 86.5% of the American public who are Christian; we have our finger on the pulse of the moviegoing public unlike the secular critics who have cut themselves off from the majority of the American people" ("Critical Voices," *Movieguide,* February 1993, p. 10).

[44]Medved, *Hollywood vs. America,* p. 306.

[45]Ibid., p. 11.

[46]*Entertainment Weekly,* July 17, 1992, p. 27.

[47]Medved, *Hollywood vs. America,* p. 261.

[48]Ibid., pp. 262-63.

[49]Chandra Mukerji and Michael Schudson, eds., *Rethinking Popular Culture: Contemporary Perspectives in Cultural Studies* (Berkeley: University of California Press, 1991), p. 2.

[50]Quoted in "Hollywood vs. the World," *Cross Currents* (Markham, Ont.: Evangelical Fellowship of Canada, 1994), videocassette.

[51]Michael Medved, "Protecting Our Children from a Plague of Pessimism," *Imprimis* 25, no. 12 (December 1995): 4-5.

[52]See Stanley Aronowitz, *Roll Over Beethoven: The Return of Cultural Strife* (Hanover, N.H.: Wesleyan University Press, 1993); Henry A. Giroux and Roger I. Simon et al., *Popular Culture, Schooling and Everyday Life* (Granby, Mass.: Bergin & Garvey, 1989).

[53]Quoted in Maxwell, "New Hollywood Watchdogs."

[54]I am paraphrasing, in a somewhat different context, Rodney Clapp, "Calling the Religious Right to Its Better Self," *Perspectives,* April 1994, p. 13.

[55]In this sense Calvin Seerveld defines culture as "the cultivation of the creation by humankind, the formative development in history of creaturely life tended by human creatures. . . . So the crux of a Christian conception of culture is that it belongs inescapably to the office or task of being human, is cosmic in scope, and is actually performed as a service of reconciliation and praise or as a wasteful, fruitless attempt to regain paradise for ourselves." Calvin Seerveld, *Rainbows for the Fallen World: Aesthetic Life and Artistic Task* (Toronto: Tuppence, 1980), p. 179.

[56]Allan Bloom, *The Closing of the American Mind* (New York: Simon & Schuster, 1987), p. 19.

Chapter 13: Back to the Future

[1]David Cook, *A History of Narrative Film,* 2nd ed. (New York: W. W. Norton, 1990), pp. xv-xvi.

[2]Father Kieser, "TV Could Nourish Minds and Hearts," *Time,* September 14, 1992, p. 80.

[3]William Fielding Ogburn, *Social Change with Respect to Culture and Original Nature* (New York: Viking, 1922).

[4]According to one report, VR could "open new worlds of learning, using simulated realities to

teach everything from driving a car to performing laser surgery. It will evolve into a new, participatory art form." See "Information Explosion Takes Place in Ethical Void," *Grand Rapids Press,* November 7, 1993, p. A16. See also Richard Corliss, "Virtual, Man!" *Time,* November 1, 1993, p. 80.

⁵This study is cited in Marc Silver, "Sex and Violence on TV," *U.S. News & World Report,* September 11, 1995, p. 64.

⁶Brandon S. Centerwall, "Television and Violence: The Scale of the Problem and Where to Go from Here," *JAMA* 267, no. 22 (June 10, 1992): 3060 (emphasis added). Centerwall lists sources and gives a summary of the research on the effect of television violence. A brief summary can also be found in "Videodrome," *The Economist,* August 13, 1994, pp. 73-74. There are too many studies to cite here, but the interested reader can consult special issues on the topic in *Journal of Social Issues* 42, no. 3 (1986) and *The CQ Researcher* 3, no. 12 (March 26, 1993). For an interesting debate see "Controversies: Television at the Crossroads," *Society* 21, no. 6 (September/October 1984): 6-40. On popular music see Elizabeth F. Brown and William R. Hendee, "Adolescents and Their Music: Insights into the Health of Adolescents," *JAMA* 262, no. 12 (September 22-29, 1989): 1659-63. On a related issue see Daniel Linz and Neil Malamuth, *Pornography,* Communication Concepts 5, ed. Steven H. Chaffee (Newbury Park, Calif.: Sage, 1993).

⁷See Jonathan Alter, "The Cultural Elite," *Newsweek,* October 5, 1992, p. 30; Don Groves, "Overseas Censors Relax Scissors in Freer Climate," *Variety,* October 25, 1993, p. 12; David Denby, "I Lost It at the Movies," *New Republic,* November 2, 1992, p. 32.

⁸David Snedden, commissioner of education for Massachusetts, quoted in Joel Spring, *Images of American Life: A History of Ideological Management in Schools, Movies, Radio and Television* (New York: State University of New York Press, 1992), p. 55.

⁹Quoted in Spring, *Images of American Life,* p. 66. Hays estimated that as many as six thousand schools and six million students were participating in a program run by a nonprofit educational agency, Teaching Film Custodians, Inc. (TFCI), that served as an advisory committee to the MPPDA. See Will H. Hays, *The Memoirs of Will H. Hays* (New York: Doubleday, 1955), pp. 480-81. According to Spring, some three million students were enrolled in film appreciation courses by 1937 (*Images of American Life,* p. 64).

¹⁰The production of instructional films was not profitable for film companies. They did, however, benefit from the good publicity TFCI brought, along with some required student attendance at local theaters. The industry also used educators' claims that they could improve the movies by enriching the tastes of the audience as another argument against federal censorship. "Better audiences mean better pictures," the secretary of the Motion Picture Producers and Distributors of America (MPPDA) told the National Education Association in 1931. "You must realize that however earnest the producers of motion pictures may be in their continuous efforts to raise the social and moral standards of motion picture entertainment, the most they can do is to set the minimum level of good taste. Above that [it] is the community itself which sets the fashion" (Carl Milliken, quoted in Spring, *Images of American Life,* p. 61).

¹¹Floyde E. Brooker, "Motion Pictures as an Aid to Education," *The Annals of the American Academy of Political and Social Science* 254 (November 1954): 105.

¹²Cary Bazalgette, "Teaching the Media in Tomorrow's Schools," *Media Development,* January 1994, p. 15.

¹³Patricia Aufderheide Rapporteur, *Media Literacy: A Report of the National Leadership Conference on Media Literacy* (Washington, D.C.: Aspen Institute, 1993), p. 1. A summary of the basic tenets of the movement and its composition and history, as well as additional resources, can be found in J. Francis Davis, "Appendix A: Media Literacy—From Activism to Exploration," contained in this report, which is also the source of the information that follows.

¹⁴The National Alliance of Media Arts Centers (NAMAC), the San Francisco-based Strategies for Media Literacy, and the Houston-based Southwest Alternate Media Project sponsored a confer-

ence to address the lack of communication between educators, artists and policymakers regarding media education. (The National Alliance for Media Education [NAME] was formed as a result of this conference.) The National Council of Teachers of English (NCTE) and the New York-based alternative media organization Educational Video sponsored a conference to combine media theory with practical lessons in teaching about the media. A series of conferences cosponsored by the University of Pennsylvania's Annenberg School for Communication summarized knowledge about the effects of the media and recent work in media research and education.

[15]Richard Corliss, "Give the Rating System an X," *Time*, August 27, 1990, p. 56. The X rating began with *Midnight Cowboy* (1969) and *Last Tango in Paris* (1973) but soon became synonymous with pornography. X was the only designation not copyrighted by the MPAA, making it available to anyone who did not submit a film for a CARA rating; pornographers use it as a form of advertising. The X rating is considered the death knell for a movie because it largely excludes the film from the marketplace. Newspapers will not advertise or review X-rated films. Few distributors will handle them, most theaters will not exhibit them, and some video outlets refuse to carry them.

[16]James M. Wall, "Movie Ratings, Freedom of Expression and Community Control," *Media Development*, April 1994, p. 37.

[17]See Timothy Gray, "Ratings Still Rankle After All These Years," *Variety*, January 10-16, 1994, pp. 1, 44.

[18]See John Brodie, "Sex! Controversy! PR!" *Variety*, August 29-September 4, 1994, pp. 7-8.

[19]Beyond the sources on visual literacy cited in this chapter, the interested reader might consult the following: Paul Messaris, *Visual "Literacy": Image, Mind and Reality* (Boulder, Colo.: Westview, 1994); Horace Newcomb, ed., *Television: The Critical View*, 5th ed. (New York: Oxford University Press, 1994); Jeremy G. Butler, *Television: Cricial Methods and Applications* (Belmont, Calif.: Wadsworth, 1994); Quentin J. Schultze, *Redeeming Television* (Downers Grove, Ill.: InterVarsity Press, 1992); Louis Giannetti, *Understanding Movies*, 5th ed. (Englewood Cliffs, N.J.: Prentice-Hall, 1990); David Bordwell and Kristin Thompson, *Film Art: An Introduction* (New York: McGraw-Hill, 1990); Bernard F. Dick, *Anatomy of Film*, 2nd ed. (New York: St. Martin's, 1990).

[20]Federal Communications Commission, "Children's Television Programs: Report and Policy Statement," *Federal Register* 39, no. 6 (November 1974): 39,399, as cited in Dale Kunkel, "From a Raised Eyebrow to a Turned Back: The FCC and Children's Product-Related Programming," *Journal of Communication* 38, no. 4 (Autumn 1988): 99. The brief summary here is drawn from this essay. See also the "Children's Programming" special section in *Variety*, January 1-7, 1996, pp. 67-76. The 1990 Children's Television Act reestablished limits on commercials during children's viewing hours but left vague a requirement on educational programming.

[21]"Movie Standards Overrated, Need Reform, AMA Says," *Grand Rapids Press*, June 15, 1994, p. A3; Jenny Hontz, "Senate Panel OKs Bills to Restrict TV Violence," *Electronic Media*, August 14, 1995, p. 2; Richard Zoglin, "Chips Ahoy," *Time*, February 19, 1996, pp. 58-61; Verne Gay, "How's It Rate?" *Grand Rapids Press*, February 16, 1996, p. A1.

[22]See Jenny Hontz, "A V-chip Family Feud," *Electronic Media*, July 4, 1995, p. 32, and "House OKs Act Rewrite," *Electronic Media*, August 7, 1995, pp. 31-32; Dennis Warton, "V-Chip, on a Roll, Puts Industry in a Pickle," *Variety*, July 17-23, 1995, pp. 21, 25, and "Senate Panel OKs 2 Antiviolence Bills," *Variety*, August 14-20, 1995, p. 28.

[23]Quoted in Benjamin Svetkey, "Bleak Chick," *Entertainment Weekly*, November 3, 1995, p. 36.

[24]Neal Gabler, *An Empire of Their Own: How the Jews Invented Hollywood* (New York: Crown, 1988), p. 173.

[25]For a fuller treatment of this point see Paul Schrader, *Transcendental Style in Film: Ozu, Bresson, Dreyer* (Berkeley: University of California Press, 1972).

[26]John Kennedy, "Editor's Letter," *George*, October-November, 1995, p. 9.

[27]Quoted in Michael Walsh, "Running Up the Scores," *Time,* September 11, 1995, p. 78.

[28]Greg Evans, "Road Shows Roll over B'way," *Variety,* May 23-29, 1994, p. 31. See also Greg Evans, "Legit Breaks Billion-Dollar Barrier," *Variety,* May 23-29, 1994, pp. 45, 47.

[29]Paul DiMaggio, "Classification in Art," *American Sociological Review* 52 (August 1987): 444-45.

[30]Judith R. Blau, "Study of the Arts: A Reappraisal," *Annual Review of Sociology* 14 (1988): 280.

[31]Warren I. Susman, *Culture As History: The Transformation of American Society in the Twentieth Century* (New York: Pantheon, 1984), p. 253.

[32]Janice Castro, "Rock'n'Roll's Holy War," *Time,* June 20, 1994, p. 46.

[33]Erwin Panofsky, "Sytle and Medium in the Motion Pictures," in *Film Theory and Criticism: Introductory Readings,* 4th ed., ed Gerald Mast, Marshall Cohen and Leo Braudy (New York: Oxford University Press, 1992), p. 244.

[34]Cardinal Roger M. Mahoney, "Film Makers, Film Viewers—Their Challenges and Opportunities: A Pastoral Letter," September 30, 1992, p. 4.

[35]T. S. Eliot, *Notes Toward a Definition of Culture* (New York: Harcourt Brace, 1949), p. 111.